Acclaim for

Ronald H. Spector's

AFTER TET

"Valuable and vital . . . smoothly written . . . Spector skillfully uses a mass of primary and secondary sources."
—*Newsday*

"Superb history . . . Mr. Spector's own service in Vietnam enriches the realism of the book, but its unique value is applied intelligence, analyzing events and the policies that shaped them."
—*The New Yorker*

"Immensely readable and thoroughly researched, this is a major contribution to the study of the war and a superb book."
—George C. Herring, author of *America's Longest War*

"*After Tet* is an absorbing and thought-provoking account of the military, political, and social forces that created the most bloody year of the Vietnam War. . . . Ronald Spector should be congratulated for painstakingly presenting a panorama of viewpoints— from archival records to compelling personal testimony—to challenge the historical record."
—Al Santoli, author of *Everything We Had: An Oral History of the Vietnam War*

"Ronald Spector is one of America's leading military historians, which he again proves in *After Tet*. It is an authoritative and above all readable account of a key period in the Vietnam War."
—Stanley Karnow, author of *Vietnam : A History*

Ronald H. Spector

AFTER TET

Ronald H. Spector is Professor of History and International Affairs at George Washington University. He served as Director of Naval History for the U.S. Navy and is the author of the classic work on the Pacific War *Eagle Against the Sun*.

Quang Tri

Phu Bai

Da Nang

Chu Lai

Bong Son

Pleiku · · An Khe

Qui Nhon

Tuy Hoa

Nha Trang

Dalat

Phan Rang

Tay Ninh

Bien Hoa

Phan Thiet

Xuan Loc

Saigon ☆ Long Binh

Vinh Long

Vung Tau

Can Tho

Bac Lieu

Map Scale in miles

0   50   100

scale   miles

—N—

Map by Shelby L. Stanton

VIETNAM 1968

AFTER TET

THE BLOODIEST YEAR IN VIETNAM

Ronald H. Spector

Vintage Books
A Division of Random House, Inc.
New York

FIRST VINTAGE BOOKS EDITION, FEBRUARY 1994

Copyright © 1993 by Ronald H. Spector

All rights reserved under International and Pan-American Copyright Conventions. Published in the United States by Vintage Books, a division of Random House, Inc., New York, and simultaneously in Canada by Random House of Canada Limited, Toronto. Originally published in hardcover by The Free Press, a division of Macmillan, Inc., New York, in 1993. This edition is reprinted by arrangement with The Free Press, a division of Macmillan, Inc.

Maps reprinted with permission from Presidio Press (505B San Marin Drive, Novato, CA 94945) from the book *The Rise and Fall of an American Army*, by Shelby L. Stanton, copyright 1985.

Library of Congress Cataloging-in-Publication Data
Spector, Ronald H., 1943–
After Tet: the bloodiest year in Vietnam / Ronald H. Spector.—
1st Vintage Books ed.
p. cm.
Includes index.
ISBN 0-679-75046-0
1. Vietnamese Conflict, 1961–1975.
2. Vietnamese Conflict, 1961–1975—United States. I. Title.
DS558.S69   1994
959.704'34—dc 20   93-27495
CIP

Manufactured in the United States of America

10 9 8 7 6 5 4 3 2 1

To my younger son Jonathan and to my older son Daniel, who was born in the year that the war ended; and to my friends and companions of 1968–69 who did not live to see that year.

CONTENTS

CONTENTS

PREFACE

On January 17, 1968, my 25th birthday, I received my orders for Vietnam. At that time I had completed boot camp at Parris Island and had just finished advanced infantry training at Camp Geiger in North Carolina. None of us was particularly surprised to receive orders for Vietnam. We had been well briefed on what to expect by our instructors at Camp Geiger, all of whom appeared to have three Purple Hearts and to speak in a monotone of expletives. We expected the worst, and Vietnam would seldom disappoint us.

Six weeks later, on my last home leave, I sat with my family in front of the television and watched Walter Cronkite deliver his personal assessment of the situation in Vietnam.

> It seems now more certain than ever that the bloody experience of Vietnam is to end in a stalemate. . . . to say that we are closer to victory today is to believe, in the face of the evidence, the optimists who have been wrong in the past. To suggest that we are on the edge of defeat is to yield to unreasonable pessimism. To say that we are mired in stalemate seems the only realistic, yet unsatisfactory, conclusion.

One month later we left Camp Pendleton, California, for Vietnam. Our planes landed in Hawaii to refuel, and we wandered around the large terminal looking for snacks and beer. In the newspaper racks, the headlines read, "LBJ TO ADDRESS NATION ON VIETNAM WAR." It was March 31, 1968.

The following morning I was awakened by another Marine's

portable radio in our transit barracks on Okinawa. I thought I heard a news broadcaster say that the President had stopped the bombing of North Vietnam and called for peace talks. I went back to sleep. Later I recalled the broadcast, but the news seemed so surrealistic, I decided it had been a dream. It was not until we landed in Vietnam two days later that I learned that the President had indeed made these historic announcements, as well as declining to run for another term.

This book is an account of the nine months following President Johnson's March speech. While a number of authors have attempted to tell the story of the American experience in Vietnam through chronological narratives spanning the years 1965–1973, this book attempts to interpret that experience through a close examination of a single year, a year that witnessed the largest and most costly battles of the war.

During most of 1968 and a portion of 1969 I was a field historian on special assignment from the Commandant of the Marine Corps, attached to the III Marine Amphibious Force. In that job I had an opportunity to see a good deal of the war in the five northern provinces of South Vietnam as well as to talk with hundreds of Marines, soldiers, and sailors, both informally and for the purpose of historical interviews. Yet while this book is informed by personal experience, it is in no sense a memoir or a personal account. In discussing attitudes and practices of American GIs in Vietnam I have frequently drawn from my own experience and memory. However, I have in no case relied on personal experience alone; all incidents, attitudes, or practices described here can be documented by independent sources.

The story told here largely confirms the accuracy of Walter Cronkite's conclusion that the war was "mired in stalemate," but the implications and results of that stalemate were to prove far more complex and tragic than anyone might have forseen. In the work that follows I have attempted to explain why the war did not go away, long after Walter Cronkite and millions of other Americans decided it should.

ACKNOWLEDGMENTS

I am grateful to the Research Grants Committee of the University of Alabama for a grant that made possible my visits to the Lyndon Johnson Library, the Indochina Archive at the University of California, Berkeley, and the Hoover Institution. I am also grateful to the Woodrow Wilson International Center for Scholars for the opportunity to spend the summer of 1990 at the Center as a visiting scholar, and to colleagues there, especially Michael Hunt, Lawrence Lichty, Dennis McLane, and Robert Timburg, for listening patiently to my ramblings about this project.

A number of colleagues and friends took the time from their own busy schedules to read parts of the draft manuscript and gave me the benefit of their advice. I thank Frederick Z. Brown, Norman M. Camp, Jeffrey Clarke, Graham Cosmas, William Hammond, George Herring, Richard Hunt, Arnold Isaacs, George MacGarrigle, Morris J. MacGregor, Samuel Popkin, Naomi Rodgers, and Nina Seavey. Special thanks to Igor Bobrowsky, Peter Braestrup, and Ed Melton, who read the chapters with an infantryman's eye and contributed some of their own memories and conclusions about the events of 1968. Many of these readers differed strongly with the author on one or more points of fact or interpretation, and they should not be held responsible for this book's conclusions or for any errors that remain.

A number of other individuals discussed the book with me and gave me the benefit of their expertise. Douglas Pike was a gracious host and infallible guide to the records of the Indochina Archive at Berkeley. Jack Shulimson was always willing to share his own unmatched knowledge of Marine Corps operations in Vietnam. Ed

Marolda and Bernard Nalty were most helpful on Navy and Air Force operations and records respectively, as was Morris MacGregor on race relations in the armed forces. Professor Ngo Vinh Long kindly allowed me to read his unpublished paper on the Tet offensive and the NLF. As will be evident from the notes, I relied heavily on the extensive material at the Marine Corps Historical Center collected over more than twenty years by Reverend Ray W. Stubbe, the former chaplain at Khe Sanh, a mine of information and a fitting memorial to those who served there. I owe special thanks to Shelby Stanton, who served as an infantry officer in Vietnam and has since become a widely read expert on many aspects of the war. He encouraged the project from its inception, made available his own voluminous files, and allowed me to use the maps that appear in this book.

Any historian of Vietnam is ultimately dependent on the knowledge and experience of records managers and archivists in attempting to cope with the voluminous yet baffling and elusive records of the war. I have been fortunate to have had the assistance of David Humphrey and his staff at the Lyndon Johnson Library; Rich Boylan, Cary Conn, and Terry Hanna at the National Archives; Mrs. Kathrine Lloyd of the Operational Archives Branch, Naval Historical Center; Joyce Bonnett of the Marine Corps Historical Center; Benis M. Frank, creator and head of the Marine Corps Oral History Collection (now Chief Historian of the Marine Corps); and Hannah Zeidlich and Jerry Harcarik of the U.S. Army Center of Military History. Special thanks to the creators and custodians of the Company Command in Vietnam Oral History Series at the Army War College and the Army Command and General Staff College Colonel Reg Schrader and Dr. Ronald Berlin.

I had the help of many people in seeing this book through its lengthy gestation period. I was fortunate to have the support of a number of resourceful and talented research assistants: Sean Morton at Alabama; Paul L. Nussbaum at the Wilson Center; and Alexis Castor, Suzanne Baughmann, and Diep Taggart at George Washington University. My agent, Gerard McCauley, and my editor, Joyce Seltzer, not only handled the logistics but read and commented on the manuscript in its various stages, as did Erwin Glickes, president and publisher of The Free Press. Cherie Weitzner, Lise Esdaile,

Eileen DeWald, and Robert Harrington at The Free Press handled various aspects of the book's publication with their usual tact and efficiency. Meredith Hartley typed the manuscript with speed and accuracy. I am especially grateful to my secretary, Elizabeth Loughney, and my research assistant, Diep N. Taggart, who cheerfully typed last-minute revisions and footnotes and whose good sense and good nature remained unshaken by the erratic behavior of the author. Finally, I am grateful to my wife Dianne and to my sons Daniel and Jonathan, who stoutly bore with the author's various mood swings and tantrums as well as his frequent absences from family activities in order to "do a little more work on the book."

INTRODUCTION

More than seventeen years after the last American GI left Vietnam, we still have no widely accepted explanation for that longest war in American history. How did the United States lose the war in Vietnam? Why were we there? Why did the war last so long? Why didn't we win? These remain fundamental questions that we have failed to answer. In a sense, then, we have no real history of Vietnam. Instead we have controversy, myth, and popular memory.

One of the most tenacious components of that popular memory is of the events of February and March 1968. Those tense and crowded weeks began with the surprise and shock of the Communist Tet attacks against dozens of South Vietnamese cities and towns and climaxed in President Lyndon Johnson's television address of March 31 announcing his decision to halt the bombing of most of North Vietnam and not to seek reelection. That was followed almost immediately by Hanoi's acceptance of Johnson's offer to begin peace talks. Ever since that time, it has become a commonplace to refer to Tet and 1968 as "the turning point," "the year of decision." Yet, if Tet was "the turning point" why did the war continue for five more years, with more Americans dead after Tet than before? What did happen in Vietnam in 1968 to make it so different from 1966 or 1967? And if 1968 was a critical year, why did the war continue until 1973?

The answer may be found in a look at the nine long months after President Johnson's speech of March 31, 1968, the speech so often singled out as the event that symbolized "the turning point." The rest of 1968 is passed over in silence as a sort of anticlimax. Yet the events of those nine months, particularly developments in South Vietnam, were far more important in shaping the course of the war for the next five years than anything done in Washington during February and March. The nine months following LBJ's historic speech saw the fiercest fighting of the war. From January to July 1968 the overall rate of men killed in action in Vietnam would reach an all time high and would exceed the rate for the Korean War and the Mediterranean and Pacific theaters during World War II.[1] This was truly the bloodiest phase of the Vietnam War as well as the most neglected one.

An examination of the events of 1968 makes clear that rather than World War II or Korea, to which it is often compared, the most appropriate analogy to Vietnam is World War I. As in World War I on the Western front, the War in Vietnam was a stalemate and had been a stalemate since the early months of the conflict. As in World War I, neither side was prepared to admit this fact, and each side grossly underestimated the determination and staying power of the other. Both sides persisted in the belief that the other side was near to collapse and that just a little more pressure, a little more perseverence, would lead to victory.

Though the fundamental stalemate remained unbroken in the aftermath of Johnson's speech, many things *did* change during 1968. A new American commander, General Creighton Abrams, assumed the task of directing—or more accurately, presiding over—the U.S. war effort, and some of his more innovative commanders, like General Raymond G. Davis, with Abrams's encouragement, were to adopt new operational methods that gave the Americans an edge, though not a decisive one, in the intense fighting in the latter half of 1968. On the battlefield, North Vietnamese came to replace Southerners in many Viet Cong units, and the North Vietnamese Army assumed a greater burden of the fighting.

With the Communists weakened militarily and organizationally by the losses in their repeated offensives, the U.S. and South Vietnam were able for the first time to gain a real measure of control in the countryside. Yet the continued weaknesses of the South Vietnamese regime, the Communist powers of recuperation, and the U.S. decision to begin troop withdrawals in 1969 made this Allied ascendancy in the countryside only temporary.

Even while American forces were experiencing greater success on the battlefield and in the contest for the countryside, American GIs were beginning to show signs of coming apart under the continued strain of fighting a costly stalemated war for objectives that were never clear or compelling. It was during 1968 that the U.S. forces began seriously to encounter the problems related to racial tensions and drug abuse which were to lead to their near disintegration in 1971 and 1972.

Many aspects of the conflict also remained constant after Tet. One was the nature of the ground war in South Vietnam. American generals and others have repeated so often the phrase that "we won all the battles" in Vietnam that they have come to believe it. Many others, taking their cue from popular books and movies, have a vague impression that American soldiers were simply hapless victims, floundering aimlessly in the jungles and rice paddies, always at the mercy of the tricks of the "wily Viet Cong." In the work that follows, I have tried to portray something of the real nature of the fighting in Vietnam and to show how the failure of most American commanders to adapt their operational methods to the peculiar conditions of warfare in Vietnam, or indeed to adapt at all, contributed to the continued stalemate which was the war's most important characteristic.

Other things remained unchanged as well: the constant determination of Hanoi's leaders to unite Vietnam under their leadership at whatever cost; the concern of the President and his advisors for U.S. credibility and reputation for power; their loyalty to their South Vietnamese ally; and the continued weakness, corruption, and disarray of that ally, which, in the end, ensured that for all the battlefield successes and advances in pacification the United States might enjoy, the war would remain stalemated. This book is the story of those nine least-known and most bloody months, a period that illuminated the true nature of the struggle in Vietnam and largely determined its course.

AFTER TET

CHAPTER 1

"I Want to Speak to You Tonight of Peace in Vietnam"

Thick morning mist was normal this time of year in the mountains, crags, and plateaus around the Khe Sanh Combat Base. On this particular morning, March 30, 1968, the Marines were counting on the fog. B Company, 26th Marines, was preparing for an attack on some high ground about 800 yards south of the Khe Sanh perimeter. The objective of the attack was to recover the bodies of some Marines killed in an earlier fight outside the perimeter. On February 26 a Marine patrol had flushed out three North Vietnamese soldiers manning an observation post. The North Vietnamese had fled, leading the patrol into a well-prepared ambush. A fifty-man reaction force was dispatched, and it too was ambushed. Thirty Marines, more than the strength of the original patrol, were killed, and seventeen wounded.

The Marines had a tradition of always bringing back the bodies of the dead, but in this fight the fire from the Vietnamese bunkers and spider holes had been so intense that no one could reach the bodies of the fallen without himself becoming a casualty. So about two dozen dead had been left on the hill that day in late February.[1]

The February 26 ambush received little attention in the press. A lot was happening in Vietnam that month, most of it bad. The Communist Tet Offensive—simultaneous attacks by 85,000 troops on five major cities, dozens of military installations, and more than 150 towns and villages—erupted on the last two days of January. At

Hue, the old imperial capital in central Vietnam, 7,500 Viet Cong and North Vietnamese troops seized control of much of the town, precipitating a savage three-week battle that destroyed much of the city and cost thousands of lives.

And all through the month the seige of Khe Sanh continued. A force estimated at forty thousand Communist troops encircled the six thousand Marines and South Vietnamese Rangers at Khe Sanh, firing an average of a hundred and fifty rocket, mortar, and artillery rounds into the base each day. On February 23, three days before the ill-fated patrol, Khe Sanh had received 1,300 incoming rounds. Marine casualties averaged more than a dozen each day, more if you counted the Marines holding the vital hilltop outposts: Hill 861 and 861A, Hill 881 South, and Hill 950 on the high ground around the Khe Sanh plateau, where the shells and casualties were a good deal worse.[2]

Still, there were those bodies on the high ground, less than a mile from the perimeter. "It got to be almost . . . the bastard child of 1/26 and the horrible family secret that you didn't want to talk about," recalled an artillery officer serving with the battalion. "There was that stigma of the ghost platoon or the lost platoon, leaving your dead on the battlefield, all those Marine myths that you didn't dare—everything was there and everything got blown way out of proportion."[3]

The bodies had now been there more than a month, and March 30 was the day to get them back.

At 7:25 in the morning, the 2d Platoon of B Company, still concealed by the enveloping fog, crossed an old French plantation road, which marked their line of departure. They were followed ten minutes later by the rest of the company. The Marines advanced behind a moving wall of artillery shells, much as their grandfathers had at the Meuse-Argonne. Indeed, by this third month of the siege the Khe Sanh battle area, with its thousands of muddy sand bags, trenches, bomb and shell craters, and incessant artillery barrages, had come to resemble somewhat a battlefield of World War I.

B Company's first objective, a Communist trench line less than a hundred yards away, was secured without difficulty. Here the company consolidated and, with two platoons deployed in a line, moved toward the next objective, "Alpha," the high ground about

800 meters away, just beyond the area containing the bodies of the February fight. As the Marines moved slowly forward they began receiving 60mm mortar fire from their direct front. The Americans answered with heavy fire from Khe Sanh's artillery, which had been presighted on the battle zone. Then, as the two platoons crossed a low knob, they were hit by intense heavy mortar and machine gun fire. Directly ahead lay a complex network of mutually supporting Communist bunkers and trenches.

Calling in their supporting artillery ever closer, the Marines used rifle and machine gun fire to pin down the defenders, while three- and four-man fire teams lobbed satchel charges at the bunkers.[4] "We got so close all we could see were Chicom grenades flying at us," recalled PFC Jeff Culpepper of the 3d Platoon,

> We started assaulting bunker after bunker. As we went we burned some out with flame-throwers . . . things were flying everywhere. We got into the first trench and cleared it and on we went. . . . We got to the third trench line and they finally pinned us down . . . about two hundred meters to our front they had mortars set up. . . . mortars dropping all over the place and nowhere to go.[5]

The B Company commander, Captain Kenneth Pipes, directing the fight from a bomb crater, was hit by a 60mm mortar shell, which killed his radio operator and two forward observers. Though painfully wounded, Pipes refused evacuation and remained on the radio directing supporting fire and seeing to the withdrawal of the other casualties.

Lieutenant J. W. Dillon, a platoon commander, assumed command of the company. The Marines were still advancing, but they had by now used up all their satchel charges and were reduced to lobbing grenades at the bunkers. The company had taken heavy casualties, including many wounded who were in urgent need of evacuation. Dillon could see that if the Marines stayed on the level ground among the bunkers they would be wiped out. Using his two strongest squads, Dillon fought his way to the top of the high ground at Alpha. The squads then formed a defensive perimeter while the dead and wounded were evacuated. As soon as this was accomplished, Dillon himself was ordered to pull back. There was no time to find all the bodies of February 25, many of which lay under piles of rubble and dirt churned up by recent air raids.

As Dillon's rear guard withdrew, North Vietnamese troops left their bunkers to follow. Dillon contacted the four 106mm recoilless rifles at Khe Sanh already registered on his position. "I'm going to pop smoke at my forward-most element," yelled Dillon, "Fire east of the smoke."[6] Caught in the open, the North Vietnamese were decimated by the hail of 106 shells. As the last Marines pulled back into the Khe Sanh perimeter, 60mm mortars joined in the slaughter.

The Communists left 115 bodies on the battlefield, and many more were probably killed in the fight for the bunkers. B Company lost a dozen killed and more than fifty seriously wounded. The 1st Battalion, 26th Marine Regiment's After Action Report made no mention of the bodies still on Alpha but praised "the aggressive fighting spirit of Company B . . . in the first planned offensive attack of a known enemy position in the battle for Khe Sanh Combat Base."[7]

The confused and desperate fighting around Khe Sanh was nothing new. It was merely an episode in the crescendo of violence that continued to envelope Vietnam for the next several months. In Washington, however, in the quiet, crowded offices of the Pentagon and the State Department, their walls decorated with safes, filing cabinets, and maps, and in the more stately Victorian rooms of the Executive Office Building and the White House, a change of mood and a gradual change of vision and purpose were taking place. While B Company was destroying the bunkers near Alpha, President Lyndon Johnson was meeting with his top advisers, including the newly appointed Defense Secretary Clark Clifford, Press Secretary George Christian, and National Security Adviser Walt W. Rostow.[8] The President's White House staff was completing the last changes to a final draft of a major policy speech on Vietnam scheduled for the next evening, a speech that would profoundly influence American expectations toward the Vietnam War even while the war itself raged unabated.

The President's speech writers had been working on such an address since February 3, and the ensuing weeks had not been happy ones for Johnson. Heavy fighting continued in Vietnam, with the death toll rising to more than five hundred each week. More and more Americans had begun to express doubt and concern about the war. At a White House breakfast for Democratic congressional leaders, Senate leader Robert Byrd told the President that, though he had never raised any question in public, he was convinced that "Something is wrong over there." The Viet Cong, said Byrd, far from suffering from declining morale as the Administration had claimed, had demonstrated that they "could attack all over the country."[9] A Gallup poll taken in March showed President Johnson's popularity to have reached an all-time low. Only 36 percent of those polled approved of his conduct of the presidency, and only 26 percent supported his conduct of the war.[10] The *Wall Street Journal* warned on February 23: "The American people should be getting ready to accept, if they haven't already, the prospect that the whole Vietnam effort may be doomed."[11]

Then, on March 10, the Sunday *New York Times* carried a three-column story on page 1, under the headline: "Westmoreland Requests 206,000 More Men, Stirring Debate in Administration."

The news that the top American commander in Vietnam, General William C. Westmoreland, had requested such large reinforcements hit the American public with almost as much impact as the Tet attacks themselves. Secretary of State Dean Rusk was summoned to testify before the Senate Foreign Relations Committee, where he was grilled for eleven hours. In mid-March 139 members of the House of Representatives sponsored a resolution calling for a complete congressional review of U.S. policy in Vietnam. Senator Robert Kennedy, the former Attorney General, privately proposed to President Johnson that the Chief Executive appoint a commission of eminent Americans to reassess Vietnam policy.[12]

For many Americans the news seemed confirmation that U.S. forces must be in desperate straits in Vietnam. "The enemy now has the initiative; he has dramatically enlarged the area of combat; he has newer, more sophisticated weapons," warned Frank McGee in an NBC News special the evening of March 10. ". . . the war as the Administration has defined it is being lost. . . ."[13]

In fact, the Communists had suffered heavy casualties in the Tet attacks, and Westmoreland, who saw the Tet Offensive as "a devastating defeat for the Communists," was feeling more optimistic than ever.[14] "We face a situation of great opportunity as well as heightened risk," he wrote to Washington on February 12.[15]

Westmoreland and the Joint Chiefs of Staff had long wished to extend the ground war in South Vietnam into Laos in order to eliminate the Ho Chi Minh Trail, the North's main supply and infiltration route, and to attack Communist base areas across the Cambodian border. Those suggestions had been repeatedly rejected by the White House, but Westmoreland believed that Washington might now be willing to consider his proposals for a new offensive. With the encouragement of the JCS Chairman, General Earle Wheeler, Westmoreland renewed his request for a large reinforcement to carry out his long-deferred plans. Wheeler, aware of the President's opposition to widening the war, presented the case for more troops not as a step toward an expanded offensive but as a necessary measure to ensure against possible "reverses."[16] The Joint Chiefs of Staff also saw "great opportunity" in the Tet crisis. They had long urged the President to mobilize the Reserves and to reconstitute a strategic reserve to deal with possible Cold War crises in other parts of the world. The North Korean seizure of the American electronic surveillance ship *Pueblo* in January had underlined the possibility of such wider dangers for the United States.

From the viewpoint of the military planners, the 206,000 troop request was prudent and reasonable and would provide for a wide variety of contingencies, whether dangers or opportunities. Few civilians saw it that way. The massive reinforcement would further Americanize the war in Vietnam while bringing the war home to the United States with greater impact than ever before. The hundreds of thousands of Reservists, National Guardsmen, potential draftees, and their families would be most immediately affected, but all Americans would feel the effects in higher taxes, more pressure on the dollar, greater inflation, and above all more domestic turmoil. For, by the beginning of 1968, Americans were deeply divided over the question of Vietnam.

Moral and practical questions and criticisms about the war and the way it was being waged had spread far beyond the traditional peace groups and critics of American foreign policy to embrace members of the House and Senate, businessmen, clergy, and even some retired military. For a significant minority of Americans, including many of the country's intellectual and religious leaders and some of the brightest college students, the war, which by 1967 had already cost 15,000 American lives and thousands more Vietnamese casualties, seemed morally indefensible. Antiwar demonstrations became a commonplace on college campuses. Protestors picketed the White House chanting, "Hey, hey, LBJ, how many kids have you killed today?" In October 1967 thirty-five thousand demonstrators staged a one-day protest at the main entrance to the Pentagon.

The disquieting thing was that not only liberals, intellectuals, and college students were turning against the war, but men known for their hard-eyed realism and dispassionate insight into power politics. These included the columnist Walter Lippmann, whose olympian pronouncements had been carefully read by half a dozen Presidents, and Soviet expert and Cold War guru George Kennan. Former Republican National Committee Chairman Thurston Morton of Kentucky had come to oppose the war, as did about a quarter of the members of the House of Representatives. Democratic power broker Thomas P. "Tip" O'Neill discovered that his college-age son and daughter opposed the war and soon became far more critical of it himself.[17] A handful of senators, led by Foreign Relations Committee chairman J. William Fulbright, were in open revolt against the war by 1967.

The shock of Tet served to reinforce the doubts and criticism of those who had come to oppose the war while giving many politicians and opinion leaders who had reluctantly gone along the impetus to change their minds. The President's apparent indecisiveness and lack of direction during the troubling weeks of February and March also served to loosen the discipline he exercised over many Representatives and Senators, who at last felt free to go their own way and publicly express long-held doubts.[18] How confused and ambiguous feelings had now become was dramatically illustrated in the New Hampshire Presidential primary in March, when Senator Eugene McCarthy, an outspoken critic of the President's Vietnam policy, came within a few hundred votes of defeating Johnson in the Democratic race. The New Hampshire primary was widely interpreted as a stunning public rejection of the President's leadership in the Vietnam War.

Whatever its meaning, the New Hampshire primary served to highlight the fact that "the Tet Offensive had legitimatized the war as a political issue."[19] Four days after the primary a far more formidable rival to President Johnson, Robert F. Kennedy, brother of the late President and a hero to millions of Democrats, announced his candidacy for the nomination.

Most Americans were neither tortured by conscience over the death and suffering of the Vietnamese nor concerned about the war's impact on the Cold War balance of power. Yet there was a nagging, growing unease. The war seemed not to be succeeding, in fact seemed not to be going anywhere. "We ought to win it or get out," was a popular sentiment during late 1966 and 1967. The problem was that the means either to win or to get out were as confused and controversial as the war itself.

When U.S. troops had first come in force to South Vietnam in the summer of 1965, it was to rescue a U.S. ally believed to be on the verge of defeat at the hands of the Communists. The South Vietnamese Army, repeatedly defeated by the Viet Cong, appeared close to collapse. Meeting in Honolulu in April 1965, the President's advisers had concluded that the introduction of U.S. troops in the south would be a key measure in the U.S. effort to "break the will of the NVA/VC by depriving them of victory." Defense Secretary McNamara had estimated that "it will take more than six months, perhaps a year or two, to demonstrate VC failure in the south."[20] General Westmoreland reported two months later that the combat troops then arriving by sea and air at Da Nang, Saigon, and Cam Ranh Bay would "give us a hard hitting offensive capability on the ground to convince the VC they cannot win."[21]

By the end of 1966 it seemed clear that the intervention of U.S. combat forces had staved off the imminent collapse of the Saigon government. They had "demonstrated to the Communists that they cannot win," as the President's advisers were fond of repeating. Unfortunately, it was also apparent that the Communists had demonstrated the same to the Americans.

North Vietnam matched the buildup of forces with stepped up infiltration of their troops into the south and new weapons supplied by the Russians and Chinese. Westmoreland, aware of the Communist buildup, asked for and received additional American troops. By mid-1966 there were about 350,000 U.S. troops in Vietnam. By 1967 there were more than 400,000, and Westmoreland was outlining plans to employ more than 100,000 more. Fierce battles erupted near the northern border of South Vietnam, in the central highlands, and in the area near the Cambodian border known as War Zone C. U.S. casualties during 1967 rose to a new high of more than 200 killed and close to 1,400 wounded each week.[22]

Both sides proclaimed their success. Washington claimed to have inflicted heavy losses on the Viet Cong and North Vietnamese and to have shaken their hold on the countryside. Yet no end to the war appeared to be in sight. The Thirteenth Plenum of the Party in Hanoi spoke of a "decisive victory in a relatively short period of time," and the Communists were pleased with what they saw as their ability to hold their own against the richer, better equipped Americans. Yet the stalemate they were able to impose seemed to have no influence on Washington, which only increased the size of its commitment to South Vietnam. In the fall of 1967, the Communists decided to gamble on breaking the stalemate through a series of widespread and repeated attacks throughout South Vietnam. At best the attacks would galvanize popular discontent with Saigon and lead to the collapse of the Thieu government and disintegration of its army. At least the attacks would serve to convince the United States that it had no hope of winning.[23] By the third day of the Tet attacks, many Americans were convinced. What the reaction of the White House would be was another matter.

Westmoreland's proposal for 206,000 more troops was turned over to the new Secretary of Defense, Clark Clifford, for study. Clifford's was a name to conjure with in Washington in 1968. A wealthy and successful lawyer, a power in the Democratic party for more than twenty years, Clifford was widely credited with engineering Harry Truman's famous upset victory in the election of 1948. Called by newspapers "the consummate Washington insider," he had overseen the transition from the Eisenhower to the Kennedy Administration in 1960 and might have had any number of posts in the Kennedy and Johnson Administrations. Clifford, however, preferred to retain his independence and his lucrative law practice until finally prevailed upon by Johnson to accept the position of Secretary of Defense. "The President and I had a frank relationship through-out," Clifford recalled in a 1972 interview. "He had nothing I wanted. I was older than he. Our relationship was on an entirely different basis than some of his other advisers."[24]

Whether Clifford's assignment was to assess the merits of the troop proposal or merely to find a means whereby the proposal could be carried out is unclear, but Clifford soon determined on the former. Moreover, he had already talked with top civilians in the Pentagon, including Assistant Secretary of Defense for International Security Affairs Paul Warnke, Under Secretary of the Air Force Townsend Hoopes, and Deputy Secretary of Defense Paul Nitze, as well as the outgoing Secretary of Defense, Robert McNamara, all of whom had become increasingly critical of the course of U.S. policy in Vietnam. In a short time, Clifford transformed his mandate into a thorough reassessment of American strategy toward the Vietnam War.

The troop request proved easiest to decide. Sending reinforce-ments would not win the war, nor would withholding them lose it, while the political and economic costs would be disastrous. On March 22 the President formally decided against all but a very small troop increase for Vietnam. On the same day Johnson announced that General Westmoreland would be brought home in midsummer from his post as top U.S. commander in Vietnam to become Chief of Staff of the Army. Ostensibly a promotion, the move was widely viewed as a clear sign that Washington had lost confidence in Westmoreland's leadership.[25] "Westmoreland Kicked Upstairs" was the headline in Saigon's English-language *Daily News*.[26]

Publicly Westmoreland declared that he was honored by the new appointment. Privately he was disappointed and angry. "This was the spot that a lot of people had him pegged for but not the one he wanted," wrote one general on his staff. "He wanted very much to stay in the mainstream of the war."[27] At a dinner in his honor in Saigon, Westmoreland "gave a rather bitter speech in which half facetiously he said he didn't think he could get confirmed in his new post because the Senate would hold him responsible for all our failures."[28]

In fact, the President had not lost faith in his Vietnam command-er. Meeting with Joint Chiefs of Staff Chairman Earle Wheeler and

Westmoreland's deputy, General Creighton Abrams, Johnson said that he believed that the request for more troops was based on the need to counter the continued and substantial infiltration of Communist troops into South Vietnam.[29] Yet the President and his advisers were easily convinced by Clifford that the troop request was strategically doubtful and politically suicidal.

The larger questions of Vietnam policy remained. Clifford had become increasingly critical of the course the U.S. was following in Vietnam. "I have grave doubts we have made the type of progress we had hoped to make by this time," he told the President. "We continue to fight at a higher level of intensity. Do you want to continue the road of more troops, more guns, more planes? I see more and more fighting and more and more casualties and no end in sight."[30] Like McNamara and other proponents of de-escalation, Clifford and his advisers soon focused on the American air war against North Vietnam as the critical factor in the search for a settlement of the war.

The United States had first begun the sustained bombing of North Vietnam in the spring of 1965. By the end of 1965 American aircraft had flown about 55,000 sorties against North Vietnam and had dropped 33,000 tons of bombs, aiming at such targets as military barracks, ammunition depots, radio facilities, rail yards, naval bases, airfields, bridges, and radar installations.[31] By the end of 1966 the totals were 148,000 sorties and 128,000 tons of bombs. By December the United States had dropped a total of 860,000 tons of bombs on North Vietnam. That was more than the 631,000 tons dropped during the Korean War and far more than the 500,000 tons dropped during the entire war against Japan.

What had all this bombing accomplished? There was heated disagreement about that. When the initial air attacks against North Vietnam had been launched, strategists in the White House had expected that the pain and shock inflicted by the bombing would soon compel the North Vietnamese to stop, or at least slow down, their support of the war in South Vietnam. They also believed that the bombing would boost the morale of the Republic of South Vietnam, sorely beset by increasingly destructive attacks by the Viet Cong.

The bombing did boost the morale of South Vietnamese leaders, or at least they told the Americans it did. Presidential adviser McGeorge Bundy, who imagined, like his fellow New Englander Longfellow, that humanity was still "hanging breathless" on every move made in Washington, was confident that the bombing "laid to rest the widespread fears among Asian nations that the U.S. lacked the will and determination to do what was necessary in Southeast Asia."[32] Unfortunately, this display of will and determination had little apparent effect on the North Vietnamese, whose commitment to the war in the south showed no sign of abating.

The bombing's economic and military damage to North Vietnam was estimated by the CIA at about $130 million by the end of 1966, and more than 35,000 North Vietnamese, 80 percent of them civilians, had been killed. Destructive as it seemed, the bombing was, in fact, carefully controlled and limited. The thousands of civilian casualties were an increasing source of anguish and embarrassment to those Americans who questioned Washington's strategy and a growing object of condemnation abroad. Yet tragic and appalling as they were, they were actually small compared to casualties inflicted in the strategic bombing of British, German, Chinese, and Japanese cities during World War II.[33] Washington leaders were acutely aware that unleashing dozens of aircraft and thousands of pounds of bombs against a country on the border of the People's Republic of China and closely allied to the Soviet Union carried considerable risks. Many of them held vivid memories of the Chinese intervention in Korea fifteen years before, and the ultimate intentions and motives of the Chinese were little clearer in the mid-1960s than they had been in 1950. For those reasons the bombings were carefully regulated and modulated from Washington. Each list of targets to be bombed was submitted one (later two) weeks at a time through a long chain stretching from the military commands to the Department of Defense, the State Department, the White House, and often to the President himself. Washington officials even determined the strength, altitude, and direction of each strike.

The President and his top civilian advisers also saw the bombing as a slow and deliberate means of compelling the North Vietnamese to ease their pressure on the south. "The pattern adopted was designed to preserve the options to proceed or not, escalate or not, quicken the pace or not, depending on North Vietnam's reaction.

The carrot of stopping the bombing was deemed as important as the stick of continuing it, and bombing pauses were provided for."[34]

But the Joint Chiefs of Staff and the Army, Navy, and Air Force commanders in Vietnam had no use for carrots and sticks. Their preference was for sledgehammers. They wanted to attack North Vietnam rapidly, unrelentingly, with overwhelming force; to destroy its airbases, planes, and anti-aircraft defenses; to cripple its few industries; to tear up its bridges and railroads; to cut off its fuel and power supplies. Instead they had to settle for a finely adjusted mix of restraints, of fits and starts emanating from Washington. Aviators saw this approach as absurd and dangerous, and the generals saw it as militarily unsound and futile.[35] "We repeatedly killed dedicated professional air officers and lost expensive and irreplaceable aircraft," wrote Jack Broughton, an Air Force fighter pilot, "because of the maze of restrictions imposed on those of us assigned the task of fighting in a nearly impossible situation."[36]

After almost three years of war neither party to the bombing debate had any accurate concept of the enemy they faced. The civilian experts, analysts, and elder statesmen in the Pentagon and the White House had made their careers handling the convoluted competitions and crises of the Cold War with the Soviets. The dynamics of the nuclear arms race, the management of competition and confrontation in Europe, and the care and nurturing of the U.S. global alliance system were the areas where they claimed, and were acknowledged to have, special expertise. They had demonstrated this expertise to their own and to most observers' satisfaction in the recent Cuban Missile Crisis. The Soviets were tough, determined, wily, and ruthless opponents. Like the Americans, they possessed the means to destroy the world in a nuclear war. Yet they were also cautious, fairly consistent, more or less rational, and fairly predictable, as the Missile Crisis had shown.

They were also familiar. Some senior presidential advisers, like Dean Rusk, George Ball, and Averell Harriman, had dealt with Soviet-related problems and issues for more than twenty-five years. Compared with the knowledge and experience concerning the Soviets or even the Chinese, the depth of ignorance about Vietnamese history, society, and motivation that pervaded the American government in 1965—from the newest Foreign Service officer or systems analyst to the most distinguished Cabinet members and congressmen—was striking.

The aviators, generals, and admirals knew even less about Vietnam, but they knew something about air power and how it could influence wars. The senior commanders had seen firsthand the destruction it had wrought in the cities of Germany and Japan, remembered how the two strongest Japanese bases in the Pacific had been isolated and crippled entirely by air, how air attacks had destroyed the German transportation system before D-Day. That Vietnam was a far different country from 1940s Germany or even Japan and was waging a far different kind of war, a war that required only a tiny fraction of the supplies consumed by a German Panzer division or a Japanese carrier strike force, was a fact only gradually becoming apparent.

With the commitment of American combat troops to Vietnam in the summer of 1965, Washington's emphasis shifted from bombing as a way of breaking North Vietnamese will to bombing as a way of depriving Hanoi of the means to wage war in the south. The list of targets was steadily increased, along with the rate and scale of attacks. Yet the increase was gradual, and entire areas of North Vietnam, including the cities of Hanoi and Haiphong, which contained important industrial and port facilities, were spared. Also off limits were areas within 25 miles of the Chinese border. President Johnson was keenly aware of the danger of inadvertently provoking China or Russia into entering the war and escalating the conflict to a superpower confrontation. "We don't want a wider war," the President emphasized, "They [North Vietnamese] have two big brothers that have more weight and people than I have."[37] Johnson and his advisers stressed that the bombing was directed at slowing and reducing infiltration and equipment into the south through attacking ammunition depots, barracks, supply depots, and lines of communication.

As the bombing continued, the North Vietnamese greatly strengthened its air defenses. China and Russia supplied them with sophisticated anti-aircraft guns, radars, and missiles, as well as jet fighter aircraft, until by 1967 North Vietnam had one of the most modern air defense systems in the world.[38] The limited bombing campaign in the north, while increasing numbers of American troops were being committed to combat in the south, seemed ineffective and illogical to the Joint Chiefs and to most military commanders in the field. The Commander-in-Chief, Pacific, Admiral Ulysses S. Grant Sharp, expressed a view that would be repeated by military leaders many times throughout the war when he declared at the end of 1965, "The Armed Forces of the United States should not be required to fight this war with one arm tied behind their backs."[39] A few weeks later Sharp called for an expanded air campaign directed at North Vietnam's road and rail links with China, destruction of the North's petroleum, oil, and lubricants ("POL") facilities, and intensified attacks on Communist military facilities and activities south of the 20th Parallel. "These three tasks well done," promised Sharp, "will bring the enemy to the conference table or cause the insurgency to wither from lack of support."[40] Sharp's recommendations and arguments were to be repeated many times throughout the next two years. They represented the thinking of many senior generals and admirals about how the air war ought to be waged now that the United States was fully committed to war in Vietnam.

Against their repeated urgings, the President and his advisers also had to weigh the consistent reports of the Central Intelligence Agency, which emphasized that North Vietnam was a primarily agricultural nation with a primitive transportation system and few industries. Almost all of the Communists' military equipment came from China and the Soviet Union. As for the Viet Cong and North Vietnamese forces in the South, they were dependent on the North for only a very small amount of supplies and equipment, estimated at about 100 tons a day. To the intelligence analysts, then, North Vietnam looked like a very unrewarding object of air attack; there simply weren't enough high-value targets.

Then, in the spring of 1966, American military leaders began strongly pushing for an air campaign that would finally have a really decisive effect: an attack on the North's petroleum, oil, and lubricants system. POL, they argued, was the Communists' Achilles' heel. Ninety-seven percent of North Vietnam's oil and lubricants storage capacity was concentrated in just thirteen sites. Sixty percent of the North's total POL was consumed by the military. The trucks and motor-driven sampans carrying supplies to the South could not run without gasoline. The President's National Security Adviser, Walt W. Rostow, was enthusiastic, and Secretary McNamara agreed, provided the strikes could be carried out without excessive civilian casualties or damage to merchant shipping.

On June 22 the President approved the proposed strikes. The attack on the POL targets was to be a maximum effort involving only the most experienced crews, supported by flak suppression and electronic countermeasures aircraft. Clear, cloudless weather was essential. Beginning on June 24, the National Military Command Center began sending McNamara written weather forecasts every few hours. On June 29 the weather finally cleared. A message from Washington went out to Admiral Sharp over a special channel: EXECUTE.

On airfields in South Vietnam and Thailand and on carriers in the South China Sea the hiss and whine of jet engines could be heard in the predawn darkness as hundreds of pilots and technicians completed their final preparations and aircraft rose into the slowly brightening sky. Tank farms at both Haiphong and Hanoi were struck simultaneously, and by the end of the day black soot and flame covered both cities. By the end of the month almost 80 percent of the North's bulk fuel capacity had been destroyed.

It was a superb job of bombing. And it made no difference to the war. Despite the destruction of much of their large storage capacity the Communists were never short of fuel. They simply didn't need all that much anyway, and their needs could be satisfied by switching to a system of dispersing already drummed fuel along transportation routes and in small underground storage sites. Less fuel might be stored in North Vietnam, but more fuel could be sent in already drummed and ready for use. Bombing might have wrecked the Haiphong docks, but tankers simply stood offshore and unloaded onto barges. By the end of September the CIA and DIA were reporting "no evidence yet of any shortage of POL in North Vietnam . . . no evidence of insurmountable transport difficulties . . . no significant economic dislocation and no weakening of popular morale."[41]

The failure of the POL campaign convinced Defense Secretary McNamara that bombing the North could never have a decisive impact on the course of the war in South Vietnam. McNamara's systems analysts calculated that the United States was spending almost ten dollars in direct operational costs for the bombing for every one dollar of damage inflicted on North Vietnam. The operational costs also included almost five hundred planes lost and hundreds of aviators killed or captured by the end of 1966. "To bomb the North sufficiently to make a radical impact upon Hanoi's political, economic, and social structure," McNamara told the President in October 1966, "would require an effort which we could make but which would not be stomached either by our own people or by world opinion, and it would involve a serious risk of drawing us into war with China." McNamara recommended that the bombing be stabilized at its present level and "at the proper time . . . I believe we should consider terminating bombing in all of North Vietnam or at least in the northeast zones for an indefinite period in connection with concurrent moves toward peace."[42]

Outside government, other voices were raised against the continued bombing. The spectacle of the world's strongest military power waging war against one of the world's poorest and most backward provoked a storm of criticism and condemnation abroad. The British philosopher and political gadfly Bertrand Russell convened an "International War Crimes Tribunal" in Stockholm to try U.S. leaders in absentia for waging "a war like that waged by fascist Japan and Nazi Germany."[43] Ho Chi Minh and the embattled peasants of North Vietnam became instant heros to students and left-wing parties all over Europe, and even British Prime Minister Harold Wilson worried that the bombing of North Vietnam "without producing decisive military advantage may only increase the difficulty of reaching an eventual military settlement."[44]

U.S. critics of the President's Vietnam policy had long since made the bombing the central focus of their protests, and even many Americans who still hoped for success in Vietnam had come, like McNamara, to believe that the continued bombing might be more of an obstacle than an aid in achieving a favorable end to the war. The distinguished *New York Times* correspondent Harrison Salisbury visited North Vietnam at the end of 1966 and reported on the extensive damage done to civilian targets (accidentally, said the

Pentagon; deliberately, said the antiwar critics) by the American air campaign.

None of the U.S. top military leaders, however, were ready to concede that the bombing could be stopped. The only thing wrong with the bombing, the military planners in the Pentagon, Hawaii, and Vietnam argued, was that it was too gradual and too limited. They argued that Communist forces in the South would be far stronger and better equipped except for the relentless pressure of the American air attack on their lines of communication.

The generals and admirals found a sympathetic audience in the Senate Armed Services Committee, headed by the veteran political leader John C. Stennis of Mississippi. Stennis and his colleagues, longtime standard bearers for the military like Senators Henry Jackson, Stewart Symington, and Strom Thurmond, listened with pained disbelief to McNamara's arguments that the bombing had already destroyed every worthwhile target in North Vietnam while utterly failing to reduce the flow of supplies to the South. They were far more receptive to the military's arguments that, but for the bombing, the Communists would have double the number of troops in South Vietnam. The committee issued a blistering report castigating Washington leaders for "the fragmentation of our air might by overly restrictive controls, limitations and the doctrine of gradualism placed on our aviation forces which prevented them from waging the air campaign in the manner and according to the time table which was best calculated to achieve maximum results."[45]

Bowing to the pressure from the Stennis subcommittee and the military, Johnson authorized the bombing of several previously prohibited targets. At the same time, however, in a speech in San Antonio, Texas, the President also announced that the United States was willing to stop all bombing of North Vietnam in return for assurances that this would lead to prompt negotiations and that the Communists would "not take advantage" of such a cessation of bombing. At the end of 1967 the bombing of North Vietnam continued at a high level, with few targets left unscathed. Defense Secretary McNamara had accepted an appointment as head of the World Bank.

Now, as Johnson and his advisers weighed their options in the wake of the Tet Offensive and Westmoreland's troop request, the bombing came up again. As in the past, a bombing halt was seen by all as an important gesture to symbolize U.S. reasonableness and willingness to negotiate. A partial bombing halt had been suggested at the beginning of March by Secretary of State Dean Rusk. Rusk argued that a bombing pause confined to the area of North Vietnam north of the 20th Parallel would do little military harm during the monsoon season and could do much to quiet public outcries against the war. If, as expected, the Communists failed to respond positively to the pause, bombing could be resumed with the United States in a stronger moral position. Clifford and his staff had also come to support a bombing halt, but as a first step toward real negotiations.

On March 20 and 22 the President met with his advisers to discuss the idea of including an announcement of a bombing halt in his policy speech, now scheduled for the end of the month. At the first meeting, both Rusk and former National Security Adviser McGeorge Bundy expressed the growing pessimism that many in the President's inner circle had begun to feel over the course of the Vietnam War. "The clement of hope has been taken away by the Tet Offensive," Rusk observed. "People don't think there is likely to be an end." Bundy agreed, adding that Washington must have something "to offer besides a new war," something that would emphasize U.S. "reasonableness versus Hanoi's unreasonableness."[46]

Yet there was little agreement on what concrete measures to take. At the March 22 meeting, the discussion of a possible bombing halt was confused and inconclusive. The President, referring to the "dramatic shift in public opinion on the war," expressed interest in some sort of change in bombing that might spare Hanoi and Haiphong "and wait two weeks on possible developments." Secretary Clifford, repeating his observation that Vietnam was "a bottomless pit," suggested a cessation of bombing above the 20th Parallel. Rusk supported Clifford's suggestion but cautioned that Hanoi was unlikely to reciprocate. Assistant Secretary of State William Bundy added that any bombing halt "would cause major difficulties in Saigon," while Rostow said that "Hanoi would know full well that we were taking advantage of the bad weather." While it "might have some effect on the doves," it would ultimately be unsuccessful. McGeorge Bundy agreed that a bombing halt would have "a short life diplomatically" but was not opposed. Supreme Court Justice

Abe Fortas, a close friend and adviser of the President, dismissed the bombing halt as "too little and too late." Instead, the President's speech ought to emphasize the acts of aggression and brutality by the Communists to remind the public "why we are in Vietnam."[47]

With the President's speech only ten days away, Clifford decided that he "needed some stiff medicine" to persuade the President to adopt his view.[48] He suggested that Johnson call a meeting of his informal group of elder statesmen and advisers, dubbed by White House staffers "The Wise Men."

The Wise Men had no formal authority but immense influence and prestige. They included men who had formerly served in the Johnson Administration—such as McGeorge Bundy, former Under Secretary of State George Ball, and former deputy Secretary of Defense Cyrus Vance—but also men of great stature and reputation from both parties, men whose names were already in the history books: Dean Acheson, former Secretary of State under Truman; Douglas Dillon, who had held high office under both Eisenhower and Kennedy; and John J. McCloy, whose record of distinguished public service stretched back to World War II. Three of the nation's famous soldiers were there as well. General of the Army Omar Bradley, one of the two living American five-star generals; General Matthew Ridgway, the miracle worker of the Korean War; and General Maxwell Taylor, a paratrooper hero of World War II and former Chairman of the Joint Chiefs of Staff. Altogether it was a group whose names were synonymous with the great trials and triumphs of the last quarter-century: the D-Day invasion, the Berlin blockade, the Marshall Plan, the Korean War. They were men from the centers of power, the great law firms, banks, and corporations, renowned for their judgment and devotion to public service.

Like their friends and younger protégés in the Administration, The Wise Men's focus was on the great issues of world politics: the management of relations with Europe and of the continuing Soviet–American confrontation, and the prudent application of American power. They knew little of the particulars of Southeast Asia and cared less. Yet they knew that the war had become a problem and a menace, a threat not only to the cohesion and rationality of American political life, but to the type of world order they had spent their careers building and maintaining.

On March 26 The Wise Men assembled over dinner and received a briefing on the Vietnam situation by senior State, Defense, and CIA officials. They were not reassured. The following day the group met for lunch with the President. They were joined by JCS Chairman Wheeler and General Creighton Abrams, Westmoreland's deputy, just returned from Vietnam. "Are we not relatively much stronger today than a year ago, two years ago?" the President demanded of the two generals. "Yes" was the reply. "If you take the five-year period from July 1965 to July 1970, are we as far along proportionally as in World War II?" Johnson asked. "Yes" replied General Wheeler, "even better off."[49]

Few of The Wise Men found this type of logic convincing. Dean Acheson summed up the group's view when he warned, "We cannot do the job we set out to do in the time we have left, and we must begin to take steps to disengage." A minority of the group favored holding the line. Justice Fortas protested: "This is not the time for an overture on our part. I do not think a cessation of bombing would do any good at this time. I do not believe in drama for the sake of drama." "This issue is not that stated by Justice Fortas," snapped Acheson. "The issue is can we do what we are trying to do in Vietnam? I do not think we can . . . the issue is can we, by military means, keep the North Vietnamese off the South Vietnamese? I do not think we can. They can slip around and end-run them and crack them up."[50]

Rostow would later complain that The Wise Men "were not focusing on Vietnam but on the political situation in the U.S."[51] His observation was in a large sense true and in a large sense irrelevant. American policy had always been decided on the basis of considerations largely divorced from the actual situation in Vietnam. Assistant Defense Secretary John McNaughton, one of the architects of the carefully modulated bombing of North Vietnam, had once listed the reasons for American involvement in Vietnam as "70 percent to avoid a humiliating defeat, 20 percent to counter Sino-Soviet influence, and 10 percent to aid the South Vietnamese." Now the domestic political and Cold War geopolitical calculations that made up 90 percent of the equation had changed. That was the true message of The Wise Men to President Johnson, and the President understood. Though he raged that "the establishment bastards have bailed out" and demanded to hear the briefings the Defense Department and CIA had presented to the group, the President knew that he must now take some action to reassure the public that the United States was not simply sinking deeper into war.

At 9:00 p.m. on Sunday, March 31, as the planes carrying his son-in-law, Captain Charles Robb, and some four hundred other Marines to Vietnam were landing on Okinawa, Johnson stepped before the television cameras to announce, "Good evening my fellow Americans. Tonight I want to speak to you of peace in Vietnam. . . ."

After repeating his San Antonio proposal, the President announced: "I am taking the first step to de-escalate the conflict." The President declared:

> We are prepared to move immediately toward peace through negotiations. . . . We are reducing—substantially reducing—the present level of hostilities. And we are doing so unilaterally and at once. Tonight I have ordered our aircraft and our naval vessels to make no attacks on North Vietnam, except in the area north of the Demilitarized Zone where the continuing enemy buildup directly threatens allied forward positions and where the movements of their troops and supplies are clearly related to that threat.

The President went on to announce, "Now, as in the past, the United States is ready to send its representatives to any forum at any time to discuss the means of bringing this ugly war to an end. I am designating one of our most distinguished Americans, Ambassador Averell Harriman, as my personal representative for such talks. I call upon President Ho Chi Minh to respond positively and favorably to this new step toward peace."

Coming to the end of his address, the President stunned the nation with his closing announcement:

> With America's sons in the fields far away, with Americans under challenge right here at home, with our hopes and the world's hopes for peace in the balance every day, I do not believe that I should devote an hour or a day of my time to any personal partisan causes or

to any duties other than the awesome duties of this office—the Presidency of your country. Accordingly I shall not seek, and I will not accept, the nomination of my party for another term as your President.

After the speech came another shock. On April 3, three days after Johnson's surprise announcement, Radio Hanoi announced that the Communists were ready to talk.

Americans were momentarily stunned, then euphoric. The "20 words that shook the world," *Newsweek* declared, "gave the nation an almost cathartic sense of relief at the prospect of a move toward peace."[52] Almost fifty thousand telegrams, most of them favorable, poured into the White House between March 31 and April 2.[53] The Dow-Jones index jumped twenty points. A poll of fifty-seven major news editors and columnists showed that forty-three approved of the speech and only five disapproved.[54]

Some active opponents of the war experienced jubilation; now Kennedy would be President. Now the war would end. Others suspected a trap, a cynical political maneuver by a President they had come to hate and mistrust. Of one thing everyone was sure, a great turning point had been reached. A British journalist visiting the United States a few months after LBJ's speech was struck by the way in which . . .

the rancorous, near hysterical atmosphere of the Tet Offensive has been entirely transformed since the President's speech. . . . People outside politics are not arguing much about the war at present. . . . Most of them appear to believe that whoever captures the presidency . . . will be obliged to end the conflict within a matter of months. How this is to be done or what concessions are to be made is very much a matter of detail.[55]

It was this matter of detail which was to prolong the war for the next four and a half years and bring thirty thousand more young Americans to an early grave. For no one really knew what the details might involve. Clifford and The Wise Men had no real solutions to offer. Their attention was elsewhere: on the war's impact on larger American policy; on its impact on politics and the economy in the

United States; on limiting the damage. The Pentagon civilian analysts also had few solutions beyond stabilizing, containing, and scaling down the war. What was to come after that was not clear. They had fought for a bombing halt and a de-escalation of the war for so long that when those were finally achieved they had little more to offer beyond the stale formulas of giving more of the burden of the war to the South Vietnamese, an exercise in wishful thinking and self-delusion that would soon be elevated to the status of a policy.

The President's decision on March 31 put a ceiling on American ground forces in Vietnam but left most other questions unresolved. Johnson's real motives at the time can never be precisely known, but whatever the media might say, he was far from abandoning hope for ultimate success in Vietnam. At the meeting with his advisers at which Johnson had insisted that we were "further along proportionally" than in World War II, the CIA analyst George Carver had suggested to the President that "1968 will be the decisive year. The next two to four months will be decisive. The political balance may tip. Our contribution must be one of attitude."[56] It may well be that Johnson's apparent change of policy was primarily a bid for time in order to see the "decisive year" through to success. Yet how would success be achieved?

In the end the details were to be settled in the mountains, jungles, and rice paddies of Vietnam itself. Both the Americans in Saigon and the Communists in Hanoi believed themselves to be on the offensive against a seriously weakened enemy. The day following the President's speech, General Westmoreland directed his commanders to make every effort to "maintain maximum pressure on the enemy in the south. . . . Maximum pressure at this point could demoralize the enemy in the south and bring about an unprecedented defection rate."[57]

On the same day, the standing committee of COSVN, the Communist high command for South Vietnam, issued a directive to all military units and leaders of the People's Revolutionary Party. The U.S. imperialists, it stated, were "being isolated throughout the world." In Vietnam, "the U.S. ground forces are now short of personnel, the negroes have risen up to oppose the government. . . . Our position is still strong. Our personnel strength has doubled." The Party Current Affairs Committee resolved "to maintain and expand the victories we have just gained by continuously attacking and pursuing the enemy. . . . We must intensify attacks in cities and towns and simultaneously seek to liberate all the areas in the vicinity of these urban zones."[58] For the Communists the Tet attacks were only the first step in a series of coordinated attacks on towns and bases, which they planned to continue throughout the spring and summer. For the Americans in Saigon, Communist military setbacks at Tet appeared to open the way at last to a knockout blow.

Over the eight weeks following the March 31 speech, 3,700 Americans would be killed in Vietnam. In the period from May 5 to May 18 alone close to 1,800 would die, almost double the number killed in the first two weeks of the Tet Offensive. During the same eight weeks nearly 18,000 American combatants would be wounded seriously enough to require hospitalization. Communist dead, according to widely disputed figures collected by Westmoreland's headquarters, totaled more than 43,000.[59] Few paid much attention to South Vietnamese military casualties, but they were usually double those of the Americans.[60]

During 1968 both sides would make their maximum effort to break the stalemate in South Vietnam. Over the next nine months, while attention in the United States was focused almost entirely on election year politics and the hope of a peace settlement in Paris, Americans in Vietnam would lift the siege of Khe Sanh and launch a counteroffensive. The Communists would stage a second wave of attacks in May and a third in August. American and Vietnamese forces would make their greatest sustained effort and would suffer their heaviest losses. American GIs, caught in a confusing, frustrating, and seemingly unwinnable war, buffeted by the winds of racial and generational conflict at home, would fight on, but their military organization would begin a slow disintegration. The people of South Vietnam would experience even greater social upheaval, terror, and destruction than they had known in the previous long years of war. America's Saigon ally, with all its chronic weakness and corruption, would weather the storm but emerge with its fatal flaws intact and as unchangeable as ever.

CHAPTER 2

"You Don't Know How Lucky We Are to Have Soldiers Like This"

B y 1968 the United States had well over a half-million fighting men in Vietnam. The nature of that Army reflected many of the confusions and compromises of the American commitment to Vietnam. In the course of 1968, as fighting in Vietnam intensified and social upheaval in the United States grew worse, the Army would begin to feel the strain.

The half-million American soldiers, Marines, aviators, and sailors who were to fight the battles of 1968 were in many respects the finest military force the United States had ever sent abroad. Their grandfathers in World War I had sometimes been sent to battle only half-trained. In World War II Americans had suffered devastating defeats on Bataan and at Kasserine Pass. In Korea many of the first American troops to fight against the North Koreans had abandoned their equipment and fled in panic.[1] Yet when the Marines and air cavalry met the Communist regulars in the Ia Drang Valley and along the central coast of Vietnam in 1965, they had held their ground, and if anyone could be said to have won those short, bloody, and confused first battles of this new war it was the Americans.

Two decades later, when they are widely regarded as "society's losers, the same men who got left behind in schools and jobs. . . . suckers having to risk their lives in the wrong war,"[2] it is difficult to recall how differently these men were viewed in 1968. Officers and career NCOs who had served in earlier wars regarded them with respect and admiration. "These young troopers coming out here straight from staging battalion or ITR [infantry training] never cease to amaze me," declared a Marine officer at the end of 1968. "They'll work themselves to death for you. They'll do anything you tell them to."[3] "The amazing thing about our troops is that they fought with all they had, never complaining," a veteran first sergeant observed in 1966. "The men out there were outstanding, and if I have to go into battle again I hope the same type of men are with me."[4] "You just can't understand how lucky we are to have soldiers like this," a captain with the First Battalion, 26th Infantry, said. "He fought as bravely if not more so than his predecessors in World War I or II."[5]

The men and women who inspired such extravagant praise from the career soldiers were not themselves professionals. They were draftees and reluctant volunteers, led by captains, lieutenants, and junior NCOs who were also on their first, and as they loudly proclaimed their only, term of service. They were the product of the peculiar military manpower system that fed the Vietnam War, a system that by 1968 had become a distorted mirror, a monstrous caricature of American short-sightedness, irresponsibility, phony patriotism, self-serving expediency, and political cowardice.

The experience of World War II and Korea and the years of Cold War crises had led military planners to base much of their planning on the assumption that a substantial number of National Guard and Reserve troops would be called to duty in the event of a major military commitment such as Vietnam.[6] That had been the pattern in all previous wars from the War of 1812, when 460,000 militia had been mobilized to support seven thousand regulars, to Korea, where 380,000 Reserves and National Guardsmen had been called to the colors to supplement the regular Army of 590,000.[7] By the 1960s Army Guard and Reserve units were better trained and equipped than ever before in American history, while the Navy, Air Force, and Marine Corps also maintained large and similarly well-equipped Reserve establishments. Yet in July 1965 President Johnson, a few days before he announced to the nation that major combat units would be committed to Vietnam, informed the Defense Department that there would be no Reserve callup and not even an extension of tours for those men already on active duty.[8] The decision was the President's own. He was concerned, he said, about sending alarming signals to the Russians and Chinese.[9] What he did not say publicly was that he was also concerned about sending alarming signals to the American people. A Reserve callup would signal that the country was really going to war, that the war would probably be long and painful, that some of the President's most cherished programs and priorities might have to be put aside. If the Reserves were to be retained for more than a year, the President would have to declare a national emergency, "something even more dramatic and decisive than calling the Reserves."[10]

All through 1965 and 1966, the Joint Chiefs of Staff pressed for a Reserve callup, and all through those years the President said no. Meanwhile, young men of draft age soon realized that the Reserves represented a safe haven. Guard and Reserve units rapidly began to fill up with affluent and well-connected young men, many of them college graduates. Major General George Gilson of the Maryland National Guard told *Life* magazine that whenever the Baltimore Colts "have a player with a military problem they send him to us." At one point in the 1960s the Dallas Cowboys had ten players assigned to the same National Guard division. By 1968 the Army National Guard had a waiting list of a hundred thousand men. Less than 1 percent of the members of the National Guard were black.[11] So bitter and resentful were the feelings about the Guard and Reserve that in 1988 the charge that vice presidential candidate Dan Quayle had used special influence to find a billet in the Indiana Air National Guard during the Vietnam conflict would create a storm of angry controversy.

Whatever his reasons, the President's decision on the Guard and the Reserve decisively shaped the composition of the forces that were to fight in Vietnam. Denied the opportunity to call up Reserves or extend tours of duty, the armed forces were obliged to depend on conscription and on recruiting, largely induced by threat of conscription, to meet their manpower requirements. In effect, the United States would create a "Vietnam-only" army to fight its war in Southeast Asia, and the engine that drove the entire process of persuading or inducing men to serve in that army was the draft.

By 1965 compulsory military service, invariably referred to as "the draft" was largely taken for granted by most Americans. The last serious congressional debate over the merits of the draft had been in 1951–52.[12] As late as August 1966, 79 percent of respondents told a Harris poll that they "favored the present draft system."[13]

Only a minority of Americans had reached adulthood in a time when the United States had not had conscription. The draft was widely regarded as a fact of life and also as an important rite of passage, like graduation, marriage, and fatherhood. Boys "became men" in the armed services, according to popular wisdom. Even rock music idol Elvis Presley had been obliged to serve his turn in the Army and could be seen in fan magazine photos of the 1950s on maneuvers with his "Army buddies" in Germany.

Despite its apparent universality and efficiency, the Selective Service System had, in fact, undergone significant changes since the Korean War. During World War II and until the mid-1950s, the draft did roughly correspond to the popular image of a near-universal conscription system. Of men who were twenty-six years old in 1958, 88 percent of those found physically and mentally qualified had served in the armed forces. However, only 79 percent of qualified twenty-six year-olds in 1962 had seen service, and in 1966 the figure had fallen to 65 percent.[14]

The main cause of the marked change in the impact of the draft was a growing proportion of eighteen-year-olds in the population. In 1955 only 1,150,000 young men reached the age of eighteen during the year. By 1965 1,700,000 males were celebrating their eighteenth birthday, and the figure had reached 2 million by the early 1970s. This growth in population, together with steady or declining draft calls, meant that, despite the continuing image of "universal service," a steadily decreasing proportion of the nation's youth was being called upon to serve.

The response of the Selective Service System was to liberalize deferments. During World War II and the Korean War deferments from service were relatively few. During the late 1950s and early 1960s, however, deferments were freely granted. College and graduate school students qualified without regard to course of study or class standing. Fathers were granted deferments, and later married men without children. Other men qualified for exemption on the basis of possessing skills or working in occupations important to the "national interests, health, and safety." At the same time, the Army raised the mental and physical standards for service, thus ensuring a higher rate of rejections on those grounds.

By 1964 the Defense Department was examining ways in which the draft might be phased out. Given the rising pool of eligible young men and steady or declining military needs, the task appeared possible in the long run, albeit expensive and difficult. Then came Vietnam.[15]

As the Vietnam buildup continued, draft calls were revised dramatically upward. Total inductions during fiscal year 1965, the last year of peace, had totaled about 120,000. For fiscal 1966 the Department of the Army projected a modest increase of about fifteen thousand men. President Johnson's commitment of major units to Vietnam in the spring and summer of 1965 quickly rendered these plans obsolete. The actual number of inductions during fiscal 1966 was almost 320,000 men, a 250 percent increase over the previous year. Three hundred thousand were for the Army, and twenty thousand more for the Marines. Inductions for fiscal 1967 continued at the three hundred thousand level. During the following fiscal year inductions reached a new high of 334,000. By the last half of 1968 levels of inductions had begun to decrease, but they still totaled two and one-half times what they had been in the "normal" years of the early 1960s.

As draft calls rose, the unevenness and inconsistency of the Selective Service System became more apparent. Instead of pictures of Elvis Presley serving as an ordinary GI, newspapers carried stories like the case of the actor who held a hardship deferment because his mother, who lived in his Hollywood mansion, needed his $200,000 yearly income as her "sole support." The draft also became a target for opponents of the war, some of whom encouraged young men to evade or "resist" induction. Public outcries against what was perceived by many to be an unfair, archaic, and discriminatory system increased.

At the heart of the Selective Service System were more than four thousand local boards whose constituencies ranged in size from twenty-seven registrants for one board in Colorado to fifty-four thousand for one in Los Angeles.[16] The three to five members of the local board were nominated by the state's governor and appointed by the President for unlimited terms. All served without compensation and were required to be residents of the county in which their board was located. By the beginning of the Vietnam buildup, almost half of the local board members had served for ten or more years, and nearly half were over sixty years of age. Almost a quarter were over seventy. About two-thirds of the board members were veterans, but only 3 percent had seen service as recently as the Korean War. Over 30 percent had served in World War I. Less than 2 percent of the board members were black.[17]

General Louis Hershey, the director of Selective Service, was wont to describe the local boards as "little groups of neighbors on whom is placed the responsibility to determine who is to serve the nation."[18] If the local boards had ever had those characteristics, they had long since lost them by 1965. By that time only a small minority of the local board members could be characterized as neighbors, or even acquaintances, of the young men they were classifying and inducting. In one survey of registrants in Wisconsin, less than 20 percent of the registrants, even in small towns and rural areas, could identify a single member of their local board by name. A study of the Chicago area found that "many board members who were originally appointed when they were South Shore residents had since moved to North Shore suburbs but still commuted to their original board." The area covered by the board had, in the interim, become populated predominantly by blacks recently arrived from the rural south.[19] One author observed the deliberations of several local boards in a large Eastern city for six months and "saw no instance in which board members knew a registrant or his family."[20]

In the great majority of cases brought before the board, classifications were routine or mandated by law. In passing on the remaining cases, however, the local boards exercised wide discretion in granting or withholding deferments and classifications. Policies varied widely from one board to the next. Two consultants to the National Advisory Commission on Selective Service observed, "Men of one age group or a particular marital status are drafted in one state, deferred in another; a group of graduate students with similar programs and records at the same institution are classified in a variety of ways by their respective local boards; teachers, artisans, and social workers may be automatically deferred in some boards and automatically drafted in other boards; the possibilities are almost infinite."[21]

The National Advisory Commission on Selective Service appointed by the President in 1966 urged an end to most deferments and selection by lottery, with the youngest called first. Strong opposition to reform among influential members of the House and Senate Armed Services Committees blocked reform efforts, and it was not until 1970 that important changes were made in the Selective Service System. Those changes presaged the end of peacetime conscription and the introduction of the all-volunteer force.

Though it was the focus of public attention, the draft did not provide all or even the majority of the men who served in Vietnam. Throughout the war the Navy, Air Force, and, with some exceptions, the Marine Corps recruited only volunteers, and men continued to enlist in the Army in large numbers. The great majority of the Army enlistments were draft-motivated and prompted by a desire to obtain a guarantee of some particular training, branch, or area of service.[22] Such guarantees were available only to enlistees.

As the Vietnam conflict grew in intensity, safety from combat became an increasingly important inducement for men to choose the enlistment option. Many believed that by enlisting they could choose a safer military occupation or career field, one unlikely to bring them to Vietnam, at least in a combat role. That popular belief was not far from reality, for Defense Department statistics revealed that a draftee's chances of serving in Vietnam were never less than 50 percent and sometimes as high as 80 percent. During 1969 an Army draftee serving in Vietnam had almost double the chance of being killed as an enlistee of the same rank, and his probability of being wounded was 70 percent higher.[23]

The requirements for officers and noncommissioned officers created by the Vietnam War were proportionally even greater than the requirements for additional enlisted men. By the time of the Vietnam buildup, the ROTC had become the primary source of officers for the active Army, and the service moved quickly to try to raise ROTC enrollments through a stepped up advertising campaign and increased availability of scholarships. The U.S. Military Academy also increased the size of its classes by about 25 percent. Yet neither expansion of ROTC nor growth in West Point class size could immediately relieve the severe shortage of officers. To deal with that problem, the Army turned to another time-honored expedient for quick expansion of the officer corps—Officer Candidate School.

During World War II the majority of officers in the Army ground forces had been commissioned through the Officer Candidate program.[24] In the late 1950s and early 1960s Officer Candidate School was used by the Army to develop promising enlisted men, particularly those with some college training, as junior officers. With the demands of Vietnam, the Army stepped up its efforts to recruit college men for Officer Candidate School. Almost 6,500 OCS candidates were enlisted under the "College Graduate Option" during 1965.[25] The output of Army Officer Candidate Schools increased sixfold during the first year of the Vietnam buildup, from three hundred candidates a month to more than 1,800. During the second year, July 1966 to July 1967, the monthly average increased still further to 3,500. During the first three quarters of fiscal 1967, the output of Army Officer Candidate Schools was equal to the entire officer production of those same schools between 1958 and 1966.[26]

While the Army acquired its Vietnam-era junior officers from traditional sources, its solution to the problem of providing the additional noncommissioned officers required for combat and combat support units in Vietnam was radical and unprecedented. The decision to wage the Vietnam conflict without drawing heavily on the Reserve forces meant that critical shortages soon developed in the middle ranks of the noncommissioned officer corps, particularly in the grades E-5, E-6, and E-7. In the peacetime Army enlisted men normally took five years or longer to acquire the requisite experience and seniority to attain even the rank of E-5, sergeant. With the demands of Vietnam, however, the Army could scarcely afford to wait five years for a new corps of middle-level NCOs to work their way up through the ranks. Instead the Army was obliged to carry out two-grade promotions by picking the most promising PFCs (E-3s) and making them acting sergeants (E-5) in command of a squad.

As an alternative to this approach the Army, in late 1967, established a Non-Commissioned Officer Candidate program whereby enlisted men who had completed their basic combat and advanced individual training could qualify for immediate promotion to sergeant upon completion of a rigorous twelve-week course at one of four Non-Commissioned Officer Candidate Schools. Those who ranked in the top 5 percent of the class were eligible for immediate promotion to staff sergeant (E-6). About 70 percent of each class successfully completed the course and were awarded their stripes. Within a week of completing their training most graduates were on orders to Vietnam. Quickly labeled the "instant" or "shake and bake NCO" course, the new program was producing thirteen thousand NCOs a year by 1968.[27]

The Marine Corps also underwent drastic expansion. In the absence of a Reserve callup, the Corps was authorized to expand from 193,000 to 302,000 men, a sudden and drastic expansion of over 60 percent. For the first time since the Korean War the Corps was also obliged to accept draftees, nineteen thousand in 1966, a small percentage of new recruits, but a serious blow to the Corps's elite image. Subject to the same one-year tour limitations as the Army—actually thirteen months—the Marine Corps soon found its manpower resources stretched thin. By 1968 there were close to one hundred thousand Marines serving in Vietnam, about one-third of the total Corps. It was popularly observed at the time that there were only three classes of Marines: those in Vietnam, those recently returned from Vietnam, and those getting ready to go.[28]

The impact of the Vietnam buildup fell hardest on the Marine Corps officers and career NCOs. To meet the need for twice as many officers as in pre-Vietnam years, the Marines commissioned thousands of NCOs and warrant officers. By 1967 the Marines had more than five thousand temporary officers, most drawn from the ranks of its best sergeants and warrant officers.[29] As a result, the Marine Corps, like the Army, found itself by the third year of the war with an acute shortage of noncommissioned officers. "At a time when experienced small-unit leadership became essential, expansion reduced the average length of service of sergeants from 10.9 to 5.7 years and the average length of service for corporals from 5 to 2.7 years."[30]

The ultimate result of the President's decision against mobilizing the Reserves and the services' adaptation to that decision was the creation of an entirely new Army of draftees, one-term volunteers, instant NCOs, and recent graduates of ROTC and OCS. The new "Vietnam-only Army" was vividly described by an infantry captain in 1968:

> The young captain, straight from the States or Germany, will be amazed at how "civilianized" his combat company is. The majority of his troops are draftees . . . and he may be fortunate to have two senior NCOs or any Regular Army lieutenants. His NCO leadership is provided by instant NCOs from Fort Benning . . . who seldom, if ever, have any intention of staying in the service. The private soldier is, as often as not, on a first-name basis with his platoon sergeant and the worst term of derision he can bestow is Lifer.[31]

The statistics bear out the captain's impression. During 1969 draftees accounted for 88 percent of the Army's infantry riflemen in Vietnam. Of the remaining 12 percent, only 10 percent were first-term enlistees.[32]

The "Vietnam-only" GI was young, far younger than his World War II or Korean War counterpart. During the first year of World War II, about 60 percent of the men inducted into the Armed Forces were over twenty-four years old, and over one-quarter had passed their thirtieth birthday. At least 30 percent and probably far more of the Army's enlistees during that same year were also over twenty-four years old, and at least 10 percent were over thirty.[33] By way of contrast, the median age of inductees in 1965 was 21.5 years, and by 1966 it was 20.3 years.[34] A 1969 survey found that 86 percent of Army draftees were nineteen or twenty years old, while less than 7 percent were over twenty-two and only a handful were eighteen or younger. Enlistees were even more youthful. Thirty-eight percent were eighteen or younger and only one-fifth were over twenty years of age.[35]

Despite the availability of college and graduate school deferments and other inequities of the draft, the Vietnam-era GI was still far better educated than his World War I and World War II counterpart. In World War I the average draftee was "more likely to be illiterate, more likely to have less than five years' schooling, and less likely to have graduated from high school" than males of the same age who escaped the draft.[36] Among World War II draftees, only 13.6 percent had attended college. For Army enlisted men E-5 and below, in 1968 the figure was over 30 percent, and the 1968 soldiers included almost three times as many college graduates. Only about 24 percent of World War II draftees had completed high school, and 35 percent had never gone beyond grammar school. The Vietnam-era Army had close to 80 percent high school graduates and virtually no one whose education had ended with grammar school.[37]

Not only was the Vietnam GI better educated than his World War II counterpart, he was better educated than the soldiers of the Korean War and Cold War years of 1950 to 1964. At the end of 1952 about 12.5 percent of all military personnel on active duty had completed some college. By 1963 the total had risen to 16.5 percent. By contrast, at the end of 1967 over one-fifth of Vietnam enlisted personnel had attended college.[38]

The surprisingly large representation of soldiers and Marines with "some college" is testimony both to the exceptional quality of the Vietnam GI and to the inequities of the 1960s draft. For while college students were almost universally accorded deferments, these were granted only to "full-time" students. Those men too poor to attend college full time or those imprudent enough to interrupt their full-time studies for whatever reason were fair game for the draft boards. "Just think of this as your junior year abroad," was the way one Marine gunnery sergeant greeted former college students joining his battalion in Vietnam.

What most forcibly impressed observers about the Vietnam GI, however, was neither his youth nor his education, but the color of his skin. The veteran war correspondent and military analyst S. L. A. Marshall declared that he had "seen too many of our battalions come out of the line after hard struggle and heavy loss. In the average rifle company the strength was fifty percent composed of negroes, southwestern Mexicans, Puerto Ricans, Guamanians, nisei, and so on. But a real cross section of American youth? Almost never."[39]

That America's armed forces had seldom, if ever, been "a real cross section of American youth" was a fact of which few Americans were aware and about which even fewer cared.[40] What was becoming scandalously clear as the Vietnam war ground on was that most of the burden of fighting and dying seemed to be borne by those who had received least from American society.

During 1966 and 1967 much attention was focused on the high proportion of blacks among Vietnam casualties. During 1966, for example, black soldiers made up about 13 percent of total Army personnel in Vietnam but suffered close to 23 percent of the casualties.[41] In every Army division in Vietnam during 1965 and 1966 the percentage of African-American deaths was higher than the percentage of blacks in the unit. In the 1st Cavalry Division (Air Mobile), which was 13.4 percent black, African-Americans accounted for 26 percent of the casualties.[42]

The reasons for the high proportion of black casualties had less to do with Pentagon policies or combat in Vietnam than with the position of blacks in the United States during the mid-1960s. In a country where racial discrimination and, often, formal segregation were still widespread, the armed forces offered blacks, in the words of the U.S. Commission on Civil Rights, "greater career opportunities than they can find in the civilian economy." Once in the military, however, blacks often found that educational deficiencies barred them from qualifying for many of the highly skilled or highly technical jobs to be found "in the rear." In addition, black career soldiers often volunteered in large numbers for the elite combat units such as the airborne, partly for the challenge and prestige of the assignment and partly for the additional pay earned by airborne qualification, which could mean a good deal to a young soldier from a large and poor rural or inner-city family.[43]

Overall, African-Americans did not serve in Vietnam out of proportion to their numbers in the general population. African-Americans *were* more likely to be drafted than whites because they were seldom in a position to obtain a deferment. However, the poor educational and health care facilities available to most blacks in the 1950s and 1960s meant that they were far more likely than whites to fail the pre-induction physical or educational tests.[44]

Beginning in 1967 the armed forces undertook a concerted effort to bring down the numbers of black casualties, primarily by reducing the percentage of black soldiers assigned to infantry, armor, and cavalry units. By mid-1969 the proportion of black casualties was reasonably close to the percentage of blacks serving in Vietnam, and by the conclusion of the war the Defense Department could truthfully say that blacks had not died out of proportion to their numbers in Vietnam.[45]

That was scant comfort to the men who died there and seemed incredible to many black veterans of 1965, 1966, and 1967, who could recall a time when, as the Army's own statistics demonstrated, many infantry battalions were over 50 percent black.[46] Sergeant Stan Goff, who served with the 1st Infantry Division in 1968, recalled that "seeing all those black guys in the infantry . . . word was getting around that blacks were being drafted for genocidal purposes; sure, just to get rid of us. And we believed it. A lot of people believed it."[47]

Yet it seemed to many who looked carefully at the question that the consideration that most determined a man's chances of fighting and dying in Vietnam was not race but class. Journalists and social scientists examining the question of who served in Vietnam consistently concluded that it was the poor who bore the lion's share of the fighting and dying. Blacks were overrepresented in line companies and in casualty lists not because they were black but because they were poor. A study of 101 communities in Cook County, Illinois, found that young men from the lowest-income communities were almost three times as likely to have died in Vietnam as men from the wealthiest communities.[48] Surveys of communities in Wisconsin, Long Island, and Salt Lake City reached similar conclusions.[49]

Yet Vietnam GIs of 1968 were not simply a collection of ill-educated, impoverished youths from the bottom rungs of society. Rather, they represented the solid middle of American society. More recent studies based on more complete data have substantially modified the stereotypes of the 1970s.[50] If high school graduates far outnumbered college graduates, they also far outnumbered high school dropouts and those with little education. Far from being an army of "losers," the Vietnam War Army was an army of achievers, of solid hard workers, men and women to whom society had given no special advantages but who were accustomed to making their own way. If they were not the social and intellectual cream of American youth, neither were they its dregs or castoffs. Only such men and women could have stood the fiery test of that spring and summer of 1968.

* * *

Unlike his father or grandfather in previous conflicts, the Vietnam GI did not go to war with his unit crowded aboard a troop ship or an amphibious assault craft. Most men entered Vietnam as part of replacement drafts sent out at regular intervals to fill the places of returnees and casualties. After 1965, most soldiers and Marines flew to Vietnam in relative comfort aboard commercial airliners chartered by the U.S. government. The incongruity of this mode of going to war forcefully impressed many servicemen and women. "Here we go to hell escorted by tight-hipped, Maybellined, hard-smiling, round-eyed stews from Never-Never Land," wrote one Marine.[51] The plane "was colored some brilliant paint," recalled a soldier, "foxy stewardesses serving us this champagne lunch and flying thousands and thousands of miles with only our fantasies and expectations and what we read about the war."[52]

As the plane approached Vietnam the mood abruptly changed. "Everybody was tense and quiet, trying to look out the window, you know, climbing all over you to look down," one soldier recalled. "So the whole flight, from the time we hit the coast 'til we landed, there was absolute silence. Even the stewardesses were silent."[53] "As our flight was coming in for final approach the pilot announced that Bien Hoa air base was under attack and that the aircraft was being diverted," reported an Army colonel. "This announcement clearly had an unsettling effect on most of those aboard."[54]

Few newcomers arrived under such dramatic circumstances, but all shared the feeling of nervous apprehension as they reached Vietnam. "All I knew was I was landing in Vietnam and didn't have a gun . . . I didn't know, when the door opened on the plane, if you were supposed to do like in the movies, hit the ground and belly down the gangplank," Jonathan Polanski, a soldier with the 101st Airborne, recalled.[55]

Most planes arrived late at night, and new arrivals were taken by truck or bus to a transit facility, where they remained until morning. "Even though the flight was twenty-three hours long and no one had gotten much sleep, as tired as we were, the hot night air, which smelled heavily of urine, made sleep impossible," wrote one soldier.[56] Marines arriving in Da Nang were kept awake not only by the heat and humidity but by the intermittent roar of jet aircraft arriving and departing on tactical missions. Servicemen arriving at other airfields often were treated to the loud, unsettling bang of intermittent artillary fire and the sudden flash of flares and illumination rounds. If, as frequently happened, the newcomer shared the transit facilities with experienced troops returning from R&R, the "new guy's" apprehension level would climb still further as he listened to the veterans' matter-of-fact discussion of wounds, leeches and mosquitoes, booby traps, dismemberment, ambushes, accidents, and other routine ingredients of life "in the bush."

Yet only a minority of new arrivals in Vietnam were in fact destined for combat. Although the United States and its allies enjoyed an advantage in total military manpower of close to six to one over their Communist opponents in South Vietnam, Defense Department analysts estimated that at the end of 1967 "friendly forces [are] roughly at parity with enemy forces in rifle-carrying infantrymen on offensive operations."[57]

Precisely what proportion of U.S. forces were engaged in combat in Vietnam in 1968 and what proportion were engaged in support or other activities remains unclear. In April 1969 the official figures were 57.5 percent of U.S. forces in combat and combat support units and 42.5 percent in combat service support units. Yet, whatever their job title and whatever the official classification, the evidence is overwhelming that only a small minority of servicemen present in Vietnam were engaged in active operations against the enemy. Even those units classified as combat (not "combat support") had large numbers of their men assigned to administrative and support roles, providing static security, in transit, sick, on leave, wounded, or undergoing special training. Lieutenant Colonel Anthony Herbert estimated that his unit, the 173d Airborne Brigade, had approximately three thousand men in its five rifle battalions. Yet the brigade's total strength was ten thousand, most of whom were counted as "combat troops" in the Pentagon's arithmetic.[58]

The distinction between combat, combat support, and combat service support was made even more inexact by the fact that while large numbers of "combat" and "combat support" troops were actually performing logistical or administrative functions, some supply and service troops were at times involved in combat. At least two Medals of Honor were awarded to truck drivers of the 1st Logistical Command, a "service support" unit,[59] while medical corpsmen with infantry companies, also classified as service support troops, had perhaps the most hazardous jobs in Vietnam. In addition, large numbers of administrative and support troops were assigned additional duties as perimeter guards, members of reaction platoons, and local security patrols. During Tet 1968, some units found that their motor pool, supply point, or workshop had become "the front lines."

A more widely used and seemingly more accurate method of assessing the numbers of combat troops was to count the number of maneuver battalions available for operations. A maneuver battalion is a combat unit of battalion size, usually infantry, armored cavalry, tanks, or mechanized infantry, that is able to move under its own resources and engage the enemy with its organic weapons. In April 1968, the United States had 112 maneuver battalions, and Department of Defense figures showed 29 percent of total Army personnel in Vietnam and 34 percent of the Marines as serving in maneuver battalions.[60]

Even the yardstick of maneuver battalions, however, failed to measure accurately the number of men actually available for operations. The authorized strength of a Marine infantry company, for example, was six officers and 210 enlisted men. Yet many former battalion commanders insist that the actual figures were far lower. Colonel Birchard B. DeWitt recalled that his four infantry companies had one officer each, not six, "except India Company, which had the luxury of having two." As for enlisted strengths, the average number of men in an infantry company of one Marine division during late 1966 was reported as just under 160 rather than 210, and, as one former officer observed, "by the time you subtracted those sick, lame, and lazy; R&R; etc., etc., and etc., you were lucky to put a hundred ten men in the field."[61] Similarly, Lieutenant Colonel Herbert estimated that no company in any battalion in his brigade "had more than seventy-five men physically present, ready to go."[62] An official study of the 9th Infantry Division in 1968 found that on any given day rifle companies within the division that had an "assigned strength" of 157 men had in fact only about 65–70 men available for operations.[63]

Why was the "tail-to-tooth ratio," as the military called it, so large? One reason was simply the time lag which often occurred between the loss of men in combat or through rotation and the arrival of their replacements. A second cause was the relatively large proportion of grunts under medical care or with temporary disabilities, which disqualified them for combat. Operating in the jungles, mountains, swamps, and flooded rice paddies, soldiers in maneuver battalions were most exposed to risk of contracting fungal and bacterial infections, malaria, hepatitis, dysentery, and other diseases. In the 9th Infantry Division about 47 percent of soldiers not available for duty were suffering from the effects of a skin disease known as "immersion foot," which resulted from prolonged exposure of the feet to the water and mud of the Mekong Delta rice paddies.[64] A third reason, often cited by critics, was the unusually high "standard of living" demanded by the American military in Vietnam. While soldiers "in the bush" enjoyed relatively few amenities, others at the division headquarters and logistics bases worked in air-conditioned offices and lived in barracks with hot showers and flush toilets. Mess halls served hot meals with fresh fruit and vegetables and ice cream made in one of the Army's forty-odd ice cream plants. Generals lived in air-conditioned trailers or, in some cases, entire houses. "The quarters will have running water, flush toilets, air-conditioned bedrooms, etc.," wrote one officer, describing a general's home away from home. "It is completely paneled in plywood—top-grade—finished in clear varnish, tile floors, concrete patio, the works."[65] At the III Marine Amphibious Force headquarters, it was forbidden to photograph the commanding general's spacious bungalow. The troops were told this was for security reasons, but many suspected it was out of fear that some envious congressman might see it.

Movie theaters, steak houses, bowling alleys, and pizza parlors blossomed at all but the most remote base areas in Vietnam, while post exchanges stocked with the latest in stereo equipment, watches, cameras, and jewelry, as well as plenty of beer and soft drinks, supplied soldiers with the necessities of life. Maintaining something approaching the American standard of living in a distant and underdeveloped tropical country, of course, called for a massive logistical effort and absorbed servicemen who might have been assigned to other tasks.

Yet even had MACV forgone many of the amenities it insisted upon for its troops, especially for its officers, it is doubtful that the tail-to-tooth ratio would have been drastically effected. In the final analysis, the striking disparity between U.S. combat and support forces in Vietnam arose not so much from the desire of U.S. generals to have more air-conditioned pizza huts and bowling alleys, or from the natural tendency of men to find jobs and necessary reasons to stay in the rear, as from the nature of Vietnam and the style of war which the United States chose to wage there.

For almost twenty years before Vietnam, the U.S. Army had trained and planned for operations "in areas such as Europe and Korea where usable road nets, railroads, and port facilities already existed."[66] In the case of Vietnam no heavy internal transportation networks and few modern airfields existed. Saigon was the only deep-water port. The entire logistics infrastructure, which eventually came to include seven jet-capable airfields, six new deep-water ports, seventy-five new tactical airfields, twenty-six hospitals, and two dozen permanent base facilities, had to be built from scratch.[67] In addition to supporting their own forces, U.S. support and service troops were also charged with supplying many of the logistical needs of the Vietnamese and other non-American allied forces in Vietnam, as well as the CIA's mercenaries, called Civilian Irregular Defense Groups, and other Vietnamese government militia and regional security forces; all together about one million troops.

The U.S. style of operations, with its emphasis on firepower and rapid aerial movement of large numbers of troops over most areas of the country, also placed enormous demands on logistical support. During a single month of 1969, for example, ground crews and maintenance personnel had to supply fuel, parts, and repairs to support 74,000 helicopter gunship sorties (a sortie is one flight by one aircraft), 25,000 sorties by fighter-attack aircraft, and eight hundred sorties by Air Force gunships. U.S. and allied artillery fired almost 1.2 million rounds, or 36,000 tons of shells; planes and helicopters expended 41,000 tons of ordnance; and more than 200,000 tons of supplies were hauled to forward bases by more than 2,700 truck convoys over roads that had been largely built and maintained by U.S. engineer units. About 100,000 tons of supplies more were transported by air. In addition to all these warlike activities, logistical support had also to be provided by MACV troops for activities ranging from Vietnamese government civic action projects to herbicide spraying to super-secret intelligence and reconnaissance missions.[68]

Men newly arrived in Vietnam generally remained at the transit facility for two or three days awaiting assignment and transportation to their units. Units that had their own aircraft or other transportation frequently utilized it to pick up their replacements from Bien Hoa or Cam Ranh Bay. Soldiers assigned to units that lacked such means had to make their way by "common-user aircraft" to their unit's area. Because replacements held a relatively low travel priority, there were frequent delays and false starts before the tired and apprehensive "new guys" finally arrived at their units.

For men destined for infantry assignments—"grunts," as they were universally called—the journey to their unit was especially discouraging. At the airfield transit facility, the grunt encountered large numbers of soldiers living in relative comfort and safety. "The view of the base [at Cam Ranh Bay] was unbelievable. It looked as if we never left the States. There were barracks, workshops, motor pools, and paved roads as far as we could see. The place was full of PXs, basketball courts, and even a beach for swimming."[69]

As he made his way into the country, the newly arrived grunt found living conditions becoming less comfortable and more primitive. Yet each place was more fortunately situated than his final destination. "He sees the large base areas, with air-conditioned offices, PXs, steam baths, and service clubs and realizes that they were not intended for his use. Even his closest comrades in arms, the tankers and artillerymen, enjoy a standard of living considerably higher than his own."[70]

Even more demoralizing to the new arrival was the sight of large groups of soldiers at the airfields and transit facilities returning home from their tours. At times the homeward-bound troops would be boarding the planes at literally the same time as new men were disembarking. An Army psychiatrist with the 1st Cavalry Division recalled that for new arrivals the replacement center at Camp Alpha near Tan Son Nhut Air Base outside Saigon was "an initial trauma to remove any vestige of military-missionary zeal. To see the naked joy in the faces of the out-going troops and hear their hair-raising combat stories, plus the sound of artillery plus the mess halls plus the latrines; why everyone doesn't turn around and go home still puzzles me."[71]

The Vietnam-only Army had fought well through 1965, 1966, and 1967 and would continue to fight well through 1968. Yet it was an organization that lacked any true sense of identity, continuity of leadership, or purpose. Its cutting edge, the infantrymen, junior NCOs, company officers, and helicopter pilots, was overwhelmingly draftees or one-term volunteers almost completely divorced from the long-service, experienced senior NCOs and officers who were expected to provide those qualities. The extremely youthful makeup of the Vietnam combatants made this lack of experienced leadership even more damaging. As early as 1955, the sociologist Roger Little had noted that combat units in the Korean War, composed largely of men twenty-one and younger, had fewer men "than in WWII who had prior experience in civilian leadership roles. There was also a corresponding lack of awareness or affiliation with reference groups in the larger society other than the family and a lack of mature role models with whom younger troops might identify."[72]

No army is immune to the influence of social and political controversies and changes in the society it serves. Yet the Vietnam-only Army, led by a young, inexperienced, and constantly changing body of junior officers and NCOs and a remote, equally transitory body of senior officers, was especially sensitive to these changes. As the war seemed to take on a life of its own during 1968, with harder fighting, heavier casualties, and no definable goal save the vague hope of negotiations, and as the fabric of society "back home" seemed to fray under the strain of increasing political and racial animosities, the Vietnam-only Army began to show increasing signs of strain.

CHAPTER 3

"You're Going Home in a Body Bag"

To the small minority of soldiers, sailors, Marines, and airmen who served in combat units fell a disproportionate share of the burden of the ordeal of 1968. Combat GIs in Vietnam inhabited a special universe with its own rules, its own heroes and villains, its own values, and its own sense of time. The GIs themselves were at least partly conscious of this qualitative difference in their environment, of the separate and special qualities of their daily lives, which set them apart not only from ordinary young Americans but even, in important respects, from other GIs "in the rear." This consciousness was summed up in the phrase that grunts and other combat troops used to describe the homes and lives they had left behind in the United States. They called it "back in the world."

The environment of the Vietnam grunt's world was as squalid, harsh, and demanding as that of any soldier in World War II. Although entire battalions, regiments, brigades, and even divisions frequently moved by helicopter in Vietnam, once in an operating area the troops deployed and moved by foot, usually breaking into company- and platoon-size units, which might patrol for many days or even weeks through jungle, mountains, swamps, or rice fields searching for enemy base camps or supplies. Specialist Ernie Boitano described one such sweep in the flooded rice paddies of the Mekong Delta: "The dikes were like four feet strips of dirt, eighty or a hundred feet long . . . and you were always humping over them. Sometimes during high tide they would go to the middle of your chest and you'd go across maybe two steps and the person in front of

46

you would help you up. And you did that all day long."[1] "Anyone over here who walks more than fifty feet through elephant grass should automatically get a purple heart," wrote George Olsen, a Ranger with the Americal Division. "Try to imagine grass eight to fifteen feet high, so thick as to cut visibility to one yard, possessing razor sharp edges. Then try to imagine walking through it while all around you are men possessing automatic weapons who desperately want to kill you."[2]

During the dry season the temperatures could often exceed 100 degrees. In May 1968, Marines on Operation ALLEN BROOK in the Go Noi Island area of Quang Nam Province south of Da Nang fought for more than a week in weather that averaged over 110 degrees. Officers and medics speculated that as many as one-third of their casualties may have been due to heat.[3] James Martin Davis recalled, "Fatigues dripping wet with perspiration, clinging to the body . . . forever being tangled in 'wait-a-minute vines,' immobilized in elephant grass, and surrounded by the muffled voices of young soldiers in the heat muttering under their breath."[4]

During the monsoon the heat abated, but the frequent torrential rains brought flooding and made living conditions even more uncomfortable. Troops frequently found their bunkers, huts, or hardback tents flooded or buried in mud. "The rainy season came . . . it was wet wherever you went," recalled a lieutenant with the 25th Division, "and you had the rats. You went in to lie down at night, you had to beat it around your poncho to make sure there were no rats."[5]

Rats were a constant nuisance in most forward areas in Vietnam. Lieutenant Elmo Zumwalt, who commanded a Swift boat, recalled;

One night when we were off patrol, we tied up at an old ferry landing and huge wharf rats crawled all over us. We couldn't fire at them because of the noise it would make, so I set a piece of cheese out on the landing and when the rats all clustered around it I fired a flare gun at them at point-blank range. I thought it would frighten them, but one of the rats, about the size of a small dog, just looked up at me as if to say, "Who do you think you're trying to scare?" and finished off the cheese.[6]

At Khe Sanh the rats had a near-mythic reputation. At the height of the siege, thousands of rats roamed the base feasting on the uncovered piles of garbage, which the constant shell fire and mortars had made too hazardous for the Marines to bury. The rats' favorite delicacy was peanut butter, one of the most common contents of C rations. Marines counterattacked with thousands of traps and globs of peanut butter mixed with zinc phosphide, a poison. A rat bite usually involved a medical evacuation out of Khe Sanh, and, as the shelling worsened, many men declared their intention to sleep with their toes out of their blankets and a dab of peanut butter on each toe.[7] Yet, since rat bites also meant fourteen days of painful rabies shots, it seems unlikely that many men actually availed themselves of this expedient.

Even more detested than rats were the mosquitoes, leeches, and red ants, which seemed to thrive everywhere in Vietnam. The most familiar ornament on the helmet band of a Vietnam infantryman was a small bottle of insect repellent with which the troops waged an unequal battle against flying pests. "Everybody would get them," recalled one infantryman of the red ants, "Your pants would be tied up at the bottom, but somehow they would still get in your legs. All you could do was hope to get through to them in a hurry and then start beating on them. They're about an eighth of an inch big and they keep on biting."[8] About 75 percent of cases of falciparum malaria occurred among troops assigned to combat missions. Those men were also the most likely to suffer from skin disorders, diarrhea, hepatitis, and scrub typhus.[9]

Even more unsettling than the insects was the presence of large numbers of snakes in certain regions of Vietnam, especially during the monsoon season, when many were washed out of their holes by rain and flooding. "Ninety-nine out of a hundred snakes in Vietnam are poisonous, and the one hundredth swallows you whole" was a staple of GI folk wisdom passed on with special relish by old salts to "new guys."

The difficulties of operations in this hostile environment were multiplied by the heavy loads many GIs were obliged to carry on their extended operations "in the bush." More than seventy years before the Vietnam War, German medical students at the Frederick William Institute had experimented with carrying the campaign load of German infantrymen on a series of marches ranging from 12 to 45 miles under varying weather conditions. The medical students concluded that any load heavier than 44 pounds was "likely to cause in the human body perturbations the injurious influence of which makes itself felt afterwards." The German soldier's normal load of close to 70 pounds "had a bad effect on the physique of a man even during average marches in cool temperatures and never ceases to cause a gradual enfeeblement of physical endurance."[10]

Following World War II the respected military analyst S. L. A. Marshall, basing his conclusions on his extensive observations of combat soldiers' performance in varying conditions, strongly argued that 48 to 50 pounds was the absolute maximum that even the strongest, best-conditioned soldier could be expected to carry on active combat operations.[11]

All these studies and experiments notwithstanding, the Vietnam GI was frequently loaded down with close to 60 pounds of ammunition and equipment. One battalion of the 1st Infantry Division required each rifleman to carry fourteen magazines of ammunition, two smoke grenades, two fragmentation grenades, a gas mask, weapon-cleaning equipment, two canteens, three boxes of C rations, a Claymore mine, trip flares, an entrenching tool, twenty sandbag covers, poncho, and poncho liner.[12] On operations where commanders expected to need extra ammunition or specialized equipment, the GI's combat load could easily exceed the normal 50–60 pounds carried in the tropical heat of Vietnam. Echoing the German medical students of seventy years before, an infantryman with the 2d Battalion, 35th Infantry in Vietnam observed: "It doesn't take long to get you run down when you're carrying everything you own on your back."[13]

"Extra gear or ammo deemed personally useless was frequently dumped at the first opportunity," recalled Igor Bobrowsky, who served with the Fifth Marines,

> . . . in spite of the knowledge that what was only dumped but not destroyed would probably end up in Charlie's hands. As frequently as possible extra loads were eased by unloading them via the expedient of "lighting up" some target of real or invented opportunity. This of course lightened the individual's load of "useless" ordnance, such as

LAWs, mortar rounds, etc.—and also tended to level a lot of the surrounding countryside. Of course, there were many times when it turned out that what had been thus unloaded was very much missed when the "fit hit the shan."[14]

To help him cope with the extremes of the Vietnam environment, the GI had several specially designed items of equipment, which varied widely in their success and popularity. By 1967 the "tropical combat uniform" had largely replaced the unloved and uncomfortable utility uniform. The essential features of the tropical combat uniform, or "jungle fatigues," were baggy pants with large extra pockets along each leg and a loose cotton-poplin bush shirt worn outside the trousers and likewise equipped with large pockets. Much cooler and lighter than the standard fatigues, they were an instant success, although their lightweight material was prone to snagging and tearing in heavily wooded or jungle environments.

Camouflaged tropical uniforms of various patterns were also being issued to some units by 1968 and would become widely used by mid-1969.[15] The standard type of camouflage uniform, called ERDL Camouflage (for U.S. Army Engineer Research and Development Lab), blended well with most Vietnam terrain and was highly effective in resisting the infrared and other thermal imaging detection devices increasingly employed by the Communists. Yet the standard American camouflage uniform was never as popular as the more dramatic and warlike appearing "tiger stripe" camouflage uniforms worn by many Vietnamese and some allied units. Such uniforms were prized by American troops despite their poorer quality and smaller, less usable pockets. Members of reconnaissance units, the Rangers, and advisory teams always found good reasons to wear the tiger stripes, and ordinary GIs wore them when they could get away with it.[16]

The Vietnam soldier's individuality was most clearly expressed, however, not in his uniform but in his headgear. Combat troops who wore the steel helmet often decorated the camouflage covers with nicknames, slogans, short-timer calendars, peace symbols, and names of states or home towns. In one Marine battalion red tassels, used in Vietnam for altar decorations, were hung from the sides of helmets.

Besides the steel helmet an almost infinite variety of hats and headgear bloomed and flowered among GIs in Vietnam. The well-known green berets of the Special Forces were soon joined by a wide variety of other berets. Advisers to ARVN airborne units wore rose-colored berets; advisers to tank, mechanized, and police units wore black berets, as did recon units and some infantry units. Company F of the 51st Infantry (Long-Range Patrol) wore tiger stripe berets. Members of mobile advisory teams wore aquamarine berets, while U.S. advisers with the Vietnamese Rangers sported garnet-colored berets, which were "often procured a size and a half too large, soaked in beer or water, and deliberately shaped into a style resembling a cock's comb. The Vietnamese considered this style of beret to represent masculine power."[17]

Not content with berets, unit commanders in Vietnam experimented with various other distinctive headgear ranging from Australian bush hats to various styles of cowboy hats. The 2d Battalion, 3d Infantry even sported a tricorner hat "designed as a link to the regiment's colonial tradition."[18] By 1968 the officially prescribed "utility cap," a distinctly unmilitary-looking beanie closely resembling a baseball hat, and almost universally despised by all soldiers below the rank of three-star general, was being gradually supplanted by the far more popular "tropical hat" or "boonie hat." The boonie hat was a floppy, full-brim hat that offered good protection from the sun and insects and could be easily cut or reshaped to meet the soldier's own ideas of style and utility. Its broad, tent-like shape proved ideal for ornamentation. The MACV commander, General Creighton Abrams, was soon sputtering angrily that "subject hat . . . was not intended as a carrier of grenade rings, colorful headbands, peace symbols, and other unauthorized items."[19]

Perhaps the most successful individual item of equipment was the tropical combat boot. The combination leather and nylon boot was light, mildew-resistant, and quick drying. It featured a spike-resistant insole, which offered some protection against Viet Cong poison punji stakes and bamboo spikes. The long-wearing, highly durable boots were much sought after by both field troops and support personnel, and although GIs might modify, trade, or disregard many other items of uniform, few indeed ever willingly parted with their tropical boots.

Far and away the most controversial item of equipment of the Vietnam war was the M-16 rifle. At the outset of the Vietnam War, the standard U.S. rifle had been the M-14, an improved version of the old M-1 of World War II fame, which fired a large .30 caliber round. Though highly accurate, the M-14 was ill adapted to the close-range jungle fighting of Vietnam. It was virtually uncontrollable when fired at full automatic. In addition, the heavy .30 caliber rounds limited the amount of ammunition an individual rifleman could carry. At the end of 1965 General Westmoreland recommended that a new rifle, the M-16, be adopted as the standard weapon for Vietnam. The M-16 was smaller and lighter than the M-14 and fired a small but highly destructive .22 caliber bullet. In a close-range fire fight, the M-16 enabled a combatant to control his automatic fire, while its smaller bullet, which had a propensity to tumble as it struck human flesh, proved highly lethal. Army Special Forces units had used an earlier version, the AR-15, in Vietnam during the early 1960s with excellent results. Yet when the M-16 began to be issued in quantity to soldiers and Marines during 1966, problems soon developed.

A large number of the weapons tended to jam or otherwise malfunction. The results in combat were often catastrophic. "I know of at least two Marines who died within ten feet of the enemy with jammed rifles," a young officer wrote to Senator Gaylord Nelson of Wisconsin. "No telling how many have been wounded on that account and it is difficult to count the NVA who should be dead but lived because the M-16 failed. [Today] we found one Marine beating an NVA with his helmet and a hunting knife because his rifle failed."[20] "I pack as many grenades as I can plus bayonet and K-bar [jungle knife] so I'll have something to fight with," another Marine told his parents. "If you can, please send me a bore rod and a one and one-quarter inch or so paint brush. I need it for my rifle. These rifles are getting a lot of guys killed because they jam so easily."[21] Some GIs even claimed that although the Communist soldiers would strip the bodies of Americans of everything useful when given the opportunity, they would always leave the M-16s, "which they consider worthless."[22]

A Michigan firm that had sent small sample packets of its new lubricant called Dri-Slide as Christmas presents to Michigan soldiers in Vietnam was suddenly deluged with hundreds of letters from GIs requesting more and describing hair-raising and tragic incidents resulting from the lack of proper lubricants to service the temperamental M-16s.

Army ordnance experts who had accepted the M-16 only grudgingly under pressure from Defense Department civilians tended to blame lack of proper cleaning and maintenance by the GIs in the field. It *was* true that units that had trained with the new rifle in the States before going to Vietnam seldom experienced the malfunctions reported by men who had been issued the rifle after some time in country.[23] A team of Army and industry ordnance specialists who visited Vietnam in the fall of 1966 declared that they had "never seen rifles with such poor maintenance. . . . On some rifles you could not see daylight through the barrel."[24] Combat troops angrily retorted that they had been repeatedly told that the new wonder-rifle required almost no cleaning or maintenance and that in any case maintenance items always seemed to be in short supply. This shortage extended not only to lubricants, made famous by the Dri-Slide episode, but even to such mundane items as cleaning rods. In one company of the 1st Air Cavalry Division, men stated "that cleaning material was hard to get and T shirts were used to make patches. Some men had even ordered cleaning material from the U.S."[25] An often-repeated anecdote concerned a Marine who was recommended for a medal because he repeatedly exposed himself to heavy enemy fire in order to pass the single, valuable cleaning rod to various members of his platoon whose rifles had malfunctioned.

In 1967, a Congressional investigating committee headed by Representative Richard H. Ichord eventually concluded that much of the problem was caused by the Army's poor management of the M-16 development program, management so poor that it "bordered on criminal negligence."[26] The committee was particularly critical of the Army's decision, against the express objections of the designer and the manufacturer, to switch to an ammunition propellant different from that for which the rifle had been designed.

The Army and Marines quickly adopted a number of emergency

expedients: cleaning and maintenance were emphasized, and supplies of cleaning equipment increased, while a new lubricant, better adapted to the humid climate of Vietnam, was hastily distributed, along with better lubricating instructions. As many rifles as possible were also fitted with chrome-coated chambers, which seemed to cut down on jamming. Yet malfunctions of the M-16 continued as a serious, often fatal problem for many combat troops well into 1968.[27]

In the field many items of equipment and uniform were sometimes discarded or drastically modified to meet the demands of the climate and the GI's own taste. Undergarments were often discarded, and troops sometimes fought stripped to the waist or wearing their protective "flak jackets" directly over their bare chests in the intense heat. The vagaries of resupply to remote areas in the field, together with a tendency of the lightweight tropical uniforms to snag, rip, or tear, further contributed to the ragged appearance of many troops "in the bush."

The conditions and intensity of combat in Vietnam varied enormously; from the World War I–style warfare of Khe Sanh to the "amphibious" riverine warfare of the Mekong Delta, from fierce clashes in the mountains and jungles to endless patrols in the agricultural lowlands, where the main menaces were often mines and booby traps. Even in a single province the pattern of battle and death could vary enormously. A study prepared for the Pentagon of operations by a single Marine division in one province during 1968 and 1969 showed wide variations in the tactics employed by the U.S. and Communist forces, the terrain, and the cost in U.S. casualties. The causes of the casualties also varied. In one operation almost 30 percent of the casualties were due to mines and booby traps. In another, there were virtually no losses to those devices.[28]

Despite the attention paid in the media to such large engagements as Khe Sanh, An Loc, and the struggles around Hue and Saigon during Tet, most of the "battles" of the Vietnam War were short, sharp clashes between company-, platoon-, or squad-size units. The majority lasted only a few hours, often only a few minutes. There were hundreds of such small engagements during 1968 in Vietnam, and, although clashes between larger units continued to capture the attention of the Pentagon and the press, these small engagements remain the characteristic "battle" for most GIs.[29]

Short as they usually were, these small battles could be bloody indeed. Most U.S. casualties occurred during the first few minutes of a fight before the U.S. unit could bring supporting artillery and aircraft to bear on the enemy. The head of the MACV operations center, Brigadier General J. R. Chaisson, estimated that, in engagements in the rugged, jungle-covered mountains of the central highlands, it was not unusual for a U.S. company to sustain twenty to fifty casualties in the first few minutes of contact. In 1967 a company of the 2/503d Infantry lost seventy killed and twenty-five wounded in a half-hour after being ambushed by a Communist battalion.[30]

Overall, the toll on men in infantry units and those in direct support of them was heavy. Although officials in Washington were fond of pointing out that the casualty rate for American forces in Vietnam was considerably lower than in World War II and Korea, that had far more to do with the larger percentage of personnel in support units and the availability of improved medical care than with any differences in the intensity of combat. Men in "maneuver battalions," the units that actually did the fighting, continued to run about the same chance of death or injury as their older relatives who had fought in Korea or in the Pacific. Indeed, during the first half of 1968 the *overall* Vietnam casualty rate exceeded the overall rate for all theaters in World War II, while the casualty rates for Army and Marine maneuver battalions was more than four times as high.[31] Marine Colonel William T. Dabney observed that "of the two hundred plus men" he had started out with in the defense of Hill 881 South during the siege of Khe Sanh, "there were nineteen of us when we got back to Quang Tri."[32] One-third of the men in the contingent that the journalist John Sack accompanied to Vietnam in 1966 were killed or badly wounded during their first six months in country.[33]

The casualty rate for wounded in action throughout 1968 and 1969 was considerably higher than that for either World War II or Korea.[34] A company commander in the 1st Cavalry Division recalled that "in one action the company lost forty-five out of one hundred and ten men, but only two killed."[35]

The surprising ratio of fatalities to wounded was one indication of the high standard of medical care available to servicemen in Vietnam. In World War II about 71 percent of men who became casualties survived their wounds. In Korea the figure was 74 percent. In Vietnam over 81 percent of men wounded in battle survived.[36]

In addition to the well-known innovation of aero medical evacuation or "dust-off," a number of other factors contributed to the excellent survival rate of Vietnam casualties. The lack of a moving front, or indeed any real front lines, and the static, repetitive style of warfare so frustrating to soldiers and strategists proved a lifesaving boon to medical care. Because combat operations occurred in the same general area month after month, field, surgical, and evacuation hospitals seldom had to be moved or relocated. This unusual stability of forward hospitals in Vietnam made it possible to install air-conditioning and sophisticated "state-of-the-art" medical equipment. "At present we have some items of equipment in Vietnam that equal what you have in Walter Reed," the U.S. Army Surgeon General declared in 1968.[37]

Another factor was the ready availability of whole blood. In World War II, whole blood was rarely, if ever, available even at division- and corps-level hospitals. In Vietnam, stocks of whole blood, packaged in styrofoam containers, which permitted storage for forty-eight to seventy-two hours in the field, were almost always available in forward areas.[38]

Yet it was aero medical evacuation that was the most important, as well as by far the most dramatic, innovation of the Vietnam War. The Korean War had demonstrated the potential of the helicopter as an air ambulance, and the Army had begun employing helicopters in Vietnam as early as 1962. In Vietnam, with its mountains, jungles, and flooded rice paddies, and its poor and insecure roads, the helicopters proved an invaluable asset. Yet the tropical environment posed formidable challenges. The warmer the air, the less "lift" achieved by the helicopter rotor blades, and Vietnam's hot climate meant that early helicopter models often lacked the power to carry more than one or two patients at a time.[39] With the arrival of the new and more powerful UH-1H in mid-1967, the medics finally had a machine that could perform well in Vietnam's demanding environment. The rugged UH-1H also was equipped with instruments for night and bad weather flying and carried skids rather than wheels to allow landings in rocky or swampy terrain.

Beginning in 1967, medevac helicopters were equipped with hoists from which a litter could be lowered up to 250 feet to pick up casualties in unusually rugged terrain. Although the hoist saved many lives, its use was always slow, nerve-racking, and hazardous for the flight crews involved. The helicopter was obliged to remain almost stationary high above the jungle in easy view of any nearby enemy, while the litter was slowly lowered and raised. A color-coded cable told the aircraft commander how much cable he had extended. The last 50 feet were colored red. A detonator charge stood ready near the hoist to sever the steel cable should the helicopter find it necessary "to make a quick exit from the area."[40] Fortunately for their peace of mind, few wounded men being evacuated by hoist knew about this special "safety precaution." The official report of the 1st Cavalry medical battalion noted reassuringly that "the cable cannot be blown without the approval of the aircraft commander."[41]

The ubiquitous medevac helicopter became almost an emblem of the Vietnam conflict. In a war long on frustration and short on popular heroes, the dust-off pilots became almost legendary for their courage, tenacity, and ingenuity. The rate of loss to hostile fire for medevac helicopters was about three and a half times the loss rate for all other types of helicopter missions, and more than a third of all flight crews of dust-off ships were killed or wounded.[42]

One episode in early 1968 epitomized the spirit and determination of the dust-off crews. At dawn on January 5, Major Patrick H. Brady left Chu Lai in southeastern Quang Nam province to evacuate casualties from a Special Forces camp in the fog-shrouded mountains near Phu To. In fog so thick that the tip of the rotor blades could not be seen from the cockpit, Brady located the camp and flew off six casualties. The following morning Brady, still flying in dense fog, landed a medical team in the Hep Duc Valley, where a company of the 198th Light Infantry had suffered sixty casualties. Ignoring Communist anti-aircraft guns, which had already shot down two gunships, and flying through fog that had defeated the attempts of four other copters, Brady made three more trips into the valley, bringing out a total of thirty-nine casualties. On the same day, Brady rescued more American troops southeast of Chu Lai in the face of machine gun fire so intense that the troops on the ground were at first unable to leave cover to load the wounded.

Picking up a new aircraft and a relief co-pilot, Brady ended his day by landing in a minefield to pick up casualties of another unit of the hapless 198th Light Infantry. Under heavy fire, Brady's crew chief and a medic collected the wounded and loaded them aboard. A mine, detonated by one of the medics, hurled Brady's crew into the air and showered the aircraft with fragments. Shaken but unhurt, the crewmen resumed the loading and flew the 198th's casualties to hospitals.[43]

In all, Army medevac helicopters carried at least 400,000 U.S. military personnel and a considerably larger number of Vietnamese troops and civilians to hospitals during the ten years from 1963 to 1973. It is impossible to say how many lives were saved by this novel method of medical management, but no one doubted that the total was large.

Once aboard the evacuation helicopter, the wounded GI received immediate emergency aid and stabilization from the medical crew and intravenous fluids if necessary. Most helicopters arrived at a casualty clearing station within twenty minutes, and no medevac flight in Vietnam took longer than thirty.[44] At the clearing station, which was equipped with a pharmacy and X-ray laboratory, doctors evaluated the wounded and provided immediate lifesaving and resuscitative care. Patients who required more than a few days' care were taken, often by air, to a surgical or larger evacuation hospital.

Most of the injuries involved multiple wounds from fragments of mines, shells, or other explosive devices or high-velocity bullets. The steel helmet and armored vest or "flak jacket" worn by most troops in the field provided fairly good protection against fragmentation wounds but not against bullets.[45]

A large share of the burden of medical management in Vietnam's military hospitals fell to the nurses. Of the 8,000 to 10,000 women who served in Vietnam, the vast majority were nurses; about 80 percent served in the Army Nurse Corps, the remainder in the Air Force and Navy. The majority were younger women 20–24 years of age, one-third just out of nursing school and new to the military.[46] In Vietnam, they were generally assigned the most stressful and demanding medical work in intensive care, operating rooms, triage, or anesthesia, and their responsibilities far exceeded those of nurses "back in the world."

Like other GIs "in the rear," the nurses were exposed to the dangers of random rocket and mortar fire and occasional sniper attacks, but their worst moments of fear and stress usually occurred within the hospital itself. Because casualties were often brought from the field to a hospital minutes after a battle, nurses saw far greater numbers of severely wounded patients than had been the case in previous wars.[47] One nurse recalled that her first exposure to war came five days after her arrival when she was assigned to examine bodies to determine the cause of death:

> That's something I still have flashbacks about—unzipping those bags. . . . A young guy had his face blown away with hundreds of maggots eating away where his face used to be. Another one had his eyes wide open. He was staring at me. I remember he had a large hole in his chest, and I knew it was a gunshot wound or a grenade injury. It had blown his heart, his lungs, everything to shreds. He had nothing left but a rib cage. . . . There were GIs exposed to flame throwers or gas explosions. We used to call them "crispy critters" to keep from getting depressed.[48]

"I was always so struck by them," a correspondent observed of the nurses she had seen in Vietnam. "Those young, young faces and those ancient eyes. Just like on those statues in Washington. Yeah. They were eyes that had looked into hell."[49]

Despite the presence of some half-million American troops in Vietnam, 30 percent of whom were at least theoretically committed to combat operations, the bounds of the grunts' universe were fixed and narrow. In a war in which companies, and even platoons and squads, often operated independently for extended periods on sweeps, patrols, and area security operations, the individual's face-to-face contacts—his primary group, as social scientists would say—seldom extended beyond his battalion and often not beyond the company. Within the world of companies, platoons, and squads relationships were intense and all-encompassing. "The combat unit is undoubtedly one of the most closely knit, interdependent groups in existence," a division psychiatrist in Vietnam wrote. "Members of the unit eat, sleep, work, and fight as a group. They share their food, equipment, feelings, and news from home."[50]

Amid the fear, confusion, loneliness, and fatigue of Vietnam, the squad or platoon was the GI's life raft. They were men with whom he could truly share his thoughts, his fears, his hopes and anxieties. Above all, they were men on whom the soldier could depend for his survival. "This battalion is good," one battalion commander told new arrivals, "Know why? Because we help our buddies. We don't let our buddies down. I want you troops to say, 'If there's anywhere in the world I want to get wounded, it's in this battalion, because my buddies will bring me in; they're not going to leave me.'"[51]

Combat soldiers almost invariably proclaimed that their squad, platoon, or company was "the tightest"; that the guys "would do anything for you."[52] And it was certainly true that members of squads and platoons frequently developed genuine and lasting friendships. Yet the consciousness of mutual dependence in battle overrode all other attitudes and desires. Personal quarrels and personality clashes were far rarer than in normal life, and overt racial antagonism almost nonexistent. "Because you need each other's support if you're in a fire fight, you keep it down to a minimum," recalled one combat veteran. "You keep your remarks and your weird looks and your ways and your crappiness down to a minimum."[53]

Many units provided distinctive rituals or rites of passage for replacements ("Fucking New Guys": FNGs) joining their unit. One unit held "court" and sat around the new man while one of the old-timers asked him whether or not he performed and enjoyed cunnilingus.[54] Another unit waited for the newcomer's first visit to the company club, where he was placed on the stage while, to the tune of "Camp Town Races," the entire company sang in his honor:

> You're going home in a body bag; Doo dah, doo dah.
> Shot between eyes, shot between the thighs.
> You're going home in a body bag; O doo dah day.[55]

In an extreme form of initiation rite, one Marine company obliged all newcomers to handle the dead bodies awaiting removal at the landing zone in order to overcome their fear of death and killing.[56] A less flamboyant method adopted by many units was to marry the FNG with a "buddy" who had been in country more than six months.[57] Whatever the nature of the group's initiation, it usually had the desired effect of helping the new man become speedily integrated into the group, overcome his outward fear, and imitate the group's techniques of survival.

Just as the FNG had the lowest status in a combat unit regardless of rank, the highest status was customarily accorded the men who had been with the unit longest. Time in country was one of the primary sources of respect in a combat unit. It was also widely believed to confer a certain wisdom or at least know-how. FNGs were constantly admonished by their squad mates to "watch the old-timers," "listen to what the old salts are saying; they know, they've been here."[58]

As in all wars, the desire to survive and to see one's comrades survive was the most widespread attitude among combat troops in Vietnam. "They didn't fight primarily for Mom's apple pie or the flag," a platoon leader in a mechanized infantry company asserted. "They were fighting for each other and for their unit, their company. They were fighting to survive."[59] "I guess my standard of success was keeping my soldiers alive," recalled a former company commander with the 3/503d Infantry.[60] It was a standard that would have been readily endorsed by almost all small-unit leaders in Vietnam and probably in many other wars as well. Yet in Vietnam, where the conventional military measures of success—ground gained, cities captured, numbers of prisoners taken—were largely or wholly absent, survivalism came to assume an almost exclusive place in a combat soldier's evaluation of success and prestige.

There were, of course, other standards of success in the confused, nasty, and endlessly repetitive war of small units in Vietnam. Officers and career soldiers might take pride in success on ambushes (and success in avoiding them), keeping the enemy out of defensive perimeters, capturing prisoners, or finding large arms caches. Doubtless many other members of the unit did too. Yet, as the war ground on through its third and fourth year, the prestige of performing a mission well proved increasingly inadequate to men who more and more could see no larger purpose in that mission, and no end to the incessant patrols, sweeps, and ambushes which appeared to result only in more danger, discomfort, and casualties. "I feel as if I've been used," a soldier with the 1st Infantry Division told a reporter in 1969. "Nothing I've seen or heard about the way we've been doing things and why makes any sense."[61] More than ten years later, two career Army officers reviewing their experiences in Vietnam reached much the same conclusion. "I didn't understand why I was in Vietnam very clearly, I really didn't," a former company commander with the 4th Infantry recalled. "And in free moments when we didn't have a lot to do, those personnel that were close to me were struggling for the same kind of explanation and that created a lot of problems."[62] "I'm not really sure that anybody in the higher-up levels knew what we were supposed to be doing," another officer said. "I'm like I say, like my troops, I just wondered, you know: okay, if we do all this, what's going to happen? What are we doing? What's the goal of the whole thing?"[63]

The lack of any tangible measures of progress such as ground gained, cities captured, and enemy armies destroyed contributed to the widespread feelings of futility and frustration about the war. There was little enough comfort to be had from the capture of features on a map for soldiers in World War II. Yet Army psychologists noted that during rapid advances, such as the movement of Allied armies through France and Belgium in August and September 1944, even combat veterans could feel optimistic. Moreover, the capture of a hill or a town could mean greater safety, comfort, or even (in the final days) war booty for the troops involved.[64] In Vietnam, in contrast, hard-won terrain was often abandoned almost as soon as it was secured, leaving the GIs with the feeling of futility and frustration. "They did not know the feeling of taking a place and keeping it" the former infantryman Tim O'Brien wrote. "No sense of order and momentum. No front, no rear, no trenches laid out in neat parallels, no Patton rushing for the Rhine, no beachheads to storm and win and hold for the duration. They did not have targets, they did not have a cause. . . . On a given day they did not know where they were in Quange Ngai or how being there might influence larger outcomes."[65]

Despite the frustration, danger, and hardship, most combat troops appeared to cope well with their deadly and alien world. At least that was the opinion of psychiatrists and other behavioral scientists who studied the Vietnam GIs' "adjustment." They noted that the incidence of psychiatric problems and "combat fatigue" among Vietnam troops in 1968 was low, far lower than the rates for World War II. During World War II 23 percent of all medical evacuations had been for psychiatric reasons, whereas the figure for Vietnam was less than 6 percent.[66] Even as fighting intensified and casualties mounted, the incidence of psychiatric problems in Vietnam remained about the same as those for military units in the United States.[67]

This pattern did not continue into the later stages of the war. After 1968 the neuropsychiatric disease rate for Vietnam began to rise and "increased more precipitously than in any other location where there were large numbers of American troops."[68] By 1970 there were more than twice as many hospital admissions for psychosis, psychoneurosis, and character and behavior disorders as there had been in 1967. In terms of man-days lost, neuropsychiatric problems had become the second leading disease problem in the theater.[69] In World War II neuropsychiatric casualty rates rose as the intensity of combat increased. In Vietnam, as fighting and casualties grew *lighter,* the psychiatric casualty rate *increased.*

While the honeymoon lasted during the early years, there was no shortage of behavioral scientists to "explain" this unusual pattern of behavior. Psychiatrist Peter Bourne declared that "the low level of psychiatric attrition . . . can be attributed directly or indirectly to the significant increase in awareness of the military command." Bourne and other psychiatrists who had served in Vietnam also attributed the scarcity of psychiatric problems to the relatively brief and episodic nature of most Vietnam combat, the provision of relatively greater creature comforts, such as hot meals flown in by helicopter and the availability of brief rests and even an overseas vacation in a neighboring country—R&R. Above all he believed that the one-year tour helped greatly to remove "the sense of hopelessness that prevailed in previous conflicts, where death, injury, or peace became the only socially acceptable way in which the soldier could find himself extricated from combat." By way of contrast, the GI in Vietnam "knows that he can merely survive for twelve months and his removal from combat is assured. . . . These policies have exerted a profound although unmeasured effect."[70]

The Vietnam soldier would have emphatically agreed. The twelve-month tour was the lodestar, the organizing principle around which the soldier built his entire existence. Every GI knew, almost to the day, when his tour in Vietnam would end, and his attitudes and behavior were powerfully affected by the knowledge. "Short-timer calendars" blossomed throughout Vietnam. Among the most common was a sketch of a naked woman divided into 365 tiny squares, one to be filled in every day as the longed-for date approached. "Short-timers," men who were approaching the end of their tours, took on the aura of an envied elite among their fellow GIs. The men themselves proudly proclaimed that they were "getting short" or were now "so short I can barely come up to your knees."

The criteria for who was entitled to be considered a "short-timer" varied widely from unit to unit. In some units men with two or even three months left to serve might consider themselves "short." In others the short-timers were those with less than a month to go. Whatever its precise meaning, once a man came to consider himself short, a characteristic pattern of behavior often set in, which commanders labeled "short-timer's fever." Soldiers who were experienced, cool, and steady suddenly became anxious and timid as the end of their tour approached. They became extremely reluctant to take risks of any type and began to recall stories of men killed in their last week or even their last day in Vietnam.[71]

Many combat units dealt with the problem by sending men to the rear during their last few days or weeks, or at least markedly reducing the demands on their performance. "Short-timers were sent back to the rear when it was clear their hearts, minds, and balls were no longer wired together," one Marine recalled. "The last thing you need behind or alongside you was some guy daydreaming about what life must be like back in the world and counting how many microseconds it would be before he was part of it."[72]

Yet such measures, although widely adopted, provided no real cure for short-timer's syndrome. A man serving in a unit where men were customarily sent to the rear for their final two weeks might simply begin his short-time anxieties some time sooner. "It gets to that point," an officer who had commanded two companies recalled, "and the guy is about ready to say, 'Well, it's about time for me to come out of the field,' and he starts looking around, 'When do I get taken out?' . . . That'll happen. It's just a psychological progression where the guy is ready to come out and if it doesn't happen and if he's a weak individual he's going to think of reasons to get out. It's very disruptive."[73]

Yet short-timer's syndrome was only one of the ill effects that the system of one-year tours and individual replacements had on the combat effectiveness of American forces in Vietnam. The constant personnel turnovers threatened and sometimes broke down hard-won unit cohesion, the feelings of familiarity and confidence that combat units worked so hard to maintain. The system also ensured that at any given time a platoon or company in the field would be made up largely of inexperienced newcomers. A former platoon sergeant recalled: "The makeup of my platoon changed almost weekly. . . . After only two months in Vietnam, I had more experience than half the men in my platoon."[74]

Most observers of fighting men in Vietnam agreed that a soldier was at his most effective after about six to eight months in country.[75] At that point, he had acquired considerable experience and began to think of himself as an old hand at jungle or mountain warfare. When "they get to the middle [of their tour] they start being the old hand," recalled a company commander with the 2d of the 60th Infantry, "and they kind of strut around a little bit to the new guys, they want to prove that they're macho types. . . . They know what they're doing so they're going to teach them stuff."[76] Yet soon after this point short-timer's fever and the end of his tour effectively removed the old-timer from the field.

Even more threatening to military effectiveness was the policy of rotating officers to rear areas (combat service support or headquarters jobs) after six months in command of a combat unit. The official rationale usually offered for the practice was that the strain of command was such that most men were likely to become tired and less effective after prolonged operations in the field. Major General Richard G. Lawrence, who commanded an armored cavalry squadron in Vietnam in 1968, still claimed, many years later, that the six-month rotation was prudent and sensible. "In my own case, personally, at the end of six months I was tired. I'm not sure I made decisions in the fifth or sixth month that were as good as decisions in the first three or four."[77]

Few other officers believed they had been so weary after six months as to impair their decision-making ability. Many attributed the policy of short command tours to the desire of the services to give as many officers as possible a chance to gain command experience and advance their careers. "If I had my way I'd have stayed in command the whole time I was there," an infantry company commander recalled of 1968. "Unfortunately, there were other officers that were standing in line to get commands and the battalion commander, of course, he had pretty much to give them the opportunity."[78] "The attitude I got [sic] was that units were training aids for training new commanders and future leaders," one former armored cavalry commander reported. "I just think that is not the way to do business."[79]

Whatever the reasons, there is almost universal agreement among officers who served at the company level that the six-month tour was "disastrous" for unit effectiveness.[80] Many believed that they had just begun to be fully proficient at their jobs only a month or two before their six months expired.[81]

The troops were well aware of the implications for them of this constant turnover of command. "Men do not like a change of leadership," a former artillery battalion commander concluded. "I would say that had as deleterious an effect on morale as anything [in Vietnam] simply because the new leader is unknown."[82]

Not only was he unknown, but he was almost certain to be inexperienced. A company commander with the 1st Cavalry Division observed that his men became very upset and depressed over officer casualties, not so much out of grief as "because they knew it meant a new, inexperienced guy was coming on the scene."[83]

Some newly arrived officers would "absolutely astound everyone with the level of their overall ignorance and very specific stupidity," a Marine who served during 1968 recalled. "The best of the newly arrived officers would basically function as just another member of the platoon or the company letting the NCOs and 'salts' run the outfit until they saw what was done and how. Of course, even the best learners who managed to survive, left all too soon to be replaced by new 'boot' officers."[84]

While the six-month tour for commanders had at least an explicit rationale ("fatigue") and a plausible motive ("careerism"), the one-year tour appears to have been largely a result of routine and accident. Twelve months had, for many years, been the standard tour for military men serving as advisers and technicians away from their families in overseas "hardship areas." Vietnam, with its inhospitable climate, primitive living arrangements, and generally unhealthful conditions, readily qualified.

During the 1950s and early 1960s, however, knowledgeable officers familiar with Vietnam had repeatedly argued that whatever the hardships twelve months was simply too short a time for an American military adviser to learn his job and become fully effective.[85] Yet, except for a few months in late 1961, the twelve-month tour remained in effect. When American combat troops began to arrive in the spring of 1965, the twelve-month tour was simply extended to them.[86]

Within a few months of the commencement of American combat operations it became apparent that, from the standpoint of efficient manpower utilization, the twelve-month tour made no sense whatsoever. Long after it was too late, an Army staff study concluded that the most efficient arrangement would have been eighteen months. For soldiers serving two-year enlistments, an eighteen-month tour would still have allowed four to five months for training and one or two months for leave, travel, and processing. Soldiers serving three years could also be utilized under such a system by combining their eighteen-month Vietnam tour with a full year in a U.S.-based unit.[87]

As it was, the Army was faced with the problem of endemic personnel turbulence occasioned by the very high turnover rates made necessary by the twelve-month tour. U.S.-based and Europe-based Army units were constantly losing their most experienced enlisted men to levies for Vietnam while receiving (in the case of U.S.-based units) large numbers of returnees from Southeast Asia with only four to eight months of service remaining. These "short-timers" were of relatively little use to their new commands and also were a frequent cause of morale and disciplinary problems. The twelve-month tour also made little sense from the standpoint of equity since all personnel in Vietnam, whether in an unhealthy swamp or at a beach resort, whether in frequent close combat or in an air-conditioned office, served an identical number of days.

Despite these problems, the services and the Defense Department never seriously considered altering the twelve-month tour. The seal of permanence was set upon the whole crazy-quilt arrangement in October 1966, when Defense Secretary McNamara, prompted by persistent rumors and growing public concern over a possible increase in Vietnam tour lengths, publicly announced, "We have no intention of changing the twelve-month tour of duty. All of the men assigned to Vietnam, with the exception of some commanders and General Westmoreland and a few of his staff and the higher echelon staffs in the field, are sent on a twelve-month tour of duty."[88] As late as the middle of 1968, General Westmoreland's assistants, preparing the testimony for his confirmation hearings as Army Chief of Staff, declared that lengthening the tour of duty in Vietnam "would be self-defeating." They also argued that a significant number of Army personnel voluntarily extended their tours in Vietnam, thus providing at least some of the benefits associated with longer tour lengths.[89]

In fact, men did extend their tours in Vietnam, and in some military specialties the proportion exceeded 10 percent. Yet few enlisted men in ground combat specialties (less than 1.75 percent) or aviation (less than 1.5 percent) were among those extending. An Army study in 1968 showed that the type of soldier most likely to extend was a senior NCO in such specialties as food services, engineer maintenance, and administration.[90] Few combat troops would have been surprised to learn that "lifers" who stayed "in the rear with the gear, the sergeant major, and the beer," were willing to extend their tour or reenlist in Vietnam, but extensions among enlisted men in the field were infrequent indeed. When extensions did occur they tended to be in circumstances like those described by Tim O'Brien in *If I Die in a Combat Zone:*

> Then the battalion re-up NCO came along. "I seen some action. I got me two Purple Hearts so listen up good. I'm not saying you're gonna to get zapped out there. I made it. But you're gonna to come

motherfucking close. Jesus, you're gonna to hear bullets tickling your asshole and sure as I'm standing here one or two of you men are gonna to get your legs blown off. Or balls. One or two of you, it's gotta happen.

"So what can you do about it? Well, like Sarge says, you can be careful, you can watch for the mines and all that, and, who knows you might come out looking like a rose. But careful guys get killed too. So what can you do about it then? Nothing. Except you can re-up."

The men looked at the ground and shuffled around grinning. "Sure, sure I know nobody likes to re-up. But just think about it a second. Just say you do it. You take your burst of three, starting today, three more years of Army life. Then what? Well I'll tell you what, it'll save your ass, that's what, it'll save your ass. You re-up and I can get you a job in Chu Lai. I got jobs for mechanics, typists, clerks, damn near anything you want, I got it. So you get your nice safe rear area job. You get some on-the-job training, the works. . . . So you lose a little time to Uncle Sam. Big deal. You save your ass. So, I got my desk inside. If you come in and sign the papers it'll take ten minutes, and I'll have you on the first truck back to Chu Lai."[91]

Although the generals often viewed a high extension or reenlistment rate as an indication of good morale in the unit, soldiers themselves usually saw it as primarily a method of escaping a dangerous or undesirable job. Soldiers facing court-martial for refusing to join their units in the field on operations sometimes offered as their excuse an intention to extend for a better job in the rear.[92]

Though it soon became obvious that tour extensions did not really provide continuity in any meaningful sense, this too had little impact on the services' commitment to retaining the twelve-month tour. However irrational from the point of view of manpower utilization, however destructive of morale and unit cohesion, whatever distortions it worked upon the overall U.S. defense posture, the twelve-month tour remained to the end. As John Paul Vann, the veteran military adviser and pacification expert, is reported to have observed, "The U.S. has not had five years' experience in Vietnam. The U.S. has had one year's experience five times."

Uncertain of purpose; skeptical of their mission and their own higher-level leadership; lacking continuity, tradition, and experience; lacking, in fact, most qualities of successful military organizations except courage, youth, energy, and resilience, the Vietnam-only GIs faced the great tests of 1968. Concealed in quiet villages or impenetrable mountains, in bamboo huts near the Laotian borders or in tunnels and bunkers a few thousand yards from Da Nang and Saigon, their enemies waited and prepared for battle.

CHAPTER 4

"Born in the North, to Die in the South"

If there was one thing the GIs of 1968 could agree on about the puzzling, frustrating war raging in Vietnam, it was that they faced a formidable enemy. "North Vietnamese are great fighters, boy," observed Richard Blanchfield, a Navy corpsman with the 26th Marines in 1968. "You'll never hear Marines say the North Vietnamese aren't tough. They're probably the toughest fighters in the world as far as I'm concerned. They knew what they were fighting for. They understood why they were there and they were there for the duration."[1]

"I still think about this North Vietnamese soldier," Charles Strong, a machine gunner in the Americal Division, recalled. "This was a brave dude. I'll never forget him. It took a whole platoon to kill him. He was held up in a tunnel. He knew he had no possible chance of winning whatsoever. And he wasn't really expecting no help. But this was the bravest dude I had ever seen. . . . When they pulled him out. . . . he had a hunk of meat out of his leg. . . . He had shrapnel all over his body. He had a hole in his side. But he wouldn't give up. Because he really believed in something."[2]

Who were these Vietnamese who had defeated the French and who, since 1965, had stood up to fearful bombing, shelling, and appalling losses in battle against the world's strongest military power?

They were a people accustomed to war, a people who indeed defined themselves by war and by struggle.

"Our curriculum revolved around the story of Vietnam's two thousand years of struggle against all kinds of foreigners," recalled one Vietnamese of his schooling in Haiphong in the 1960s. "We studied, case by case and story by story, the lives of all Vietnam's national heroes—Tran Quoc Tuan, Tran Hung Dao, who chased out the Mongols in the thirteenth century, and especially Emperor Quang Trung, who surprised and defeated the Chinese at Tet in 1789. . . . Everybody learned these stories with tremendous pride and enthusiasm. . . . Our national heroes had loved freedom and were ready to sacrifice everything for it. That feeling got instilled into us, into our bones, that we had to be worthy of our history."[3]

Martial tales and legends formed the subject matter of songs, narratives, and plays performed by minstrels and actors in villages throughout the country. Ellen Hammer recalled that even in the 1960s boatmen on the Perfume River "still sing nostalgic songs about the Emperors Ham Nghi and Duy Tam and how they resisted the French during the colonial period."[4]

"We children knew that our ancestral spirits demanded we resist the outsiders," wrote Le Ly Hayslip, whose parents were rice farmers in a village near Da Nang. "Our parents told us of the misery they had suffered from the invading Japanese . . . and from the French who returned in 1946. These soldiers destroyed our crops, raped our women and tortured or put to death anyone who opposed them . . . now, the souls of all those people who had been mercilessly killed had come back to haunt Ky La—demanding revenge against the invaders."[5]

The Vietnamese thought of themselves as giant-killers, more resolute, more courageous, and also better organized and smarter than their opponents.[6] The odds mattered little. They were accustomed to winning against odds. The Vietnamese had thrown off the Chinese yoke and had turned back Kublai Khan's Mongol hordes; they had defeated and almost exterminated their powerful Indianized neighbors to the south, the Chams. They had wrested other parts of their country from the Thais, Burmese, and Khmers, and in the modern era they had defeated the French.

In 1964 the Vietnamese Communists believed themselves to be on the verge of yet another victory, this time against the American "puppet" government in Saigon. Beginning with fewer than two thousand armed adherents in 1959, Communist forces in the south, formally designated the People's Liberation Armed Forces by the party, labeled Viet Cong by the Americans and Saigon, had grown to seven thousand in 1960 and more than one hundred thousand by early 1964.[7] As early as January 1960, four PLAF battalions, totaling about two hundred men, had successfully attacked the headquarters of the South Vietnamese Army's 32d Regiment in Tay Ninh province, killing or wounding nearly seventy South Vietnamese troops, capturing large quantities of weapons, and leaving the barracks and headquarters in ruins.[8] Two years later the Communists scored an even more impressive success near the hamlet of Ap Bac, in My Tho province, where three PLAF companies and local guerrillas held off a South Vietnamese force four times their size. The South Vietnamese, though supported by American helicopters and armored personnel carriers, were held at bay. They suffered more than sixty casualties and the loss of five helicopters before the Communists successfully disengaged in the gathering darkness.[9] An American adviser called it "the Fort Benning school solution of how an outnumbered infantry unit ought to organize a defense."[10]

By late 1964 PLAF troops, now operating in units of battalion and regimental size, defeated elite South Vietnamese Ranger and Marine units in a month-long series of engagements near the village of Binh Gia, about 40 miles southeast of Saigon. U.S. military advisers estimated that by the end of 1964 the South Vietnamese government was losing the equivalent of about one battalion a week to enemy action and widespread desertion. A major ingredient in the rapid growth and success of the Viet Cong was the leadership and organizational skills supplied by southern-born soldiers and political experts infiltrated from the north. Veterans of the Viet Minh struggle against the French, these dedicated and skilled combat leaders, who had regrouped in the north after the signing of the Geneva Accords in 1954, began slipping back into the south in late 1959. They brought with them weapons and equipment to begin a new war against the Saigon regime.

Yet it was not the skill of the Communist cadres so much as the incompetence, corruption, and oppression of the South Vietnamese government that enabled the Communists to grow from a few thousand to a formidable army in less than four years. The Republic of Vietnam, headed since 1954 by Ngo Dinh Diem, dubbed "the miracle man of Southeast Asia" by the American media, was venal, reactionary, inefficient, and corrupt. Diem himself was a Catholic in a country that was 90 percent non-Catholic and where the Catholics were looked on with suspicion as the toadies and protégés of the French.

Like many members of the Communist leadership, Diem was born to a mandarin family in central Vietnam. Unlike his Communist rivals, however, Diem adopted no new leadership style, no new ideology or political techniques. He was a mandarin of the traditional sort, personally honest, patriotic, and hard-working but incapable of dealing with the problems of a nation torn by nine years of war and revolution. Although South Vietnam received lavish U.S. aid after Diem consolidated his power in 1955, much of the aid money found its way into the pockets of Army officers, provincial officials, and members of the Ngo family.[11] In the countryside and villages, Diem replaced many local officials with outsiders, often Catholic refugees from the north. The new officials were as oppressive, arrogant, and corrupt as their predecessors but carried the additional stigma of being strangers without local ties.

An ambitious land reform program was begun but was so slow in starting and so ineptly administered that it ended by alienating both peasants and landowners alike. Ferocious efforts to root out Communist agents and sympathizers by Diem's police and security forces resulted in the capture of many Communists and the disruption of their organization. Yet the anti-Communist campaign was conducted in such a heavy-handed, brutal, and capricious manner that many non-Communists were arrested, imprisoned, and even executed.[12] "Not only were local officials and police agents incompetent at singling out active Viet Minh [Communist] agents," a study commissioned by the U.S. Defense Department declared, "but many were also arrogant and venal in the execution of their tasks and by their offensive behavior generated sympathy for the Viet Minh."[13]

On this fertile ground, the Viet Cong insurgency quickly took root. By November 1963, when Diem was overthrown by his own generals in a coup actively encouraged by Washington, the Viet Cong had some seventy thousand active adherents and virtually controlled large portions of many provinces.[14]

To the leaders of the Communist revolutionary movement in the south, all Vietnamese, whether young or old, male or female, were potential fighters in the struggle against the Americans and their puppets in Saigon. The struggle had two complementary forms, political and military, each dependent on the other. All of the population, whether called on to participate in demonstrations, engage in sabotage, act as scouts or spies, or spread propaganda, were equally combatants in the war against Saigon. Douglas Pike observed: "The Vietnamese Communists erased entirely the line between military and civilian by ruling out the notion of noncombatants. . . . Not even children were excluded— particularly not children one might say. All people became weapons of war."[15]

While the Communists regarded all of the people of South Vietnam as being in the front lines, only a portion were to be provided with modern arms and formal training. The military arm of the Viet Cong was composed of several different types of forces, each working in cooperation and each coordinating with and supporting the political activities of the party. The lowest level of military organization was the guerrilla squad or platoon, controlled by the party hamlet or village leadership. The guerrilla squad or platoon was a permanent organization, but its members were clandestine, part-time soldiers who supported themselves as farmers, shopkeepers, or artisans. Guerrillas possessed a variety of weapons and were capable of carrying out local attacks on government outposts, protecting party members, collecting taxes, and scouting for larger local and main force Viet Cong units.[16]

Supporting the guerrillas were various unarmed self-defense and militia organizations usually composed of older men, younger teenagers, and women. Their primary purpose was to provide the guerrillas and other Viet Cong forces with intelligence, assistance, propaganda, and sabotage activities and to provide labor for construction of trenches, tunnels, and fortifications.

Far better armed and trained were the full-time military forces of the PLAF: the Regional or Local Forces, and the Main Force. The

Local Forces were organized in companies and operated within the bounds of the province or region; the Main Forces were organized in battalions, regiments, or even occasionally division-size units.[17]

Normally young men were recruited first into guerrilla units, to be assigned to Main Force units only after acquiring some experience in the guerrilla forces. This was done in order to provide the Main Forces personnel with combat experience but also as a means accommodating the recruit's strong attachment to his family and village. Such a system allowed him to begin his military service while still living in his home region.

The process of "upgrading" both men and entire units from village guerrillas to Local Force to Main Force was continuous, with the pace varying according to the scale of combat and the Communists' manpower needs. The process could also be reversed, and members of the Local Force and Main Force units could be introduced into guerrilla platoons and squads. This was done on occasions when the Local Force or Main Force unit had suffered severe losses or when the guerrillas needed to be trained, supported, and led on a special mission that called for the skills and firepower of the higher-echelon soldiers.[18] During the preparations for Tet, guerrillas and Local Force units that normally provided replacements to Main Force battalions were instead reinforced themselves by higher-echelon units in preparation for the attacks they would spearhead.

In 1968 Viet Cong recruits, whether guerrilla or full-time, were overwhelmingly rural in origin. Eighty-three percent had been farmers in civilian life. Only 13 percent had progressed beyond the fourth grade, and only 2 percent had completed secondary school.[19] The intense fighting and the rising demand for recruits during 1967 and 1968 resulted in the enlistment of many younger men. Over one-third of the sixty thousand new entrants into the PLAF during 1968 were estimated by U.S. intelligence to be seventeen years old or under, a number being as young as thirteen.[20]

Before 1966 the Viet Cong had found many willing volunteers who joined for reasons of patriotism and belief in the Communist exhortations to free the country of the American imperialists. By 1968 it was clear to Vietnamese in even the most remote and backward areas that service in the PLAF meant hardship, danger, privation, and increasing risk of death. "When our enthusiasm for resisting got too cool, the Viet Cong simply turned up the heat," Le Ly Hayslip recalled. "By the second year of this new war, we could not go to another town or talk to anyone from outside the area without first getting permission from the cadre. If a stranger came to the village—even someone's long-lost relative or an orphan from another district—everyone wanted to know who it was and how long he or she was going to stay. It was OK to visit your friends and relatives, but if you stayed too long the cadre leaders were sure to ask about it later."[21]

District party committees continued to provide recruits, often through appeals to families or thinly veiled threats. The Communists also played on personal grievances against the Saigon government, desire for revenge against corrupt or brutal officials, and fear of the South Vietnamese draft. When other inducements failed, recruits were often abducted or blackmailed into joining.[22]

To replace the grim losses suffered in the Tet attacks, the Communist high command began to reinforce Viet Cong units with large infusions of replacements from the north. Although Hanoi stoutly denied it, the Peoples' Army of Vietnam, Hanoi's regular forces, had long played an important role in the war in the south. As early as the autumn of 1964 an entire PAVN regiment had departed for the south, followed by three more during the winter, so that by May 1965 the number of northern-born regulars in the south was estimated by U.S. intelligence at more than six thousand.[23] The first complete North Vietnamese Army unit, the 808th Independent Battalion, entered the south in the fall of 1964, and the first regimental-size unit in December of the same year.

With the introduction of U.S. combat troops in 1965, the North Vietnamese rate of infiltration increased dramatically. By 1967 the rate averaged more than seven thousand a month. The intensive fighting inaugurated by the Tet attacks made even greater demands on North Vietnamese manpower, and during the first six months of 1968 an average of twenty-nine thousand North Vietnamese combatants a month entered South Vietnam.[24] These new arrivals from the North were required not only as replacements for the North Vietnamese Army units in the South, which by 1968 totaled nine divisions and at least a dozen independent regiments, but also to fill the gaps in the ranks of many Viet Cong units, which had suffered heavy losses in the Tet battles.[25] By the spring of 1968 U.S. intelligence estimated that some thirteen thousand to sixteen thousand North Vietnamese Army fighters were serving in Viet Cong Main Force units, with some Viet Cong regiments having over 70 percent North Vietnamese personnel.[26]

To supply the manpower for war in the South the Democratic Republic of Vietnam drew heavily on its population of some 20 million. About one hundred thousand males fit for military service reached draft age each year, and Hanoi expanded the pool of eligible men still further by recalling former military personnel, lowering induction standards, and extending terms of service. Women replaced men in many local defense units, thus freeing more males for service in the South.

Most of the men who came South in 1968 were draftees, although a few were volunteers. Since 1965 the DRV's draft laws had been steadily tightened. Catholics and ethnic Chinese who had formerly been exempted as unreliable were now often conscripted. Many students and professionals lost their exemptions, and the age limits of draftees were extended from ages 18–25 to ages 17–35. There were some Communist prisoners of war who spoke of infiltration groups in which the majority of the personnel were over thirty years old.[27]

The Viet Cong and North Vietnamese forces were outnumbered by their American and South Vietnamese foes. They also lacked aircraft and, except near the Demilitarized Zone, tanks and heavy artillery. Yet they remained a formidable fighting force. They excelled in defense and in a wide variety of carefully prepared ambushes. An often-employed Communist tactic was to allow an American unit on a patrol or sweep to blunder onto carefully prepared field fortifications. A captured North Vietnamese officer expressed the view that the "American infantry units are weak," because they "cannot take or destroy a machine gun position in a properly prepared bunker except by calling for air or artillery. However, the NVA can destroy any American bunker with its B-40 rockets."[28]

"They were masters at aligning weapons with fields of fire," a former company commander with the 1st Air Cavalry Division recalled. "They were superb at masking their true position. The Americans would move up, you would kill a couple and the rest would run and it was a natural tendency to take off after them. . . . In close terrain against enemy like the North Vietnamese that will get you your nose bloodied. . . . They were absolute masters at choosing the right terrain at the right place at the right time to blow your crap away."[29]

Although the Communists' skill and tenacity in defense inspired awe and respect, their performance on the offensive was often weak and ineffective. Their supporting fires were almost always weaker than the Americans', and they often lacked the ability to coordinate attacks of larger than company size.[30] A Defense Department study found that Communist-initiated attacks on U.S. positions, though they often achieved surprise, still cost the Communists an average of five soldiers for every U.S. casualty.[31] On the infrequent occasions when Communist units were taken by surprise, they often proved incapable of rapidly adapting to the situation, frequently suffering heavy losses and sometimes disintegrating in panic. Communist losses in U.S.-initiated ambushes averaged more than twenty-five times those of the American units opposing them.[32]

Thus while American battalions and even companies could range far afield in search of the enemy, confident in the support of their massive artillery and airpower, the Communists relied on careful preparation, surprise, and defense in depth to give them the edge against American firepower. Another asset that enabled the Communists to survive on the battlefield was their excellent and sophisticated employment of electronic warfare. There was more than a little irony to that. During World War II it had been the United States that, together with its allies, had gained a clear lead in communications intelligence, breaking the most sophisticated codes and ciphers of the Japanese and subtly exploiting the combined intelligence work of British and American code-breakers who eavesdropped on Axis communications from Berlin to Tokyo.[33]

Yet in the Vietnam War it was the Viet Cong and PAVN who made the more skillful use of electronic warfare. The Communists generally employed three types of electronic warfare against the Americans: "jamming," or the introduction of various disturbances on the frequency being used by the enemy to prevent or interfere with his transmission; "intercepts," or the clandestine monitoring of enemy radio communications; and "imitative deception," or broadcasting bogus messages on the enemy's frequency to confuse or deceive him.[34]

Although jamming was sometimes used effectively by the Communists, the practice required high-powered radios with new batteries which many Communist signal units lacked. Intercepts were employed far more frequently. The Communists' task was made easier by the fact that the American forces seldom took precautions to safeguard the security of their transmissions. Most messages were sent by voice radio and were seldom encoded or enciphered. The units of the 1st Air Cavalry Division, for example, employed the same call signs and frequencies from late 1966 until March 1970.[35]

"We discussed everything in the clear," recalled an artillery battalion commander. "Well, the attitude was 'so what if they can hear us, we can out-maneuver them and get there faster than they can do anything about it.' The battalion and brigade commanding officers, they all had these [code] names. I remember the brigade CO's name was 'Cherokee.' Well, Christ Almighty, by the time the guy has been in the area for only a few days, the enemy knows who the hell Cherokee is. They could follow him all over the battlefield."[36]

Viet Cong and PAVN interception operations enabled them to gain advance knowledge of American and South Vietnamese troop movements, attacks, ambushes, and air strikes. Despite the speed with which the American forces could move and strike in Vietnam, the Communists were seldom surprised or caught napping.

The Communists' monitoring of American communications enabled them to acquire a thorough knowledge of American slang, call signs, names, voice patterns, and phonetic alphabet. In December 1969, a platoon from the First Brigade of the First Infantry Division captured a twelve-man Viet Cong electronic warfare team together with its equipment and logs near the outskirts of Saigon. Examination of the captured documents and records revealed that the team, known as A3, had been monitoring the voice and Morse code transmissions of American and South Vietnamese forces for several years. Indeed, the captured logs suggested that "members of the team knew more about the communications of local American and South Vietnamese units than did most allied communicators."[37]

The Vietcong frequently employed this knowledge of U.S. communications procedures to enter the radio net and redirect American artillery fire or air strikes. During a fire fight in Lam Dong province in 1967 members of a MACV advisory team requested artillery support. As the Fire Direction Center prepared to direct the mission, they "received another call in clear and distinct English requesting the fire be shifted to a different set of grid coordinates. Luckily the team overheard the request and were able to contact the Fire Direction Center in time to prevent an artillery attack on their own position!"[38]

The Viet Cong also made skillful use of caves and tunnels as supply centers, headquarters, hospitals, and schools. The famous "tunnels of Cu Chi," hundreds of miles of passageways, workshops, living quarters, and storage rooms dug into the dry laterite clay of Hau Ngia and Binh Duong provinces near Saigon, formed an underground network stretching from the outskirts of the capital to the Cambodian border.[39] The tunnels were superbly camouflaged and featured multiple exits and entrances with dead-end tunnels and booby traps to confuse attackers.

By 1968 all North Vietnamese Army and Main Force Viet Cong units were almost entirely equipped with weapons supplied by China and Russia, notably the redoubtable AK-47 assault rifle and the RPG-2 (B-40) rocket launcher, as well as 60, 82, and 120mm mortars and a variety of rockets for standoff attacks.[40] Nevertheless, the Communist forces in the South continued to provide much of their own supplies and equipment. Vietnamese living in or near "liberated zones" were expected to supply the Communist forces with grain and other foodstuffs, medicine, building materials, and transport.[41]

Much material was also obtained through a "shadow supply system," which relied on clandestine procurement of supplies from the South Vietnamese and Americans themselves. South Vietnamese plantation operators, mine owners, and logging companies operating in or near Communist-controlled areas often paid large bribes to the Viet Cong for the privilege of being permitted to conduct business unmolested. One logging company concluded a formal agreement to supply the Communists with weekly shipments of rice, salt, printer's ink, and newsprint, as well as a 500,000-piaster monthly protection fee, in return for woodcutter's rights. In another district, the Communists charged a flat fee of three hundred piasters per meter of wood.[42] In other districts, the Communists levied a "tax" on trucks and other commercial vehicles using portions of certain roads controlled by the Viet Cong. South Vietnamese trucking companies were also often hired to haul supplies for Viet Cong rear service units. In one province, the Viet Cong provided Honda motorcycles to their suppliers. After a certain number of supply runs, the messenger was allowed to retain the motorcycle.[43]

A not inconsiderable quantity of supplies and weapons for the Communists came from their South Vietnamese opponents. "During the very first days of the war of resistance our party pointed out the battlefield as the major source of equipment for the revolutionary army," a North Vietnamese general wrote. "Even when fighting reached a peak in the spring of 1975 our forces continued to consider the use of war booty as one of the best and timeliest means to meet combat requirements."[44]

By 1968 most of the people of North Vietnam knew that the struggle in the South had become grim, bloody, and protracted. "The villages were emptying out," recalled a Communist journalist. "The young people were all going to fight in the South and they weren't coming back. It began to seem like an open pit. The more young people who were lost there, the more they sent. There was even a kind of motto that the whole generation of army-age North Vietnamese adopted—they tattooed it on themselves and they sang songs about it—'Born in the North, to die in the South.' "[45]

The government continued to report only victories and to conceal the costs of the war from the population. "We all believed in the mission of liberating the South," recalled Hoang Tat Hong, a clerk in a rural cooperative in Than Hoa province who was drafted in 1967.[46] Cadres and troops infiltrating from the North were told that the front controlled three-quarters of the land and four-fifths of the population and that they would receive a warm welcome from the people of the south. They were warned to "move fast or there will be nothing left for them to liberate and they will lose the honors reserved [for the liberators] by the people."[47] Mai Van So, a Viet Cong logistics officer and veteran of the war with the French, was surprised and amused when "a number of newly infiltrated cadre told me they thought the war in the South was over."[48]

Deaths in combat were seldom reported. Most often families would learn of casualties only through word of mouth or from wounded comrades brought back to the North.[49] Disabled or badly mutilated veterans were kept away from heavily populated areas and sent to special centers in the highlands around Lang Son and Vinh Phuc. One story, told all over Hanoi, concerned a wounded soldier brought back from the South to one of these special areas. Somehow his wife learned of his return and, after much effort, discovered that her husband was in a hospital for the severely wounded. Making her way to the hospital, the wife found her husband and discovered that he had lost both legs and both arms. The wife fled in shock and horror. "The husband, feeling utterly abandoned, took his own life in despair." The wife was brought before a court and sentenced to seven years in prison for having caused the death of her husband.[50]

"Many parents tried to keep sons out of the army. They would hide them when they were called up," a university student recounted. "Anyone who didn't show up automatically had his [family's] rice ration cut. But, families would buy food on the black market or just get along. . . . They would survive that way while they tried to scrape up enough to bribe a recruiting official. . . . Other draftees mutilated themselves. . . . People with money were able to pay doctors to disqualify their children."[51] Highly placed party leaders arranged for their sons to be sent overseas to study when they came of draft age. A former PAVN sergeant claimed that "almost every district or party committee member had a son studying abroad."[52]

For the great majority of North Vietnamese youth who lacked sufficient opportunities or sufficient desperation to try such expedients, the draft remained a common fate. Most young men received a letter on their seventeenth or eighteenth birthday ordering them to report for a physical examination. The letter was usually delivered by a member of the hamlet or village party committee or, in a large city, by the party section chief, who often accompanied the youth to the examination center.[53] If he was found physically qualified, a recruit could be called to service within a few days or after as long as several months.

As Phan Than Long was about to leave his home on the outskirts of Hanoi to report for induction, his sister burst into tears. "We were hugging each other and crying. At that point a recruitment cadre showed up and ordered me to hurry up. Then he told my sister that she should be encouraging me to go instead of making things so painful. My sister let him have it. 'We love each other in this family,' she told him. 'Don't be so rude to me.' She really put this guy in his place. Of course, I had to leave anyway."[54]

Despite the pain of leaving their homes and families and despite their anxieties about military service, new recruits usually found the regimen of basic training not unpleasant. Housing and sanitary conditions were good, and the food was superior to anything many of the poorer recruits had ever had at home. The training schedule was rigorous, with emphasis on maintenance and use of weapons such as rifles, grenades, and mines; ambush tactics; and penetration of barbed wire obstacles—all with a heavy dose of political indoctrination. Yet the trainees got plenty of sleep, access to newspapers and magazines, and opportunities to engage in sports and see movies or plays.[55]

The relative amenities of basic training little prepared the PAVN soldier for what he would experience on his journey south. Although the army attempted to prepare infiltrators for their ordeal with a special course of preinfiltration training in rugged mountain areas, few were really prepared. Only a handful of hardened veterans of the Viet Minh had ever faced hardships comparable to those that awaited the PAVN infiltrators as they made their way south, through the Truong Son mountains of Laos and western Vietnam along the jungle tracks and roads the Americans had named the Ho Chi Minh Trail.

The peaks of the Truong Son mountains varied in height from 1,800 to 3,000 feet. All but the highest were covered by dense tropical forests thick enough to block the sun's rays. More than two hundred streams and rivers cut deep ravines and valleys through the range. In the rainy season the streams would overflow their banks, sending torrents of water down the valleys and mountainsides.

Through this inhospitable land the PAVN infiltrators, organized into infiltration groups of about four hundred to five hundred men, made their way to the south.

Some members of the groups had received both basic training and special infiltration training. Others had completed only part of their infiltration training, while still others had arrived fresh from basic training as the group was about to depart. A few unfortunate last-minute arrivals had not even completed all of their basic training.

Whatever their level of preparation, the PAVN infiltrators found their two to three months on the trail an ordeal. Most of the northerners had grown up in the lowland coastal regions or the Red River delta and were no more prepared than American GIs for the rigors of the highlands. Vu Van Mong, a thirty-one-year-old army veteran and father of five who had reenlisted in 1968 after the school at which he was headmaster had been destroyed by American bombing, noted in his diary that "one day in the mountains of Laos has four seasons. The morning is spring; at noon it is summer; in the afternoon it is autumn; and at night it is winter."[56]

Through rain and cold the march to the South inexorably continued. Attacks by allied aircraft were a constant menace. Hoang Tat Hong's infiltration unit was attacked by twenty-two cells of B-52s in the space of about six hours. "We continued to look for dead bodies until two or three days later," Hong recalled. "The survivors all felt very frightened and embarrassed. We all thought that since such horrible things could occur in a resting place, the real battlefield should be very fierce."[57] "Truly one month in a land of tears. Nothing but bombs and bullets," wrote one infiltrator in his diary.[58]

Many nights the soldiers slept on the bare ground. Fires for warmth or cooking were usually forbidden to prevent detection by allied aircraft.

Food soon began to run short, and the regular diet was reduced to a small quantity of rice and an even smaller quantity of salt. Some soldiers were reduced to eating roots, leaves, and moss, while others burned the roots of the tranh plant and used the ashes as salt.[59] "At first three balls of pressed rice mixed with salt and a canteen of water were given every day," wrote a platoon commander who infiltrated in 1966. "Now at each meal only one ball of rice mixed with salt and a little fresh water are served. However, it is better than to eat moss as a rice substitute, taste ashes of straw as a substitute for salt and drink urine instead of water."[60]

Because fires for cooking and boiling water were usually forbidden, many PAVN troops developed intestinal disorders. Skin diseases were also common. Malaria was rampant, and though most infiltrators were supplied with a quantity of quinine pills and some other medicines, these often proved ineffective or inadequate. Sometimes 80 percent of the men of an infiltration group contracted some form of malaria. A soldier of the 12th PAVN Regiment told allied interrogators that almost 40 percent of the men in his company had been left behind on the trail at various aid stations because of malaria. "I have a constant fever, my body is emaciated, my wrists are thin, my eyes are sunken, my hair falls out," Vu Van Mong wrote after five weeks on the trail, "but I must still carry a load weighing over thirty kilograms."[61]

Upon arrival in South Vietnam the members of the infiltration group sometimes remained together as a fighting unit but more often were sent as replacements to various PAVN or Viet Cong formations already in the South. The PAVN soldier usually ate better in the South. A typical diet consisted of rice and vegetables with canned meat. Sometimes the local population would sell or give additional food to the troops, and soldiers often used periods of stand-down to go fishing to supplement their diet.[62] Yet periods of hunger and privation were far from rare, and disease continued to be an everpresent problem. The elite 141st North Vietnamese Regiment, dug into caves in the mountains of southwestern Quang Nam province, suffered an almost 100 percent incidence of malaria during the fall of 1968.[63] About 120 members of the 101st NVA Regiment, one of the first major North Vietnamese units to fight in the south, were stricken with malaria within a month after their arrival in South Vietnam. "For lack of beds and mats in the dispensary, all patients lay on hammocks fastened to trees." Two medics cared for all 120 patients until the two were assigned to care for combat casualties. The patients were then left to take care of themselves. "The moderately ill patients looked after the more seriously sick. The only medication was two quinine tablets and some rice soup with salt or sugar. As the patients 'recovered' they were returned to combat."[64]

In addition to the hazards of combat, disease, and malnutrition, the North Vietnamese soldier in the south suffered from acute homesickness. Although the party relentlessly hammered home the theme that all Vietnam was one country, to men who had seldom been far from their native towns and villages the south seemed foreign indeed. The southerners had strange accents and differing customs, nor were they always welcoming or friendly. The North Vietnamese soldier knew that he was in the south "for the duration," and the long separation from friends and family was particularly hard to bear. "Do the people living in the beloved socialist land know that more than sixty of our youths and teenagers who left the North to go on duty never returned with us because they were killed in action in the deep forests of western Nam Bo?" a radio operator with a PAVN battalion wrote. "I wonder why I am here while my friends are now sitting in the classroom listening to interesting scientific lessons."[65]

What kept the Communist soldiers going in the face of such fearful dangers and hardships? A study commissioned by the Defense Department in 1967 had concluded "that the enemy's morale was well-nigh indestructible and therefore not likely to be significantly lowered by pressures on soldiers in battle."[66] Follow-up studies with almost one thousand Viet Cong and North Vietnamese prisoners of war in 1968 and 1969 suggested that despite the heavy casualties of Tet the morale of the Communist soldier had not been seriously shaken. Almost all Communist combatants viewed the Tet attacks as "a success." None could even conceive of the Communists losing the war, and all expressed confidence in the ultimate victory of the liberation forces. "I never think that the front could lose the war," said an NVA private. "This war is a war of the Vietnamese people fighting against American imperialists. As long as the Vietnamese people still exist and as long as the American people are still in Vietnam dominating the Vietnamese people, the war will go on." Even the addition of more American troops and planes could only serve to prolong the war, not win it for the Americans. "Everybody in the world, not the Vietnamese alone, know that

America is a rich country and has all modern weapons," said a Viet Cong cadre, "but modern weapons do not make the United States win this war. . . . I think the war will last a long time and the Vietnamese people will certainly win it."[67]

Two ingredients for maintaining the Communist soldier's seemingly unshakable morale were strict indoctrination and supervision. From the time he entered the PLAF or PAVN a soldier was continuously and closely watched by his officers and NCOs and by the ever present political officer for signs of low morale, homesickness, malingering, illness, or unhappiness. A platoon leader reported that "we are very careful with men of our unit who are worried or whose morale appears to be low. We watch them closely and accompany them continuously."[68] The officers and political cadre played a complex role as therapist, informer, father figure, heroic leader, propagandist, and social worker. "The fighters are watched very closely from the lowest squad level up," a Viet Cong cadre reported. "By watching them very directly and indirectly, that is to say by following up the reports made on them, we cadres knew whether a man had good morale or not. Even if a man pretended or hid something, he would eventually be found out, no matter how well he pretended or how carefully he hid."[69]

Most Communist combatants confessed warm feelings of friendship and admiration for their leaders despite the leader's multiple roles and his unquestioned position as a figure of authority. American interrogators noted that Viet Cong and NVA enlisted POWs "discuss with great familiarity the detailed backgrounds, personalities, habits, and interests of as many as thirty officers in their regiments."[70] One prisoner observed that "between cadre and soldiers the relations were very friendly, there was no discrimination at all. We even wrestled with the company commander."[71] Nguyen Van Thong, a young second lieutenant commanding a platoon in a reconnaissance company of the 1st PAVN Division, reported that his men "complained frequently about their life and many times I have seen men talk back to cadre," yet he had "never heard the soldiers criticize their leaders and I've never had anyone disobey my orders." When asked to give an example of how a man was disciplined when he failed to carry out an order, Nguyen replied that he could not as he "had never seen it happen."[72]

All soldiers also engaged in frequent self-criticism sessions designed to relieve anxieties and hostilities and help cadre to eliminate sources of discontent and fear. The soldier was first criticized by his fellow soldiers under the guidance of a political leader and was then encouraged to criticize himself and acknowledge his errors and failings. He was then free to criticize others, including his superiors. Under the guidance of the political cadre, the meeting was skillfully guided toward reinforcing each member's resolve to work harder for the party's aim and to put aside personal differences.

The final and most important means of enforcing desired behavior was the three-man cell. The cell was both a strong primary group—"three best friends," as one Viet Cong soldier described it—and a tactical unit that functioned as a fire team in combat and an instrument of party control.[73] The cell leaders watched the cell members, who in turn observed the behavior of the cell leader. "If the cell leader did something wrong, the two members of his cell would report him to the higher cadres to have him demoted," a PAVN private declared. "If the two other members were ill-behaved the cell leader also reported it to higher cadres. That is the collective command and individual accountability policy."[74]

In addition to the pervasive system of surveillance, thought control, and indoctrination, the Communist armed forces also offered many positive inducements for soldiers to continue to perform at a high level of effectiveness. Promotion and advancement within the PLA and PAVN were largely based on performance, and all officers were selected from the ranks. To men whose possibilities of social and economic advancement had been limited by the bounds of their village or their tiny farm, the opportunity to obtain additional education, to become officers and party members with steadily increasing status and power, seemed appealing indeed, as did the promises of a happy, prosperous, and egalitarian society that would follow a Communist victory.

Yet the Communist system of rewards and punishments, indoctrination and motivation, could not alone account for the steadfastness of the Viet Cong and North Vietnamese soldiers under the steadily increasing pressure of combat in 1968. Chinese Communist forces in Korea had employed a very similar system of motivation and control. That army had nevertheless come close to disintegration under the superior firepower of the United Nations forces in the bloody battles of early 1951.[75] The Communist forces in Vietnam did not disintegrate. One explanation was that, although at times subject to heavier firepower than anything employed in Korea, they could often ease the pressure and control the tempo of fighting by withdrawing to bases in inaccessible swamps and jungles or to sanctuaries in Laos, Cambodia, and North Vietnam. Viet Cong and PAVN units were normally required to mount only a limited number of major attacks each quarter, together with a somewhat greater number of small-scale actions.[76] A study of the combat experience of Viet Cong and PAVN prisoners during 1966 and 1967 found that they fought an average of less than three engagements in twenty-six months.[77]

Like their American opponents, the Communist cadres proclaimed almost every military encounter a "victory." When asked about three unsuccessful attacks made by his unit on a district town, a Viet Cong private told his interrogator: "Generally speaking we didn't lose. We were just unable to take the targets." Another prisoner of war, a squad leader, described a withdrawal under fire following his unit's unsuccessful attack as "our most successful battle."[78] Even where heavy losses were undeniable, Communist soldiers were assured that they had won a victory by demonstrating their determination and willingness to die for the people.[79]

The final and most important factor reinforcing the determination of Communist fighters was the mixture of xenophobia and patriotic wrath they directed at the American "invaders" of Vietnam. In a country where hostility to foreigners and resistance to foreign rule were venerable traditions, the presence of hundreds of thousands of Americans on Vietnamese soil was enough to stir patriotic feeling in the most politically indifferent Vietnamese. Hostility to the Americans for their bombing of the north and "oppression" of the south was mentioned by almost all Viet Cong and PAVN prisoners. They saw the war as an entirely defensive one against foreign invaders who, like the French, were attempting to impose their rule upon them through a puppet regime. "When I got the draft notice I knew I was destined to go south and I knew the chances of coming back were very slim," a PAVN private from Hai Doung province said, "but once I was at training camp I began to understand that the fight for the south had to be done. Actually, I must say I already believed the

Americans were a hundred times crueler than the French."[80] Even soldiers who had voluntarily surrendered to the Americans continued to voice such feelings. "Facing the sympathetic welcome of our compatriots, facing the crimes done by the Americans, we wanted to hurry up to Saigon and to liberate this city," wrote one POW whose entire company had recently surrendered to the South Vietnamese.[81]

Combined with patriotic resolve was a profound fatalism. "We all wanted to see our loved ones again, but we all knew that the country was being invaded, that many people in the South were being dominated by the Americans," a PAVN private said, "so all we could do was to fight the war."[82]

During 1968 the PAVN and the remnants of the Viet Cong were to suffer even more grievous losses to the Americans and South Vietnamese. Desertions increased, war weariness spread, more formations were obliged to regroup to Laos and North Vietnam or to spend much of their time securing food and supplies. Yet the Viet Cong and North Vietnamese did not yield or disintegrate, and the continued presence of 550,000 American soldiers in South Vietnam continued to provide the Communist soldier with his strongest incentive to keep fighting.

CHAPTER 5

"Corruption Is Everywhere"

If the Americans possessed, after three years of war, a wary respect for and interest in the fighting abilities of the Vietcong and North Vietnamese, they had little interest in or understanding of their South Vietnamese ally. General Westmoreland's strategy during the first three years of the war had been to shunt aside the Vietnamese armed forces and have American troops take on the strongest Viet Cong and North Vietnamese units while the South Vietnamese assumed responsibility for territorial security.

Now, in the wake of Tet and Johnson's March decisions, the South Vietnamese forces took on a new significance for those who still hoped for some favorable outcome to the war. The Tet attacks marked the beginning of a new American attitude toward the South Vietnamese armed forces. South Vietnamese units had been the special targets of Communist attacks in their nationwide offensive, yet they had fought well, far better than their American advisers had anticipated. Desertion rates soared during the intense fighting of February and March, but Americans noted with satisfaction that no South Vietnamese unit, "not a single platoon," had defected to the Communists. A strange reason for pride perhaps, but one that accurately reflected the attitudes and expectations of senior Americans in Saigon after four years of dealing with the South Vietnamese army.

Yet if the prognosis for the South Vietnamese among Americans in Saigon remained guarded despite a good performance during Tet, in Washington, harried and frustrated leaders were eying the South

Vietnamese armed forces with new interest as a key component of a new strategy to extract the United States from its entrapment in an open-ended conflict.

As early as July 1967 Pentagon officials had expressed impatience with the measured pace of expansion of the Vietnamese armed forces. When one of Westmoreland's aides suggested to Defense Secretary McNamara that some of the Secretary's proposals for quick expansion of the Vietnamese army might not be psychologically acceptable to the Saigon government, McNamara exploded. "Psychologically I can't accept it. . . . I am sick and tired of having problems in what the GVN will accept when American society is under the strain it is under today."[1] To the men in the White House and the Pentagon, "the ability of the South Vietnamese to rally and meet the challenge," in the words of National Security Adviser Walt Rostow, "was one of the few welcome surprises of Tet."[2] Their performance suggested to President Johnson that "the South Vietnamese were clearly improving militarily and getting in shape to carry a heavier combat load."[3]

The public outcry over General Westmoreland's request for 200,000 additional troops in March 1968 had demonstrated the limits of American commitment to the ground war in Vietnam. To those in Washington who still hoped for success in the war, a greater role for the South Vietnamese appeared necessary, indeed unavoidable. Lieutenant Colonel Herbert Shandler, who served in the office of the Assistant Secretary of Defense, International Security Affairs, during this period, later wrote that "making the war the responsibility of the Vietnamese became an important, perhaps the only, means to continue the struggle without massive increases in American forces and with the support of the American people. . . . American forces . . . would continue to provide a shield behind which the South Vietnamese forces could rally, become effective, and win the support of the people. But now, resources would be made available to them and pressure would be applied to allow, indeed to require, progress in this long-neglected area."[4] Yet the task would prove difficult, for the South Vietnamese army was both more and less than the American idea of an army.

In the eighteenth century, a Frenchman observed that Prussia was not so much a country that had an army as an army that had a country. The same might have been said of the American-supported regime in Saigon. In 1968 the Republic of Vietnam, or "South Vietnam" as it was invariably called, was fourteen years old. Most of that time it had been at war.

No one knew for certain when the war had begun. Perhaps it was in December 1960, when the National Liberation Front of South Vietnam was officially founded. Perhaps it was in May 1959, when the 15th Plenum of the Central Committee of the Communist Party in Hanoi authorized cadres in the south to begin the armed struggle against Ngo Dinh Diem. Perhaps it was even earlier.[5] The South Vietnamese armed forces had grown from less than 500,000 men at the beginning of 1965 to close to 700,000 by 1968, or 1 million, if all the men in the various police and paramilitary forces were counted. South Vietnam had a greater proportion of its population under arms in 1968 than South Korea, the Soviet Union, Israel, or the United States.[6]

Since 1963 the armed forces had openly ruled South Vietnam. In November 1963 a coalition of colonels and generals with active U.S. encouragement and support had overthrown the Ngo Dinh Diem government and had murdered Diem and his brother Nhu. There followed eighteen months of confusion and instability, as one government succeeded another in Saigon. The military junta that had overthrown Diem lasted barely two months before it was overturned in a bloodless coup led by General Nguyen Khanh. In August 1964 Khanh's inept and heavy-handed rule touched off widespread rioting in Saigon, forcing the general to resign.

During the following two weeks there were three different governments in Saigon, as mobs of Buddhists, Catholic Youth, and gangs of thugs clashed in the streets. When the smoke had cleared General Khanh was back in place. In October he engineered the installation of a "civilian government" headed by Phan Khac Suu, a venerable fossil from the prewar era of anti-French nationalism, and Tran Van Huong, a former mayor of Saigon. By December the generals had scrapped the Suu government, much to the distress of Washington, and had returned to a military junta headed by the ubiquitous Khanh. Khanh's turn finally came in February 1965, when a coalition of younger generals led by General Nguyen Cao

Ky, the thirty-five-year-old commander of the air force, and General Nguyen Van Thieu forced him to resign and leave the country to become a "roving" ambassador.

The younger generals also installed a civilian government, headed by Dr. Phan Huy Quat, who had served in the French-created government of Emperor Bao Dai, but after a few months the military again assumed direct control. By June 1965, as thousands of American combat troops began operations in Vietnam, that nation was openly and directly under the control of a military dictatorship. A junta of ten generals called the National Leadership Committee or the Committee for the Direction of the State, led by Ky and Thieu, ruled the country, with Ky as *de facto* prime minister and Thieu as head of state and chairman of the committee. Various other consultative bodies existed to advise and assist the generals, but they were of no real consequence.[7]

No one in the spring of 1965 expected the Ky government to last. Ky himself was a flamboyant and controversial figure. An aviator who looked and talked like an American fighter ace, he was a native of North Vietnam and a Buddhist. Impetuous and outspoken, he was a natural focus of American media attention and was always ready to talk to the first newsman who caught his eye. Although he lived scarcely 2 miles from the prime minister's office, he insisted on commuting to work in a helicopter, "engulfing the entire government complex in a deafening roar each morning as he arrived."[8]

Thieu was older, shrewder, and more reserved than Ky and more attuned to the realities of Saigon's military politics. A former division commander and a southerner, Thieu was willing to yield the limelight to Ky while he patiently developed his power base behind the scenes.[9] The two generals neither liked nor trusted each other, and their disparate backgrounds and military careers added to their estrangement. A common saying in Saigon was that if the two could be placed in a blender, "what came out would be a good deal better for the country than what went in."[10]

Although it appeared at first as simply another in the string of short-lived military juntas, the Ky–Thieu government had the considerable advantage of American support and military resources on an altogether unprecedented scale. Other than the Communists, they also had few organized political rivals. In April 1966 the directory government successfully put down a challenge to its authority by militant Buddhist factions in Da Nang, Hue, and Saigon. In I Corps, where the Buddhists had the open support of the corps commander, General Nguyen Chanh Thi, a powerful rival of Ky and Thieu, order was restored only after five battalions of marines and rangers loyal to Saigon were flown into the north and put down the uprising by force. More than eight hundred Vietnamese were killed or wounded in the fighting before government troops regained control.[11]

Although the spectacle of troops and tanks putting down a popular movement did little for the regime's public image, the suppression of the revolt in I Corps removed the Buddhists as a serious political challenge to the Thieu–Ky regime, much as Ngo Dinh Diem had destroyed or neutralized the political-religious sects in 1955. From 1966 until the final collapse of South Vietnam, the army and its factions represented the only real source of political power in Vietnam. Among the generals, however, rivalry remained intense.

Stung by charges of dictatorship and spurred on by their American allies, Thieu and Ky began to move toward creating a constitutional government. In September 1966 elections were held for a constituent assembly to draft a new constitution for the republic. Buddhists announced a boycott of the election, and the Viet Cong threatened violence, but voter turnout was high. Both Saigon and Washington pronounced the election a success. Within a few months the new constituent assembly had completed work on a new constitution for South Vietnam. Elections for a bicameral legislature and a president and vice president were scheduled for early September 1967.

With a popularly elected government actually on the horizon, Americans in Saigon began to fear that the Vietnamese might be in danger of introducing too much democracy. A MACV study completed during the summer of 1967 warned that a rapid transition to civilian rule would be ill-advised. Only the military had the requisite experience and administrative skills to function effectively in a country "at war, divided, underdeveloped, with a long authoritarian tradition."[12] Ambassador Henry Cabot Lodge worried that the military would stage another coup if it were denied "a proper role." The United States had to ensure that either Thieu or Ky was elected president, although a civilian vice president would probably be acceptable.[13]

The Americans need not have worried. Civilian opponents of the regime were too disorganized and divided to mount a significant challenge to the military leadership. Almost 1,200 candidates ran for a seat in the election for the 137-member lower house. In the Saigon area alone, 236 candidates vied for fifteen seats.[14] The largest demographic group, the Buddhists, were hopelessly divided among themselves and lacked permanent political organizations.[15]

Although many American observers believed that elections would be a new and valuable experience for the South Vietnamese, one that would "train them in democracy," the Vietnamese were already quite familiar with the institution. Yet their concept of "elections" was quite different from that of the Americans. In the United States, elections were a critical element of the political process and a means of deciding important questions of state. In Vietnam elections were a means not of settling political disputes but of signifying that they had been settled—a ritual, and not a process, of government.[16]

The real question revolved around the matter of which general the military would agree to back for president. The leading contenders, Thieu and Ky, both claimed to have the support of their fellow generals and the approval of the Americans. American leaders in Washington wrung their hands over the prospect of an open split between the generals, which might lead to new coup attempts and renewed unrest.

Westmoreland and the new U.S. Ambassador, Ellsworth Bunker, although just as worried, wisely refrained from intervening in the quarrel, and in June 1967 the South Vietnamese finally settled things among themselves. Forty-eight generals met in Saigon behind closed doors for almost three days and nights to hammer out a deal. At one point in the stormy discussions Thieu reportedly delivered a scathing attack on the corruption of Ky and his close associates, "which reduced the Air Vice Marshal to tears."[17] In the end the generals agreed to back Thieu as the presidential candidate, with Ky as his running mate for vice president. However, Ky was to be allowed to have a say in cabinet appointments, and the generals established a secret military council composed of senior officers to advise the new president.[18]

On Sunday, September 3, 1967, the citizens of South Vietnam again went to the polls, this time to elect a president and the upper house of the legislature. A close observer of the elections concluded that they "demonstrated the bankruptcy of most established political parties and organizations in South Vietnam."[19] Thieu and Ky managed to win only 35 percent of the popular vote, but their ten opponents fared even worse, averaging about 7 percent. The most popular civilian candidate was neither the venerable Dr. Phan Khac Suu nor former premier Tranh Van Huong, nor even Dr. Phan Quang Dan, who had achieved a certain celebrity by openly opposing Diem in 1959 when it was still dangerous to do so and had gone to prison for his effort. Instead the top opposition vote getter was an obscure, Buddhist lawyer, Truong Binh Dzu, who ran on a platform of peace and negotiations with the National Liberation Front. He received 17 percent of the vote. The generals dismissed Dzu as "a dog who should be put in a cage." A few months later Dzu was arrested and convicted by a military court of "conduct detrimental to the anti-communist spirit of the people and the armed forces." He spent five years in jail.

An American apologist for the regime hailed the election and the mediocre showing of the Thieu–Ky ticket as proof that real democracy had come to South Vietnam. Less sympathetic critics argued that the outcome demonstrated that the generals were so incompetent they could not even properly rig an election.[20]

Thieu was exasperated and humiliated by the election results. Ky was angry at what he rightly viewed as an attempt to shunt him aside. The civilian candidates banded together to denounce the government for fraud and vote-rigging. All sides blamed the Americans. In this awkward and inauspicious fashion, the last and most long-lived of all South Vietnam's military regimes began its eight-year rule.

Despite the election, Thieu's position was by no means unchallengable. He could not openly fire or transfer Ky's supporters, but he took full advantage of the Americans' zeal for rooting out corruption and improving efficiency to ease out some of the men loyal to Ky under the guise of administrative reforms. Nevertheless, the Thieu–Ky balance of power might have lasted longer had not renewed Communist attacks on Saigon in the spring of 1968 dealt Thieu a winning hand.

Ky's most powerful supporter was General Nguyen Ngoc Loan, Director of the National Police, who controlled much of South Vietnam's security apparatus, including the Saigon Police, port authority, and customs with their accompanying networks of protection rackets, bribes, and kickbacks. Loan achieved international fame during Tet when he took custody of a high-ranking Viet Cong cadre who had been captured after murdering some of his civilian hostages, relatives of South Vietnamese police and officials. Loan shot the prisoner through the head at close range with a revolver. The moment was captured in a still photo by Eddie Adams, an Associated Press photographer, and in even more gruesome color film footage by an NBC cameraman, Vo Suu. An estimated 20 million people watched Suu's film of the shooting on NBC's *Huntley–Brinkley Report* on February 3, 1968, and the photo became the most famous and talked about picture of the Vietnam War.[21]

During later fighting in Saigon–Cholon, Loan was seriously wounded while leading his men against some Viet Cong in a Cholon alley. Loan was forced to resign from his position in order to undergo surgery and extended hospitalization. A month later, ten senior Vietnamese officials were killed or wounded when a U.S. helicopter gunship mistakenly fired a rocket into their Cholon command post.[22] Among the casualties were most of Ky's top supporters, including the director of the Saigon port authority, the director of the municipal police, the commander of the 6th Ranger Battalion, and the mayor of Saigon. All were speedily replaced by Thieu loyalists.[23]

By the end of 1968 Ky's influence was clearly on the wane. By that point his functions had been reduced to chairing three powerless advisory committees, and by early 1969 his last supporter had left the cabinet.

Almost four years after the ouster of Diem, the United States had finally achieved its objective of a stable government in Saigon. Yet it was a government without real substance. Thieu himself was a friendless and suspicious man living in constant dread of a coup or of abandonment by the Americans. "He never trusted anybody in his entourage or in the armed forces," General—later Senator—Tran Van Don observed, "yet he did not trust the Americans either. . . . He was scared every day he would lose their support and therefore was no more comfortable with them than he was with his compatriots."[24] A man wedded to procrastination and inaction, Thieu once declared to Ky his fear that the Americans "may kill me at any time if I do something against them."[25] "After all these years of war," an American journalist observed in 1970, "the Saigon government remains a network of cliques, held together by American subsidies, a group of people without a coherent political orientation, bent on their own survival."[26]

As a military force, the army also remained a weak reed upon which to base American hopes of building a strong, independent, non-Communist Vietnam. Most of the generals and senior colonels in the army owed their positions to political and family connections rather than to military competence. American advisers to Vietnamese division commanders routinely recommended their relief for cowardice, dishonesty, or incompetence, usually to no avail.[27] A veteran news correspondent reported "something of a running competition among American advisors as to who could claim to be with the absolute worst South Vietnamese division."[28] As late as 1970 one senior American official in Saigon rated only one Vietnamese general officer as "fully competent" for his job. Other advisers more generously rated as many as three in that category.[29]

South Vietnamese generals were drawn from a class as far removed from the average Vietnamese farmer or artisan as John D. Rockefeller from the average oilfield roughneck. They were sons of the great landlords of the Mekong Delta, the French-educated business and professional elites of the cities, and a few survivors and descendants of the traditional Mandarin classes.

Over half the generals had entered the army in the late 1940s and early 1950s as officers in the French armed forces or in the newly formed "national army" of Emperor Bao Dai, the French client ruler of Vietnam; 40 percent of the colonels had entered in that period; as had almost 70 percent of all field grade officers.[30] None of these men, indeed almost no member of the officer corps, had joined the great struggle for national independence from 1946 to 1954.[31] Instead they had been the subordinates and collaborators of the French, just as they now appeared to many Vietnamese to be the tools and proxies of the Americans. It was a group whose behavior was shaped by the firm conviction that no duty or obligation of citizenship was so compelling that it could not be avoided through judicious use of money and family connections, nor any position of trust so exalted that it could not be obtained by those same means.[32] Promotions and assignments depended upon personal, regional, and family connections and the intricate balancing of factional interests and demands within the ruling elite. Premier Nguyen Cao Ky was exaggerating only a little when he observed to a reporter that "before I can fire even a driver I have to check with eight generals and their families."[33]

Each senior general had his coterie of supporters and relatives among the lower ranks, whom he sought to protect and promote. Promotion boards generally divided the available positions among the protégés of the various generals on the board through a process of horse-trading and compromise.[34] For those officers lacking wealth or family and personal connections, there was little or no advancement and only the prospect of endless years of service in remote or dangerous areas, while the better-connected enjoyed staff duty in the towns and cities. "We have officers who spend fifteen years in Saigon and they get medals and get promoted," one disgruntled Vietnamese told an American reporter. "We have soldiers who spend ten years in Dak To and they get nothing. It is a matter of knowing the right people and paying the right people."[35]

Entry into the officer corps was open only to holders of the "Baccalaureate II," requiring twelve years of formal schooling. Most of the schools that awarded such degrees could be found only in the larger towns and cities. During the early 1960s only about 15 percent of Vietnamese school-age youth were enrolled in such schools, which were often private institutions with high tuition rates. Even in 1970, after American aid had somewhat increased the availability of secondary education, less than 10 percent of South Vietnamese students ever progressed as far as the Baccalaureate II degree.[36]

The relative scarcity of secondary school and college graduates, together with Saigon's rigid insistence that all officers must come from this group, meant that many baccalaureates and college graduates had to be conscripted into the ranks of the officer corps to meet the needs of a steadily expanding army. A Rand Corporation study estimated that by 1968 more than three thousand teachers and professors had been lost to educational institutions in South Vietnam through this process.[37]

The conscripted scholars were generally poorly motivated and ill-suited to their new responsibilities. As early as 1960 a British observer reported that "officers recruited by this method displayed, in some cases, more interest in the perquisites and privileges attached to their rank than in the efficient discharge of their duties, an attitude which was combined on occasion with a townsman's disdain for the peasant soldiers whom they were appointed to command."[38]

By contrast, officer candidates in the North Vietnamese People's Army were required to serve five to six years as enlisted men before becoming eligible for commissions. Battle experience, combat leadership, and courage were considered the most important criteria for selection.[39] An officer corps dominated by the educated urban elite was hardly the ideal choice to lead one peasant army against a tougher, more experienced peasant army in the swamps, jungles, and mountains of South Vietnam.[40] "The Vietnamese officer corps," a Rand study noted, "tends to be unable to relate to the rural environment."[41] Many American advisers would have used considerably stronger language.

Yet it was not the class bias of the Vietnamese officer corps that would prove its undoing, but rather the rampant corruption which by the late 1960s had enveloped all agencies of government and most institutions of South Vietnamese society. As more and more American goods and money flowed into South Vietnam during the 1960s, opportunities for graft, fraud, and extortion multiplied. The military controlled most of the higher branches of civil administration in South Vietnam. Region chiefs, province chiefs, and district chiefs were all active duty officers, and their control of the organs of civil government greatly widened the opportunities for graft and corruption.

The most widespread form of abuse was the misappropriation of funds. Unit commanders routinely pocketed the pay of dead, missing, or discharged soldiers on their rolls and also did a lively business in the sale of military assignments, early discharges, and draft exemptions. Like eighteenth-century European officers, Vietnamese colonels and generals paid large sums for choice assignments and fully expected to recoup their investment many times over from the rich opportunities for graft and extortion offered in the wealthier provinces and towns.

Once he had secured a desirable command, the senior officer installed his loyal underlings in key positions. They, in turn, were expected to recompense their chief with a share of the graft they secured through their own discharge of their duties.[42] Beside the sale of jobs and misappropriation of funds and materials, South Vietnamese generals engaged in a wide array of other rackets, including the use of their military forces to protect or promote criminal activities. In Long An province the generals used army trucks, escorted by military police, to transport smuggled goods from the coast to Saigon.[43] The commandant of the large Quang Trung training center, Colonel Vu Ngoc Tuan, was discovered to have used his trainees to construct an ice-making plant with military building material.[44]

Drug trafficking was widespread, and many of Saigon's top officials and generals were rumored to be heavily involved in smuggling and protection of the opium trade.[45] The deputy province chief at Kien Tuong, Major Tran Tien Khang, "was accused of operating an opium smuggling ring that extended from Cholon (Saigon) to Cambodia."[46] At the end of 1967 the attractive young niece of the director of customs, who worked as a stewardess for Royal Air Lao, was arrested at Tan Son Nhut Airport with 200 kilos of raw opium in her luggage.[47]

Another source of profit was trade with the Viet Cong. Large quantities of food, gasoline, medicines, and equipment, much of it supplied by the United States, were sold to the Communists by South Vietnamese soldiers, usually through middlemen. A liter of gasoline or a case of batteries could usually be sold at a 300–400 percent profit, and Army officers sometimes utilized military vehicles to help move contraband goods. In the Mekong Delta, militia troops sank a Vietnamese navy patrol boat after the crew had refused to share the profits from the boat's diesel fuel drums, which they were selling to Viet Cong middlemen.[48]

Occasionally, as in the case of Colonel Quang, an instance of corruption might become so blatant and American complaints so vociferous that the government was obliged to take action and remove the offending individual from his post. That was "punishment" only in the formal sense, however, since the culprit almost always obtained a new job at comparable or even higher rank. The commander of IV Corps, Major General Nguyen Van Manh, was removed from his post in February 1968 after repeated scandals, blatant incompetence, and complaints by his American advisers. He was then appointed Inspector-General of the army with the mission of "rooting out corruption within the military commands."[49]

Highly publicized incidents like Colonel Quang's ice house were the exception, but graft, corruption, and nepotism permeated all levels of Vietnamese officialdom. Not only were they the rule rather than the exception, they were the very essence of the whole system of South Vietnamese politics and administration. Several months after the collapse of South Vietnam, in 1975, staff members of the Rand Corporation interviewed a number of former senior officials and generals of the Saigon regime who had managed to escape to the United States. They found that "there was not one high-ranking person in the Saigon government who was not accused by at least some of the respondents as having participated in the corruption and profited from it. Indeed, one former colonel suggested that the hope and expectation of benefiting from racketeering, bribery, and kickbacks was often the principal motivation for men to enter government service.[50]

Because of the considerable time and effort involved in managing the various rackets, businesses, and other financial schemes with which many South Vietnamese officers were connected, family members were often drawn in to help. Officers' wives were especially active in helping their husbands to acquire money and property. The wives of at least four generals served on the board of the French concern that distributed beer and soft drinks throughout the country, and officers' wives also controlled the lucrative laundry business at American military bases. Even Colonel Ma Sanh Nhon, the Hau Nghai province chief, a fighting soldier who had risen from the ranks and was often held up as a model leader by his American advisers, had found time to establish his sister in a lucrative import–export business based on contacts he had established for her while in the United States.[51] Two South Vietnamese generals, reflecting on the problems of South Vietnam, wrote bitterly of "high-placed ladies," wives of officials and general officers,

> . . . who took over the management of their husbands' business affairs. Officials in general conveniently pretended knowing nothing about their wives' wheeling and dealing. . . . Naturally the wives' ability to make money depended on their husbands' clout. These ladies formed their own cliques, rivaled [sic] among themselves, and were a major cause of rivalry among their husbands. Around each of these there formed a small court made up of influence peddlers, common fund subscribers, and money seekers who, more often than not, were the wives of their husbands' subalterns.[52]

Even if he had no ambitious wife and no desire for illicit gains, the South Vietnamese officer would still have been hard put to support himself and his family on the meager pay offered by the government. American-style fringe benefits such as commissaries, free medical care, and post exchanges were almost nonexistent. Officers and men received a food allowance of a few piasters a day to purchase their rations in shops or on the open market, but this allowance was inadequate even to provide for the soldier himself, let alone for his family. Faced with a miserably inadequate salary and slow or nonexistent promotion, in a society experiencing rapid inflation and a flood of American consumer goods, it was a rare officer who could resist the temptation to supplement his income in various illicit ways.

By 1968 the Vietnamese army had become quite adept at extending and consolidating its political power and enriching its generals, but its performance on the battlefield remained unsatisfactory. In the two years following the arrival of American combat forces, the ARVN casualty rates had remained almost static, while American casualties had increased by 400 percent the first year and 100 percent the second year.[53] During the entire period, only twenty majors and lieutenant colonels of the South Vietnamese army had been killed in action. The U.S. Marine Corps, with only one-seventh the number of troops as the ARVN, had lost seven times as many officers of the same ranks.[54]

Although total South Vietnamese casualties remained considerably higher than those of the Americans, many critics attributed this to heavy losses among the local security forces, the increasing aggressiveness of the Viet Cong, and general South Vietnamese ineptitude rather than to any real effort to win the war. John Paul Vann, a province senior adviser known for his outspoken views, demonstrated in one study in late 1967 that the number of engagements between South Vietnamese forces and the enemy on ARVN-initiated operations had actually decreased by about 75 percent between January 1966 and June 1967. In one twelve-day period between March 17 and 28, 1967, South Vietnamese soldiers and security forces conducted a total of 13,200 operations ranging from small ambushes to battalion-size sweeps. Only about sixteen contacts with the enemy had resulted from all this effort.[55] The ARVN 25th Division claimed to have inflicted a total of seventeen enemy casualties while suffering seventy of its own, most due to accidents.[56]

To Americans familiar with the South Vietnamese army, these figures came as no surprise. The ARVN's skill at "search and avoid" operations, as they were cynically labeled by GIs, had long been known. The South Vietnamese superior knowledge of the local area and familiarity with the language made it easy for them to avoid known Communist operating areas and bases. Often tacit truces existed between the regional security forces and local Viet Cong.

A former Vietnamese company commander admitted after the war that he had deliberately avoided battle with a large Viet Cong force by moving his men away from the probable area of contact. He reported next morning that he had seen no enemy and that the intelligence provided him must have been incorrect. "I performed a balancing test," he recalled. "I weighed the recommendations made by American intelligence advisors against [the loss of] human life. Their information had no value when compared to saving human lives. With the understanding that I could be court-martialed for what I had done, I still lied to headquarters."[57]

What was surprising was not that Vietnamese soldiers sometimes avoided combat, but that they often fought hard and well and managed to hold together as a military force. "Given the political dynamics of the last three years," a State Department expert observed in 1968, "it is surprising that Republic of Vietnam armed forces have not succeeded in destroying themselves."[58]

Like most other undesirable aspects of life in Vietnam, service in the military could be avoided if one had sufficient connections and sufficient money. Although Vietnam possessed a draft and, after 1968, the Saigon government had decreed a "general mobilization," conscription was fairly easily avoided. As in the United States, a large number of deferments were available on the basis of health, education, occupation, or family hardship, and these were easily obtained through bribery or outright purchase. The price of avoiding the draft varied from about 10,000 piasters to as much as 100,000 piasters, depending upon the province and region. Like the rich and the very rich, the very poor also enjoyed some advantage in evading the draft, because inept record-keeping and inadequate census data in the more remote rural areas made it easy to avoid registration altogether.

For those who did find themselves in the military, it was possible to purchase false leave or discharge papers so as to remain at home or at civilian jobs for extended periods. Soldiers who availed themselves of this opportunity were referred to as "the potted trees" or the "ornamental soldiers."[59] For those who could afford neither a draft exemption nor potted-tree status, there remained the option of desertion.

Desertions from the Vietnamese army continually ran at several thousand men a month, and infantry combat units often lost 10 percent of their personnel each month to desertion. During 1968 desertion from the armed forces averaged more than 10,000 a month, reaching a peak of 15,060 during October.[60]

The South Vietnamese took a philosophical view of this massive monthly exodus. Occasionally at the urging of their American advisers they would launch periodic sweeps of the larger towns to round up deserters. In response to American pressure, punishments for desertion were gradually stiffened. A large number of suggestions for reform and improvement in personnel management and leadership were also pressed upon the Vietnamese by Westmoreland and his experts in order to cut down on the staggering desertion rate. The Vietnamese generals listened attentively, considered the measures carefully, and then did nothing.[61]

The unfortunate remnant of South Vietnamese soldiers, those who neither fled nor bought their way out, were often committed to combat with little or no formal training. Medical care was primitive, sometimes inadequate; promotions were rare and slow, leaves and passes almost unknown. After 1968's "general mobilization," infantry soldiers had little to look forward to except years of endless war. If his family was dependent upon him, the soldier had little choice but to move his family with him to his army base. At the base camp his dependents would be spared the danger of Viet Cong reprisals and be able to share whatever meager pay and rations he received. South Vietnamese divisions and regiments also normally recruited within local towns and villages, and most volunteers joined units likely to be closest to their village or hamlet.

Most Vietnamese army units thus occupied a permanent installation, which was home not only to the soldiers but to their families as well. When the base camp was threatened, soldiers fought fiercely in its defense, but they were reluctant to operate very far from the base for any considerable period of time. The battalions, regiments, and divisions of the South Vietnamese army were, in effect, tied to specific geographical areas near their bases.

The only truly mobile forces the Republic of Vietnam possessed were an airborne division and several battalions of marines. Better paid, better equipped, and better trained than other South Vietnamese troops, the marines and airborne were normally employed as a general reserve and committed to reinforce and assist other units in difficult or important operations. They also played a significant role in preserving the political balance of power in Saigon. General Le Nguyen Khang, commander of the marine division, was a Ky supporter, while General Du Quoc Dong, who commanded the airborne division, was loyal to Thieu. (Khang, considered one of the few really competent generals by the Americans, managed to survive the eclipse of Ky and to keep his job as head of the marines.)[62]

For most South Vietnamese soldiers, with their low pay and uncertain supplies, food remained a constant concern. One American adviser recalled that Vietnamese GIs constantly foraged to supplement their meager rice ration, "a large rice-fed paddy rat was relished much as a U.S. Marine might enjoy hot turkey at Thanksgiving."[63] The same adviser once observed a fire fight between

Vietnamese marines and several Viet Cong cornered in some farm buildings. "I observed a member of the enveloping assault squad hand his rifle to a fellow marine while he stalked a couple of chickens. Flushed, the chickens ran toward a shed containing the VC. The marine continued the pursuit, unarmed, while his squad covered him. . . . He returned with it intact and squawking loudly! I asked the [Vietnamese] major why they didn't shoot the chicken in lieu of taking the risk of losing a marine. He replied, 'Must play first. Also bullets mess up meat, no good!' "[64]

Not all chickens were obtained in so heroic a manner. Well-founded reports of ARVN soldiers stealing or extorting food from Vietnamese villagers were so common as to be almost a staple of American advisers' suggestions and complaints.[65] Soldiers of Lieutenant Nguyen Ngoc Ngan's company operating in the Mekong Delta "thought nothing of stealing chickens and fruit from the villagers or of trampling their rice fields even while their officers were assuring them of their good will."[66]

For all that, there were good units and fighting soldiers in the South Vietnamese army, like the 1st Division in the northern area of I Corps, which conducted its own basic training program and provided troops with monthly furloughs and dependent housing. Nearly half the division's personnel were volunteers.[67] The Vietnamese marine battalions, another example, spent months in combat in the malaria-infested swamps and jungles without rest or respite, and prided themselves on never losing a weapon.[68]

There were fine leaders like Major Nguyen Van Be, district chief of Tui An district, a former enlisted man and son of a sergeant major in the French colonial army. Although his district was a reputed Viet Cong stronghold, Be refused ever to sleep anywhere but the district headquarters. "He was proud of the fact that he had been wounded fighting the Viet Cong and believed he had bought the district with his blood. His family lived very austerely in his bunker, the furniture made from old ammo crates."[69]

Another much-admired soldier was Colonel Bu Van Giai, commander of the 2d Regiment of the 1st Division, who, according to soldier folklore, once personally led his men in an assault on a North Vietnamese position in the DMZ area, capturing a rocket battery and turning it around to fire into North Vietnam.[70] And there was

Lieutenant Colonel Chau Minh Kien, commander of the 1st Battalion, 8th Regiment, who so impressed the men of the U.S. 1st Infantry Division that they named a fire base in his honor.[71]

There were even a few good generals. The commander of the 1st Division, General Ngo Quang Truong, an austere and relentless fighter, had been known to imprison officers who failed to measure up. General Le Nguyen Khang, commandant of the marine corps and an associate of Ky, had a professional reputation so high that Thieu never dared replace him.

Still, few believed that South Vietnam's armed forces were a match for their Communist opponents. Since 1965, the South Vietnamese had been relegated to a secondary role, while American troops took on the strongest Viet Cong and North Vietnamese units.

At first sight this approach seemed to make sense. The Americans, better trained and equipped with massive firepower and superior mobility, could be employed fighting the enemy's big units in something approaching conventional battles in the remote western jungles and mountains, while behind the "shield" provided by the American Army, the South Vietnamese forces could get on with the job of territorial security and reasserting government control. After all, the South Vietnamese were presumed to know their own people better than the Americans and would do better at the task of winning hearts and minds.

Yet from the first Westmoreland's plan proved unworkable. The Viet Cong refused to confine their activities to the highlands and border areas, and American forces soon found themselves obliged to fight many battles in the densely populated coastal lowlands. As for the South Vietnamese armed forces, their normal relationship with the rural population remained one of hatred and suspicion as the troops continued their practice of stealing or extorting food from the population and destroying property and livestock in real and imagined battles with Communists. In Ghia Dinh province, units of the South Vietnamese army spent much of their time helping absentee landlords collect rent and taxes from farmers and tenants in formerly Viet Cong–controlled areas, an activity that would win few hearts and minds but brought handsome kickbacks from the landlords.[72]

In the Mekong Delta, Lieutenant Ngan found that hostility toward his battalion had "become so intense in our area that whenever a patrol passed a village it was usually attacked. Then reinforcements would be rushed in and in the ensuing battle the entire village would be leveled."[73]

With the Tet offensive and Washington's new attitude toward the South Vietnamese forces, MACV produced a flurry of plans for beefing up the Vietnamese armed forces by activating new units; rounding out those already in existence with more transportation, artillery, and tanks; and adding more planes and helicopters to the air force. In addition, most first-line ARVN infantry would receive the new M-16 rifle. In all, South Vietnam's armed forces were scheduled to grow to more than 800,000 men by the beginning of 1970, an increase of about 20 percent.[74]

Yet how was the United States to compel the South Vietnamese forces to become more effective? How was the required progress to be achieved? The American effort to "improve" the South Vietnam-ese army was far older than the war. In 1954 American soldiers had been confident that they would quickly be able to turn the Republic's army into a first-class fighting force as they had just done for Syngman Rhee's troops in South Korea. General John W. "Iron Mike" O'Daniel and General Samuel D. Williams, hard-driving veterans of World War II and Korea, tackled the job with enthusiasm as heads of the U.S. Military Assistance Advisory Group in Vietnam.

Williams, who headed the Advisory Group from 1955 to 1960, knew relatively little about Asia but a great deal about public relations and bureaucratic survival. He proceeded to organize and train the South Vietnamese army along American lines to meet an invasion from the north and began the tradition of optimistic assessments and rosy predictions that would be followed by many of his successors in Saigon.[75] In April 1960 Williams told a reporter for Time-Life that the South Vietnamese army was "whipping" the Viet Cong "right now." One month later he informed Senator Mike Mansfield that the situation in Vietnam had improved to the point where it would probably be possible to begin withdrawing about 15 percent of the advisory group during 1961.[76] By 1968 the Vietnamese army had increased immeasurably in size and equipment, but its ability to "whip" the Communist enemy was still problematical.

As in General Williams's day, the principal American instrument for improving and assisting the Vietnamese army remained the advisory system. By the end of 1965 there were already more than eight thousand U.S. military personnel serving as advisers to Vietnamese divisions, regiments, battalions, logistical installations, schools, and training centers. In addition, many top U.S. officials and major unit commanders were technically advisers to their equivalents in the Vietnamese government or military. Thus Westmoreland, in addition to his operational duties, was senior adviser to the chief of the Vietnamese Joint General Staff, the III MAF; I and II Field Force commanders were senior advisers to the Vietnamese corps commanders; and MACV staff sections advised their counterparts in the Joint General Staff. Every Vietnamese army unit larger than a company had its complement of U.S. advisers, ranging from five men at battalion level to more than fifty at division headquarters.

In theory the adviser's role was to "appraise the situation and give sound advice based on fundamental military knowledge." Advisers were selected on the basis of their professional expertise and attainments and assigned according to their rank and military specialty. Few advisers had more than a superficial knowledge of Vietnamese history or customs before their arrival in Vietnam, and even fewer could speak or understand Vietnamese. The Chief of the Joint General Staff, General Cao Van Dien, remarked after the war that he could recall no instance "in which a U.S. adviser effectively discussed professional matters with his counterpart in Vietnamese."[77] Interpreters were hard to find and not always reliable. Though many Vietnamese officers spoke a smattering of English, misunderstandings were frequent.[78] A story that was often repeated during the early days of the U.S. advisory effort told of an American officer who was attempting to teach basic facing movements to a group of recruits.

> He instructed the interpreter to tell the men, "about face." The interpreter looked at the major rather quizzically, then spoke rapidly to one of the trainees. The man broke from the ranks, went over to a

pail of water, washed his face, and then returned to the formation. Each time the advisor would attempt to teach this facing movement the same act would be repeated. Finally, after the third attempt, the trooper broke down. He told the major that there was nothing wrong with his face, that it was clean because he had washed it three times.[79]

Nevertheless, the misunderstanding between Americans and Vietnamese, as one adviser declared, went "beyond language."[80] It was not, as most Americans imagined, a case of dealing with an Asian army that was less advanced and less proficient than the U.S. Army. In fact, two entirely different systems were involved, one based on promotion according to merit, strict adherence to a hierarchical chain of command, and separation from and subordination to civil authority, and the other based on alliances and arrangements between families and cliques, promotion and assignment based on patronage and political compromise, and the performance of the most important political functions by the military. In the American tradition military officers were men who sacrificed opportunities for wealth and material gain to serve their country. Vietnamese tradition held that wealth and opportunities for gain were the normal rewards of higher rank. American officers regarded field command as a recognition of accomplishment and the best opportunity for advancement; Vietnamese officers regarded it as a penalty for their missteps or lack of political clout.[81] The confusion was compounded by the fact that in organization and nomenclature the Vietnamese system closely resembled the American. In operation they were and had to be drastically different.

The success of an adviser depended primarily on his ability to gain the respect of and establish rapport with his Vietnamese counterpart. The most successful relationships were usually at the lower levels, where advisers ate, slept, and fought with their Vietnamese units. Even the most successful advisers experienced frequent frustration in attempting to get their units to "do the right thing" in a timely manner. "I have used every approach I can think of since I have been here," one district adviser declared at the conclusion of his tour. "From being a nice guy, giving things, from being the bad guy and telling my counterpart that he is not doing his job, from reporting him, and I have yet to find a way that will convince a

Vietnamese to do what is right."[82] A Special Forces officer in Loc Ninh recalled that at first "I thought I was the worst military advisor in history because . . . so far as I knew everybody who had preceded me had been getting along just fine with all their doggone counterparts and here I couldn't even get the crap picked up off the street." He later learned "that everybody [else] was meeting the same goddam problem."[83]

In practice, if not in theory, the most important task of most advisers was to serve as unofficial coordinators of fire support, medevacs, and other U.S. military assistance to his unit. The adviser's "main function is to provide gunship support, medevac, and coordinate on air strikes if planned," observed a U.S. Army adviser in 1968, "providing support on operations. This is what the Vietnamese want. In the long run, this is what you end up doing."[84]

Advisers often attempted to use their control of access to fire support and transportation to influence their counterparts, but even here their success was limited. In an incident that caused considerable embarrassment in Saigon and Washington, the senior adviser to the 25th Division, Lieutenant Colonel Cecil F. Hunnicutt, withdrew some of his advisory teams from the division's subordinate units. Hunnicutt had long been at odds with the division commander, General Phan Trong Chinh, whom Hunnicutt considered incompetent and ineffective. He complained that many of Chinh's battalion commanders deliberately avoided contact with the enemy. He also believed that Chinh was protecting corrupt and drunken subordinates who were his friends or relatives. Many other Americans shared Hunnicutt's view that Chinh was one of the worst division commanders in the Vietnamese army, yet no one on the MACV staff raised the question of how to address the serious defects in the advisory system revealed by the Chinh–Hunnicutt affair. Instead Americans in Saigon worried mainly about the publicity surrounding the incident when General Chinh chose to make the dispute public by complaining of Hunnicutt's "sneaky reports." Chinh also complained of the tendency of some Vietnamese to be overly influenced by American wealth and power.[85] Chinh's remarks soon found their way into the Vietnamese and American press.

Far from worrying about the incompetence and corruption complained of by Hunnucutt, American generals devoted most of their attention to ensuring that American advisers would have even less leverage against their Vietnamese counterparts in the future. A new MACV directive issued in the wake of the Chinh affair warned U.S. advisers to "avoid becoming involved with their counterparts over minor, everyday problems," to "be discreet," and "under no circumstances" to use the threat of removing advisory teams or advisers "as a means of exerting pressure on a counterpart."[86]

Having reduced the adviser's function to one of persuading, nagging, bluffing, and cajoling, Westmoreland and Abrams devoted much thought and effort to measuring their success. Beginning in early 1968, MACV required advisers to complete an elaborate multiple choice questionnaire on subjects ranging from the morale of their units to the amount of time it took to call in fire support. The new reports, called SEER (System for Evaluating the Effectiveness of the RVNAF), together with the detailed monthly reports on operations already required of advisers, provided Saigon and Washington with a wealth of statistics by which to measure the "progress" of Saigon's armed forces. Yet there was only a tenuous connection between the SEER reports and actual events on the battlefield. Although they had the appearance of scientific measurements, the reports were, as the Army's official history points out, "inherently subjective" and ill-suited for comparing the performance of different units.[87] Yet the great attraction of the SEER reports was that they produced masses of quantifiable information, and in a war run on statistics this was a virtue sufficient to assure the system's survival.

General Westmoreland and General Abrams consistently rejected the one action that might, in fact, have enabled the Americans to compel "progress" in the performance of the South Vietnamese Army: a unified command. Such a command would have empowered American generals to transfer, promote, and replace South Vietnamese commanders, reorganize and redeploy units, and directly control operations. General Matthew Ridgway had exercised such power in Korea with good effect. Washington had proposed a similar arrangement for Vietnam in 1965, on two occasions in 1967, and in the wake of the Tet Offensive, but Westmoreland had always demurred. He insisted that he had sufficient personal influence with Vietnam's top generals to ensure unity and coordination in military operations. Although he acknowledged that "corruption is everywhere" in the South Vietnamese military, Westmoreland believed that the problem was a political one and therefore beyond any solution that the Military Assistance Command could provide.[88]

The real reason for Westmoreland's reluctance may have been his conviction, shared by many U.S. military leaders, that once U.S. forces had been committed the active participation of the Vietnamese army was neither necessary nor desirable. Westmoreland "refrained from using his influence to correct incompetence and corruption so gross that even he acknowledged their existence," wrote Neil Sheehan, who had covered the war since the early 1960s, because "he and nearly all his generals wanted as little as possible to do with the Vietnamese on their side. . . . Rather than taking over the ARVN and . . . reforming them . . . Westmoreland was intent on chucking the Saigon forces out of the way so that he could win the war with the U.S. Army."[89]

By mid-1968 this approach had been noisily repudiated in both Washington and Saigon, and General Abrams had proclaimed the new doctrine of "one war" with identical missions assigned to U.S. troops and South Vietnamese regulars. Yet no new mechanism had been introduced to ensure that the South Vietnamese armed forces would be reformed and improved to the point where they could take over the major burden of the war.

So, despite their proclamations of respect and interest, despite the new measures of progress, and despite the massive infusion of U.S. weapons and equipment, the South Vietnamese armed forces were left with their basic structure and practices intact. For the next five years, until the final departure of U.S. forces in 1973, there were unmistakable signs that despite lavish American aid the ARVN would ultimately fail to live up to U.S. expectations. The Vietnamese armed forces continued to close its officer ranks to all but the well-educated, continued to experience massive desertion, and continued to suffer from corrupt and incompetent leadership. It was an army that had learned a good deal since 1963 about how to rule, but too little about how to fight.

CHAPTER 6

The Relief of Khe Sanh and After, April 1968

Even as the President concluded his March 31 speech, one of the largest operations of the Vietnam War was beginning in the rugged mountains of Vietnam near the Laotian border. The operation was labeled PEGASUS, and its objective was to reopen the land route to Khe Sanh. To the media and to many Americans who followed the war, the siege of Khe Sanh and this endeavor to "lift the siege" were dramatic, significant, and consequential military developments, like the relief of Bastogne in World War II. Yet Vietnam was not World War II, and the battles in the mountains near the western border would highlight not only the dramatic story of Khe Sanh but also the essential continuity and inconclusiveness of the type of war the Americans were waging in Vietnam in the spring of 1968.

One reason the Tet attacks came as such a surprise to most Americans was that the attention of top military leaders had been focused elsewhere, on Khe Sanh, where fighting had begun ten days earlier. "The biggest battle of the war is shaping up near Khe Sanh," the director of the MACV Operation Center wrote two days before the Tet attacks. Even after heavy fighting erupted in the cities, many at MACV "sort of suspected that [the Communists] were doing it to get our attention away from the Khe Sanh area where he is stacking up troops for a big push."[1]

As the battles for the cities raged, the eyes of American generals in Saigon remained focused on the northernmost provinces of Quang Tri and Thua Tien. These provinces, along with their more southerly neighbors Quang Nam, Quang Ngai, and Quang Tin, formed parts of the narrow central neck of Vietnam, traditionally the poorest and most xenophobic region of the country. The old imperial capital of Hue, where the powerless emperor and his mandarins had held court less than thirty years before, was in Thua Tien, and the important port city of Da Nang, now swollen beyond recognition by American airfields and bases, was a little farther south, on the other side of the Hai Van Pass, where the Annamite mountain chain came down to touch the South China Sea. Across the mountain passes a narrow, winding highway, Route 1, provided the only overland line of communication to the two northernmost provinces. Away from the narrow ribbon of agricultural lowlands along the coast, much of the area was sparsely populated mountain and jungle, stretching away in thick blue-green forests to the Laotian border. To MACV this area constituted the I Corps Tactical Zone, or I Corps, as it was universally called, one of the four principal military regions of South Vietnam.

Of the four Corps areas, I Corps had long been considered the most critical and dangerous area of Vietnam. Westmoreland and his deputy, General Creighton Abrams, believed that the Communists hoped to seize control of Quang Tri and Thua Tien and to organize them as liberated zones, bargaining chips for future negotiations.[2]

As the fighting around Khe Sanh increased in ferocity, Westmoreland fed more and more troops into I Corps. During January and February, the 1st Cavalry Division (Air Mobile) and two brigades of the 101st Airborne Division arrived to join two reinforced Marine divisions and a large Army division (the Americal) already there. An additional Marine regiment and an Army airborne brigade, newly arrived from the United States, were also deployed to the northern provinces. By March 1968, over 50 percent of all U.S. maneuver battalions, half of the total U.S. combat power on the ground, were located in I Corps, three of the divisions—the 3d Marine Division, the 101st, and the 1st Cavalry—crowded into the area north of Hai Van Pass.

This region was nominally the responsibility of the III Marine Amphibious Force, with its headquarters at Da Nang. Yet Westmoreland did not fully trust the Marines to direct the battle in this critical sector, so in late 1968 he established a forward command post at

Phu Bai outside Hue and put his deputy, General Abrams, in charge. At the beginning of March, Abrams turned over command of what had by then become a full-fledged corps headquarters to Lieutenant General William B. Rosson, much to the annoyance of the Marines, who felt little need for a three- or four-star Army general to hold their hands. "Those of us at III MAF regarded it as a transparent effort to diminish the importance of III MAF," a Marine officer recalled. "We . . . saw it as a 'power grab,' an effort to move into the publicity limelight at a time when considerable media attention was focused there."[3] Rosson's Provisional Corps, Vietnam (later XXIV Corps) reported to III MAF but was in direct charge of operations in Quang Tri and Thua Tien, including Khe Sanh.

As the Communists stepped up their artillery and rocket fire at Khe Sanh, the Americans answered in kind. Giant 175mm guns at nearby Camp Carroll and "the Rockpile" fired round the clock in support of the base. Navy, Marine, and Air Force planes flew more than three hundred sorties against targets around the base. On an average day, 1,800 tons of bombs were dropped on the Khe Sanh area. By the end of March the besieging Communist forces had been subject to almost twice the total tonnage of bombs dropped during the entire first two years of the war against Japan.[4] Most fearsome were the strikes by B 52 bombers, code-named Arc-light. The giant bombers were capable of carrying approximately 60,000 pounds of bombs in the form of high explosives, delayed-action ordnance, cluster bomb units, antipersonnel canisters, or all of these combined. A formation of six B-52s dropping their bombs from 30,000 feet could utterly devastate an area half a mile wide and almost 2 miles long.[5] Air Force analysts later claimed that ten thousand to twelve thousand North Vietnamese soldiers had been killed by the bombing, which also destroyed bunkers, gun positions, supply dumps, and ammunition.[6]

Radio Hanoi boasted that North Vietnamese soldiers had little fear of the B-52s, and the Communists did receive frequent timely warnings of impending raids from Soviet intelligence trawlers in the South China Sea.[7] Yet even with warning, the Vietnamese Communists found the B-52s to be the most terrifying weapon in the American arsenal. "Even if an individual is not directly injured by the blast, he may experience secondary effects such as temporary

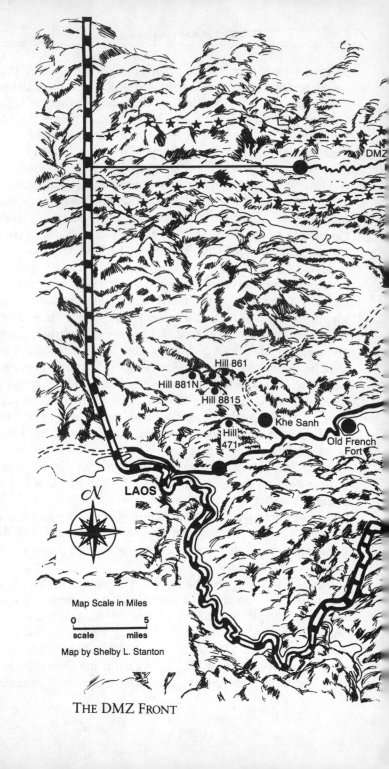

THE DMZ FRONT

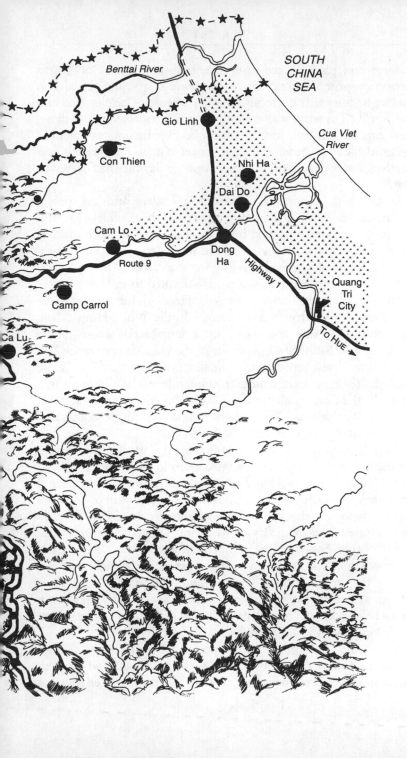

deafness and pains in the chest," allied interrogators of North Vietnamese prisoners concluded. "The noise, shock, and destruction produce an intense fear accompanied by a sense of helplessness and isolation."[8] "The terror was complete," recalls a former high-ranking Viet Cong official, "one lost control of bodily functions as the mind screamed incomprehensible orders to get out. . . . It was not just that things were destroyed; in some awesome way they had ceased to exist."[9]

As the siege continued, Washington leaders and the public became increasingly apprehensive about the base. Television and newspaper reporters shuttling back and forth to Khe Sanh made it the most heavily reported story of the war. *Newsweek* ran a piece on "The Agony of Khe Sanh" as its cover story, and 50 percent of all CBS TV film reports on Vietnam were devoted to it.[10]

There were constant references to the French defeat at the siege of Dien Bien Phu fourteen years before.[11] In the White House, "the Situation Room was dominated by a large aerial photographic mosaic of Khe Sanh showing details of the U.S. Marine trench line [*sic*] and the latest reported Communist positions. . . . The White House had also acquired a large terrain model of the Khe Sanh area for use by the Commander in Chief." The President and his advisers were, as *Washington Post* reporter Don Oberdorfer observed, "mentally in the trenches with the boys."[12]

On February 7, a few days after the Tet attacks had begun, Communist forces supported by tanks overran the Lang Vei Special Forces Camp, killing two hundred of its five hundred defenders and ten of their two dozen American advisers. The swift fall of Lang Vei sent psychological shock waves through many Americans already apprehensive about the safety of Khe Sanh. "Jesus, they had tanks. Tanks!" wrote *Esquire* correspondent Michael Herr. "After Lang Vei how could you look out of your perimeter at night without hearing the treads coming? How could you patrol in the dark without remembering every story you ever heard about ghostly enemy helicopters . . . about the tracks cut in the floor of the A Shau Valley big enough to hold trucks . . . ?"[13]

At the end of February the respected CBS anchorman Walter Cronkite returned from a two-week visit to Vietnam and warned: "Another standoff may be coming in the big battle expected south of the Demilitarized Zone. Khe Sanh could well fall with the terrible loss of American lives, prestige, and morale and this is a tragedy of our stubbornness there."[14]

Yet the big battle never came. Instead, by mid-March U.S. intelligence analysts began reporting the withdrawal of major enemy units away from the Khe Sanh area.[15] Journalists and some military men speculated that the enemy's sudden withdrawal indicated that the attack on Khe Sanh had been a feint to draw U.S. attention and troops away from the areas of the impending Tet attacks. Westmoreland and his commanders contended that the heavy losses the enemy had suffered were what compelled him to break off the siege. Twenty years later the argument over the Communists' real intentions and their degree of success at Khe Sanh still rages.

Despite the easing of the threat to Khe Sanh, Westmoreland pressed on with a plan for an attack westward to relieve the garrison. The operation would also reopen Highway 9, the only east-west road to the base, and would destroy or drive off the besieging enemy forces. The attack was code-named PEGASUS, and to carry it out Westmoreland had allocated more than thirty thousand troops under Major General John J. Tolson, commanding general of the 1st Cavalry Division (Air Mobile). In addition to his entire division, with its four hundred helicopters, Tolson would have the 1st Marine Regiment, the 26th Marine Regiment, a Vietnamese Ranger battalion, and a Vietnamese airborne unit.[16]

The jumping-off point for the operation would be the village of Ca Lu on Route 9, about 15 miles northeast of Khe Sanh. Here since mid-March Army and Marine Corps engineers and Navy SeaBees had been carving out a major operating base, Landing Zone Stud. Within a few days they had constructed a 1,000-meter airstrip, ammunition storage areas, fuel bladders, communications centers, repair shops, and a complex of bunkers. By March 25, when it was completed, Stud "was a forward operational base that looked better than most permanent installations in I Corps."[17]

On the morning of April 1, 1968, LZ Stud's 1,000-meter airstrip was covered by rows of helicopters, their rotor blades partly hidden by the dense morning fog, their engines emitting the distinctive staccato whump-whump-whump of the Huey. Packed inside were troops of the 1st Battalion, 7th Cavalry of the 1st Cavalry Division.

"The Cav," with its large and distinctive yellow-and-black shoulder patch, was known all over Vietnam—it had in a sense been born in Vietnam. In a year or two, when the Army's divisions in Vietnam would begin to experience serious disciplinary problems, the 1st Cavalry would contribute more than its share of drug problems, courts-martial, and racial incidents, but in the spring of 1968 its troops were still proud and cocky. They called themselves "horse soldiers" and liked to remember their links to General Custer and the frontier Army. They thumbed their noses at the old "straight-leg" infantry and especially at the Marines whom they considered plodding, unimaginative, and old-fashioned. The Marines returned these feelings with interest and were enraged at suggestions that they were being "rescued" at Khe Sanh by The Cav. Yet as they watched wave after wave of helo-borne troops pass overhead, most Marines felt not a little envy at this new style cavalry that had more helicopters than the Marines had in all of Vietnam. Within a few months the Marines would adopt a more mobile style of warfare that closely mirrored The Cav's.

General Tolson's plan was to have two battalions of Marines, 2d Battalion, 1st Marines and 2d Battalion, 3d Marines, attack down Route 9 toward Khe Sanh, closely followed by engineers to improve the roadway. At the same time, the 26th Marines at Khe Sanh would attack and secure Hill 471 just south of the base. The brigades of the air cavalry would leap-frog into positions south and southeast of Khe Sanh where the remnants of the 304th North Vietnamese Division were reported to be deployed. The Cav troopers would roll up any enemy in their path as they advanced toward the base. The Vietnamese airborne would be airlifted into the area southwest of Khe Sanh and attack toward Lang Vei.[18]

On the morning of April 1 the Marines of 2/1 and 2/3 began their movement down Route 9 through the thick morning fog, closely followed by the bulldozers, graders, trucks, and cranes of the engineers and SeaBees. As the fog finally began to lift, waves of helicopters whined and roared overhead carrying an entire brigade of The Cav. Less than twelve hours after Lyndon Johnson's peace address on March 31, the largest military operation ever undertaken in I Corps was under way.

Like the Great Siege, the Great Relief was something of an

anticlimax. Most of the enemy troops around Khe Sanh had withdrawn to Laos, and the Marines and cavalry troopers often found that their most formidable opposition was the heavily wooded mountain terrain. "Elephant grass, bugs, snakes, and shit all over the place," as one Marine described it.[19]

The Americans found extensive enemy bunker complexes and large quantities of ammunition and supplies, especially food. And there were bodies. Official American reports claim to have found "over eighteen hundred dead bodies on the hills around Khe Sanh." Intelligence analysts speculated that as American bombing and shelling intensified, "a point was reached where casualties to the necessarily large burial details became unacceptable to the NVA command."[20] Marine chaplain Ray Stubbe noted that at one point Khe Sanh's celebrated rat population suddenly disappeared, not for any lack of garbage and C rations at the combat base, but "because all the enemy bodies and body parts strewn so close to the combat base made better food."[21]

As the relieving forces neared Khe Sanh, the Marines at the base began their own offensive by attacking Hill 471, a critical piece of terrain that commanded a view of much of the Khe Sanh Valley. In the predawn darkness of April 4 three companies of Lieutenant Colonel John J. Cahill's 1st Battalion, 9th Marines left Khe Sanh for Hill 471, about 3,000 meters south of their position. Their approach covered by the thick morning fog, the Marines reached the base of the hill undetected, and Company A moved up the slope to the attack. Heavy air and artillery strikes had been directed at the hill, but the enemy bunkers, positioned on the forward face, were impossible to knock out except by a direct hit. Reaching the crest of the hill, A Company found North Vietnamese with machine guns dug in in the bomb craters left by the incessant American bombing. The Marines and NVA traded fire and showers of grenades in a brief but bloody fight which left ten Marines and thirty soldiers of the 66th North Vietnamese Army Regiment dead among the bomb craters.[22]

Sergeant William Lanier, diving headfirst into a crater to escape the heavy machine gun fire, found himself face to face with four NVA soldiers. They appeared to be thirteen to fifteen years of age and seemed "scared to death, paralyzed with fear" especially upon seeing a 6-foot, 3-inch "elephant." The four immediately surrendered and were taken to Khe Sanh.[23]

Other North Vietnamese fighters were made of sterner stuff. Two battalions of the 66th Regiment, which had just completed a thirty-six-hour march from their base near Hue, were directed to recapture Hill 471 at all costs. One battalion was caught in the open by U.S. artillery and decimated. The survivors then joined the other battalion in an attack on the hill in the early morning hours of April 5.

The Communists' approach was revealed by American illumination shells, and the North Vietnamese attackers were devastated by artillery and automatic weapons already registered on their route of approach. Unshaken, the Vietnamese advanced to within 15–20 meters of the Marine defenders before finally breaking before the superior firepower of the Americans.[24]

While the Marines were securing Hill 471, the 2d Brigade of The Cav was running into stiff resistance. The 3d Brigade's 2/7 Cavalry fought a day-long battle against enemy blocking positions along Route 9, while the 2d Brigade found itself meeting heavy resistance when it air-assaulted into a landing zone near an old French fort just south of Route 9 a little east of Khe Sanh. Yet the Communists could not long hold out against the air cavalry's combination of heavy firepower and fast-moving helicopter assaults on their flanks and rear.

One after another, the Communist-held positions around Khe Sanh fell to the Americans or were abandoned without a fight. The 2d Battalion, 26th Marines, sending out its first long-range patrols since January, cleared enemy bunkers between the combat base and the Marine outposts on Hills 861 and 881 South, to the northwest of Khe Sanh. On April 8 the commander of The Cav's 3d Brigade, Colonel Hubert Campbell, arrived at Khe Sanh with the first elements of his command to effect the formal relief of the base. Two days later a battalion of The Cav's 1st Brigade seized the Lang Vei Special Forces Camp, knocking out one of the vaunted Communist tanks in the process. On April 12 Route 9 was reopened to vehicular traffic for the first time since September 1967.[25]

The final battle of Operation PEGASUS was fought on Easter Sunday, April 14, when the 3d Battalion, 26th Marines attacked Hill

881 North. The hill was on the high ground northwest of Khe Sanh. Unlike most of the hundreds of other nameless hills, peaks, and ridge lines upon which Americans had fought and died in Vietnam, Hill 881 North had real meaning for the Marines of 3/26 and indeed for everyone who had been at Khe Sanh. On January 20, I Company, 3/26th Marines, on a reconnaissance in force under Captain William H. Dabney, had fought an engagement with elements of a North Vietnamese division in the low saddle between Hills 881 South and 881 North. That battle had marked the opening of the Khe Sanh campaign.

During the next eleven weeks more than five thousand rockets would be fired at Khe Sanh from the Hill 881 North complex. Meanwhile Dabney's I Company, dug in on Hill 881 South, kept the Communists' firing positions both on 881 North and in Laos in the Co Roc mountain range under constant observation, providing timely warning and adjusting counterbattery fire.[26] In return, 881 South underwent a rain of fire that exceeded even the most intense bombardments at Khe Sanh.

Each morning Dabney and his men emerged from their bunkers to stand stiffly at attention while Dabney shouted, "Attention to colors." Two Marines tied a pock-marked and torn ensign to a radio antenna, which was then solemnly raised while a Marine played "To the Colors" on a bugle. The entire ceremony took approximately thirty seconds, the time it would take for the first giant 120mm mortar rounds from 881 North to impact on the outpost. The second the bugle call ended, the Marines dived for cover as the hilltop rocked with the explosions of incoming shells.[27]

Now, on this Easter Sunday, it was the Marines' turn. Three companies of the 3d Battalion, 26th Marines had moved into attack positions at the base of 881 South under cover of darkness. Shortly before daylight, scouts from L and M companies, picking their way up the mountain, made contact with elements of the North Vietnamese battalion defending 881 North. The chatter of AK-47s, M-16s, and machine guns erupted all along the front as the Marines advanced up the hill. "A rain of Chinese Communist grenades began falling on us, so heavy that it appeared that it was just raining grenades," recalled Lieutenant Charles King, who commanded the L

Company point platoon.[28] Supported by heavy mortar fire and 106 recoilless rifles, the Marines cleared the enemy bunkers one by one. Corporal Eldridge Patterson of L Company was knocked momentarily unconscious by a grazing blow to his head. "I came to, I saw blood all over me but I knew I wasn't dead. I picked up my rifle and went after [the NVA who had shot at me]. Got to the top of the hill and he took his second shot at me and I heard a whine past my ear. I was shooting from the hip with my M-16 rifle and put a round right through him."[29]

More than a hundred North Vietnamese soldiers died on Hill 881 North that day.[30] Others fled, attempting to find cover in the tall elephant grass from the waiting Marine fighters circling near the hill. In the late afternoon, Lance Corporal Dennis Mannion of K Company performed a brief victory ceremony. He "took down his brownish-green jungle pants and shit on the hallowed NVA high ground of 881 North—it wasn't too difficult a job. I had to take a shit anyway—and it was very satisfying."[31]

Had the Vietnam War been a World War II movie, the story would have ended here, with the exhausted but triumphant Marines atop Hill 881 North where it all began, with the siege of Khe Sanh lifted by fast-moving sky cavalry and the North Vietnamese routed. In fact, however, the PEGASUS fighting marked the midpoint, not the end, of the ordeal of Khe Sanh. More than four hundred American troops would be killed in or near Khe Sanh in the ten weeks following the commencement of Operation PEGASUS, and 2,300 others would be seriously wounded.[32] That was more than twice the casualties officially reported for the period of "the siege" from late January to the end of March.

The truth was that Khe Sanh, though no longer cut off or threatened with imminent attack, remained under siege. Communist artillery, dug deep into the crags and peaks of the Co Roc mountains in nearby Laos, continued to bombard the base at will, while the Americans could never successfully locate or destroy those guns. NVA regiments, badly mauled during PEGASUS or in the winter fighting, could withdraw at will to refit and regroup across the Laotian border, then return to fight another day.

That Khe Sanh was more a liability than an asset had long been obvious to both General Rosson and his nominal superior, the III

MAF commander, Lieutenant General Robert E. Cushman. As PEGASUS went forward, Cushman and Rosson made preparations to abandon Khe Sanh and to shift to a more mobile posture of operations. Naval gunfire experts and Air Force liaison officers arrived at the base to plan for the destruction of all fixed installations at Khe Sanh. Marines and support personnel began packing equipment and filling in fighting holes. "The general attitude of people in the base is that it is wrong to abandon the base after fighting so long for it," Chaplain Stubbe wrote in his diary. "Was it all worth it? Sic transit gloria mundi."[33]

Chaplain Stubbe's misgivings were mild indeed compared with the reaction of General William Westmoreland when he learned of plans for "Retrograde." "Sunday we went up to Phu Bai for a meeting on Khe Sanh," General Chaisson wrote to his wife. "I never saw Westy so mad. They were working plans under Rosson to pull out. Westy lowered the boom. He was so mad he wouldn't stay around and talk with them. Instead he told me what he wanted and left me to push it with Rosson and Cushman."[34]

The following morning a Marine engineer officer at Khe Sanh "received a very great shock" at the morning staff meeting. "Late last night word came down from 'high levels' that Khe Sanh Combat Base would not be abandoned. So we had to unpack all our personal gear and then this p.m. we started digging in again. The trenches from which we had pulled our CONEXs [large metal storage boxes] had all been filled in already and our organic [metal] mats had been staged for helo-lift. . . . It will take at least a week to get our area built up again."[35]

Instead of closing the base, a new operation, "SCOTLAND II," would begin on April 15. Marines would continue to occupy Khe Sanh and some of the surrounding hills and to conduct reconnaissance and search-and-destroy operations.[36] The four battalions of Marines that had held Khe Sanh before PEGASUS would be relieved by three fresh Marine battalions and two battalions of The Cav's 1st Brigade.

SCOTLAND II opened with a battle that rivaled in sheer misery, pain, and bloodshed any of the events of the winter just ended. It began as a routine patrol by A Company, 1st Battalion, 9th Marines, near the battalion's base on Hill 689, a few miles from Khe Sanh.

The patrol was checking an area where a few North Vietnamese soldiers, possibly forward observer teams for the ubiquitous Communist mortar batteries, had been recently spotted. Like many Marine companies in early 1968, Captain Henry D. Banks's Company A had only two platoons with a total strength of about eighty-five men. However, that was more than enough to handle the few scattered Communist soldiers who were all the Marines expected to find in the area.

The platoon left Hill 689 at 7:00 A.M., passed through a valley, and reached the base of a neighboring hill at about 10:00 A.M. Two-thirds of the way up the hill, Banks halted the company and sent his 1st Platoon under Second Lieutenant Francis B. Lovely on ahead. Just before reaching the crest, Lovely stopped and sent one fire team ahead to check out the reverse slope. Dropping to a low crawl, the fire team approached the ridge line and soon came under fire from their direct front.

Believing he had run into a sniper, Lieutenant Lovely deployed his platoon to outflank the enemy position, only to be met with heavy small arms and grenade fire. An attempt by the 2d Platoon to sweep around the right of the enemy position also met heavy fire. Within a few minutes Banks had lost a dozen men, including the 2d Platoon commander and platoon sergeant, and about twenty others were wounded. The wounded and dead were so close to the enemy positions that they could not be reached. Nor could Banks call in artillery support without endangering his own wounded.

Captain Banks, realizing that he had run into an enemy bunker complex, called for assistance in evacuating his wounded and extracting his platoon from the trap. Lieutenant Colonel John Cahill, the battalion commander, brought his two remaining companies in to help. D Company was ordered to move to back up A Company and assist in the evacuation. Meanwhile C Company would attack the rear of the enemy bunker complex to relieve pressure on A Company.

But the battalion was not dealing with a single bunker complex, as Cahill believed.[37] It was in fact engaged with at least a company of North Vietnamese troops in mutually supporting bunker complexes. The bunker complex facing A Company was U-shaped and therefore could not be outflanked. Its rear was protected by other

U-shaped bunker complexes, all concealed by the heavy vegetation and elephant grass.

The North Vietnamese had already won the first part of the battle by luring A Company's successive elements into a deadly crossfire and pinning them down so close that they could not call in supporting arms. Now they were to repeat the performance with C Company.

Without knowing the exact position or strength of the enemy, C Company was committed to the attack up the wooded rear of the hill on which A Company had been pinned down. Captain Lawrence Himmer, the company commander, placed his two platoons on line, with 1st Platoon leading. As the line cleared the crest of the hill, the Marines came under heavy fire from a second enemy bunker complex to its left flank. Within a few minutes Captain Himmer, the two platoon commanders, a platoon sergeant, and most of the squad leaders were killed or wounded. The Marines traded grenades with the enemy and blasted them out of bomb craters and spider holes. First Lieutenant David Carter, who led the 1st Platoon, estimated that only eight of his thirty-two men came away alive and unhurt.[38] Finally, under fire from both front and flank, C Company halted, its ranks heavily depleted, its center squads barely in contact with A Company.

A Company had meanwhile made good progress in evacuating its wounded, and Colonel Cahill, who had been wounded himself but refused to be evacuated, ordered D Company to attack around the other side of the hill in order to relieve the pressure on C Company, now in as precarious a position as A.

Making their way through the 4-foot elephant grass, Captain Cargill's D Company was soon immobilized by heavy and accurate sniper fire and mortars. With five men killed and unable to see the enemy, D Company was also halted.

With darkness approaching, Colonel Cahill now had no choice but to attempt to extract his scattered and badly hurt companies. As Corporal Dewey E. Troup, a squad leader with C Company bitterly observed, "By evening there was bodies everywhere . . . and we really hadn't did what we came up there to do: we still hadn't got the gooks off the hill . . . 'cause we didn't have anything left to take the hill."[39] Company A had largely completed its withdrawal, and

Company B had retrieved its wounded but not its dead. Company C was in worse shape, its dead and wounded in scattered pockets, its company commander missing.

The evacuation of the wounded had become a minor nightmare. The single landing zone was under intermittent mortar fire and was so small that CH-46s could not land safely. Only UH-1s, smaller and handier but with less carrying capacity, could be used. With Khe Sanh fogged in, the choppers had to make the long flight all the way back to Dong Ha before returning. As darkness settled in, evacuation became even more difficult; eventually some casualties had to be brought back or carried to Hill 689.

Departing from Marine Corps tradition, 1/9 had been obliged to leave some of its dead behind. What was not realized at the time was that some of the living had been left as well. The following morning Marines of C Company on Hill 689 were startled to hear a man yelling across the valley from the area of the previous day's battle. Corporal Henry Casteneda recognized the voice of his squad-mate, Corporal John Hunnicutt, thought to have been killed in the previous day's fighting. Sergeant Thomas Dubrey quickly organized his platoon for a rescue. As the lead squad approached Hunnicut's position, they suddenly heard a single rifle shot. At the same time Corporal Hunnicut's yells ceased. The Marines called to Hunnicut but heard no reply, and they were now beginning to receive scattered sniper fire. Convinced that Hunnicut was dead, Sergeant Dubrey withdrew to Hill 689.

Less than two hours later a spotter plane, checking the area of the previous day's fighting, noticed a Marine who appeared to be alive about 50 meters down the slope from the U-shaped bunker complex that had been the objective of A and D companies' unsuccessful assaults. A number of American bodies could also be seen scattered near the bunker.

While fighter-bombers and helicopter gunships strafed and rocketed the area, volunteers from 1/9 boarded two CH-46s to attempt to rescue the Marine and recover as many bodies as possible. The first CH-46 landed in a swirl of dust and sand directly atop the bunker complex. One North Vietnamese soldier was crushed to death as the 46 lowered its heavy rear tailgate, and the Marines emerged, rifles and machine guns blazing. Four more Vietnamese were shot by the Marines as they raced around the left side of the helicopter toward a half-dozen Marine bodies. The single live Marine remained on the right of the helicopter, too far away to be reached, and the CH-46 had now become the target of enemy mortar and machine gun fire. With seventeen bullet and shrapnel holes in its fuselage and part of the hydraulic system shot away, the CH-46 could not reposition itself for a second try. The rescue party scrambled back aboard and the 46 limped back to Hill 689.

The live Marine was still on the ground, and the second CH-46 requested permission to make a try, but the battalion air officer had now concluded that the large, slow CH-46s would have little chance of making a successful rescue in such a confined space.

But other helicopters could. Early in the afternoon Air Cavalry gunship pilots in the area who had been listening to the radio traffic volunteered to attempt a pickup. A flight of eight Huey gunships, collectively called Blue Max, slowly circled the area blasting away with rockets and machine guns while a ninth swooped down to rescue the Marine. Medevaced to Khe Sanh, the rescued Marine proved to be not Corporal Hunnicut but PFC Panyaninec, another C Company survivor.

The following morning, Corporal Casteneda again heard Hunnicut's voice calling for help. C Company dispatched another patrol to rescue Hunnicut. By this time, however, the planned transfer and replacement of Marine battalions at Khe Sanh was well under way. Lieutenant Colonel Cahill was about to get a new regimental commander. So the patrol was halted a few hundred yards from Hunnicut while two colonels and a general discussed its next move. While the discussion continued, Blue Max repeated its performance of the previous day and rescued Hunnicut. In all, 1/9 had lost forty-one killed and thirty-two wounded on Hill 622. Corporal Hunnicut's C Company had twenty-six of its eighty-five-odd Marines killed, including the company commander, Captain Himmer. More than two dozen dead had been left on the battlefield.

The failure to recover the dead and the long delays in evacuating the wounded were unusual and prompted an investigation, but in most other ways 1/9's nameless battle on a nameless hill near Khe Sanh was fairly typical of Marine battles in Vietnam in the spring of

1968. A platoon or company would stumble onto a well-prepared enemy unit in a strong, mutually-supporting bunker complex. The Americans would take heavy casualties in the first few minutes and would be hindered in using artillery by fear of hitting wounded near the bunkers. The wounded, in turn, would be unreachable because of heavy enemy fire. Other American units would be committed to the battle without benefit of reconnaissance or intelligence and would themselves be ambushed or pinned down.

That 1/9 failed to occupy the hill and force the Communists to retreat was no doubt galling to the pride of Marines like Corporal Troup and many others, but in practical terms this failure made little difference. The Marines would have left the hill within a few days in any case. As a squad leader with 2d Battalion, 26th Marines commented a few days after his battalion's successful assault on Hill 881 North, "First of all I'd like to say that I feel this operation was successful. But it was needless, due to the fact that after we had taken our objective we just left it. . . . We ran them off the hill and they came right back and occupied the position."[40] In victory or defeat, the pattern of ground warfare near the DMZ remained the same.

Further south, however, in the coastal lowlands of Thua Thien province near Hue, Brigadier General John H. Cushman's second brigade of the 101st Airborne was experimenting with new methods. Since arriving in the area in mid-March, Cushman had attempted to work closely with the South Vietnamese, establishing close ties between his units and local government officials. Unlike many American commanders, Cushman encouraged close cooperation with the South Vietnamese military, even undertaking joint operations and arranging for South Vietnamese Regional Forces and militia or "Popular Forces" to accompany American platoons and companies.[41]

The result was that Cushman began to receive good intelligence on the whereabouts of the enemy. On more than one occasion his men were able to locate North Vietnamese Army forces precisely in a village or hamlet and surround the area. Yet the majority of the enemy was almost always able to slip through the American encirclement or "cordon" during the night.

Unsuccessful or at best partly successful, cordon operations had become a commonplace since the U.S. forces first began large-scale operations in Vietnam three years before. Cushman was determined to change that. He and his battalion commanders attempted further cordon operations and carefully analyzed their experiences. It soon became apparent that night-long continuous illumination of a village by air-dropped flares would be necessary for success. Even eight to ten minutes of darkness would be sufficient for the enemy to shift position and escape. It was also necessary to ring the village completely with foxholes only 10 meters apart. Finally, every man in those foxholes would have to remain awake and alert, even though many of them might have been fighting all the previous day.

At the end of April, Cushman's men finally got the chance to apply their hard-learned lessons. In Huong Tra district near Hue, at a bend in the Perfume River, two companies of the American 1/501st, the elite Black Panther company of the South Vietnamese First Division, and three platoons of Popular Forces trapped an entire North Vietnamese battalion in two villages, Phuoc Yen and Le Van Thuong.

For five nights the North Vietnamese struggled desperately to escape the noose, losing about four hundred men before final resistance collapsed on May 3. The Americans and South Vietnamese captured 107 prisoners, the largest haul of the war to that point. The brigade repeated its success one month later, when it encircled and destroyed the command group of a North Vietnamese regiment and a battalion in the village of Le Xa Dong in Phu Vang district, capturing forty-one prisoners.

The Second Brigade's achievement was hailed as a great success by Saigon and was played up for the media, but Cushman's innovations were not passed on. Indeed, MACV lacked any effective mechanism for passing them on, and his achievements were never repeated. Within a few months, failure, sometimes disastrous failure, had become the rule for attempts at cordon operations in Vietnam.

While the Marines were settling in to more of the same in the hills and valleys near Khe Sanh, and the Second Brigade of the 101st was conducting its successful experiments with cordons, the 1st Cavalry Division had been assigned a new mission. The biggest Communist success of Tet had come at Hue, the old imperial capital, where

HUE AND THE A SHAU VALLEY

Map by Shelby L. Stanton

Hue

2
3
1

Bon Tri

Perfume River

Phu
Bai

Huang
Thoi

North Vietnamese and Viet Cong forces had seized a large proportion of the city. They had held out for three weeks in the older fortified part of the city known as the Citadel, which contained the imperial palace. General Westmoreland and his commanders were convinced that the staging area and supply base for the Communist forces that had attacked Hue and for others which continued to menace Thua Tien province was the A Shau Valley. The A Shau was a remote, mile-wide finger of bottom land running northwest to southeast between the jagged mountains near the Laotian border. An old French road, Route 527, snaked its way from the valley across mist-covered mountains to Hue.

From 1963 until 1966, the Americans had maintained a Special Forces camp at the southern end of the A Shau Valley, but in March 1966 the Communists had overrun the camp. Using materials from the former American airstrip to improve their main road, Route 548, the Communists turned the valley into a major base and terminus of the Ho Chi Minh Trail.[42] Now for the first time since 1966 Westmoreland was ready to again attack the A Shau Valley with his Air Cavalry.

To General Tolson the sudden order to terminate his 1st Cavalry Division's operations around Khe Sanh and move to the A Shau came as an unwelcome surprise. "I had scheduled more than thirty-eight additional operations to extend our control of the Khe Sanh area," he wrote four years later. "There was great potential for the continued air assault operations that were abruptly brought to a close."[43]

The great haste in dispatching The Cav to the A Shau was due to calculations about the weather. Even in a region of Southeast Asia renowned for its bad weather, the A Shau Valley had a special reputation. Its peculiar location and topography made it subject to both the northeast and southeast monsoon with their heavy rain and hail. The brief interval between monsoons, mid-April to mid-May, was believed by Westmoreland's planners to be the only suitable time for operations in the valley.[44]

The 1st Cav's descent into the A Shau, code-named Operation Delaware, began with a near disaster as two battalions of The Cav air-assaulted into the northern end of the valley on April 19. Despite more than two hundred tactical air strikes and twenty-one B-52 raids during the preceding five days, North Vietnamese antiaircraft batteries were alive and kicking as the assault helicopters worked their way down through the fog and low-lying clouds. Mobile 37mm antiaircraft guns, which could fire three rounds a minute, and dozens of heavy machine guns destroyed ten helicopters and damaged more than a dozen others.[45]

Once on the ground the two battalions, 1-7 Cavalry and 5-7 Cavalry, found themselves unopposed but virtually walled in by the steadily deteriorating weather. During the next four days high winds, thunderstorms, and torrential rains made aerial resupply a nightmare. For the helo pilots "what should have been a simple twenty-minute flight" from The Cav's staging area to the valley "was usually an hour and twenty minutes of sheer terror." The Hueys picked their way through fog and rain squalls, always hoping to avoid the jagged peaks and ridge lines obscured by the clouds and murk.[46]

Despite the weather, 5-7 Cavalry, whose direct support artillery had been airlifted in an hour after its assault, was able to receive some supplies. Lieutenant Colonel Joseph E. Wasiak's 1-7 Cavalry was not so lucky; their position at LZ Vicky was so weathered in that the battalion could neither be resupplied nor evacuated. Colonel Wasiak had no choice but to move his battalion overland to a more favorable spot 4 miles south, LZ Goodman. The trek through the thick jungle in the pouring rain took four days. (In The Cav's after-action report this movement was described as "1-7 Cav commenced an attack over land to secure LZ Goodman.")[47] Along the way, 1-7 troopers discovered two Soviet-built bulldozers carefully concealed in the hillside.

As 1-7 arrived at LZ Goodman the weather moderated, and on April 24 two battalions of The Cav's 1st Brigade air-assaulted into the central part of the valley near the abandoned airstrip at the village of A Loui. Meanwhile the 3rd Brigade in the northern end of the valley took advantage of the better weather to bring in their remaining supporting units and artillery. In both the northern and the central portions of the valley Cav soldiers were finding massive amounts of supplies as well as trucks, construction equipment, and the AA guns that had earlier given them so much trouble.

The North Vietnamese forces in the valley, mostly engineer and transportation troops, put up little resistance on the ground except at a large depression in the valley called the Punch Bowl, which housed a major logistics complex. The North Vietnamese company defending the Punch Bowl was well entrenched in mutually supporting bunkers and had at least one tank in support.

Using massive air and artillery support The Cav blasted the North Vietnamese from the bunkers in three days of hard fighting. Sergeant Hillery Craig of D Company 1/8 Cav knocked out a tank with two rounds from his M-72 rocket launcher. The Punch Bowl proved to be the major supply and support center for the entire A Shau Valley with a truck park, hospital, administrative, and logistical sites.[48]

By May 10, as the rains of the southwest monsoon forced The Cav to begin extracting its units from the valley, the horse soldiers had captured more than 71,000 pounds of food, over two hundred thousand rounds of ammunition, seventy-six vehicles including a tank, and more than a dozen large antiaircraft guns.[49]

The 1st Cavalry Division commanders believed that Operation Delaware had been a severe blow to the Communists, not only in the material but also in the psychological sense. "The 1st ACD has effectively demonstrated to the enemy that he has no sanctuaries. His operations are under constant threat of assault by air-mobile infantry," read The Cav's after-action report.[50] In fact, the North Vietnamese were back in a few weeks. American and South Vietnamese forces would not return to the A Shau for almost a year. When they did return, the operation there would lead to one of the most fateful encounters of the war on a mountain called Dong Ap Bia, which the GIs would soon rename Hamburger Hill.

By the time The Cav had departed the A Shau in mid-May the North Vietnamese had begun to return to the area around Khe Sanh in considerable numbers. By early May four North Vietnamese regiments totaling more than 4,500 men, together with supporting artillery, were in the immediate vicinity of the base. The 3d Marine Division commander, General Rathvon McC. Tompkins, compared the situation "to that experienced during late CY 1967."[51] The overland supply route along Highway 9 from Ca Lu to Khe Sanh remained open but was the scene of "almost nightly ambushes and fire fights."[52] More than two hundred Marines and soldiers had been killed and almost one thousand wounded since the siege had been officially lifted in mid-April. Khe Sanh was once again experiencing heavy shelling by artillery, mortars, and rockets. "No one here is unaware," remarked Brigadier General Carl W. Hoffman, commander of the Marine forces in and around Khe Sanh, "that 'Long-range Charley' would like to put one of his 130mm rounds right on your head."[53]

Less than one month after the conclusion of PEGASUS, after all the dramatics of "air-mobile assaults," Marines taking back the high ground, and "lifting the siege," the war in the mist-covered mountains on the Laotian border was back to business as usual.

CHAPTER 7

The May Offensive: Dai Do

On May 13, 1968, five weeks after Operation PEGASUS had officially lifted the siege of Khe Sanh, the long-heralded peace talks opened in Paris. The previous weeks had been filled with surprises and frustrations. "Many of the State Department's senior officers, including those with longest experience in dealing with the communists," had doubted that Hanoi would respond at all to the President's invitation to begin negotiations.[1] The Communists' prompt response caught many of the President's advisers off guard, and some suspected that Hanoi was engaged in a propaganda ploy.[2]

Although the President had declared his readiness to "go anywhere, any time," to talk peace, it soon became apparent that the two sites proposed by Hanoi, Phnom Penh and Warsaw, were totally unacceptable for U.S. purposes. Poland was a Communist country and a staunch backer of Hanoi. Cambodia was ostensibly neutral and had no diplomatic relations with either the United States or South Vietnam. U.S. diplomats insisted that the talks had to be held in a country with a U.S. Embassy able to handle the large volume of secret communications likely to be generated by the American negotiators, and one in which Americans could move freely without the constant monitoring and surveillance routine in Iron Curtain countries. Hanoi for its part vetoed all fifteen sites suggested by Washington. In an effort to break the deadlock, Indonesia offered to provide a warship as a site for the talks, which could then take place "in neutral waters." This proposal Hanoi also declined.

As the deadlock dragged on, President Johnson once again came in for impatient criticism from foreign governments and members of Congress. Foreign Relations Committee Chairman J. William Fulbright urged Johnson to accept Warsaw, while presidential hopeful Robert Kennedy urged Johnson not to worry about losing face "by agreeing to a site we have not selected. The important thing is to get the talks started; each week of delay costs the lives of hundreds of men."[3]

Then, unexpectedly, Ambassador William Sullivan reported from Laos that the North Vietnamese had agreed to send delegates to Paris to begin talks. The French were delighted. Spokesmen for President Charles de Gaulle reminded reporters that Paris was the natural setting for international negotiations of first importance. *Time* magazine sourly noted that it had also been the site of the unsuccessful Fontainebleau talks of 1946 between the French and Ho Chi Minh, whose failure had led directly to the first Indochina war.[4]

To head their negotiating team in Paris, the Democratic Republic of Vietnam named Xuan Thuy, a onetime Foreign Minister and close associate of Ho Chi Minh, who had headed the North Vietnamese delegation at the Laos talks in Geneva in 1962. A small, soft-spoken man, he could nonetheless deliver unflagging tirades of denunciation and propaganda for hours on end.

The head of the American delegation, W. Averell Harriman, was suffering from a slight hearing impairment, a condition that newspaper wags observed might be an actual asset if the negotiations became protracted. At seventy-six, Harriman had held more important government jobs than any other member of the Johnson Administration. The son of the railroad baron E. H. Harriman, he had been Ambassador to Great Britain and Russia and Governor of New York. "Averell looks terrific," a friend told Mrs. Harriman shortly after his seventieth birthday. "You'd look terrific too," she replied, "if you did nothing but play polo until you were forty."[5] "Relentless, restless, ruthless, expert in the care and feeding of presidents," Harriman was unfailingly courteous and utterly unflappable.[6] He was also a tough, sometimes brutal, bureaucratic infighter. With Clark Clifford, Dean Rusk, and Walt W. Rostow, he would soon become one of the major figures in the Administration's Vietnam discussions.

The opening round of talks quickly deadlocked, with the North Vietnamese repeating their earlier pronouncements that the sole purpose of the meetings could only be to arrange for "the unconditional cessation of the U.S. bombing raids and all other acts of war so that talks may start." President Johnson, who had approached the idea of negotiations with misgivings, now angrily observed that the North Vietnamese "made a pretty good trade. They get partial suspension of the bombing for merely sitting in Paris talking."[7] Secretary of Defense Clifford, however, argued that the Paris talks were a propaganda asset for the United States. He pointed out that after three years of declaring that they would never talk until all bombing ceased, the North Vietnamese had come to Paris with part of their country still under air attack. Moreover, the concentrated bombing of the areas just north of the Demilitarized Zone was "causing them more damage than our previous bombing program."[8] For once the military agreed with the White House. The Commander-in-Chief Pacific Fleet reported good results in interdicting enemy supply lines south of the 19th Parallel by concentrating on "traffic control points"—highway bridges or ferries located in areas where marshy or watery terrain prevented an easy detour or bypass. With all their forces now available to attack the narrow area south of the 19th Parallel, the air commanders were able to make concentrated and repeated attacks on these choke points.[9]

Clifford also warned the President that the American public had placed great hope in the talks, and "if we do anything to wreck [them] Bobby [Kennedy] shoots up and public opinion goes against us." It was imperative to maintain the talks until at least the end of the Democratic convention in August.[10]

Under Secretary of State Nicholas Katzenbach took a different view. The fate of talks in Paris, he observed glumly, "turns on the military situation in Vietnam."[11] The Communists may have agreed, for in early May they unleashed a new round of attacks.

"The war has entered a very fierce complex stage of strategic offensive attacks aimed at securing final victory," a resolution issued by the Communist high command in April declared. The Viet Cong and North Vietnamese forces were exhorted to follow up the attacks of February with further blows against the still reeling enemy.[12] The Americans were equally determined to keep the pressure on the

Communists, who were bound to "be hurting" after their heavy losses during Tet. Each side saw itself as still on the offensive, ready to try again for a knockout blow. Thus while the "normal" war of platoons and squads continued unabated throughout most of Vietnam, the month of May also witnessed some of the largest and most costly battles of the war.

They began with an attempt by the North Vietnamese to seize control of the eastern region of Quang Tri province just south of the DMZ around the important American base at Dong Ha. Over the next month, from April 30 to the end of May, U.S. and Communist forces in that region would fight the largest and one of the most costly battles of the Vietnam War, a battle that began at an obscure river village called Dai Do.

Along the 700-mile crescent of South Vietnam from the military demarcation line in the north to the tip of the Ca Mua Peninsula, across the mountains, swamps, jungles, and coastal rice paddies, almost three hundred maneuver battalions, the cutting edge of the enormous American and allied military establishment, faced about 120 Communist battalions. The allied battalions, overwhelmingly American or South Vietnamese but also including Thais, South Koreans, Australian, and New Zealand units, averaged about eight hundred men, the Communists' generally less than four hundred.[13]

These figures are misleading, however, for the allied battalions had a lengthy "tail" of administrative, communications, and local security personnel, while the Communist battalions were almost all "tooth."[14] In most regions the numbers were far more even *at the point of contact*, and it was American firepower and not numerical strength that gave the allies whatever advantages they enjoyed.

In the Mekong Delta region, the richest, most politically volatile region in Vietnam—IV Corps in the allied military terminology—were three South Vietnamese divisions, the 7th, 9th, and 21st, along with five Vietnamese Ranger battalions and a number of Vietnamese Marine battalions. Relatively few North Vietnamese Army or Viet Cong Main Force units were permanently stationed in the Delta. Instead, VC Local Force units and guerrillas carried on an active campaign of raids and ambushes operating from bases in the seven mountains in the Plain of Reeds near the Cambodian border and in the almost impenetrable U Minh Forest.

The U.S. military presence in the Delta consisted of two brigades of the 9th Infantry Division with its headquarters near the town of My Tho. One brigade patrolled the area along Route 4, while the other brigade formed part of a special Army and Navy mobile riverine force, which operated on the Delta network of rivers, creeks, and streams.

North of the Delta, the allied III Corps area included some seven provinces, as well as the capital, Saigon. In May 1968 some thrity-three allied maneuver battalions were stationed in the vicinity of Saigon awaiting an anticipated attack by Viet Cong and North Vietnamese forces. American intelligence estimated that the Communists had about fifteen battalions operating from long-established bases in Hau Nghia province. Other Communist bases were in the "Iron Triangle" on the eastern banks of the Saigon River north of Saigon and in Cu Chi district, with its famous tunnels on the western side of that same river.[15]

The U.S. Army's 1st Infantry Division, "The Big Red One," normally operated in III Corps, as did the 25th Infantry Division, the 11th Armored Cavalry Regiment, the 199th Light Infantry Brigade, and elements of the 9th Infantry Division.

II Corps, stretching almost 400 miles from Dak To in the Central Highlands to Nha Trang, Phan Rang, and Phan Thiet on the South China Sea, included a dozen provinces and a number of large bases like Cam Ranh Bay, Tuy Hoa, Phu Cat, Qui Nhon, and Nha Trang, most of which had large, jet-capable airfields. Yet it was the Central Highlands, the rugged, sparsely populated mountain areas of Binh Dinh, Pleiku, Contum, and Darlak provinces, the last three bordering on Cambodia, that was considered by both sides to be the critical area. The first major battle between U.S. forces and North Vietnamese regulars had been fought here in the Ia Drang Valley in 1965. In May 1968 American intelligence experts believed that at least two full PAVN divisions, the 1st and the 325C, were operating in the Highlands, periodically withdrawing to neighboring Cambodia to resupply or to replace losses. The U.S. 4th Infantry Division with a brigade of the 101st Airborne was stationed in the Highlands, while the 173d Airborne Brigade and several Korean Army battalions patrolled the coastal lowlands.[16]

I Corps, comprising the five provinces of Quong Nhi, Quong Tin,

Quong Nam, Thua Thien, and Quang Tri, which formed the narrow northern tip of South Vietnam, was geographically the smallest part of the country and had been, since 1966, the scene of the heaviest fighting. The Ben Hai River, which formed the demarcation line between North and South Vietnam, had proved an insignificant military barrier, and U.S. and South Vietnamese forces were obliged to defend virtually the entire length of the DMZ against attack or infiltration. Almost half of all U.S. combat forces in Vietnam, thirty Army and twenty-four Marine Corps maneuver battalions, were concentrated in I Corps. Here the North Vietnamese had also concentrated their striking power, close to fifty battalions, and here all but one of the major battles of May were to be fought.

The complicated two-tiered command system established by Westmoreland in January continued to prevail in I Corps. Lieutenant General Robert E. Cushman's III Marine Amphibious Force directly controlled the large U.S. Army Americal Division and the 1st Marine Division and Aircraft Wing in southern I Corps. An Army corps headquarters, XXIV Corps, now under Lieutenant General William B. Rosson, controlled the 3d Marine Division, the 1st Air Cavalry, and other Army and Marine units in the northern half of I Corps. Rosson, in turn, was nominally subordinate to Cushman's III MAF.

Through April and into May, the focus of attention for the allies in northern I Corps remained the Khe Sanh area, where patrols by Marines and Cav troopers were uncovering an impressive complex of bunkers and caves housing barracks, headquarters, supply dumps, mess halls, and hospitals, all seemingly unscathed by the massive American bombing of the previous months. The chief of staff of Task Force Hotel estimated that his forces had found more than a thousand bunkers by early May, ranging in size from small two-man fighting positions to what he termed "apartment houses under ground." Many of the well-equipped hospitals and aid stations proved to be stocked with American medicines.[17] Most of the bunkers had been abandoned, but the Communists still made their presence known at Khe Sanh by almost daily shellings.

The Communist high command was not planning another major attack there, however. Costly struggles at Khe Sanh and Hue had taught it the difficulties of trying to reinforce and resupply their forces through the rugged mountain jungles of the western DMZ region. This time they would try the flat, narrow coastal lowlands stretching south from the DMZ to the Hai Van Pass, where the mountains of the Annamite chain came down to meet the sea.

That the Communists' interests had shifted to another part of the DMZ was abruptly signaled in the early morning of April 30 when a Navy river patrol boat on a routine patrol received small arms fire from the banks of the Bo Dieu River near the small villages of Dai Do and Dong Huan. The previous day, Marines of D Company, 1st Battalion, 9th Marines, and soldiers of the ARVN 2d Regiment had clashed with North Vietnamese forces near the village of Cam Vu, about 7 miles west of Dong Ha. Although no one was aware of it, the largest and one of the bloodiest battles of the war was about to begin. It long remained a battle with no name, but many years later it was labeled Dai Do after one of the tiny villages along the Bo Dieu where determined North Vietnamese fighters were digging in for a prolonged defense.

The North Vietnamese had committed almost an entire division to battle in the narrow, 15-mile-wide corridor along the Bo Dieu between Nhi Ha, a few miles from the South China Sea on the east, and Cam Vu, a few miles west of Route 1. The Communists' ultimate intentions remain obscure. Certainly their presence along the Bo Dieu threatened the main supply route to the large 3d Marine Division bases at Dong Ha and Quang Tri City. Almost 63,000 of the 67,000 tons of supplies required by the division's units operating in Quang Tri province came by sea to the mouth of the Cua Viet River and thence by smaller naval LCUs up the Cua Viet and Bo Dieu to Dong Ha. Perhaps the Communists intended to interdict this supply route, or perhaps they merely intended to draw Americans into a battle on the Bo Dieu River, which would open the way to an attack on Dong Ha or at least would oblige the division to abandon its barrier positions guarding the DMZ.

The Americans were initially slow to recognize the new threat at the eastern end of the DMZ. A platoon from H Company of Lieutenant Colonel William R. Weise's 2d Battalion, 4th Marines, was dispatched to investigate the ambush site on the Bo Dieu.[18] Lieutenant Colonel Weise, acting on a hunch that this was more than a routine incident of harassment, ordered Captain James L. Williams, the H Company commander, to bring his entire company against the ambush site, reported to be at the small hamlet of An Lac. At the same time, Weise requested and received permission to pull his other three companies, E, F, and G, from their other assignment and move them to An Lac. Weise, with his command group, boarded an armored LCM-6 "Monitor" of the Navy River Assault Group and positioned himself on the Bo Dieu immediately opposite An Lac.

As Captain Williams's lead platoon moved toward An Lac, it received heavy rocket, mortar, and automatic weapons fire from the neighboring hamlets of Dong Huan and Dai Do. Lieutenant Colonel Weise ordered Williams's H Company to seize and hold Dong Huan while F moved up by amphibious tractor to help.

The two companies traded fire with Doug Huan across a small stream to the south of the Marines. Williams's plan was to use two tanks of his attached tank platoon and the heavily armed Monitor to provide supporting fire while H Company, partially hidden by the stream bank, worked its way 700 meters upstream to a fording point and attacked Dong Huan from the rear.

F Company, mounted on its amphibious tractors (amtracs), would also cross the stream to a small cemetery east of Dai Do to keep down enemy fire from that hamlet and create a diversion for H's assault.

Crouched in the stream bed, PFC Cecil P. Whitfield, fire team leader with 1st Platoon of H Company, watched the tanks pour fire into Dai Do. Maybe the heavy tank and artillery fire would be enough to drive off the NVA, Whitfield thought wistfully. Maybe the whole thing would be over by evening. They would stand down, sit around, and have cocoa.[19] 2d Battalion, 4th Marines, was a tough, experienced outfit, but it had seen a lot of action since Tet, and most of its companies were under strength. H Company had only two officers, and its platoons were led by NCOs. Like many other Marines at this point in the war, the men of 2/4 were also having difficulties with their M-16 rifles; because they had expected only a routine patrol, many Marines had not taken all their cleaning gear with them to Dai Do.[20]

Getting across the stream in good shape, Captain Williams turned his company south toward Dong Huan, 700 meters away across an open paddy. Their movements partly obscured by smoke and white phosphorus, H Company advanced toward Dong Huan while Marine tanks and artillery, joined by the heavier guns of warships in the river, poured a hail of shells into the village. The inhabitants of Dong Huan and its neighboring hamlets had been evacuated almost six months before. Now it was the perfect battleground, a place of fire and death, where more than a dozen companies of frightened, determined North Vietnamese awaited the attack of equally determined, equally frightened Marines.

When H had reached a point 150 meters from Dong Huan, Williams ordered supporting fires lifted. The platoons formed a line with machine guns and light automatic weapons (LAWs) directly in the assault line and advanced on Dong Huan.[21] Captain Williams was wounded by an enemy grenade, but his exec, Lieutenant Alexander Prescott, assumed command, and the attack continued. The Marines methodically cleared the enemy from their bunkers, trenches, and spider holes. Sweeping through the hamlet, the company consolidated its position and set up a hasty 360-degree defense.

The relatively easy success of H Company at Dong Huan proved a deceptive beginning. F Company failed in its attempt to gain a foothold in neighboring Dai Do, and G Company, which Weise had hoped to use as reinforcements, was delayed in reaching the battlefield because it was itself under attack by enemy units near Nhi Ha. In the end the Communist attacks forced the cancellation of G's planned helo lift. Instead, the company was obliged to conduct a fighting withdrawal by foot south to Mai Xai Chanh on the Cua Viet, where the Marines boarded Navy landing craft and arrived at Dai Do the following morning.

The 3d Marines commander, Colonel Milton E. Hull, a tough, canny veteran of World War II, arrived at Dai Do in the late afternoon and visited H's precarious positions ashore. Hull had twice refused Weise's request for another battalion to clean out the Dai Do–An Lac complex, because Hull felt he needed troops to secure the south bank of the river as well as the north. Viewing the situation firsthand, however, Hull agreed to release another company, B, 1st Battalion, 3d Marines, to Weise for the operation at Dai Do.

At 3d Marine Division headquarters, the division commander, Major General Rathvon McC. Tompkins, had also concluded that a major fight was developing in the Nhi Ha–Cam Vu corridor. A company of the 3d Battalion, 9th Marines, patrolling near Cam Vu, had run into an L-shaped ambush, and it had required the entire battalion to extricate them at the cost of almost a hundred casualties. General Tompkins also learned that prisoners taken in the fighting near Cam Vu were members of the 320th PAVN Division, a unit new to the eastern DMZ area. The best that Tompkins could do, however, was to borrow an Army battalion of the 196th Light Infantry Brigade from the III MAF general reserve. He placed this battalion, the 2d Battalion, 21st Infantry, under Colonel Hull's control and ordered it airlifted to the area of Nhi Ha, from which Colonel Weise's G Company had withdrawn under fire several hours before. So situated, the 2/21st Infantry would be in position both to block reinforcements of the Dai Do area and to prevent the escape of enemy forces from the hamlets.

At Dai Do, Weise had launched B/1/3 in a late afternoon attack against An Lac to relieve the pressure on H and F companies. Mounted atop amphibious tractors, B Company "crossed the river in a classic amphibious assault wave." The Marines had long since come to prefer the risk of riding atop the amtracs exposed to enemy fire to the dubious safety of the armored hull, whose troop compartment was located just above the gas tank. The scene reminded Col Weise, watching from his command post aboard the *Monitor*, "of films of the Iwo Jima assault in World War II. As the assault wave neared the northern river bank, the enemy opened up with heavy small arms, mortars, rockets, and artillery fire from across the DMZ. The direct-fire weapons of the river assault group boats gave excellent support as B Company dismounted and fought its way into the fortified positions."[22]

B's assault carried it well into the center of An Lac, but with mounting casualties it was unable either to clear the hamlet or to link up with F. As night fell, F withdrew under heavy fire to join with H in Dong Huan, and the three companies hung on grimly through the night, supported by artillery and mortars. During the night a 106mm recoilless rifle round fired by Marines across the river fell short, landing in H Company's positions and setting off a 60mm mortar round. Five men were wounded "and you could hear the screams through the night."[23]

Morning found Colonel Weise with a fresh company to throw into the struggle at Dai Do. G Company, under Captain Jay Vargas, having completed its overland movement from Nhi Ha, was resupplied and landed by amtracs south of An Lac. Passing around the right flank of B Company, 1/3, Vargas led his men across the open rice paddies and into Dai Do, supported by a hail of fire from the river assault boats. A-4 Skyhawk attack planes roared overhead, leaving huge napalm fireballs in their wake.

Once in the village, the Marines encountered the same formidable defensive positions with which the Marines in the western DMZ had already become unhappily familiar: concrete and log bunkers, pillboxes, spider holes, and tunnels, all with mutually supporting fields of fire.[24] Snipers, concealed in spider holes, would allow several Marines to pass unaware over their position, then would open fire from the rear.[25]

In heavy fighting, G fought its way into Dai Do and dug in for the inevitable Communist counterattack. It came in the late afternoon and was beaten back, as was a second probe an hour later. Weise ordered Captain Vargas to pull G Company, now reduced to about sixty men, back into a more defensible 360-degree perimeter. For the next twenty-four hours the four understrength Marine companies in the riverside hamlets fought grimly to hold their position and to push back the enemy. Fighting was so intense that the normal medevac helicopters could not be used, and casualties were carried by hand back to the river, where they were evacuated by small skimmer boats. Although this method created additional hardships for the wounded, it gave the beleaguered Marines the advantage of not being obliged to lift supporting fires to allow for the arrival of helicopters.

Combat was often close and confused, with some platoons sometimes finding that their flanks were opened and that they were taking fire from two or three directions. One group of Marines took cover in a trench line, only to discover that the North Vietnamese had a machine gun concealed under some straw at the end of the trench at right angles to their position. "We found them next morning," reported a Marine of H Company, "lines of bodies from the river to way back in the 'ville."[26]

Many Marines were short of ammunition, and their M-16s often failed to function. "We were stuck in a trench with rifles that wouldn't work," PFC Whitfield of H Company recalled. "The lieutenant ordered us to take any C-rations that had grease in them and use them to grease the bolt. The rifle would fire a few rounds and clog up again."[27] In an ironic reversal of the traditional Communist military practice, the Marines quickly began arming themselves with captured North Vietnamese weapons, which were plentiful and often brand new. A sergeant of H Company estimated that almost three-quarters of the men of his platoon were firing captured Communist weapons by the close of the second day's fighting.[28]

The North Vietnamese were feeling the pressure as well. Groups of PAVN soldiers were obliged to traverse the relatively open ground when attempting to attack, reinforce, or withdraw from the river hamlets. Once in the open, they were subject to the merciless attack of American aircraft and artillery. Captured PAVN soldiers reported that they found the attack by aircraft and the napalm especially terrifying and that their units had suffered heavy casualties and run short of medical supplies.

Early on May 2, E Company, the last of 2/4's widely scattered companies, finally arrived at Dai Do, having been released from its task of guarding a vital bridge. In a predawn attack on May 2, E broke in to the south of Dai Do, linked up with G, and succeeded in clearing the hamlet. Lieutenant Colonel Weise now called for the other two Marine battalions across the river, 2/3 and 3/3, to reinforce his assault and for other battalions to be lifted in a few miles north of Dai Do to close the trap on the elements of the 320th Division holding the riverside hamlets. The only reinforcement Weise received, however, was a mechanized battalion of the 2d ARVN Regiment. The ARVN were to seize the hamlets of Dong Lai and Thuong Ngia, a little to the west and north of Dai Do across a shallow stream that emptied into the Bo Dieu River. Weise's battalion was to take Dinh To and Thuong Do, also north of Dai Do on the east side of the stream.

Weise placed E and H companies, which had just made an

unsuccessful attack on Dinh To, in reserve. G Company, with only forty men but commanded by the redoubtable Captain Vargas, would spearhead the attack, followed closely by F, which was in the best shape after two days' fighting.

The attack began at 3:00 with G Company in the lead, followed by Weise, his sergeant major, his radio operators, and other members of the small command group. Dinh To was occupied without difficulty, but as the Marines crossed the opened area between Dinh To and Thuong Do the North Vietnamese sprang their trap. Enemy mortars, rockets, and artillery burst on the Marines, while at the same time North Vietnamese troops attacked from across the stream. The ARVN mechanized battalion had successfully taken Dong Lai but, perhaps discouraged by the stiff enemy resistance, had hastily withdrawn without notifying the Marines, who now were subject to heavy attack from their front and their left flank. Other North Vietnamese slipped between G and F companies, which had become pinned down in the rice paddies east of Dinh To and Thuong Duc.

Attacked from three different directions, Weise and G Company formed a tight perimeter and began a fighting retreat, picking up survivors of F Company on the way. Heavy artillery and naval gunfire "boxed in" the Marines with shells landing as near as 25 meters, while helicopter gunships made repeated passes at the attacking North Vietnamese. Colonel Weise was badly wounded, and his sergeant major was killed. Most of the remaining officers and men were also hit. Captain Vargas, wounded for the fifth time in three months, completed the withdrawal, bringing the wounded with him. By nightfall 2/4's four rifle companies had been reduced to about forty men each, and all had lost their original company commanders.

The following day, Colonel Hull moved the two remaining companies of the 1st Battalion, 3d Marines into position to relieve the exhausted remnants of 2/4. All around the corridor between Cam Lo and the seashore, sharp battles erupted as units of the 320th Division, attempting to withdraw or reinforce, collided with allied units placed across their path. From May 4 to May 13, the 320th fought at least one major engagement a day against elements of half a dozen Marine, Army, and ARVN battalions. The 2d Brigade of the

1st Air Cavalry, moved at General Tompkins's request from the Khe Sanh area to an area just north of Dong Ha, joined in the hunt on the May 8, utilizing its fast scouting helicopters and gunships to good advantage.

By mid-May action had fallen off sharply around Dong Ha. The 320th was estimated by U.S. intelligence officers to have lost at least 2,300 men and more than forty prisoners. Yet the division was to return for yet another try only a week later. Early in the morning on May 22, a platoon of I Company, 3d Battalion, 3d Marines ran into a large force of North Vietnamese about 3 miles east of Con Thien, the scene of fierce fighting in 1967. Major General Raymond G. Davis, who had just relieved General Tompkins as commanding general of the 3d Marine Division, quickly deployed four battalions against the North Vietnamese around Con Thien. In almost continuous fighting on May 23, the Marines killed more than two hundred North Vietnamese while suffering about one hundred casualties, including twenty-one dead.

As the fighting died down around Con Thien, other elements of the 320th picked a fight with their old enemies, the 2d Battalion, 4th Marines, now commanded by Lieutenant Colonel Louis A. Rann. Moving quickly to block any repetition of the early week's seige of the Cua Viet, General Davis moved four Marine battalions to bolster 2/4 and to drive north to sweep up the advancing elements of the 320th Division. In a hard-fought and bloody series of company engagements over the ensuing three days, the 320th was pushed back across the DMZ with heavy losses.

Considered as a single engagement, the fighting between April 29 and May 30, 1968, in the Dong Ha corridor constitutes perhaps the single largest battle of the war. The Americans suffered more than 1,500 casualties, including 327 dead, a figure equal to the number of Marines killed at Khe Sanh over the entire seventy-seven days of the so-called siege. The North Vietnamese were estimated to have lost almost 3,600 men killed or captured.

Marine commanders involved in the battle considered it a major victory.[29] Certainly the Marines had fought magnificently in the riverside hamlets against a superior North Vietnamese force in strong, well-prepared positions and supported by their own formidable artillery from across the DMZ. In a narrow sense the Marines had achieved their aim, eliminating the threat to Cua Viet line of communication. Yet the effort had cost an entire Marine battalion, and the enemy forces, far from being destroyed, had pulled out in good order, delivering a devastating counterattack against the Marines as they withdrew. Elsewhere in the confused clashes between Cam Vu and Nhi Ha it was difficult to say who really had the upper hand. On several occasions soldiers or Marines supposedly pursuing an entrapped NVA force walked into costly ambushes.

What the 320th Division really sought to achieve remains a mystery. A common speculation was that their real objective was the large but poorly defended 3d Marine Division base at Dong Ha. The seizure of Dong Ha, even for a few days, would have been a major psychological victory similar to Hue or the attack on the U.S. Embassy during Tet. Yet if the Communists were aiming at Dong Ha, why did they deliberately signal their presence to the allies by shooting at river traffic from Dai Do? This action, plus the elaborate fortifications at Dai Do, suggests that the North Vietnamese fully intended to fight there, perhaps as a diversion for the second round of attacks launched in early May, which the Americans dubbed "Little Tet." The second and almost certainly more costly foray by the 320th Division across the DMZ in late May might have been an act of desperation, or it may have been launched by Communist leaders encouraged by what they saw as their successes in the first round of fighting.

Whoever "won" the confused and bloody "Battle of Dai Do," the fighting left the eastern end of the DMZ line firmly in the hands of the Americans for the first time in more than two years. The North Vietnamese were not to return in force until 1972, and then they would be far more successful.

CHAPTER 8

Lessons of the May Offensive

Around 5:00 A.M. on May 5, 1968, a Marine lookout on a hilltop observation post near Da Nang spotted the telltale orange flash of a rocket exhaust. Snatching up the receiver of his radio telephone, he called, "Rockets, rockets, rockets!" At Army and Marine firing batteries in the circle of bases surrounding Da Nang, crew chiefs yanked the lanyards of their loaded 105mm and 155mm guns already sighted on known enemy launching sites. Even as the guns sent their first shells hurtling into the darkness, spotters on other observation posts were plotting the azimuth of the rocket flashes and feeding the information to the fire support coordination centers to adjust fire.[1] As Communist rockets and American artillery batteries exchanged fire near Da Nang, other Communist mortar shells and rockets were already falling on more than a hundred South Vietnamese cities, towns, and villages and at military bases and compounds from the Mekong Delta to the Demilitarized Zone. The countrywide attacks for which the Dai Do battle had served as a prelude and perhaps a diversion had begun.

"It is my view that Hanoi and the NLF are now engaged in a great gamble," Ambassador Ellsworth Bunker declared at the height of the May attacks. "This is the year of climax. Perhaps most important in terms of their gamble is that they now hope to win because of what they regard as our desperate desire for peace."[2]

Although the number of attacks was impressive, the Communists' May offensive was far less formidable than their earlier efforts at Tet. There were only about a dozen ground assaults, most of them minor, and the Communists mainly confined themselves to shelling their targets from a distance. Within a day or two of the first attacks of mini-Tet, it became clear that the Communists were concentrating their efforts in three areas of South Vietnam: the eastern portion of I Corps, the Central Highlands, and above all Saigon.

It was the ordeal of Saigon during the coming weeks which captured the attention of Washington and the world. The simultaneous and prolonged fighting for Dong Ha and the Communist assaults in the Central Highlands barely registered on the American consciousness, but Saigon was a different matter. The fighting there was to test the limits of American patience and deepen the frustration and anger felt by American leaders in Washington and Saigon at the spectacle of peace talks in Paris and intensified fighting on the very doorstep of the South Vietnamese government.

The South Vietnamese capital had already been the scene of fierce fighting during Tet. Viet Cong attackers had assaulted the large U.S. bases at Long Binh and Bien Hoa and the giant, sprawling Tan Son Nhut air base at the western end of the city. Inside the capital itself, they had attacked the Presidential Palace and the American officers' quarters, had held the radio station for several hours, and had even penetrated the U.S. Embassy compound.

In May, Saigon was still reeling from the impact of those Tet attacks. Since 1964 the former colonial capital from which the French had administered Cochin China had been transformed into a sprawling urban anthill. The population had doubled since 1961 with close to 3 million people crowded into the city and its suburbs. In the crowded slums, two thousand squatters would sometimes occupy less than 4 acres of land. By the 1960s Saigon led the world's large cities in the combined incidents of cholera, smallpox, bubonic plague, and typhoid. Health officials calculated that Saigon's children had a one-in-three chance of reaching the age of four.[3] The city had one hundred thousand motor bikes, twenty-five thousand motor scooters, twenty-five thousand trucks, and more than four hundred thousand bicycles and pedicabs, making a total of more than 2,700 civilian vehicles for every mile of paved road.[4] There were several hundred bars and fifty-six thousand registered prostitutes. Garbage piled up in the streets "until the stacks were half a block long. Late at night, after curfew, when the streets were still, the tops of the stacks would move as one walked by. The feeding rats would be disturbed by the sound of approaching footsteps and scurry about."[5]

An island of relative peace and safety until the Tet assaults, the city was now gripped by fear and uncertainty. "Commercial life is still functioning at no more than half-speed," the veteran correspondent Robert Shaplen reported. "My room boys at the Hotel Continental daily bring me new reports and show me leaflets advising them and their families to get out of town."[6]

Early in April, in an effort to prevent a repetition of the Tet attacks, the U.S. and South Vietnamese high commands launched operation Toan Thang ("Complete Victory"), a major sweep by more than eighty U.S. and South Vietnamese battalions intended to clear the countryside around Saigon of enemy troops.

Whatever success Toan Thang may have had in destroying or displacing Communist regular units, it could not seriously disrupt the extensive Communist underground within the city itself. "Literally thousands of people, including prostitutes and 'cowboy' hoodlums, are part of this intricate organization," Shaplen reported. "Secret caches of weapons are still being established everywhere in the Saigon area and different parts of [the Chinese district of] Cholon are said to be connected by tunnels running from street to street and house to house."[7] There was in fact no way effectively to cordon off Saigon from the surrounding countryside. The city's southern and western districts bordered directly on open rice paddies, swamps, and woodlands, while the entire metropolitan area was surrounded by a network of canals and rivers where the incessant coming and going of barges and sampans were impossible to control.[8]

Late at night on May 4, a taxi filled with 100 pounds of TNT exploded outside the Saigon radio and television station, signaling the start of "mini-Tet" in the capital. During that night and the early morning hours of May 5, Saigon was hit by more than thirty rockets and mortar shells. Over the next three days fierce fighting erupted in sections of Cholon near the Phu To race track, at Tan Son Nhut airfield, and at key bridges connecting downtown Saigon to outlying districts and bases like Bien Hoa and Long Binh.

Tan Son Nhut was attacked on May 5, 6, 7, 8, and 10. On the night of the sixth, a sharp fight developed between South Vietnamese Marines and a Viet Cong battalion dug in at an old French cemetery about a mile from Tan Son Nhut's main gate. In one of the

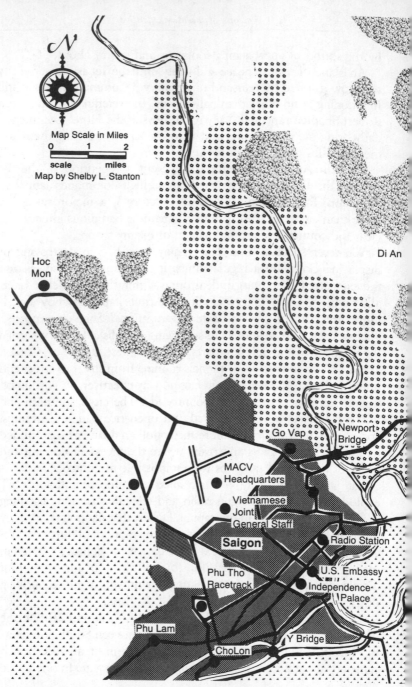

THE SAIGON–BIEN HOA–LONG BINH AREA

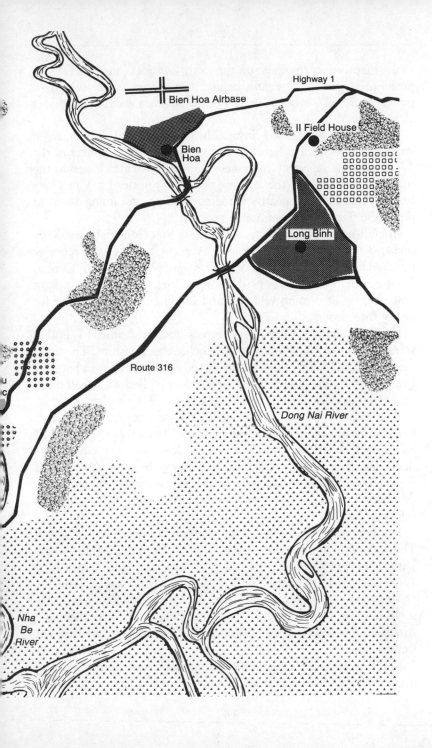

more macabre encounters of the war, Marines and Viet Cong positioned their machine guns behind tombstones and crawled past graves inscribed "Mort Pour la France" as they exchanged fire at close range.[9]

Rocket and mortar fire invariably preceded and accompanied ground attacks on Tan Son Nhut. On May 6, while soldiers of the 377th Combat Support Group were fighting off an attack against the southern perimeter of the air base, an officer noticed a Viet Cong boldly perched on a nearby building holding an aiming stake to direct the fire of the Communist mortars.[10]

In built-up areas of the city, clandestine Viet Cong units suddenly surfaced to spread fear and havoc. A *New York Times* reporter watched as "a small squad of Viet Cong rampaged through Cholon firing at three police stations, hoisting a Viet Cong flag on a light pole, sniping at passing vehicles, and holding a refugee center for nearly three hours."[11]

U.S. and South Vietnamese forces fought house to house, sometimes supported by planes and helicopter gunships. The allies employed armored personnel carriers and recoilless rifles to batter at Communist strong points. The Communists replied with their usual superbly sighted machine guns, mortars, and B-40 rockets.

At a restaurant atop the Caravel Hotel, customers vied for seats near the windows, munching on steak and lobster as they watched helicopters and fighter-bombers swoop low over the city streets delivering their deadly cargoes of bullets, high explosive, and shrapnel. Air strikes, artillery, and helicopter gunships leveled entire city blocks. Thousands of panic-stricken refugees fled toward the center of Saigon.

Frightened by the approach of Communist troops, Mrs. Nguyen Thi Bai rushed into the street hoping to find a three-wheel Lambretta taxi to move her and her household goods to safety. While she searched, two rockets demolished her house, killing her teenage son.[12] No quarter was entirely safe. Rockets and mortar shells fell near the Presidential palace and on Tu Do Street near the American Embassy and the residence of U.S. Ambassador Ellsworth Bunker.

In all, according to U.S. official estimates, about thirty thousand homes were destroyed or heavily damaged by the fighting in Saigon and the immediate vicinity. About eighty-seven thousand people were left homeless in the face of the impending monsoon rains and their normal accompaniment of floods, insects, and disease.[13] The city's eighth district, the site of the highly publicized self-help project called "New Life Construction Project," which provided well-built, low-cost housing and employment opportunities to the city's poor, was completely devastated.[14] "The Viet Cong has no air force of its own," Saigon's Police Chief Nguyen Van Luan remarked bitterly to a U.S. newsman, "so he uses ours."[15] More than five hundred civilians, "a good portion children," were killed, and almost 4,500 wounded, victims of the deadly house-to-house combat.

The worst of the street fighting had ended by mid-May, with the Viet Cong rooted out of most of their strongholds and their attacks on bridges and airfields turned back, but the rain of rockets and mortars continued. In these attacks, the main Communist weapon was a Soviet-made 122mm rocket, a simple and highly versatile weapon with a range of up to 11,000 meters. An experienced Viet Cong or PAVN rocket company could set up a rocket firing site on almost any type of terrain in about an hour and fifteen minutes. The attackers normally remained concealed in their staging area, often a nearby village or a wooded area, until after dark, then proceeded on foot to the launching site, usually less than two hours away. Two men were required to carry the launching tube, two more to carry each rocket, and two others to carry the rocket's tripod mount. To free up the men, or if the unit was short-handed, the mount was often left behind, and the launching tube would be positioned on a wooden cradle or on a mound of dirt at one end of the firing pit.[16]

The 122mm rocket had an excellent sight; when an experienced crew could receive reliable data from a forward observer, it could be fairly accurate.[17] Yet Communist gunners seldom had the opportunity to systematically adjust fire. The telltale bright orange rocket exhaust, which was visible for nearly 300 meters from the launch point, enabled allied air observers to pinpoint the location of the launch sites quickly and direct air strikes or artillery fire onto those positions. An experienced Viet Cong rocket company commander estimated that a maximum of only five rounds could be fired before a rocket battery risked discovery and destruction.[18] Where Communist attackers could get closer to their targets, they also employed their excellent 60mm and 82mm mortars. These were somewhat more accurate than the rockets but had a range of only about 3,000 meters, or 1,500 in the case of the 60mm.

At least 379 rounds of rocket and mortar fire struck Saigon between May 5 and June 8, 1968. Rounds landed in all eight of the city's precincts, damaging a hospital and killing or wounding about 260 civilians and about fifty U.S. and South Vietnamese soldiers.

At the end of May the Communists renewed their ground attacks in the Saigon area in Cholon and near the Phu Tho race track. Communist guerillas, reinforced by the Viet Cong Sixth Battalion, seized positions near Dong Khanh Street in Cholon, where some of Saigon's best-known Chinese restaurants were situated, and exchanged heavy fire with South Vietnamese Rangers and Marines. On June 29, a group of high-ranking South Vietnamese officials took up a position on the porch of Thuong Phuoc High School to view the progress of the fighting. A Vietnamese Ranger officer was radioing instructions to a U.S. helicopter gunship circling overhead. "We are marking our position with a blue smoke grenade," the Ranger told the chopper in English. "Target is a tall concrete building 200 yards north of the smoke." The gunship circled the area three times, then swooped in to fire a rocket directly at the school, followed by a burst of machine gun fire. The rocket struck the school, killing the commander of the Saigon police and the commander of the 5th ARVN Ranger group and wounding many others.[19] Many South Vietnamese attributed the incident to a deliberate attempt on the part of the Americans to kill off men who were loyal to Vice President Nguyen Cao Ky, thus affording political advantages to his rival, President Nguyen Van Thieu.

The Saigon Daily, *Cong Chung,* declared that "it was impossible for a mistake to have occurred" and demanded a joint Vietnamese–American investigation to determine the facts.[20] The official American explanation was that the rocket fired by the helicopter malfunctioned, but many GIs and newsmen speculated that the gunship had deliberately fired at the blue smoke because the pilot had misunderstood the instructions radioed to him by the Vietnamese Ranger in English in the midst of the noise and confusion of battle.[21] On this bitter and divisive note, the ordeal of Saigon reached its end.

The attacks of mini-Tet added greatly to the pain and anguish of the people of Saigon and left the American military frustrated and angry. News reports in the United States emphasized the enormous destruction wrought by American firepower in attempting to repulse the Communist assault. NBC's Howard Tuckner stood with a group of refugees on the banks of the Saigon River as they watched tanks pour "a rain of fire into their homes. What the tanks missed, helicopter gunships found."[22] "These weapons create more problems than they solve," a Vietnamese officer told *Newsweek*. "We cannot go on destroying entire blocks every time a Viet Cong steps into a house."[23] At the beginning of June Defense Secretary Clifford directed General Wheeler to determine "whether there was not some way to deal with the enemy attacks without causing so much destruction to Saigon." Wheeler passed on Clifford's request to Abrams and described "the very real concern here in Administration circles and the bad play we are receiving in the media."[24]

Abrams had already issued an order in the wake of the helicopter incident prohibiting all use of air strikes, artillery, and helicopter gunships in the Saigon area without his personal approval or that of the two general officers commanding operations in the city. He now replied angrily to Wheeler:

> I feel constrained to point out that while I do not have the benefits of TV and newspapers that are available in Washington, I live here. I ride over the city in a helicopter and see parts burning. I walk among refugees overwhelmed with personal disaster that has been their lot; I visit among the dog-tired and grimy soldiers who have survived the fight; I talk with the wounded in hospitals and I visit the bereaved and write letters of condolence. I am fully aware of the extent to which horror, destruction, sacrifice, and pain have risen in the war this year. . . . I need no urging to look into it, investigate it, or explain, or explore other ways. I live with it 24 hours a day.[25]

Abrams called for a graduated renewal of bombing of North Vietnam as "payment in kind" for the enemy's "callow and indiscriminate" attacks on Saigon.[26] Yet those attacks, cruel and persistent as they were, had proved militarily fruitless for the Communists and left many Viet Cong battalions in tatters.

In the eastern DMZ and at Saigon, the Communist efforts had

been spectacular yet unsuccessful. In the Central Highlands, however, the story would be different.

Far from the urban centers and coastal farmlands, just 10 miles from the Laotian border, the Special Forces base of Kham Duc sat in the center of a mile-wide green bowl in the rugged border country of northwestern Quang Tin province, about 90 miles southwest of Da Nang. After the much-publicized fall of Lang Vei in February 1968, Kham Duc, with its satellite camp Ngoc Tavak, 3 miles closer to Laos, was the last remaining Special Forces camp on the Laotian border of I Corps. The two outposts sat astride Route 14, the principal north-south road through the border region. Just across the border, the roads and tracks of the Ho Chi Minh Trail extended their fingers south and east, some already reaching to Route 14 itself. From there the North Vietnamese forces could continue east to the coastal plains south of Da Nang, or southeast to the Central Highland towns of Kontum and Dak To.

Like Khe Sanh and Lang Vei, Kham Duc and Ngoc Tavak did not truly "block" the enemy's infiltration into South Vietnam. The border country was too rugged, the Communist lateral roads too numerous, and the camps' garrisons too small to do that, yet the camps kept the Communists under observation and frequently interdicted their movements. Their presence meant that there would always be some sand and gravel thrown into the smoothly meshed gears of the Laotian infiltration system.

Since early April, U.S. Army engineer units had been at work upgrading Kham Duc's runway and constructing a hard-surface base for a radio navigation facility. As the improvements to the base progressed, so did Communist preparations for attack. By late April U.S. intelligence was reporting large enemy units in the area, including elements of the 2d PAVN Division. A prisoner taken on May 3 reported that his unit was planning to attack Kham Duc.[27] Four months before, when Khe Sanh had been similarly threatened, the Americans had poured in reinforcements and air support. After the besieged base held, General Westmoreland would declare the battle for Khe Sanh "a Dien Bien Phu in reverse." Kham Duc, however, was to prove a Khe Sanh in reverse.

As at Khe Sanh, the Americans began by reinforcing. A battalion task force of the Americal Division, consisting of the 2d Battalion,

1st Infantry, an additional infantry company, and some supporting artillery, began arriving by air at Kham Duc late in the morning of May 10. Lieutenant Colonel Robert B. Nelson, commander of the 2d Battalion, assumed command of the camp.[28]

Nelson's men joined about sixty Army engineers and about four hundred Civilian Irregular Defense Group (CIDG) soldiers with their South Vietnamese and U.S. Special Forces leaders and advisers. The CIDG were mercenaries recruited and organized by the Special Forces from among the various highland non-Vietnamese tribal, ethnic, and religious minorities. Neither as well-armed nor as well-trained as the North Vietnamese and Viet Cong, the CIDG group's primary mission was surveillance, scouting, patrol, and local security. Although their leaders were sometimes bound to the Special Forces and the government by personal ties or political deals, they were primarily freelance soldiers and were hired as a group on a contractual basis. Their behavior in a crisis varied from cowardice and treachery to stalwart heroism depending, on the specific situation and the tribal group involved.[29]

Even as reinforcements were arriving at Kham Duc, Ngoc Tavak was already under attack. Located on the site of an old French fort, Ngoc Tavak was defended by a 113-man CIDG "Mobile Strike Force Company" with eight U.S. Army Special Forces and three Australian Training Team advisers. Thirty-three U.S. Marines of Battery D, 2d Battalion, 13th Marines, manned two 105mm howitzers, which had recently been moved to Ngoc Tavak to interdict nearby North Vietnamese routes and trails. The howitzers, however, were short of ammunition and could be resupplied only by air from Kham Duc.[30]

At 3:00 in the morning of May 10, the Communists opened a heavy artillery and mortar barrage against the base, followed by a ground attack some thirty minutes later. During the height of the action some of the CIDG troops abandoned their positions and fled toward the compound yelling, "Don't shoot, don't shoot, friendly, friendly." Once inside the compound, however, the "friendly" troops unleashed a hail of grenades and tossed satchel charges at the Marine positions, causing heavy casualties. Some of the surviving Americans believed that they could also hear the distinctive sound of carbines being fired at them by the CIDGs. (Only the CIDGs had carbines. All NVA troops carried AK-47s, whose high-velocity rounds sounded quite different from those of a carbine.)[31]

The Special Forces commander, Captain Christopher J. Silva, and the commander of the Marine battery, Lieutenant Adams, were both badly wounded during the night. As the North Vietnamese attackers penetrated the perimeter and advanced into the eastern end of the camp, the remaining defenders pulled back and called for support from Air Force gunships and fighter-bombers on station above the camp. The defenders believed that some of the wounded were still on the western side of the camp, but as the North Vietnamese closed in the Americans had no choice but to call for the gunships to blast the western side with their deadly flechettes and cannon.[32]

At dawn, two Australian warrant officers managed to organize a counterattack by the loyal CIDG troops, which cleared the perimeter and recaptured the howitzer positions abandoned during the night attack. Yet the Marines were almost out of shells for their 105s.

Four CH-46 helicopters carrying reinforcements from Kham Duc arrived later that morning to be greeted by a hail of fire from the North Vietnamese forces surrounding Ngoc Tavak. The first chopper managed to land safely and unload about twenty-five CIDG troops, but as the second CH-46 approached the landing zone its fuel line was severed by automatic weapons fire. The damaged chopper, its fuel streaming from the fuselage, settled safely to the ground and unloaded its troops. The third helicopter landed along side and discharged its reinforcements as the crew of the crippled CH-46 jumped aboard. As the third chopper was about to lift off, however, it was hit by an RPG round and burst into flames.[33] The helicopter landing zone was now unusable, and only small UH-1 medevac helicopters could land at the camp to take off the severely wounded. As one medevac chopper came in to hover off a nearby hill, a large number of panicky CIDG soldiers rushed aboard; others held on to the skids as the helicopter lifted off, then fell to their death several hundred feet below.[34]

Captain White of the Australian training team, the senior surviving officer, was now in command. Requesting permission to evacuate the camp, White was told to "hang on." With the helo pad unserviceable, water and ammunition nearly exhausted, most of the

Americans killed or wounded, and the steadiness of the CIDG a doubtful proposition, White believed he had no choice but to abandon the camp before darkness brought renewed attacks.[35]

Avoiding the obvious routes to Kham Duc, where the enemy was almost certain to be waiting in ambush, White led his men southeast through heavy jungle to a hill about a mile from Ngoc Tavak, where they hacked out a landing zone. CH-46s quickly swooped in to bring the survivors back to Kham Duc.[36]

The loss of Ngoc Tavak had been costly. Of the forty-four Americans and Australians at Ngoc Tavak, fifteen had died, twenty-three had been wounded, and two were missing. Of the hundred-odd CIDG troops, sixty-four were missing or had deserted and thirty were killed or wounded.[37] By the time the dazed and exhausted survivors reached Kham Duc, that camp, too, was under attack.

Scattered mortar fire rained down on the camp on May 11 as the last of the Americal reinforcements and additional supplies were flown into the besieged base. By the end of that day there were a total of some 1,500 U.S. and CIDG soldiers at Kham Duc plus almost three hundred dependents of the CIDG troops, who had been evacuated from their village near the base. Many of the Americal troops had been sent to reinforce the outposts in the hills surrounding the camp's bowl-shaped valley.

Late at night on May 11, troops of the 1st NVA Regiment began their final preparations for an assault on Kham Duc. Around 4:00 A.M. the Communists overran the first of the outposts, Number 7, on a hill northeast of the base. By that time General Westmoreland had already decided to abandon the camp.

Since the arrival of U.S. forces in Vietnam, some of the largest and most stubborn battles had begun as contests for the control of such Special Forces camps as Plei Me, Bu Dop, Bac Po, and Khe Sanh. Kham Duc appeared likely to be the next such battleground, with powerful enemy forces converging on the base, U.S. reinforcements arriving, and support and strike aircraft being summoned to aid the defenders.

Yet as U.S. commanders studied the impending battle, they began to have second thoughts. When Colonel Jonathan Ladd, commander of Special Forces in Vietnam, met with the III MAF commander, General Robert Cushman, he found Cushman unwilling to commit more troops to Kham Duc. Colonel Ladd pointed out that strong reinforcements would be needed to hold the camp against an attack by a reinforced PAVN regiment. General Cushman, however, had few uncommitted troops to spare and was concerned about a new threat posed by the buildup of Communist forces in the An Hoa basin area southeast of Da Nang. A reserve CIDG Mobile Strike Force company had already been dispatched to another threatened Special Forces camp, Thuong Duc, located on the main western approaches to Da Nang. General Cushman also pointed out that Kham Duc would be difficult to resupply and was beyond artillery range of friendly supporting bases.[38]

The following afternoon, Ladd accompanied Deputy MACV Commander Creighton Abrams to a meeting with Cushman and Americal Division commander Major General Samuel Koster. Koster had now assumed operational control of the Kham Duc battle. At the meeting the III MAF staff briefed the generals on the situation at Kham Duc. They recommended that the camp be abandoned or, as they phrased it, "relocated." Colonel Ladd strongly disagreed, pointing out that Kham Duc was the last South Vietnamese outpost in the western mountains of southern I Corps. He also emphasized that it was an important launching site for MACV's super-secret SOG teams, which conducted reconnaissance missions and raids into Laos and other parts of southeast Asia to observe and interdict lines of communication, capture prisoners, assess bomb damage, and collect intelligence. By 1968 the number of such missions had risen to more than three hundred a year.[39]

Colonel Ladd suggested that a Communist victory at Kham Duc might be put to propaganda use, especially in view of the opening of peace talks in Paris. Unmentioned but ever present during the deliberations were the recent vivid memories of the siege of Khe Sanh. Although American generals had always spoken of the battle with confidence and enthusiasm when addressing Washington or the media, they had found it an anxious and wearing experience, superimposed as it was on the widespread and bloody fights of Tet. Now, with the new "mini-Tet" looming, neither Abrams nor Cushman was inclined to begin another protracted battle. "The decision to evacuate was brought on considerably by the Khe Sanh experience," General Westmoreland's operations officer wrote.[40] At the conclusion of the discussions, Abrams instructed Cushman to prepare plans for a withdrawal. Westmoreland approved the decision a few hours later.[41]

By the time word of the decision to evacuate reached Colonel Nelson at Kham Duc, all of the hill outposts were under heavy attack. Squads and platoons of American soldiers reinforcing the CIDG troops on the hills fought desperately, supported by C-47 gunships, which dropped flares to illuminate the area and peppered the attackers with their mini-cannon. As the outposts were overwhelmed, the defenders directed gunship and artillery fire onto their own positions. A few managed to escape into the Kham Duc perimeter, but many died on the hill outposts.

The fate of the outposts added to the sense of terror and foreboding within Kham Duc. The morning began with a fresh disaster as the first evacuation helicopter, an Army CH-47, was hit by heavy ground fire as it landed on the runway. The chopper exploded in flames, and its burning hulk blocked the runway for more than an hour.

As the sun rose over Kham Duc, burning away some of the morning fog, aerial observers beheld a grim sight. The camp was under almost continuous mortar fire, and heavy ground attacks were under way against the northwest perimeter. The burning CH-47 sent clouds of black smoke into the sky. On the nearby hills radio antennas sprouted above the newly established NVA command posts.[42]

Inside the perimeter the men of E Company, 2/1 Infantry, tensely awaited the ground attack they knew would come. The enemy mortar barrage increased in intensity, and a near miss showered one squad with shrapnel. An 82mm mortar round scored a direct hit on a nearby mortar manned by CIDG personnel, killing or wounding all three of the crew. Specialist 4 Todd Regon, leader of the E Company mortar team, quickly rounded up some American infantry men, led them to the pit, and gave them a crash course in mortar firing. Scrambling back to his own mortar position, Regon was astounded to see illumination rounds bursting over the daytime battlefield. An instant later the mortar man recalled that he had failed to show his infantry trainees the difference between high explosive and illumination rounds for the CIDG mortar. Despite his grim situation, Regon managed to chuckle, "This ought to confuse the hell out of the enemy."[43]

As enemy pressure on the base increased, MACV directed all available air support to Kham Duc. Fighters and attack planes from Pleiku, Da Nang, Cam Ranh Bay, and Phu Cat and from bases in Thailand converged on the beleaguered base in answer to Seventh Air Force commander General W. W. Momyer's call for a "Grand Slam" maximum air effort. An airborne command post in a converted C-130 coordinated the air attacks as dozens of aircraft responded to Momyer's call. At times there were as many as twenty fighters over Kham Duc. Two forward air controllers in light planes flew parallel to each other at opposite sides of the Kham Duc runway, each controlling fighter strikes on its side of the field. "There was such an abundance of fighters by late morning that the FACs could choose the fighter they wanted, based on whether it carried napalm, cluster bomb units, five-hundred- or seven-hundred-fifty-pound bombs, or high drag bombs."[44]

"We've got a small Khe Sanh going here," an Air Force officer at Kham Duc wrote in his diary. "I hope we finish it before night comes."[45] The evacuation, when it came, was marked by confusion, panic, and tragedy. Many of the defenders at Kham Duc were not informed of the decision to abandon the camp until many hours after it had been made. The CIDG forces, panicky and on the verge of mutiny or surrender, feared that the Americans would abandon them.

The Air Force's 834th Air Division, whose giant C-123s and C-130s would have to make the actual evacuation, was also dogged by confusion and last-minute changes. At 8:20 A.M. on the twelfth, the 834th was alerted for an all-out effort to evacuate the beleaguered base. Two hours later, fighting at Kham Duc had grown so intense that the Seventh Air Force canceled the evacuation and directed the transports to fly in additional ammunition to Kham Duc. By the time the MACV operations center directed the 834th to resume evacuation operations, around 1:30 P.M., transports were already on their way to Kham Duc loaded with ammunition. Other planes on the ground had to unload their cargoes before proceeding empty to Kham Duc to bring out the defenders. To complicate matters further, Colonel Henderson's command post could not

In the wake of the Tet Offensive in Vietnam and widespread domestic dissent and disillusionment with the war, President Johnson meets with his advisers to hear a briefing by General Creighton Abrams, Westmoreland's deputy. At the end of March 1968, Johnson announced that he would not run for reelection, that bombing of North Vietnam would cease, and that peace talks should begin. (l. to r.: Secretary of Defense Clark Clifford, Secretary of State Dean Rusk, the President, and General Abrams)(Defense Dept.)

Men newly arrived in Vietnam generally remained for two or three days at a transit facility equipped with air-conditioning, hot showers, and ice cream, while they awaited assignment to their units. It was demoralizing for the grunt to leave the relative comfort and safety of these bases for the primitive conditions and danger of life "in the field." (USMC)

Military operations in Vietnam were often carried out in rugged and inhospitable terrain. The temperature could exceed 100 degrees in the dry season, while the monsoon season brought torrential rains and mud. Rats, mosquitos, leeches, and snakes infested the jungles, mountains, swamps, and the flooded rice fields. Elephant grass could grow 15 feet high with razor-sharp edges. (National Archives)

Man-made dangers made matters worse; the North Vietnamese set deadly road mines wrapped in plastic to avoid discovery by mine detectors (above) and built elaborate well-concealed tunnel systems (below). Artillery fire has stripped away the dense foliage that protected this Viet Cong bunker. (USMC & National Archives)

A common complaint of the war was the widely held perception that American soldiers were drawn from the least advantaged sectors of society and that blacks and Hispanics were overrepresented in combat units. Although racial problems were few during the first two years of American involvement in Vietnam, racial tensions increased markedly during 1968. (USMC)

South Vietnamese soldiers, shown here with their American advisor, became the focus of new attention and expectations by Washington following the Tet attacks. In 1968 the U.S. began providing M-16 rifles to the Army of the Republic of Vietnam. In the photo, the American carries an M-16 while Vietnamese infantrymen have older M-1s. (National Archives)

In response to the destruction caused by U.S. firepower, out of fear of Communist terrorism, or both, hundreds of thousands of South Vietnamese had fled their homes by 1968 or were forcibly relocated by the U.S. and Vietnam. (National Archives)

Some South Vietnamese survived the social and economic disruptions of the war by working for the Americans as maids, skilled technicians, bar girls, saloon keepers, drivers, or in other lucrative jobs. Here a Marine gets a haircut from a Vietnamese barber. (National Archives)

Soldiers of the 1st Battalion 501st Infantry board the rugged and versatile UH-1H "Huey" helicopter in the Rockpile area near the DMZ. One of the best known symbols of the War, the Huey could serve as transport, air ambulance, gunship, or airborne command post. (U.S. Army)

A GI cleans his M-16 rifle. Serious malfunctioning of the M-16 led to a Congressional inquiry. (National Archives)

April 1968: During Operation Delaware, a 175mm gun fires into the A Shau Valley. A large cache of North Vietnamese supplies was captured, but the Communists soon returned to the area. (Defense Dept.)

May 1968: Marines wade ashore near the hamlet of Dai Do, scene of one of the bloodiest battles of the May Offensive. The series of engagements in the eastern DMZ area during May, sometimes called "the Battle of Dong Ha" or "Dai Do," were the largest of the war. (National Archives)

Marines question a captured North Vietnamese soldier. During the first six months of 1968, over 29,000 North Vietnamese soldiers made the harrowing journey to the South down the Ho Chi Minh trail to fight the U.S. and A.R.V.N. forces. Many never returned. (USMC)

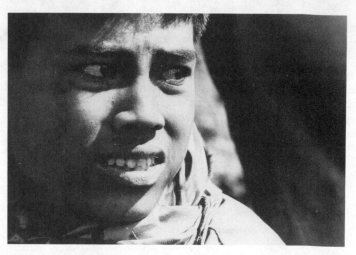

A Viet Cong soldier shows the strain of hours under U.S. air attack. Some Viet Cong soldiers in 1968 were as young as 13. Most were tenacious, skillful fighters. (National Archives)

The King's Cross section of Sydney was popular with GIs on R&R. During 1968, almost 32,000 men per month took the free commercial 707 flights to R&R sites in Bangkok, Kuala Lampur, Honolulu, Manila, Singapore, Sydney, and other Pacific and Asian destinations for a five-day vacation in the midst of their Vietnam tour. (National Archives)

Air power was vital to the U.S. in the Vietnam War, but airfields were always vulnerable to rocket, mortar, or sapper attacks.
(National Archives)

By 1968, Main Force Viet Cong and North Vietnamese army forces in South Vietnam were well supplied with Soviet and Chinese weapons. Here South Vietnamese troops survey an array of captured machine guns, mines, and ammunition. (National Archives)

Following the defeat of the Communist attacks in August and September 1968, General Creighton Abrams advised President Johnson that a further bombing halt in return for substantive peace talks would be militarily safe and "the right thing to do." (U.S. Army)

communicate with many of the supporting aircraft because the America's radios were incompatible with those used by most of the planes. Messages had to be relayed from the Special Forces command post, whose radios could talk to the planes. At times, the heavy volume of incoming message traffic "almost jammed" the two nets.[46] The communications mess made it almost impossible for ground commanders to coordinate transport and helicopter landings with supporting air strikes.

That complete disaster was averted could be credited largely to the deadly skills of the fighter pilots and their controllers and to the iron nerve and brilliant improvisation of the tactical airlift crews. The first C-130 into Kham Duc landed about 10:00 A.M. in a hail of mortar and automatic weapons fire and blew a tire on the debris-strewn runway. Lieutenant Colonel Daryll D. Cole's plane, dispatched before the evacuation order had been reinstituted, had a full load of cargo for Kham Duc, but panic-striken civilians and CIDG troops rushed the plane as soon as it taxied to a stop, preventing either orderly unloading or evacuation. With mortar shells landing ever closer to the aircraft, Cole decided to attempt a takeoff with his overloaded plane crowded with CIDG personnel and much of the remaining cargo. His first attempt was unsuccessful, and the increased attention the plane was attracting from NVA gunners persuaded the passengers to make a hasty exit. In the meantime, the crew had succeeded in cutting away part of the ruined tire. Dodging the runway debris, with fuel streaming from the wing tanks, and under heavy fire, Cole managed to get his striken C-130 airborne and safely back to Cam Ranh Bay.

Cole was followed by a C-123 piloted by Major Ray Shelton, which managed to load about sixty Army engineers and Vietnamese civilians in less than three minutes and to take off under heavy enemy fire.

Throughout the day Army and Marine helicopters continued to dodge the heavy fire to bring in ammunition and evacuate the wounded from Kham Duc. Yet the helicopters could not carry the large numbers of people now desperate to escape from the doomed camp. Only the large transports of the 834th could do that, and since 11:00 A.M. there had been no planes. Then, around 3:00 P.M., a C-130 piloted by Major Bernard L. Butcher landed at Kham Duc.

CIDG troops, women, and children swarmed aboard the plane. The CIDG soldiers and their families were convinced that the Americans intended to leave them behind and were in a state of utter panic. Two hours earlier, Special Forces Sergeant Richard Campbell had watched in horror and disbelief as a woman and her small child who had fallen while climbing the rear ramp of a CH-46 helicopter were trampled by fear-maddened CIDG soldiers in a rush to board the chopper.[47] Now, nearly two hundred women and children crowded aboard Butcher's bullet-riddled C-130.

Because he had received heavy fire from the southwest corner of the field on landing, Butcher elected to take off to the northeast. A few minutes before Butcher's takeoff, fighters had raked the NVA machine guns on the low ridges north of the runway with loads of cluster bomb units. The deadly CBUs killed the gun crews but failed to silence the guns, which were soon manned by replacements from nearby enemy positions.[48] Butcher's plane, struck by heavy machine gun fire, crashed and exploded in an orange ball of flame less than a mile from the runway. There were no survivors.[49]

Watching Butcher's crash, Lieutenant Colonel William Boyd, Jr., pilot of the next C-130 into the camp, decided on a steep, side-slipping descent onto the field. Just as Boyd's plane was about to touch down a shell exploded 100 feet ahead on the runway. Pushing his throttle forward, Boyd climbed steeply into the air for a second attempt. Landing successfully on his next try, Boyd loaded about one hundred CIDG and Americal soldiers and took off under heavy fire for Cam Ranh Bay.

The fourth C-130, commanded by Lieutenant Colonel John Delmore, had been forced to make a second pass to avoid Boyd's takeoff, and this time the Communist gunners were ready. Their .50 caliber bullets ripped 6-inch holes in the sides of the fuselage as the giant C-130, its hydraulic system shot away, bounced along the runway, glanced off the wreckage of the CH-46 destroyed that morning, and plowed into a dirt mound on the side of the runway. Miraculously the entire crew escaped. A few minutes later Delmore's crippled plane burst into flames.

The remaining C-130 pilots orbiting above Kham Duc awaiting their turn to land had seen Butcher's plane crash and burn, Delmore's wrecked on landing, and two helicopters hit by ground fire and destroyed. The runway was littered with debris and burning wreckage.

Undeterred, Lieutenant Colonel Franklin Montgomery brought his C-130 into Kham Duc, followed by two more C-130s, which, together, brought out more than four hundred people, just as the Seventh Air Force was issuing orders to cancel further C-130 landings because of the high losses. A final daring flight by Lieutenant Colonel Joe M. Jackson in a C-123 brought out the last Air Force ground control personnel. The Special Forces command group, which had insisted on remaining to the last so as to exercise some control over the terrified and near-mutinous CIDG forces, escaped by helicopter shortly afterward.

Before 5:00 P.M. it was over. Communist troops advanced cautiously into Kham Duc and along the runway perimeter as explosions from the burning aircraft and ammunition dumps lit up the twilight sky. The following morning sixty B-52 bombers, the entire force available in Vietnam, rained 12,000 tons of bombs on the camp, and MACV proclaimed that the enemy had suffered severely. Yet nothing could disguise the fact that Kham Duc had been an American defeat—a Khe Sanh in reverse. American commanders had vacillated between reinforcing the camp and evacuating it, finally opting for evacuation under the worst possible circumstances. Command, control, and communications had been confused and often ineffective. General Abrams termed the operation "a minor disaster."[50] "This was an ugly one and I expect some repercussions," the chief of Westmoreland's operations center wrote.[51]

Yet the repercussions were few. Abrams angrily ordered I Corps commanders to review their command, control, communications, and planning in order "that when your command is confronted with a similar imminent problem, appropriate action would be taken so that we would not lose another camp."[52] The general's expression of unhappiness, however, was confined to Top Secret messages. No heads rolled, no investigations were launched. Saigon and Washington remained unruffled, barely concerned. The news media, preoccupied with the Communist attacks in Saigon and the peace negotiations in Paris, paid little attention. In a war in which the distinction between success and failure, victory and defeat, had long been blurred and confused, even an unequivocal debacle like Kham Duc could be obfuscated, obscured, and ignored.

One reason General Cushman could ill spare troops to reinforce Kham Duc was that he was expecting an attack on Da Nang similar to those the Communists had already launched against Saigon. By 1968 the entire 1st Marine Division existed almost solely for the defense of Da Nang. That city, with its giant airfield, port facilities, and complex array of military headquarters and logistical support facilities, had become the nerve center of the war in the north.

The 1st Marine Division's regiments were deployed in a fanlike fashion to the southwest, south, and southeast of the city, facing at least five North Vietnamese and Viet Cong regiments, some thirty-thousand men, concealed among the heavily populated lowland rice country or in the scrub and elephant grass of the river valleys of the Thu Bon and An Hoa or the jungle-covered Que Son mountains.

Over the past three years the Marines and the Army Americal Division to the south had launched numerous forays against these base areas. Always difficult, often harrowing and bloody, the operations were invariably declared "successful." Yet the Communist threat remained.

Now Cushman prepared to launch another spoiling attack, code-named ALLEN BROOK. For this operation the Marines deployed elements of the 5th, 7th, and 27th Marines in the broad valley of the Thu Bon River, which flowed into the sea near Hoi An, about 20 miles south of Da Nang. The objective was a suspected Communist base complex located on Go Noi Island, an island formed by the Thu Bon River in Dien Ban district near Route 1, the main north-south highway of South Vietnam.

In Dien Ban district the coastal rice paddies gave way to flat, open fields covered by grass and scrub, broken by the occasional thick stand of trees. The flat, sandy soil was used for growing crops of corn, peanuts, and tobacco, and the civilian population was relatively sparse and scattered. In mid-May, when two battalions of the 7th and 27th Marines began Operation ALLEN BROOK, the average daily temperature in Dien Ban district hovered above 110 degrees each day.

I Company, 3d Battalion, 27th Marines, was the first to find the enemy. Landed by helicopter onto a grassy knoll, the company fanned out by platoons into the valley. Moving toward a small hamlet with his squad, Lance Corporal Lewis Carpenter, the point fire team leader, noticed a woman gesturing and shouting vigorously to some unseen persons in the hamlet. Yelling for the squad to follow, Carpenter's fire team raced to the hamlet, surprising a platoon of North Vietnamese soldiers at their meal. As Carpenter's men opened fire, the Communists fled in all directions while the women screamed and vainly attempted to retrieve the NVA rifles from their hiding places in the village and throw them to the fleeing soldiers. In a few moments the one-sided fight was over. More than a dozen North Vietnamese bodies lay scattered through the hamlet, and the women, later identified as members of a medical unit, had been taken prisoner.[53]

I Company pushed on through a dry river bed and on toward a tree line on the far bank. About midway across the river bed the company was hit by a hail of rifle and machine gun fire from the tree line. Only the point squad of the lead platoon managed to reach the far side of the dry river before the entire company became pinned down by heavy fire. Enemy snipers in the tree line began picking off the Marines as they vainly sought cover in the river bed. A steady rain of grenades issued from the tree line as well.

Unable to advance or withdraw, I Company called for air strikes. For almost an hour fighters bombed and strafed enemy positions in the wood. Then the company attempted a second assault but was again met by heavy fire.[54] Almost half the company was killed or wounded in this second attack. The Marines could make little headway against the North Vietnamese defenders fighting from bunkers whose ordinarily strong log-and-concrete construction had been reinforced by railroad ties and iron rails from a nearby abandoned rail line.[55] I Company's survivors remained pinned down in the river bed for more than eight hours tormented by the heat and running low on water.

Two more companies of the 3d Battalion, 27th Marines, were lifted in by helicopter to link up with and relieve the pressure on I Company. As the CH-46 transports, their motors still roaring, lowered their rear ramps to debark the men of K Company, 3/27,

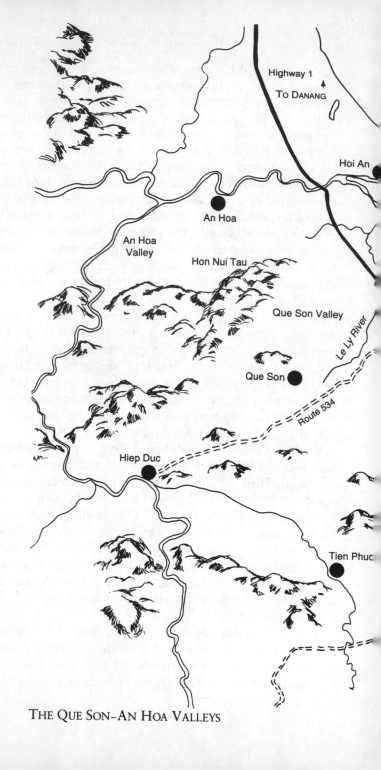

THE QUE SON–AN HOA VALLEYS

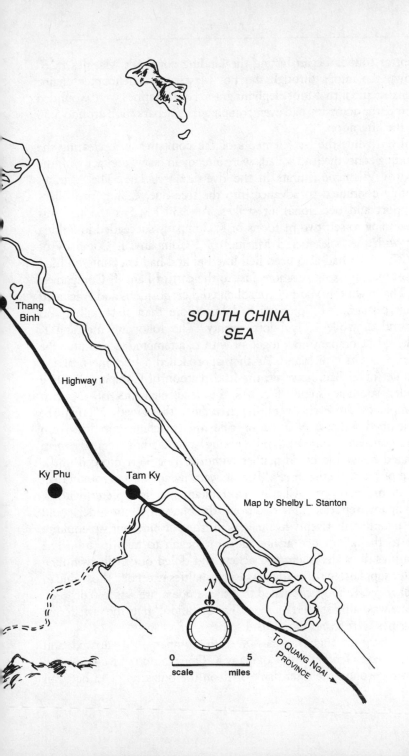

SOUTH CHINA
SEA

Thang
Binh

Highway 1

Ky Phu   Tam Ky

Map by Shelby L. Stanton

N

0   5
scale   miles

TO QUANG NGAI
PROVINCE

mortar rounds began hitting the landing zone. K's Marines raced down the ramps through the hot blast of the helicopter engine exhaust and into 7-foot elephant grass. Four Marines were wounded before the company had even completed its debarkation around 5:30 in the afternoon.

Even while the last elements of the company were clearing the landing zone, the lead squads were already in heavy contact with the North Vietnamese units in the riverside tree line. The Marines grimly continued to advance into the tree line, calling in artillery support and occasional air strikes. At 7:30 P.M., as the sun was beginning to set, two platoons of K Company succeeded in linking up with the beleaguered Marines of I Company. L Company of 3/27, which had also been heli-lifted in and had encountered little resistance, took up positions just to the east of I and K Companies.

That night the Marines consolidated their positions and evacuated their casualties. I Company had lost more than sixty killed and wounded, while K had lost twenty. The following morning K relieved I Company and, together with L, attempted to continue the sweep of Go Noi Island. As they approached a tree line near the hamlet of Li Bac, however, the lead platoon of Company K came under sporadic sniper fire. As the lead elements of the two companies drew closer to the tree line, the North Vietnamese unleashed a heavy volume of rifle and machine gun fire from well-concealed bunkers and fighting holes. Entire squads were pinned down and could neither withdraw nor be reinforced in the face of the withering fire.[56] "People were dying and we couldn't get to them," Corporal Charles D. Hukaby, an interpreter with K Company, reported. "At one point the platoon commander could see people only twenty-five meters in front of him, but we couldn't get to them."[57] Once again, the heat began to take its toll. The Marines discarded their flak jackets and doled out their dwindling water supplies. In some squads heat casualties exceeded those due to enemy fire. Rumors circulated that the temperature was 130 degrees. That was almost certainly an exaggeration, but the sweltering Marines were in no mood to dispute it.

Midway through the day a fresh company, M, arrived and attempted to link up with Company K. One platoon of M Company, moving around the right flank of K on the outskirts of Li Bac, ran into a box-shaped ambush and suffered heavy casualties. The platoon commander and all three squad leaders were killed or wounded. A handful of survivors, of whom only three were uninjured, managed to fight their way to the shelter of a large hut, which proved to be a North Vietnamese command post. Before the startled North Vietnamese could react, the Marines hurled grenades into the hut and barricaded themselves inside. Seeing the brief struggle, Hospitalman Third Class James Walters, the platoon medic, sprinted into the hut carrying a wounded Marine, then left again to drag two more wounded into the hut, where the Marines were now surrounded on all sides by the Communists. Observing this action, Captain B. K. Thomas, the company commander, directed helicopter gunships onto the area surrounding the trapped Marines. With the fire of the gunships falling within 10 feet of the hut, the Marines were able to make a hasty withdrawal, the walking wounded helping to carry the more seriously injured.[58] It was only after dark that the embattled Marines were able to disengage fully and recover all their wounded.[59] In two days of fighting, the four companies of 3/27 had lost 179 men killed or wounded.

The battles of May 17 and 18 set the pattern for the rest of ALLEN BROOK, which continued intermittently over the next two weeks as additional companies and battalions were fed into the hot, airless plain of the Thu Bon. "In all cases," a battalion reported, "contact with the enemy followed the same general pattern. Friendly forces would approach a tree line from across an open field. The lead elements of the friendly forces would enter the tree line and would be taken under fire and pinned down. The follow up elements would be taken under fire as they attempted to move forward across the open ground to assist those units already in contact. The ranges would always be under one hundred fifty meters and, in many cases, less than fifty meters."[60] It was the perfect demonstration of the North Vietnamese fighting doctrine, which aimed to surprise and pin down the Americans at ranges so close that there could be no help from the deadly U.S. artillery and aircraft.

The NVA tactics were never wholly successful. Eventually the Marines would be able to disengage, and the deadly rain of fire from the sky would begin. After one air strike against a group of NVA bunkers one Marine recalled that he had "never in my life seen an area more flattened out and devastated. The bunkers were burning on the inside and collapsing."[61] After the first days of the operation the Marines were joined by tanks, whose armor and 90mm guns proved more of a match for the bunkers. Yet the fighting in the river basins south and west of Da Nang remained among the most harrowing and sanguinary combat in Vietnam. Here, even more than in the mountains on the Laotian border or at Dai Do, the Americans were fighting the war on the enemy's terms. The United States held the initiative and could invade any Communist outpost or base area. Yet the tactical advantages in these forays usually rested with the Communists, who would allow the Americans to spend lives against their elaborately prepared defenses in terrain that the Communists knew intimately and the Americans very imperfectly.

American generals argued that these forays kept the enemy off balance and disrupted his supply system and bases. ALLEN BROOK was also credited with having preempted an enemy offensive against Da Nang. Yet, given the lack of coordination, staying power, and imagination the Communists had repeatedly demonstrated in their attacks on towns and cities, compared with their formidable fighting qualities on the defensive, one may wonder whether such preemptive operations were worth the cost. Worth it or no, ALLEN BROOK set the pattern of warfare in the river basins and coastal lowlands of Quang Nam, which was to continue almost unabated for two more years.

On the face of it, the general trend of the May fighting appeared to go in the Americans' favor. The North Vietnamese had failed, at heavy cost, to gain a foothold in Saigon or in the border provinces of the north. Allied spoiling attacks such as ALLEN BROOK had eliminated any direct threat to Da Nang. Only at the remote Special Forces camp of Kham Duc had the Communists scored a success. Yet the battles of "Little Tet" gave Americans small cause for celebration. Saigon had been devastated, and allied casualties were near an all-time high.

If the generally unsuccessful attacks of "mini-Tet" demonstrated that the Communists had learned little from their defeats at Tet, the near-record U.S. casualties suggested that the Americans had not learned much either. Infantry units were still sent against superbly concealed and protected Communist bunker complexes without benefit of adequate reconnaissance and sometimes without appropriate supporting arms. Units were often fed into battles piecemeal without any clear idea of enemy strength and dispositions. Despite overwhelming allied numerical superiority on paper, Westmoreland and his commanders frequently found their available combat forces stretched thin, as at Kham Duc and Dai Do, where adequate numbers were simply not available to meet the threat in a timely manner. Nor, despite U.S. technological superiority, were American GIs particularly well-equipped for the battles in which they were engaged. U.S. infantry lacked a weapon like the Communist B-40 rocket launcher, which was able to penetrate bunkers, while the superior reliability of the AK-47 rifle to the M-16 was already the subject of a considerable body of GI folklore. U.S. artillery was often unable to locate and silence Communist guns across the DMZ or concealed in Laos. A Marine general later observed, "It appeared unbelievable that the mighty United States, with all its technical expertise and awesome military power, was unable to at least neutralize the artillery fire from a third-rate little nation. Nevertheless the incoming artillery shells continued to arrive. U.S. target-locating equipment had not been improved since World War II. In fact, a strong case can be made that the capability had deteriorated."[62]

Air attacks could be devastating against bunker complexes, but they had to be delivered with great skill and precision and with the right mix of weapons. In costly battles in the hills around Khe Sanh during the spring of 1967, the Marines had discovered that only 750-pound to 2,000-pound bombs with delayed fuses could smash the strongest bunkers.[63] Yet weather often made attacks with such weapons hazardous or impossible, even when ground or air commanders had the insight to ask for them.

Both sides had repeated many of their mistakes of February and March in the bloody battles of May, and neither side appeared much closer to victory. Yet now the Communists were beginning to run short of men and the Americans to run short of time. A slow and painful period of learning and adjustment for both sides was about to begin.

CHAPTER 9

"The People in the Middle" *

Despite the fierce battles for the cities and towns at Tet, despite the rain of rockets against Saigon and Da Nang, almost all influential Americans in Washington and Saigon believed, or professed to believe, that the war would be won or lost not in the cities and towns but in the 2,100-odd villages, which still contained more than 60 percent of South Vietnam's population and which, during 1968, were the scene of struggles as protracted and bitter as any in the cities.

The village was the basic political and economic unit of the state. A network of hamlets inhabited by closely linked families, it was traditionally the most independent and vital element in Vietnamese political life. Under the emperors the village councils, self-perpetuating bodies of the wealthiest and most prominent village residents, conducted almost all day-to-day functions of government except for national defense and certain large-scale public works projects. "The law of the Emperor is less than the custom of the village" was a well-known Vietnamese maxim.[1] Within the villages, with their wood and thatched houses surrounded by paddy fields, narrow shaded paths, and small pagoda-like shrines, life appeared timeless, primitive, and unchanging.

Yet many villages in the provinces south and west of Saigon were

---

* "Because we had to appease the allied forces by day and were terrorized by Viet Cong at night, we slept as little as you did. We obeyed both sides and wound up pleasing no one. We were people in the middle. We were what the war was all about." Le Ly Hayslip, *When Heaven and Earth Changed Places*, p. xiv.

not even as old as Boston or New York, and all, whether in the narrow coastal plains near Da Nang or the rich and fertile rice lands of the Mekong Delta, had been profoundly affected by the impact of colonialism, war, and Western trade.

With French rule had come new links to a world economy. The French introduced a western-style money system, individual taxation, private property, and commercialized agriculture. Soon a new class of rich landlords grew up in the south, along with a much larger class of poor or landless agricultural workers and tenant farmers. During the war against the French the Viet Minh had uprooted the last vestiges of village government by notables and French-appointed functionaries. They killed or drove away landlords and their agents, and redistributed their holdings to local farmers and agricultural laborers.[2] The Diem era had brought further upheavals, the influx of refugees and officials from the North, the return of the landowners and notables to some areas, and a new insurgency, which was well under way by the end of the 1950s.[3]

Those Americans who recognized that village life and traditions had been changed by colonialism, war, and revolution almost always assumed that the rural Vietnamese desired nothing more than to "return" to their "traditional" way of life. They had suffered from bad or ineffective government and the inability of Saigon's regime to "protect" them and yearned for a return to the harmony of the old order.[4] General Samuel T. Williams, head of the U.S. Military Assistance Advisory Group in Vietnam from 1955 to 1960, asserted that "the Vietnamese farmer . . . if secure from threat would live as he has for thousands of years in the past, content with his lot on his rice paddy."[5] Similarly, the 1971 "Handbook" for U.S. advisers in Vietnam emphasized that a key ingredient in U.S. pacification policy was "the revival of strong village communities."[6] William Colby, Westmoreland's deputy for development and security programs and a veteran CIA official in Vietnam, believed that the hopes of rural Vietnamese "were largely limited to the family and the village community." Colby was confident that they "did not want to live under communist direction if they had an alternative."[7]

Yet the war in the villages was not a contest between a government attempting to restore the traditional order of the good old days and rebels attempting to overthrow it, but rather a war between two competing social systems. The NLF's appeal was focused not so much on obtaining more good things (medicine, land, education) for the peasants as on changing the whole system of distributing wealth, power, and status in the rural community. The Saigon government, backed by generous American economic and technical assistance, was in a far better position than the insurgents to offer technology, food, fertilizer, improved public health, and education, but this "large-scale relief effort," as one American expert called it, was unlikely to win the hearts and minds of the people.[8] "Those unsympathetic to the government were glad to have dispensaries, roads, loans, and farmer's associations," the most perceptive American student of the village war observed, "but they went right ahead and cooperated with the revolutionary movement for the same groups were still going to be at the bottom no matter how much assistance the government provided."[9]

The rural Vietnamese knew that the traditional village government had been an instrument of the landlords and the wealthy—when it had not been simply a vehicle for graft and extortion. Far from yearning for the good old days, farmers who had been exposed to the Viet Cong's programs and organizing efforts or who lived under NLF control understood that the NLF stood for a drastic reordering of the system of power, prestige, and wealth. For the old system based on family, wealth, custom, and corruption, the NLF substituted one based on xenophobia, loyalty, and individual competence and performance. Le Ly Hayslip observed that while many Americans saw the war as "democracy against Communism," "for us, that was not our fight at all. We knew little of democracy and even less about Communism. For most of us it was a fight for independence, like the American revolution." As well as a "battle between city people and country people—the rich against the poor–a war fought between those who wanted to change Vietnam and those who wanted to leave it as it had been for a thousand years."[10]

How far the NLF's revolution would go, that its ultimate aim was a new system of oppression in the form of collectivization and the search for ideological purity, was a fact carefully concealed by the inner circle of Communist operatives who directed the movement. The former deputy secretary of the party's Central Committee for the Western Provinces of South Vietnam observed that communists in the south "never propagandized communism. . . . Instead they say: the peasants are the main force of the revolution. . . ."

> If the party were to say: in the future you will be a laborer, your land will be collectivized, you will no longer own any farm animals or buildings, but will become a tenant farmer for the party or the socialist state—if the party were to say that, the peasants would not heed them. Thus the peasants never think of the distant future of communism. Indeed, party cadres are instructed never to mention these things, because according to the teaching of Lenin, the peasant is the greatest bourgeois of all: he thinks only of himself. Say one word about collectivism, and he already is against it.[11]

The Diem regime's attempts to suppress Communist insurgency often simply played into the hands of the insurgents. The more suspects rounded up by the police and security forces, the more hamlets searched and vandalized by government troops, the more potential recruits there were for the new Communist insurgency called the Viet Cong. As the insurgency worsened, the United States began to furnish greater quantities of arms and equipment to the Saigon government. Many of these rifles, BARs, mortars, machine guns, shotguns, and grenades soon fell into the hands of the Viet Cong when they were abandoned in panic by the ill-trained and ineffective Saigon security forces or soldiers, were stolen, or were sold outright on the black market. As early as May 1960, General Williams complained that the Communists were actually "arming themselves from captured weapons."[12]

From 1962, when the seriousness of the situation in the countryside could no longer be denied, until 1968, when the Tet Offensive brought the war to the cities, there had been at least six major campaigns to assert government control in the countryside, eliminate the network of Communist political and paramilitary organizations, and win the loyalty of the rural population to the Saigon regime. These campaigns and their programs were generally referred to by the Americans as "pacification" or "counterinsurgency."

In the early 1960s many of the more verbose and bellicose members of the Kennedy Administration, along with similarly inclined academics and journalists, had proclaimed that the problem of Communist-inspired insurrections in the developing nations constituted the great challenge for American foreign and military policy in the coming decade. President Kennedy agreed. "This is another type of war," he told cadets at West Point in 1962, "war by guerrillas, subversives, assassins, war by ambush instead of combat, by infiltration instead of aggression, seeking victory by eroding and exhausting the enemy instead of engaging him. . . . It requires, in those situations where we must counter it, . . . a whole new kind of strategy, a wholly different kind of force."[13] The word spread quickly. Government agencies from the Agriculture Department to the Central Intelligence Agency, from the Air Force to the State Department professed to be studying and preparing for the great task of counterinsurgency.[14]

Counterinsurgency, the experts explained, was far more difficult and complex than conventional warfare. The objective was not an enemy fortress or a hilltop or a town or a bridge or even the enemy army. The object of counterinsurgent warfare was control of the population, whose poverty, deprivation, or exploitation was being manipulated by wily Communist organizers and propagandists. What was required was an imaginative combination of unconventional warfare techniques, political reforms, and economic and social programs, which would enable the threatened government to win the struggle, "fought not merely with weapons, but in the minds of men who lived in villages and in the hills."[15]

Though American generals continued to proclaim that the war in Vietnam was a struggle against insurgency, a war for the people, they spent most of their time and energy attempting to transform it into the more comfortable and familiar war they had known in World War II and Korea.[16] Whenever possible "the people," the rural civilians of Vietnam, were brushed aside, abandoned, evacuated, imprisoned, or ignored so that U.S. combat forces could strike at large units of the main force Viet Cong and the North Vietnamese Army. During 1965–68 about 47 percent of all U.S. expenditures on the war in Vietnam went to air operations, hardly the subtle instrument of special warfare the experts had in mind. Only about 4 percent went for civilian programs, and only 2.5 percent for police and territorial security forces.[17]

Expressing the views of many military and civilian leaders, Under Secretary of State Nicholas Katzenbach observed in June 1967 that the war of attrition against the Viet Cong main force units and the North Vietnamese Army was "the key," and that the United States should "recognize that pacification is not the ultimate answer—we have neither the time nor the manpower."[18]

There was one dissenting voice. The Marines, while as enamored of firepower and mobility as the rest of the American military establishment, doubted that those factors alone could win the war. Experience in other civil wars in Nicaragua, Haiti, and the Dominican Republic had taught the Marines the lesson that the people, however backward and passive they might appear, could not be ignored.

In their base areas around Chu Lai, near the border of Quang Ngai and Quang Tin provinces, around Da Nang and Hue; and later farther north toward the DMZ, the Marines established Combined Action Platoons, rifle squads stationed for indefinite periods in villages, where they worked as part of a team composed of the Marine squad and a Popular Forces Platoon. The Combined Action Platoon's mission was to identify and root out the Viet Cong shadow government within the village, win the support of the people, protect them from Viet Cong coercion, train and encourage the Popular Forces, collect local intelligence, and participate in various local self-help projects referred to as "civic action."

In 1968 the Marines assigned to a Combined Action squad of thirteen infantrymen and one Navy corpsman were all volunteers. After completing a course about two weeks in length on basic infantry skills as well as Vietnamese customs, history, and language, the Marines were assigned to a Combined Action Platoon in which they remained for the rest of their tour.[19] By 1968 the qualifications for Combined Action volunteers had been firmly established. Volunteers were expected to be "mature and responsible individuals" with a clean record, at least two months' experience in Vietnam, and six or more months remaining on their current Vietnam tour. They could not have earned more than one purple heart, since the chance of receiving another while in the Combined Action program was very high. Three purple hearts meant an automatic return to United States.[20]

The thirteen-man squad, usually commanded by a sergeant in his early twenties, operated with a degree of autonomy and isolation unusual in Vietnam, or indeed in any military organization. Except for brief visits by the Combined Action company commander and a resupply truck or helicopter, the Combined Action Platoon was alone; absorbed within the daily routine of village life. "Women sweep and cook, children play, the farmers work the fields or sit and talk, the sun beats down, the bugs bite."[21]

Quartered in a small barbed wire and sandbag compound in or near a hamlet, the Marines spent their days sleeping, attending to personal chores, maintaining their weapons and equipment, and occasionally conducting civic action programs or rudimentary training for the Popular Force soldiers. As evening fell, the pace of activity quickened as the Popular Force Platoon and the Marines departed for night ambush patrols and listening posts.

The Marine squad leader was the first and final authority, with no hierarchy of command behind him, "nowhere to go to pass the buck and nowhere to hide (such as an NCO club) if things go wrong."[22] He was at once tactician, planner, authority figure, and battlefield leader. The relationship between the Marine squad and the PF platoon ranged from one of close alliance to one of grudging tolerance, depending on the particular personalities, politics, social makeup, and war experience of each village. Neither the Vietnamese platoon commander nor the American squad leader could exercise any formal authority over the forces of the other. The Marines normally took the lead in planning patrols and ambushes, in which the PFs might or might not agree to participate.

The Popular Forces were a part-time militia composed primarily of poor farmers, laborers, and fishermen, who often joined to escape the draft, to earn extra money, or because of real or fancied grievances against the Viet Cong. They were poorly armed and usually lacked all but the most rudimentary training.[23] The Viet Cong forces with whom they were nominally at war were frequently composed of their neighbors, friends, or relatives.

In these circumstances it was not surprising that many PF platoons had long since reached some sort of informal accommodation with the Viet Cong in their villages. "Between August and December [1967] I achieved the distinction of leading more than 60 night ambush patrols and at least as many day patrols without ever once finding the enemy," recalled one Combined Action veteran. "Only one night ambush was ever triggered. . . . our unsuspecting victims turned out to be a group of wild VC pigs. They squealed in terror, but even they got away unhurt."[24] Almost half of the Combined Action Platoons surveyed in a 1968 DOD-sponsored study reported little or no contact with the enemy.[25] At the other extreme, some CAPs reported up to twenty enemy contacts per month.

In villages whose people had long-standing feuds or grievances against the Communists, such as those inhabited by Catholics or refugees from North Vietnam, the Marines sometimes found the Popular Forces willing partners. In a few such cases, Popular Forces would themselves plan and initiate operations, precisely targeting the known hideouts and operating areas of Viet Cong members.[26]

The wide-scale suffering and destruction inflicted by the Communist attacks at Tet served to alienate some villagers who had endeavored to remain neutral in the war in the countryside. In a village near Cam Lo, the PF platoon had for weeks refused to cross the Cam Lo River to patrol with the Marines in areas known to be frequented by the Viet Cong, much to the disgust and frustration of the Americans. A few weeks before Tet, the Popular Forces were suddenly ambushed by the Viet Cong and suffered three casualties. "After we evacuated their casualties," a Marine recalled, "they shocked us with the announcement that they were going back out to settle the score with the VC. What is more, they asked us to come along."[27]

When the Communists and PFs chose to contend actively for control of a village, whether out of a desire for revenge, party policy, accident, or local hatreds, the resulting struggle could sometimes take on the intimacy, endurance, and lethality of a blood feud. Igor Bobrowsky, who served with a Combined Action Platoon in Quang Tri province in 1968, recalls that "the local VC were operating like 1930s gangsters—a little kidnapping here, a little extortion there, blowing someone's brains out once in a while. It was like turf warfare between gangs in the villages."[28]

In Binh Nghia village in Quang Ngia province, a Combined Action Platoon conducted a two-year struggle for control against two local Viet Cong companies supported by a local force battalion, a struggle made famous in Francis J. West's *The Village*. Established in an abandoned villa, which the Marines renamed Fort Page after their first casualty, the Marines and PFs waged a continuous night war of ambushes and patrols against the Viet Cong. The Communists struck back with ambushes of their own and attacks on Fort Page. During July and August 1966 the Combined Action Unit engaged in more than seventy firefights, averaging eleven contacts a week.[29]

On a night in September 1966, eighty Viet Cong, reinforced by a North Vietnamese company, passed undetected through a nearby hamlet and attacked Fort Page from two directions. In the ensuing battle, all six Marines in the fort were killed or wounded, but the surviving PFs repulsed the attack "on their own, throwing rocks and using fists and rifle butts when they ran out of ammunition."[30] The six remaining Marines, who had been out on patrol when the fort was attacked, refused all offers of relief or reinforcement. Two nights later the Viet Cong, emboldened by their success, openly entered the marketplace of the main hamlet and were caught in a murderous ambush by the Marines and PFs.[31]

In other villages, the struggle could be equally bitter and deadly. In the village of Cho Tui Loan, the Viet Cong put a price on the head of the PF platoon leader. The platoon leader's wife "carried a grenade taped to her side with orders to pull the pin if captured. Every so often he would change the grenade to make sure she had one that worked."[32]

It was a common practice for the Communists to put a price on the head of the Marine squad leader, his Vietnamese counterpart, and sometimes individual members of the Combined Action Platoon.[33] In the small, closed world of the village, the existence of such awards and the precise sums offered were soon common knowledge. Among the Marines it became a sign of success and a token of prestige to have a price on one's head, so much so that men without such distinction felt slighted, while those who had one worried that their price might be lower than those of others.

As might be expected, the casualty rate for CAP Marines was high, higher even than in most line units. Marines in the Combined Action program constituted only 1.5 percent of all Marines in

Vietnam but accounted for 3.2 percent of the casualties.[34] In 1968, a CAP Marine had a 75–80 percent chance of being wounded at least once and an 18 percent chance of being killed in action.[35]

During the Tet offensive, the Combined Action Platoons became a common target for Communist attacks. Altogether the Combined Action Platoons sustained more than two hundred major attacks by Viet Cong and NVA forces, ranging in size from 150 to 700 men.[36] In some hotly contested areas, the attacks continued intermittently through the end of June. A handful of CAPs were overrun, and a few others relocated, but most held their own.

To the Marines, the Combined Action program appeared a decided success. The Marines assigned to the CAP program amounted to only about 1.5 percent of the total serving in Vietnam, but they accounted for almost 8 percent of the total estimated enemy casualties.[37] Similarly, only 12 percent of PFs in I Corps were involved in the program, but that 12 percent accounted for nearly 29 percent of all enemy casualties inflicted by Popular Forces.[38] For a military command preoccupied with numbers, this was indisputable proof of success. The Combined Action program was steadily expanded from six Combined Action Platoons in 1965 to fifty-seven at the end of 1966 and to seventy-nine by the beginning of 1968.[39]

Judged by the criteria of enemy casualties, the CAPs were a great success. Judged by the more ambiguous yardstick of extending and securing government control of the countryside, their performance was more problematic. The village area assigned to the Combined Action Platoons was almost always too large for them to effectively control every hamlet, and there were never enough Combined Action Platoons to assign to all villages.[40]

By 1968, less than one-third of the Combined Action Platoons had managed to "work themselves out of a job" and move on to another village, having rid their area of any significant Communist activity.[41] "The truth, I suspect, is that where it seemed to work, Combined Action wasn't really needed, and where it was, Combined Action could never work," one veteran of the program wrote many years later. "Combined Action came as too little and too late. The VC infrastructure was too deeply entrenched literally as well as figuratively in some places. They had had more than twenty years to win hearts and minds before we blundered onto the scene."[42] "I don't think the VC have ever left this village," one CAP Marine observed. "We're all just sort of living here together. Oh, we like to think if we got clobbered one night, somebody would come and warn us."[43] Combined Action units that became too troublesome to the Communists could always be targeted for attack by strong regular forces, as happened at Binh Ngia. The CAPs' relative isolation and meager numbers made them always vulnerable to such attacks.

Yet if the CAPs' success in "protecting" the villagers from the Communists was sometimes open to question, they did enjoy fairly good success at protecting them from the Americans and South Vietnamese. "The CAP presence substantially reduces the threat to the villagers from other friendly forces, American, Vietnamese, and free world military armed forces who have been known to terrorize and even destroy villages on operations and even on casual passage throught the area," a Navy-sponsored study concluded. "CAP Marines tend to become extremely protective of 'their' village and do much to halt the ugly incidents that always occur between indigenous populations and occupying forces."[44]

At MACV and elsewhere in Saigon, the CAP program was viewed with considerable misgivings as a well-meaning but misguided effort that had the unfortunate effect of scattering small groups of U.S. troops in static positions all over the country and involving them too closely in what should have been a Vietnamese security effort. "I simply had not enough numbers to put a squad of Americans in every village and hamlet," Westmoreland later wrote. "That would have been fragmenting resources and exposing them to defeat in detail."[45]

Resources for Combined Action therefore were never lavish and were almost always confined to what the Marines themselves could spare. Yet even had the program undergone early and significant expansion, it is doubtful that the Marines would ever have found enough suitable men. Chaplain Richard McGonnigle, who was intimately involved in establishing the training program for Combined Action, observed that "when you take a group of civilians and transform them into Marines and get them to kill—and then somehow re-transform them into people that can kill discriminatingly and go through some kind of identification with people—that's an amazing psychological trick."[46]

The ideal CAP Marine was a cool and efficient infantry fighter, not only expert in the skills of combat but able to impart these skills to an untrained, uneducated farmer who spoke little or no English. At the same time, he was a patient, subtle, and resourceful community organizer, able to overcome cultural barriers and prejudice to win the hearts and minds of the villagers. Such men, if they existed at all, were in short supply. More common were men who volunteered for CAP duty to escape life in a line company or the tedium and horseshit of life in the rear, or men who were volunteered by their commanding officers to rid themselves of marginal performers or troublemakers.[47] "We were hardly the combat-tested ambassadors-in-green described in books and official accounts," recalled one CAP veteran of 1967–68. "Our experience was varied, our motives mixed. I believe we never could have found sufficient numbers of Marines with the intelligence, sensitivity, and tolerance to make Combined Action work on a large scale. We were having difficulties and at best mixed results as it was."[48]

Yet if the Combined Action program constituted something less than a "highly effective and efficient counterinsurgency method" as its promoters claimed, it was still among the most effective, imaginative, and humane approaches to the Vietnam struggle the Americans ever devised. In a conflict in which the United States and the South Vietnamese frequently waged war *on* the villages, Combined Action opted for war *in* the villages. "[Our company] managed to keep the VC out of all hamlets in Phu Thu district in which the six CAPs operated with a force of no more than 75 Marines," the former CAP leader Tom Harvey recounted. "I do not recall any of our CAPs calling in artillery, other than illumination a few times, and no gunships and no jet airstrikes."[49]

With all its bitterness and ferocity, the war waged by the CAPs was a human war against a human enemy, not the anonymous war of firepower and attrition waged by the line battalions. That was why, despite the high casualty rate, almost 60 percent of all CAP Marines extended their tour in Vietnam and why most veterans of the program continued to have positive feelings about their experience.

The Marines in Combined Action were among the few GIs to come close to experiencing the Vietnam War in a way that fulfilled the traditional American expectation of war as a personal encounter with a human enemy. "I now see all Combined Action as largely futile and even Quixotic," one Marine wrote in 1988, "but personally I don't regret a day spent tilting at the VC infrastructure. . . . I feel privileged to have had a close-up view of a part of the war only glimpsed by those in line battalions merely passing through."[50]

Though the Americans by 1968 appeared to have largely forgotten the people in their zeal to come to grips with the "real threat," the people could not as easily forget the Americans. The violent meeting between the American style of warfare and the Communist practice of People's War produced bloodshed, suffering, and social dislocation on a scale that made the earlier war with the French seem almost like a medieval tournament. Although General Westmoreland hoped to confront the enemy in the remote jungle and mountain regions, much heavy fighting inevitably occurred in or near populated areas. Given the American practice of using artillery fire and air support in almost all operations, the destruction in the villages and hamlets was bound to be heavy.

MACV had established "Rules Of Engagement" governing when and under what circumstances U.S. forces could employ artillery, air strikes, or naval gunfire, and even when they could reply to enemy fire. The Rules Of Engagement, based on generally recognized principles of the law of land warfare and frequently updated, were legally "impeccable."[51] Yet few officers even at the highest level were thoroughly familiar with these Rules of Engagement, which, in any case, were open to conflicting interpretations and left much to the judgement of the soldier on the scene.[52] "If we were fired at, at night . . . even if it was a built-up area, my policy was to put artillery on it, quite a bit of it," a company commander with the 9th Infantry Division recalled. "I pretty much stuck with that policy. That's a question, what value was gained, because in all those times only once did we find evidence that we killed anybody, in terms of enemy soldiers. We did a lot of damage to houses, did a lot of damage to local populace."[53]

"You'd get a couple of rockets shot from the center of a town. Well, it's very easy for me to say they will not be responded to by fire," observed Admiral Arthur Salzer, who commanded naval forces in the same area. "But it's very hard for the boat crew that's been hit and perhaps lost its captain, had one or two men seriously wounded to remember that when they have guns in their hands and see their friends bloody and dead."[54]

Any hamlet might be a "Viet Cong hamlet" if it happened to be occupied by Communist forces, if American troops took fire from the hamlet, or even if tunnels or bunkers were found there. Moreover, the distinction between a bunker or shelter constructed by a villager for the protection of his family and a Viet Cong fighting position was usually left entirely to the judgment of the angry, frightened, and tired GIs searching the hamlet.

Le Ly Hayslip's family bunker was larger than usual and attracted the attention of some American soldiers searching her village. "Because it was so big they thought Viet Cong might be hiding inside. [They] threw in some grenades. One of them didn't go off right away and the two Americans who went in afterwards were killed."[55] The angry American GIs took Le Ly's father into custody as a Viet Cong suspect and brought him to the district headquarters for interrogation, where he was badly beaten.

The veteran pacification expert John Paul Vann observed that the Communists' "specific objective is to get our friendly forces to engage in suicidal destruction. . . . I have walked through hundreds of hamlets that have been destroyed in the course of battle, the majority as a result of the heavier friendly fire. The overwhelming majority of hamlets thus destroyed failed to yield sufficient evidence of damage to the enemy to justify the destruction. . . . Indeed, it has not been unusual to find a hamlet destroyed and find absolutely no evidence of damage to the enemy."[56]

In addition to artillery and air support in active battles and against clearly identified enemy targets, the Americans employed a large volume of firepower in "unobserved" missions, that is, against areas where no specific target had been identified and the effectiveness of bombs and shells could not be determined. "One night at a division or brigade base camp will provide proof of the omnipresence of artillery in Vietnam," wrote one battalion commander. "It is not uncommon for the artillery in the base camp to pump out 500 to 600 rounds of artillery a night and with questionable results."[57] "During a recent trip to Vietnam I came away with the impression that [only] about six percent of artillery fires were observed," Army Chief of Staff General Harold K. Johnson reported in 1967. "Artillery school says ten percent. [We] are writing checks for a quarter of a billion dollars every month to pay for ammo."[58] Defense Department analysts, somewhat more generous, estimated that about 15 percent of artillery--but only 4 percent of air support— was delivered in support of U.S. and allied forces in contact with the enemy.[59]

Large numbers of artillery rounds were employed in "harassment and interdiction" (H&I) fire at suspected enemy supply routes or bases or to shake up the enemy. A postwar study of this practice found that "most H&Is were developed haphazardly by plotting targets based on day- or week-old sightings or random map inspections."[60] Certain areas of Vietnam that Saigon considered to be under the control of the Viet Cong were designated "free fire" or "specified strike" zones. Once such a zone was established, anyone remaining in the area was considered an enemy combatant and was subject to attack by aircraft or artillery without prior approval by the Vietnamese government or higher headquarters.

In theory, specified strike zones were established by the Vietnamese province chief for limited periods in uninhabited regions or well-known Viet Cong base areas. In fact, many Vietnamese villagers refused or were unable to leave their homes in or near the "accepted VC bases." They thus became subject to sudden and repeated artillery and air attacks.

In the delta, American helicopter pilots routinely strafed and sank junks loaded with rice simply because they had been sighted traveling a portion of a canal in a free fire zone. The crews of the junks, well aware of this practice, abandoned their craft and jumped into the water at the first sight of choppers. Such unusual behavior confirmed to the pilots that the crews were Viet Cong, and they proceeded to attack them in the water.[61] In instances where the Viet Cong and North Vietnamese troops chose to dig in and fortify hamlets or villages for a sustained fight, as at Dai Do, the destruction could be devastating indeed. In a four-day fight at the village of Chau

Nhai in Quang Ngai province, four companies of the Americal Division called in air strikes, which dropped 64,800 pounds of bombs and called for two thousand rounds of artillery fire.[62] During a single month in the same province three hundred civilians were killed, four hundred wounded, and 3,100 houses damaged. By 1969 about one-third of Quang Ngai's population was classified as refugees, their homes destroyed or abandoned due to the war. By 1968, Senator Robert Kennedy declared, the United States had dropped 12 tons of bombs "for every square mile in North and South Vietnam."[63]

Not all civilian deaths in Vietnam occurred as a result of villagers being caught in the midst of a battle or of careless or indiscriminate use of firepower. Some civilians died as a result of deliberate acts of cruelty, malice, or anger by American GIs.

The Americans who went to Vietnam in the late 1960s brought with them ideas and expectations about war they had learned from reading, television, and movies, and from conversations with veterans. Among these was the expectation that, in war, civilians would behave like civilians and soldiers would behave as soldiers. When the other side failed to live up to those expectations, there was trouble. In the Korean War, North Korean troops sometimes masqueraded as civilians, especially as refugees. The result of this practice was to "force upon our men in the field acts and attitudes of the utmost savagery," a Time-Life correspondent noted. "This means not the usual, inevitable savagery of combat in the field, but savagery in detail—the blotting out of villages where the enemy *might* be hiding; the shooting and shelling of refugees who *may* include North Koreans."[64] In January 1951, airmen in Korea were surveyed by researchers about their feelings about "attacking supply lines operated by North Korean women and children." Only 10 percent felt that the Air Force should avoid such targets. Only 20 percent expressed any unwillingness to attack "targets composed [*sic*] of South Korean women and children operating against their will as supply agents for enemy forces."[65]

In Vietnam, Americans once again faced soldiers (the Viet Cong) who sometimes looked and acted like civilians, and civilians who sometimes secretly acted as soldiers or auxiliaries for soldiers. To some Americans this made the Viet Cong not only threatening but treacherous and dishonorable. "You really didn't know where they were," one former infantryman recalled. "Like you might be going through what you would call a friendly village and all of a sudden all hell breaks loose on you. You never did know who the Viet Cong were."[66]

Americans often compared the Viet Cong unfavorably with the North Vietnamese Army in this regard. The North Vietnamese at least behaved more as expected. "I think the VC were worse than the North Vietnamese," one soldier in a tank battalion declared. "The North Vietnamese stood right out and said 'We are the North Vietnamese' and they were trying to win a battle. The Viet Cong would sneak around and ambush whenever they could."[67] Marines who had served both in the sparsely populated mountains near the DMZ and in the heavily cultivated coastal lowlands drew a similar distinction. "Up north when you made contact . . . it was like going up against your own men," observed a Marine squad leader. "Here (south of Da Nang) . . . you don't know who to fight. Old poppasan might bump you off. . . . The NVA, they fight more like we do. You respect them a little bit. The VC, I don't have any respect for them."[68]

Yet often it was not just the Viet Cong or the North Vietnamese but all the people of Vietnam who seemed to be "the enemy." This was especially true in the heavily populated rice-growing areas of Vietnam, where American troops frequently mingled with the local population, patrolling, searching villages and hamlets, or providing security for roads and bridges. In those regions American troops soon discovered a wide gap between the official Washington rationale for the war, which stressed the American aim of aiding and protecting the people of South Vietnam, and the actual behavior and attitudes of the Vietnamese they had ostensibly come to protect.

Most GIs found the rural Vietnamese primitive, unfriendly, and unappealing. Some rural Vietnamese defecated in the open, seldom washed thoroughly unless they lived near rivers or other abundant sources of water, and took long midday rests, necessitated by the climate and by their limited caloric intake. "The people live like pigs," one infantryman wrote to his parents from the Mekong Delta. "They don't know how to use soap. When they have to go to the bathroom, they go wherever they're standing. . . . The houses they live in are like run down shacks. You can see everything. They have no doors or curtains. . . . We are more than millionaires to these people—they have nothing. I can't see how people live like this."[69] Americans found most Vietnamese practices repellent if not incomprehensible. "They would eat anything," an Army nurse recalled. "They ate worms and stuff. I'm serious. Like my mommasan, who would make me so mad because all that old grease and stuff from that old rotten fish with rice—well, she'd do my uniforms and instead of using spray starch, she'd spit."[70] Vietnamese who worked for the Americans were frequently accused of theft or of spying for the Viet Cong.

The sociologist Charles Moskos, who spent several weeks with an infantry battalion in Vietnam in 1966, found in interviews that the soldier "definitely does not see himself fighting for Vietnam. Quite the contrary, he thinks South Vietnam a worthless country."[71] A *Washington Post* correspondent observed that "open expression of American contempt for Vietnamese is common. An Army major driving a jeep in Saigon after a heavy rain deliberately drives along the edge of the road so . . . he can splash pedestrians. A sergeant in Can Tho taunts a Vietnamese girl with lurid sexual insults, knowing she doesn't understand him and basking in the laughter his insults evoke from his buddies."[72]

Among GIs in the field, it was taken as axiomatic that most villagers secretly aided and protected the Communists while lying to and misleading the Americans. "The Viet Cong in this area are experts in the use of explosives for booby traps and mines," an American general reported.

We have had approximately 300 booby traps and mines explode during our operations . . . Apart from casualties the booby traps are very bad psychologically for our young paratroopers and commanders in that the men develop a sometimes bitter hatred for the local villagers. The men have every reason to believe, and are sometimes correct in the belief that, the booby traps are made by the very people they see living in the villages. The situation is worsened by the fact that the Viet Cong use certain other tactics that frustrate my men.

When our troops receive fire from a hut in a village and prepare to return fire, women and children burst out of the entrance to the hut and smile and wave their hands, because they know the soldiers will not fire. While this is happening the enemy escapes through a tunnel complex.[73]

Faced with an enemy that did not "fight like us" and with the possibility that any Vietnamese might be the enemy, some Americans reacted with outbursts of hatred and brutality. The number of deliberate acts of murder, rape, torture, or other abuse committed by American GIs against Vietnamese civilians is impossible to determine with any degree of accuracy. A 1989 survey of Vietnam veterans found that approximately 12 percent reported that they had witnessed or participated in abusive violence toward civilians.[74] During the period from 1965 to 1973, 201 soldiers and 90 Marines were convicted of serious crimes against Vietnamese.[75] These figures are almost certainly far too low to provide any accurate measure of the extent of such abuse. For example, according to Marine Corps figures only three men were convicted of rape during the entire six years the Marines were deployed in Vietnam.[76] At the other extreme, the numerous reports of alleged atrocities that originated with Vietnam veterans often could not be substantiated. Those who testified about the alleged abuses were often former GIs now active in the antiwar movement, who were understandably reluctant to cooperate with investigators from the very services they believed guilty of perpetrating war crimes. On the other hand, government spokesmen pointed out that many accusations were based on hearsay or were so general as to be impossible to substantiate.[77] And, for every veteran who insisted that murder, rape, and torture were "standard operating procedure," there was another who insisted that he and the men in his unit never engaged in such practices and that the rare breakdowns in discipline were swiftly dealt with.[78]

One area in which there is strong evidence of continued wrongdoing is in the treatment of prisoners of war. Torture and abuse of POWs and Viet Cong suspects by South Vietnamese military and police organizations had been commonplace since the beginning of American involvement in Vietnam. Yet as the war dragged on, evidence began to accumulate that Americans had sometimes engaged in similar practices. In May 1971 the Army Judge Advocate General reported that an investigation had confirmed that "on occasion electrical devices" had been used to extract information from Vietnamese during interrogations.[79] Another investigation of "Torture of Prisoners of War by U.S. Officers," undertaken by the Army's Directorate of Military Personnel Policies, concluded "the rationalization of this conduct by others who testified, indicates very certainly that violations of the Geneva Convention and ordinary views of humane treatment in handling PWs is more widespread. Various coercive pressures varying from a slap in the face to use of torture described by the witnesses [appears] to be standard practice." Those officers and NCOs involved in such practices "appeared to feel righteously justified . . . and sneer at those who condemned [torture] as being too squeamish to do what is militarily necessary." The investigators impatiently dismissed the rationale of "military necessity," pointing out that in many cases "torture has been used to make the most insignificant intelligence gains." As for reliability of any information obtained, the investigators caustically observed that, using the same methods of torture employed in Vietnam, the existence of "a Viet Cong cell could be established in Fairfax, Virginia, with any number of people admitting participation and naming or confirming other conspirators."[80]

Almost all war crimes and atrocities, proven and alleged, involved violence against a single individual or a small group of individuals. Most of the time the perpetrators claimed that their leaders, officers or NCOs, had encouraged, condoned, or even ordered the acts they committed. Most of the time these leaders were found to be either young and inexperienced or on the verge of breaking under the strain of too many operations, too many friends lost.[81] Then, in March 1968, as the Tet battles had all but died away, an event occurred which, for sheer scale and horror, stood out from all others.

At a hamlet in the coastal lowlands of Quang Ngai Province called My Lai, a company of the 11th Infantry Brigade shot, bayonetted, burned, or beat to death at least two hundred unarmed civilians, many of them women and children, in the space of a few hours.[82] More than seventy Vietnamese were herded into a ditch just east of the hamlet and shot down by members of one platoon, while another platoon moved through the settlement shooting as they went. "In some instances, grenades were thrown into family shelters. In others, the occupants were called out and shot down as they emerged. . . . In one instance ten to twenty women and children were rounded up and forced to squat in a circular formation. Then one of the men in the platoon fired several rounds from his M79 grenade launcher into their midst. Those not killed by the grenades were shot by other men of the platoon."[83]

Two weeks after the slaughter at My Lai, the Quang Ngai National Liberation Front Committee issued a propaganda leaflet, "Concerning the Crimes Committed by the U.S. Imperialists and Their Lackeys," which described the killings by the "American pirates" of five hundred civilians at My Lai. "The heavens will not tolerate this. The blue ocean waters will not wash away the hatred."[84]

For almost a year the truth of what had happened at My Lai was effectively concealed by commanders and their staffs within the Americal division. An official Army inquiry, headed by Lieutenant General William Peers, concluded that the coverup extended to every level of the division's command structure.[85]

At the end of March 1969 a former serviceman, Ronald L. Ridenhour, who had heard stories of the incident from friends and acquaintances who had been at My Lai, wrote a letter to the Secretary of Defense and other Washington officials giving a detailed account of the massacre as he had heard it from former participants. The Army Criminal Investigation Division began an investigation, and General Westmoreland, by then Chief of Staff, ordered General Peers to head a commission to determine why the incident had taken place and remained concealed for so long. In November 1969 Seymour Hersh published the first accounts of the incident in the *New York Times,* and one month later *Life* magazine published color photos taken at My Lai by a former Army photographer. The photos showed the bloody bodies of Vietnamese as they lay in ditches or by the side of a road. Others showed the terrified faces of Vietnamese women and children huddled together just prior to their murder by the men of C Company. After the publication of these articles, few Americans could doubt that something terrible had happened at My Lai.

Over the next eighteen months Americans watched in horrified fascination as the story of the atrocities at My Lai unfolded through Congressional investigations, the media, and the courts. In the end only one man, Lieutenant William R. Calley, a platoon leader in C Company, was convicted of a crime committed at My Lai. Five others were tried by court-martial and acquitted, and charges were dismissed against eleven others for lack of evidence.[86] Calley received widespread expressions of support from members of the public, who proclaimed him a "scapegoat." He was granted parole in November 1974 after having served about a third of his sentence of ten years, most of it under "house arrest" in his quarters.

Many Americans, shaken by the revelations of My Lai, tried to dismiss the event as an inexplicable aberration, an instance in which soldiers, subject to the strains of combat against the treacherous and elusive enemy, lacking proper training and leadership, had gone berserk. Others, especially critics of the war, argued that My Lai was simply an especially lurid example of routine American military practices in Vietnam.

The argument has continued to the present day, unresolved and probably unresolvable. If My Lai was an aberration or a product of poor leadership, why did studies by the Army Deputy Chief of Staff for Personnel conclude that there were no significant differences between the men of C Company and "the normal cross-section of first term enlistees and inductees."[87] If the men of C Company were frightened, angry, and frustrated at the death of their friends at the hands of Viet Cong mines and booby traps, this was an experience shared by many GIs who operated in the coastal lowlands.

As for leadership, much was made of the fact that Calley and his fellow platoon leaders were young and inexperienced. Yet the company commander, Captain Ernest Medina, was described by General Peers as a "strong, effective leader, with considerable experience." The noncommissioned officers were also considered "experienced and above average."[88]

Yet if My Lai was really "no big deal," as Calley is reported to have declared, it is hard to account for the reaction of virtually all GIs to the event. Even those hardened to the horrors of the war and convinced that all Vietnamese were treacherous and untrustworthy reacted to the news with revulsion and disbelief. "My Lai was beyond the bounds of permissible behavior, and that is recognized by virtually every soldier in Vietnam," wrote Daniel Ellsberg, an outspoken critic of the war who had spent considerable time in Vietnam as an associate of Edward Landsdale and John Paul Vann. "They know it was wrong. . . . The men who were at My Lai know there were aspects out of the ordinary. That is why they tried to hide the event, talked about it to no one, discussed it very little even among themselves."[89] "How did the men react to My Lai when the story broke?" the Americal Division psychiatrist was asked years later. "That's easy," was the reply. "Nobody wanted to be in the Americal Division."[90]

In addition to those who fell victim to American firepower, carelessness, or malice, many Vietnamese civilians also died at the hands of the Viet Cong who continued their program of terror and intimidation against anyone suspected of opposing them. Saigon reported that between 1957 and 1968 the Communists had murdered about 16,000 civilians, including 3,700 in 1967 alone. Robert Santos, a platoon leader with the 101st Airborne Division near Hue in early 1968, recalled entering a village and finding a row of Vietnamese bodies. "When you walk in and find them lined up there on their stomachs with their hands tied behind their backs, we know it was the NVA who did that. . . . They killed the water buffalo, everything."[91] Many victims of Viet Cong terror were government officials, police, or security forces, but the majority were ordinary civilians.[92] Teachers, for example, were a favorite target of Communist terror. "Why were there assassinations of teachers, many of whom did not even work for the government?" a member of the Tay Ninh Province committee wrote. "Because they were people with a profound understanding of politics, people who were pure nationalists, who might be able to assume anti-communist leadership in their area. Such people are very dangerous and are classed as traitors."[93]

Communist murders and terrorism against "traitors," "tyrants," and "reactionaries" seldom received much attention except when carried out in a particularly striking manner, as when six hundred Viet Cong troops wielding Russian-made flamethrowers attacked the Montagnard hamlet of Dak Son in Phuoc Long Province, killing more than 250 people.[94] During the battle for Hue the Communist forces rounded up almost six thousand civilians. Most were never seen again.

Pham Van Tuong, who worked as a part-time janitor in the Government Information Office, was summoned from his house by a squad of Viet Cong together with his five-year-old son, three-year-old daughter, and two of his nephews. "There was a burst of gunfire. When the rest of the family came out they found all five of them dead."[95] Four hundred men of the Catholic Phu Cam section of Hue on the right bank of the Perfume River were marched away to the south by Communist troops. Nineteen months later, Viet Cong defectors led U.S. troops "to a creek bed deep in the double canopy jungle ten miles from Hue. There spread out for nearly a hundred yards in the ravine were the skulls, skeletons, and shards of bone of the men of Phu Cam, washed clean and white by the running brook. The skulls showed they had been shot or brained with blunt instruments."[96] In all, about 2,800 bodies were eventually recovered in well-concealed graves around Hue. Many of the victims had been bludgeoned to death or buried alive.[97]

By 1968 at least 25,000 civilians a year were dying in the war and about 100,000 were injured.[98] How many of these casualties were caused by American bombs and shells and how many by Viet Cong mines, booby traps, and murder, was the subject of heated controversy. In 1971 the U.S. Agency for International Development obtained records from the Vietnamese Ministry of Health that purported to show the cause of injuries among Vietnamese admitted to government hospitals. They showed that at least 38 percent of the injured in 1968 had been wounded by shells or bombs.[99] Since the Americans had a near-monopoly of those weapons (except for occasional shells used as booby traps), it seems safe to say that at the very least 40 percent of civilian casualties were caused by U.S. forces. Administration critics and antiwar activists insisted on a much higher percentage.

Along with casualties came more than 3.5 million refugees and displaced persons.[100] Saigon claimed that these people were fleeing Communist terrorism and tyranny, and many, especially Catholics, members of the political-religious sects, relatives of soldiers and government officials who were the favorite targets of Viet Cong terror, may indeed have come for that reason. Others moved to the cities and towns seeking a share of the wealth and opportunity that the American war had brought to urban areas near U.S. bases. "Everyone in my village was saying how easy it was to make a living" near the giant U.S. base at Cam Ranh Bay, one Vietnamese woman told reporters, "so I decided to join the gold rush."[101]

Yet an Army staff study in 1966 concluded that the "immediate and prime causes of refugee movement into GVN-controlled urban areas was U.S.-RVNAF bombing and artillery fire in conjunction with ground operations."[102] "We were forced to come here," one refugee, an elderly woman, told a pair of American relief workers. "The enemy came to our old village four times. Twice it was the men from the jungle and twice it was you foreigners. Each time we suffered. You came last and brought us here."[103]

The province of Quang Nam in central Vietnam, containing the large American base complex at Da Nang, had the largest refugee population, with about 80,000 crowded into refugee camps and almost as many living elsewhere. By 1968 some districts in central Vietnam had lost almost seventy-five percent of their population. "For every soldier who went to battle, a hundred civilians moved ahead of him," Le Ly Hayslip observed. "To get out of the way; or behind him—following in his wake the way leaves are pulled along in a cyclone, hoping to live off his garbage, his money, and when all else fails, his mercy."[104]

Many large population movements were carried out deliberately by the Americans and South Vietnamese to remove civilians from the battle zone or to deny access to them by the Viet Cong. During Operation Cedar Falls in the 60-square-mile "Iron Triangle" northwest of Saigon, more than six thousand people were forcibly evacuated by elements of the 1st and 25th Infantry Divisions early in 1967.[105] As the villagers were herded into helicopters and river patrol boats, bulldozers and Rome plows—special tractors that could cut down entire trees with their blades—demolished the abandoned houses and farm buildings.

At the village of Rach Bat . . . the bulldozers would plow into the groves of palm trees, and then discovering a house, crush it. Columns of heavy black smoke rose from the burning village. . . . The villagers had been assembled next to a masonry building in the center of this activity. . . . Standing or crouching without speaking, their faces drawn tight in dead masks, the people seemed not to see or hear what was happening around them.[106]

Near the Demilitarized Zone more than two thousand families were evacuated from the area northwest of the town of Cam Lo in order to allow construction of the "McNamara Line" barrier system. Farther south, the South Vietnamese Army's Operation Lam-Son 87 resulted in the relocation of more than 10,000 people in Thua Thien province.[107]

Sometimes the evacuations were well planned and orderly. The Catholic hamlet of Lang Binh in Quang Tri province near Gio Linh made a well-planned and orderly move to their resettlement under the leadership of their priest. Warned well in advance of their impending evacuation, they had already completed the construction of more than eighty new houses at their resettlement site.[108] Yet most evacuations were sad and squalid. In most cases the people to be evacuated had only a few days, sometimes only a few hours' warning. Often the first notification that villagers received of their impending move was when soldiers, trucks, and helicopters appeared in their hamlet to begin their evacuation.

Some evacuees, relocated near American bases and airfields, found jobs working for the Americans; others earned money by providing services to GIs ranging from laundries, car washes, and barber shops to drugs and prostitution. Refugees who did well in the new urban environment soon found themselves the owners of radios, refrigerators, sewing machines, televisions, and other luxuries unheard-of in the countryside.

For most refugees, however, relocation meant an economic disaster. In most cases evacuees could bring away only what they could carry with them: livestock, furniture, rice paddy, and farm implements, which often represented most of a family's real wealth, had to be left behind. Craftsmen often had to leave their tools, and shopkeepers could seldom, if ever, bring much of their stock with them. Sometimes families lost everything. One-quarter of the people evacuated from the site of the McNamara Line reported being unable to take any personal possessions with them. South Vietnamese officials seldom made any attempt to inventory the abandoned property in order to compensate the owners.[109]

Once at the resettlement site, the evacuees faced problems ranging from disorientation and depression to unemployment to physical privation. The villagers evacuated from the DMZ to the Cam Lo area, overwhelmingly farmers and farm laborers, quickly found themselves without a livelihood. No school had been provided for their 2,500 children, and a water shortage soon developed as all but one of the shallow wells in the area dried up in the summer heat. South Vietnamese army engineers had prepared rows of tin-roofed wooden houses for the evacuees, and in the process had bulldozed all existing vegetation, "giving the area a desolate 'military camp' appearance. The wind blew constantly over the barren site, carrying with it the loosened soil, and since it was the dry season there was no rain to alleviate the dusty conditions."[110]

Unemployment rates among refugees surveyed by a Defense Department study in 1968 ranged from 47 percent to 53 percent, and over 95 percent of those refugees who had managed to find work reported their employment situation to be worse than before evacuation.[111]

Despite the economic hardships and social dislocations, many American leaders at first were inclined to view this massive population movement as an advantage to the United States and its South Vietnamese ally. A State Department message to Saigon contended that the movement of refugees away from Viet Cong–controlled areas "helps deny recruits, food producers, porters, etc. to the VC and clears the battlefield of innocent civilians."[112] The III MAF Command Chronology for 1966 observed that "the influx of refugees has had the favorable effect of denying the VC a needed labor and agricultural force."[113]

The idea that the mass of frightened, homesick, impoverished, and demoralized women, children, and old men who monthly swelled the towns and refugee camps was somehow an asset and "a reflection of the growing confidence of the Vietnamese people in their government" took a surprisingly long time to die.[114] As late as June 8, 1967, Under Secretary of State Katzenbach called for "stimulating greater refugee flow through psychological inducements to further decrease the enemy's manpower base."[115] By 1967, however, the Pentagon's own studies were casting grave doubts on the "advantages" that the thousands of displaced persons conferred on the Saigon government.

It was undoubtedly true that Vietnamese moved from their farms and their hamlets would not be available to work as laborers and porters or to add to the ranks of Communist fighters. Their rice would also be unavailable for the Viet Cong to seize as taxes or contributions. The villagers of Ben Suc alone produced approximately 1,300 metric tons of rice a year. Yet these setbacks to the Communists were more apparent than real. Only a small proportion of the refugees were men of military age; over 70 percent were women, and many were elderly or children. The fertile rice land abandoned by the refugees often did not remain abandoned long, as farmers from neighboring areas moved in to claim it and the Viet Cong extracted their cut from the new proprietors. In the refugee camps themselves, families continued to contribute food to friends and relatives in the Viet Cong, "only now they will be offering USA bulgar rather than home-grown rice."[116] The Viet Cong in areas that had been permanently depopulated simply increased taxes in neighboring districts.[117]

It was also obvious to even casual observers that the experience of forcible relocation, leaving the refugees bereft of their possessions, frightened, angry, and often living in squalor, was unlikely to produce enthusiastic supporters of the Saigon government. Far from giving Vietnamese increased confidence in Saigon, the masses of refugees seemed to imply "the failure of the government to protect the rural population from the Viet Cong," as one Defense Department study observed. "For a people as pragmatic as the Vietnamese peasants appear to be, the message is clear—the GVN is not able to protect even its supporters . . . so one had best withhold making any overt commitment."[118]

In the United States, congressional critics of the war, journalists, clergymen, and academics harshly stigmatized the encouragement of refugees as cynical, inhumane, and probably a violation of international law. By mid-1968 MACV and the American mission were in full reverse gear concerning the refugee question. Commanders were now cautioned to avoid needless evacuations and actions likely to cause large-scale population displacement. Resettling refugees and returning them to their homes became a priority, and progress was now measured by rebuilding and resettlement.[119] Yet the fierce fighting of 1968 was to exacerbate the refugee problem and bring the struggle for the villages into sharper focus.

Although the Americans still spoke of a war to win the people and safeguard their "traditional" way of life, the war in 1968 was to bring only more suffering, more disruption, and more death, including those at My Lai, where, in a sense, the American war effort reached its high point of pointless destruction. For the people in the middle it was indeed the bloodiest year.

CHAPTER 10

The August Offensive

General Creighton Williams Abrams. They never promised him a rose garden. He grew up in rural Massachusetts, the son of a railroad mechanic, and entered West Point in 1932. Like all entering plebes, he was subjected to merciless hazing, but Abrams, unshaken, gave as good as he got, once smearing an upperclassman's radiator with Limburger cheese. He graduated in 1936, average in academic subjects, third string in football.[1]

He was not slick, he was not glamorous. "Chances are if he was in civilian clothes, sitting on a park bench, a cop would tell him to move along," a close associate once observed. But he was a ferocious fighter and a brilliant combat leader who "could inspire aggressiveness in a begonia."[2] Commander of a tank battalion in the 4th Armored Division of General George Patton's Third Army, his tanks were the first to break through the German lines and relieve the besieged American paratroopers at Bastogne during the Battle of the Bulge in 1944. In Korea, Abrams served as a corps chief of staff during the year just after the conclusion of that conflict, an appropriate preparation for Vietnam.

An even more thankless job awaited him in the early 1960s, when, as a major general, he oversaw the Army troops and federalized National Guardsmen deployed to Mississippi and Alabama in the wake of riots touched off by attempts at racial integration of schools and colleges in the deep South. Tempers were strained, Washington was nervous, and Southern politicians took advantage of the moment to grandstand—or to run for cover.

Abrams remained firm but sympathetic, tough, confident, and unflappable. He threaded his way unerringly through the social and political minefields, earning the respect of many in the Kennedy Administration. By 1964 he was Vice Chief of Staff of the Army, and in 1967 he was named Westmoreland's deputy in Vietnam, succeeding him in July 1968. Abrams took over less than two months after the end of the Communist May offensive. A brief lull had settled over many of the old battle areas, but there were increasing reports from U.S. intelligence of Communist plans for a new offensive in August, "envisioned to be of longer duration than his Tet and May attacks."[3]

Saigon journalists, whose relationship with General Westmoreland had progressed from mild skepticism to barely concealed hostility, were quick to point out the contrast between Abrams and his predecessor. Westmoreland was portrayed as "the very model of a modern major general," always crisp and immaculate in appearance, controlled and confident in manner. (One writer reported that he sometimes breakfasted in his underwear to keep his uniform properly pressed.)[4] Abrams, in contrast, was usually portrayed as a homespun, earthy, no-nonsense soldier's soldier.

Westmoreland had devoted considerable thought and effort to cultivating the media, attempting, as he put it, to "demonstrate through candid exchange that I appreciated their responsibility to keep the American people informed and intended to help." Yet Westmoreland seldom enjoyed a happy relationship with the media. Reporters delighted in pointing out what they believed to be inaccuracies, half-truths, and contradictions in Westmoreland's statements. Abrams, on the other hand, appeared never to waste a moment's worry on the media and, paradoxically, seldom ever had a bad press. Reporters emphasized the thoughtfulness and keen intellect beneath his gruff exterior, his love of reading and classical music. When things went wrong, reporters tended to emphasize the extraordinary difficulties and constraints under which Abrams labored. Their attitude was well expressed in the title of one article by a *Newsweek* reporter, Kevin Buckley: "General Abrams Deserves a Better War."[5]

If he seldom engaged in hyperbole or extravagant predictions, Abrams seldom confided in anyone either, preferring to keep his cards close to his chest. "The overall public affairs policy of this command will be to let results speak for themselves," he told his generals soon after taking over MACV. "Achievements not hopes will be stressed. There is no objection to commanders talking to the press, however considerably more extensive use could be made of the phrase, 'No comment.'"[6]

In private the general was even more explicit. "Gentlemen, we had a very sad thing happen this week. The finest division commander we've ever had in Vietnam made a mistake," Abrams told his commanders and staff officers at one Saturday morning meeting. "That fine division commander had a friend and that friend was a member of the press. . . . He confided in that friend, and the next day he found himself in the headlines. That commander has been embarrassed and this command has been embarrassed, and gentlemen, with regard to the press, that magnificent commander forgot just one thing: THEY'RE ALL A BUNCH OF SHITS."[7]

Abrams directed his vast and complicated empire of soldiers, bureaucrats, engineers, and scientists from a windowless office in the MACV headquarters, a large, rambling prefabricated steel building near Tan Son Nhut Airport, which media wits had dubbed "Pentagon East." Like its Washington namesake, Pentagon East was a baffling maze of offices and corridors "filled with officers carrying attaché cases or sheaves of paper, striding briskly in starched fatigues. Vietnamese janitors, dozing in the stairwells at lunch time, are all that jar the otherwise perfect ambience of air-conditioned efficiency."[8] The Military Assistance Command staff directory was more than fifty pages long. It included a chief of staff, two deputy commanders and their staffs, a deputy chief of staff for economic affairs, a staff secretariat, and three complete "staff groups," a general staff, a "special staff," and a "personal staff."[9] "The MACV compound was the be all and the end all of their existence," recalled Vice-Admiral Arthur Salzer, who commanded the riverine forces in the Delta. "They used to call it 'Pentagon East'; it might as well have been Pentagon West so far as realism or understanding of our problem areas was concerned."[10]

It was easy to come away from this warren of buzzing activity with the impression that here was a nerve center from which the U.S. war effort was being systematically directed. Reporters and casual visitors were not the only ones who thought so. "What precisely is Abrams' mission? Has it been spelled out?" Defense Secretary Clifford demanded on the eve of his first visit to Vietnam in July. "What is his program for winning the war? Is the there such a program?"[11]

Abrams and his close associates would probably have had an ironic chuckle over the idea that COMUSMACV could, on his own, devise "a program for winning the war." Like Westmoreland, Abrams believed the power and authority of his position to be severely limited. As one of Abrams's key staff officers wrote, "COMUSMACV's authority to command or significantly influence the utilization of those resources which relate realistically to the achievement of his mission is circumscribed severely in this unique politico-military struggle."[12]

Abrams and his staff were well aware that their ability to control and influence the war was limited. Decisions that vitally affected the war, such as the extent and nature of the bombing of North Vietnam, were effectively outside Abrams's control. Like Westmoreland, he could not pursue the enemy into North Vietnam or cross the border into Laos and Cambodia to cut the Ho Chi Minh Trail and wipe out Communist bases and supply points. More important, his ability to control the actions of the South Vietnamese government and its armed forces was also severely constricted. During the Korean War, American military commanders had effectively commanded the South Korean Armed Forces as well as their own. Following the near disastrous defeats at the hands of the Chinese in the bitter winter battles of 1950–51, General Matthew Ridgway, the top U.S. commander in Korea, exercised ultimate control over Korean army operations, organization, and training.[13] Westmoreland had proposed a more modest version of this arrangement in March 1965, calling for "a small, single, combined staff headed by a U.S. general officer" to plan and direct military operations.[14] Yet the Saigon government refused to accept even this modest effort at unifying military operations. Westmoreland did not insist, and the proposal for the unified command, although fitfully revived from time to time within the Pentagon or the MACV bureaucracy, was never seriously considered again.

In the absence of a unified command, COMUSMACV could only rely upon persuasion and argument, combined with the judicious use of American military aid, as a carrot and stick. The entire process, referred to as "leverage," was awkward, imprecise, and often ineffective. On matters that were truly important to the South Vietnamese government and its generals, "leverage" availed little.

MACV itself was far from a tightly centralized control structure. It was, in fact, the apex of a system of decentralized command and control, which included elements of the four armed services, the CIA, and the State Department. Within the Vietnam command hierarchy, most of the actual decision-making authority devolved upon the division commanders and senior province advisers. Both Westmoreland and Abrams tolerated a high degree of variation and experimentation on the part of these subordinates. This was, in part, the product of the military tradition in which the two generals had been trained, a tradition that called for a large measure of autonomy to be afforded to a battlefield commander. Yet it was also true that MACV, as an organization, was ill-suited to the task of either absorbing or institutionalizing significant change.

A striking example of the U.S. military's inability either to learn from experience or pass on lessons could be found in the experience of the 101st Airborne. As described earlier, Brigadier General John H. Cushman's brigade of the 101st airborne had perfected the art of cordon operations in June 1968 at Thua Thien province, achieving two spectacular successes, which netted a record number of prisoners. Less than three months later seven companies from another brigade of the same division surrounded a village northwest of Saigon believed to be occupied by a battalion-size enemy force. Cushman's men had learned through bitter experience that fighting positions in a cordon could be little more than 10 meters apart. This information was never passed on or was disregarded, and the Americans organized their cordon in three-man fighting positions, 50–75 meters apart.

At 2:00 A.M. the Communists launched a sudden assault aimed at the gaps between the surrounding American platoons and fighting positions. In less than thirty minutes, three waves, totaling about five-hundred Communist fighters, moved through the gaps, shooting as they went. Each succeeding wave "picked up enemy dead and wounded, weapons and other equipment that was lying on the ground." As they swept past positions where American wounded lay, they policed up "the American weapons, equipment and supplies and fired into the bodies of the wounded men." Two U.S. platoons and a company command post were overrun, and fifty-six men, including the company commander, were killed or wounded.[15]

What attempts MACV did make to encourage experimentation and adaptation usually took the form of "lessons learned," compilations and recommendations that were circulated on a periodic basis to forces in the field. Those commanders who had the time or inclination to read such publications were always perfectly free to disregard them. Another frequent device was the periodic commanders' conference, meeting, or seminar, in which senior commanders reported on their recent operations and passed on any special successes or lessons. An OSD official described one such meeting:

A division commander rose to explain the success his division had enjoyed as a consequence of silencing the battlefield and not alerting the enemy by preparatory fires of the imminent arrival of U.S. troops. The commander particularly stressed the inadvisability and wastefulness of harassment and interdiction fires, H&I fires. Saying that his unit's most difficult task lay in finding the enemy, the commander went on to report that his troops had come to prefer a silent battlefield and to move without air and artillery and helicopters announcing their arrival.

The speaker was followed by another major general whose division had fought the same enemy units as the first. He averred the opposite, saying that his men never moved anywhere without massive doses of air and artillery preceding them, and that this had saved countless casualties by disorganizing and exposing enemy troops waiting in ambush. His favorite method of fighting was to find the enemy by ground contact, then pull back and let air and artillery destroy the enemy. No effort was made, publicly or privately, to resolve the issue. Each division commander remained free to choose his fire support and fighting method as he chose.[16]

Yet while MACV and his staff appeared to tolerate limitless variation and initiative on the part of the division commanders, this tolerance was not generally afforded to lower-echelon commanders.

Indeed, the heavy hand of overcentralized command appeared to reach out far from Saigon to the mountainous jungles, lowland rice paddies, villages, and swamps where the real war was waged.

In the everyday war of sharp, short clashes between small units, company and platoon commanders frequently found themselves distracted and harried by higher-echelon commanders attempting to advise and direct them, often from helicopters circling thousands of feet above the miniature battle. A former brigade commander recalled that "it was a common practice in Vietnam for general officers to rush to the sound of the gun, take command from their subordinate commanders, and run the battles themselves."[17] One former platoon leader recalled:

> The company I was platoon leader with was engaged and taking some casualties, pretty big fight, and the battalion commander was almost forced off the air, and the brigade commander was on the net controlling one of the platoons, the division commander was talking with the company commander. All this was going on and the company commander was getting pretty frustrated. He couldn't even talk to his own platoons because everybody was on his net.[18]

In 1968 the Department of the Army reviewed the Vietnam command and control structure and found "duplication and overlapping of functions" and excessive layering of headquarters, which "had the effect of reducing responsiveness and draining away skilled talent required at lower-level headquarters."[19] "You could not get them to understand what was going on on the ground," another former company commander said of his superiors. "They were always somewhere in the rear or somewhere above you."[20]

Lacking most conventional measures of military success, such as ground gained or positions captured, Abrams and his subordinate commanders relied on statistical reports to measure the progress of the war. This was a practice encouraged, perhaps demanded, by the White House and the Pentagon. Secretary of Defense MacNamara's managerial reforms in the early 1960s had encouraged a strong bias toward quantitative reports and an almost insatiable appetite for statistics throughout the military and the Washington National Security bureaucracy. With the American commitment to Vietnam came the demand for quantitative reports to measure the progress of the war.

In 1968 hundreds of officers and enlisted men at all command levels were kept gainfully employed churning out periodic statistical reports on the war. Sorties flown, bombs dropped, shells fired, toothbrushes distributed, gasoline consumed, and many other items were dutifully reported each month to Saigon and Washington.[21]

Sometimes the demand for statistics appeared to create, rather than simply measure, activity. The commander of an artillery battery recalled that division headquarters advised him "on a number of occasions that I wasn't firing enough. My reply was, in my judgment, the targets are just not there to warrant expenditure of any more ammo. And their reply was 'you will fire more rounds.' I was given a quota of rounds."[22]

Statistics were routinely employed to measure the unmeasurable. John Limond Hart, who served as CIA station chief in Saigon, remembered one occasion when the Embassy had to decide "what figure to use for the population of South Vietnam. We had only the vaguest notion of how many people lived in that benighted country and there was certainly no way of taking a census in the midst of war. Yet to make our statistics work we needed this figure. After brief discussion we settled. . . . on fourteen million—as good a guess as any other. . . . acutally we didn't even know how many people there were in Saigon itself."[23]

The best-known and most controversial statistical document was the "body count," a report on enemy casualties supposedly verified by American forces actually counting the bodies to guarantee accuracy. The reliability of these reports was widely questioned, particularly by members of the press. Douglas Robinson of the *New York Times* reported on an announcement by MACV that ninety-two enemy had been killed in an action that ended at 7 P.M. "The casualty announcement was ready at 8:30 this morning, indicating that American soldiers apparently had stayed up all night counting enemy bodies by flashlight in an area that was probably within sniper range and certainly exposed to possible mortar or rocket fire."[24] A 1977 survey of 110 generals who served in Vietnam found that 61 percent believed the body count to be "often inflated," and only 26 percent felt it was "within reason, accurate."[25]

While some commanders insisted on a literal interpretation of the body count, many other units included bodies seen from the air, bloodstains on the ground, and estimates by the combatants. In some cases the body count was deliberately exaggerated. "Sometimes the score was in the enemy's favor, and this is when the cry came in from higher headquarters for another count."[26]

Analysts in Saigon and Washington compared the number of U.S. and enemy dead in each engagement to determine the "kill ratio." Many officers complained that their superiors tended to judge their performance solely by their kill ratio and that the obsession with these statistics corrupted the military and distorted its evaluation of the effectiveness of operations. "It was part of the environment," Admiral Salzer observed. "That was the measure of effectiveness— number of weapons captured, number of bodies, ratio with your side. It was ghoulish. I told you about making Colonel ——— deploy some battalions to dig up a graveyard. That was the kind of degenerate statistical specter we had foisted on us."[27]

Some suspected an even more sinister aspect to the preoccupation with body count. The pressure for a large number of kills might lead to the inclination to include civilians in the count of "enemy dead," and perhaps weaken whatever restraints may have existed against killing unarmed civilians. In operations in the Mekong Delta from December 1968 to June 1969, the Ninth Infantry Division reported a body count of almost eleven thousand enemy dead and only 267 U.S. fatalities, a kill ratio of 40.8 to one.[28] Strangely enough, only about 751 weapons were captured. Pacification advisers in the Delta suspected that many of those killed were not Vietcong fighters but civilian "supporters willing or unwilling and innocent bystanders."[29]

Admiral Salzer concluded that one brigade commander of the Ninth Infantry Division was "psychologically . . . unbalanced. He was a super fanatic on body count. He would talk about nothing else during an operation. . . . maybe he was a good commander but you could almost see the saliva dripping out of the corners of his mouth. An awful lot of his bodies were civilians."[30] In 1972 Kevin P. Buckley of *Newsweek* charged that close to half of the eleven thousand "enemy" killed by the Ninth Infantry Division had been civilians.[31]

With his freedom of action circumscribed, with Washington and his own troops growing increasingly weary and impatient with the war, lacking any accurate measure of progress or any organization for imposing change, Abrams was faced with the task of holding together the vast but increasingly directionless American war effort in Vietnam.

Shortly before Abrams took over as MACV, the hard-pressed Marines along the DMZ also got a new commander. He was Major General Raymond G. Davis, who, on May 22, 1968, became Commanding General, 3d Marine Division. He was a hero of World War II and of the grim winter battles near the Chosin Reservoir in Korea. Davis had earned the Medal of Honor there for holding a vital mountain pass with his battalion for three days and three nights, allowing the withdrawal of two entire regiments. In the morning of the fourth day, Davis led his men down the ice-covered slopes and through the pass to safety, bringing all his wounded with him. He was a natural fighter, able to grasp the essentials of a battlefield situation with a mind unclouded by custom, routine, or preconceptions. Of all the generals who came to Vietnam, Davis would be among the very few who emerged with his reputation enhanced.

By 1968 Davis's 3d Marine Division had grown to be the largest combat unit in the Marine Corps, with eleven infantry battalions and numerous support units deployed along the trace of the Demilitarized Zone from Cua Viet in the east to Khe Sanh and its supporting bases in the west. Most of the battalions manned a series of fixed positions along the trace, often referred to as "the McNamara Line." At the eastern end of the line engineers had cleared a 600-meter-deep zone blocked by wire and other obstacles extending some 11 to 12 kilometers from the South China Sea. Behind the trace were company strongpoints labeled A1 to A6, and farther back still three fortified battalion base camps. Farther west, in the hills and mountains, the Marines occupied key terrain features leading west toward Khe Sanh and the Laotian border.

From the beginning the Marines had hated the line. The idea of an "anti-infiltration barrier" had originated with a group of scientist advisers to Secretary McNamara in the fall of 1966. McNamara and his advisers initially envisioned the barrier as a possible alternative to the bombing of North Vietnam. It was to be a technical marvel combining the latest mines and acoustic detection devices and supported by sophisticated air-dropped munitions. General Westmoreland soon changed the concept to that of a more conventional defensive line of observation posts, strongpoints, and artillery positions.[32] Westmoreland's initial plan called for an additional division and an armored cavalry regiment to man the barrier and serve as a reserve and reaction force, in addition to the engineer units needed for the actual construction work.

The Marines remained skeptical, arguing that a mobile defense of the DMZ area would be more effective. Both the Marines and CinCPac insisted that the level of infiltration across the DMZ was not high enough to justify such elaborate efforts, and, in any case, the barrier would be ineffective. "With these bastards you'd have to build the zone all the way to India and it would take the whole Marine Corps and half the Army to guard it," declared Marine Commandant Wallace M. Greene, Jr. "Even then they'd probably burrow under it."[33]

The Marines' misgivings turned to consternation in the spring of 1967, when they discovered that there would be no additional troops to build or man the barrier. Instead the task would be given to the 3d Marine Division, already fully committed to trying to defend its 300-square-mile area of operations.

As a first step, more than 2,700 families, more than 12,000 people, would have to be uprooted from their hamlets on or near the site of the proposed strongpoint-obstacle system and moved to a site near the village of Cam Lo along Highway 9, about 14 kilometers east of Dong Ha.[34] South Vietnamese officials and their American advisers had carefully planned each phase of the evacuation and resettlement. The South Vietnamese Army sent an engineer company to construct a refugee camp and a medical team to care for the health needs of the evacuees. U.S. Marines and Army provided trucks for transportation as well as tents, food, cement, and aluminum roofing.

The evacuation began smoothly, but after two days intensified fighting along the DMZ prompted the Vietnamese government to shorten the schedule for the movement from one month to ten days. As a result, many of the evacuees received little advance warning and no explanation of the sudden relocation. The hasty movement out of the hamlets obliged most of the villagers to leave many of their possessions behind. Many could bring only money and extra clothing. Only a few could bring rice, livestock, or furniture. A census following the evacuation showed that only one in five villagers was able to bring a chicken with him to the resettlement site, although in their home villages even the poorest families had owned a few fowl.[35] As the evacuees departed, their homes and possessions, often representing the accumulated wealth of several generations, were demolished to prepare the way for bunkers, observation towers, and fields of fire.

The villagers' new home was a cluster of tents and tin shelters on a barren strip of hot, wind-blown land, totally unsuited for rice-growing. Although most evacuees were eventually provided with more substantial housing, a planned school never materialized, and a serious water shortage soon developed, which was not alleviated until the following year.[36] Unemployment, which had been nonexistent in the people's native hamlets, now reached 48 percent. The more fortunate eked out a living as laborers at the nearby American bases or as members of various South Vietnamese paramilitary organizations. Uprooted from their ancestral lands, bereft of their meager possessions, unable to work at their traditional occupations or even to work at all, apprehensive, confused, and depressed, the evacuees were the earliest casualties of the McNamara Line.

By December 1967, the 3d Marine Division had devoted about 75,000 man-days to the construction effort, filling sandbags; hauling timbers, rock, and cement over the primitive dirt roads of Quang Tri Province; clearing jungle; installing barbed wire and minefields; and building watch towers. Most of this activity took place within artillery range of Communist units in the DMZ and Laos. As work on the line progressed, the North Vietnamese kept the DMZ outposts under intermittent rocket, mortar, and artillery fire. Marine positions from Camp Carroll and Khe Sanh in the west to Cam Lo, Con Thien, and Dong Ha in the east were all subject to heavy shelling. At Con Thien, which occupied the northwest corner of the McNamara Line, about 14 miles east of the South China Sea, the Marines were subjected to some of the heaviest shelling of the war. On a single day, September 25, 1967, 1,200 shells rained down on the base.[37] In mid-September, III MAF headquarters informed Westmoreland that, based on actual casualty rates for the last few weeks, about 670 Marines would be killed and 3,800 wounded by November in operations in support of the Line.[38]

It was not only the necessity to man and support the McNamara Line that kept 3d Marine Division's forces scattered and immobilized. It was also lack of helicopters. At the end of August 1967 serious structural problems in the Marines' CH-46A "Sea Knight" helicopters led to two fatal crashes and to the grounding of all CH-46s. The CH-46 constituted almost half of all Marine helicopters in Vietnam.

For months the Marines were forced to rely on a handful of CH-53s and a few dozen aged UH-34Ds, while the 46s underwent emergency modifications to strengthen their fuselage structure.[39] Poor weather conditions during the winter and spring in the western DMZ area even further limited helo operations.

Davis was determined to restore mobility to his division, "to get out of those fixed positions and go and destroy the enemy on our terms—not sit there and absorb the shot and shell and frequent penetrations that he was able to mount."[40] Like most successful military leaders, Davis benefited from favorable timing. The architects of the "barrier approach," McNamara and Westmoreland, had left the scene. Davis enjoyed the full confidence of his immediate superior, XXIV Corps commander William B. Rosson, had in fact served as Rosson's deputy, and had had the opportunity to observe the Army's "air mobile" operations at close hand. Davis knew he could count on Rosson for help, particularly for the loan of the Army's heavy lift helicopters when necessary. The Marines' own helicopter situation was gradually improving. The rebuilt CH-46s were returning, and a more advanced model, with far greater lift capability, was beginning to arrive in Vietnam.[41] Finally, the dry summer weather provided for better conditions for air operations.

Davis lost no time in implementing his new concept of operations for the division. Within twenty-four hours battalion positions had become company positions, and the troops thus freed were made available for mobile operations. The differences could be clearly seen in the second phase of the Dai Do battles. Whereas the 320th PAVN Division's first incursion had been met by a handful of scattered companies and battalions committed piecemeal, Davis met the second incursion with three entire regiments drawn from all parts of

Quang Tri province.[42] The Marines claimed to have completely destroyed one PAVN regiment and inflicted heavy casualties on two others.

Even before the conclusion of the battles with the 320th Division, Davis and his staff were planning an operation to test their concept of high mobility. The battleground would be the area south of Khe Sanh, where two newly arrived regiments of the PAVN 308th Division menaced the vital overland supply route, Route 9, between Ca Lu and Khe Sanh. Intelligence reports indicated that the two regiments, the 88th and the 102d, were also protecting a major roadbuilding effort from Laos eastward toward Hue. The North Vietnamese road was already 30 kilometers into South Vietnamese territory when it was discovered by the Americans. Intelligence analysts speculated that the road might even be capable of supporting tanks.[43]

The operation planned by the 3d Marine Division's Task Force Hotel was to move one regiment, the 1st Marines, into the mountains south of Route 9 to eliminate the enemy threat to that highway, then to move another regiment, the 4th Marines, farther south to find and destroy the road, which the North Vietnamese were pushing rapidly through the deep jungle. Most of these operations would be outside the range of friendly artillery, so the Marines planned to construct two temporary fire support bases or "fire bases," called Robin and Loon.

The fire base was an Army innovation that the Marines were adopting for the first time in this operation. An entire battery of 105mm howitzers or larger, longer-range 155s would be lifted by helicopter onto a high mountain pinnacle, which engineers had already bulldozed as flat as possible. Often the bulldozers themselves would have to be delivered in pieces to the tops of the remote, jungle-covered mountains. Once the guns were in place, the gun crews and their supporting infantry, normally one company, busied themselves with constructing a protective berm of dirt-filled ammunition boxes or sandbags, building bunkers, and sighting their weapons. Under the protective fan of the fire base's artillery, infantry operating from the base would spread out to find and engage the enemy or break up his supply caches.

The operation itself was labeled "Robin North" and "Robin

South," referring to the location of the two regiments, the 1st generally north and the 4th generally south of Fire Base Robin. Robin North and South began on the morning of June 2 as Marines assaulted by helicopter into Robin and Loon while one battalion occupied blocking positions along Route 9. The enemy response came quickly. Fire Support Base Loon was attacked the morning after it was occupied by elements of the 88th North Vietnamese Regiment. On June 5 the North Vietnamese launched an entire battalion in an attack on Loon, which was defended by Companies C and D of the 2d Battalion, 4th Marines. In a two-hour battle, the Marines beat back the attack, killing over 150 enemy troops. But Fire Base Loon was by now under constant heavy fire from 130mm guns on Co Roc Mountain. By a stroke of bad luck, the Marines had chosen a mountain top within easy sight of enemy observers on Co Roc.[44] By the June 6 Loon had become untenable. C and D Companies were lifted off by helicopter during the afternoon in the face of increasingly heavy fire from the surrounding North Vietnamese. A CH-46 carrying the last elements of the two companies was hit by .50 caliber machine gun fire and crashed, killing twenty-four of the sixty Marines aboard. A final flight to retrieve the bodies of Marines killed defending the base had to be canceled. A few weeks later, after the completion of Robin South, the Marines slipped back into Loon and retrieved the bodies.[45]

Despite this inauspicious beginning, the 4th Marines launched Robin South on schedule. A new fire support base, "Torch," was established south of Robin almost on the Laotian border. After a few days of searching, one of the companies of 3d Battalion, 9th Marines, attached as "opcon" to the 4th Marines for the operation, found the enemy road. It was an impressive feat of engineering, up to 18 feet wide in some places, with stone bridges and culverts, all concealed by layers of bent trees tied together to protect the road from aerial observation. Bunkers built along the side of the road housed the construction crews, along with kitchens and a large hospital. Captured documents revealed that the North Vietnamese expected the road to reach the city of Hue by July 30.[46]

The North Vietnamese reacted with heavy attacks against the Marines threatening the road. On June 15 elements of the 88th Regiment attacked the 3d Battalion, 4th Marines' position, overran

M Company, and set up their machine guns in the company's command post. The Marines counterattacked, supported by aerial gunships, and took back the command post in fierce, close-in fighting. Morning light revealed more than two hundred North Vietnamese dead. The Marines lost sixteen killed and about sixty wounded. They took more than a dozen prisoners. Undeterred, the North Vietnamese renewed their attack the following night. This time they attacked Fire Base Torch, which was occupied by a company of 1st Battalion, 4th Marines, and a battery of 105mm howitzers. The North Vietnamese again penetrated the American lines, but deadly "beehive" rounds fired from the level muzzles of the howitzers drove them back with heavy losses.

The final Communist effort came on June 18, when the North Vietnamese attacked K Company of the 4th Marines near the unfinished road. This time the attacking troops made too much noise getting into position. Flares from the Marine fire base revealed the Communists forming up for attack. Artillery and A-4E Skyhawks decimated the North Vietnamese as they attempted to penetrate the wire.[47]

In all, the PAVN 88th and 102d Regiments had lost more than six hundred dead, according to Marine claims, and almost fifty prisoners captured, including a battalion commander. American estimates of enemy casualties were far from precise, but in this case the unusually large numbers of prisoners suggested that the North Vietnamese had been severely hurt and their forces badly disorganized.

To General Davis Robin North and South appeared an all-out success, notwithstanding the loss of Fire Base Loon. The mobile concept had been shown to be feasible. For the first time in the war, the Marines had mounted and supplied a lengthy operation involving several battalions entirely by air in some of the wildest and most dangerous terrain in Vietnam.

Davis, Rosson, and Abrams were now ready to take a step that Abrams had decided on many weeks before: to close the Khe Sanh combat base. In mid-June Davis received the green light to begin the long-desired move out of Khe Sanh. The operation would be complicated and difficult. The nine U.S. and Vietnamese Army and Marine battalions operating in or near Khe Sanh had to be redeployed in such a way that the North Vietnamese "wouldn't figure out what was happening and realize that once they had us out-numbered they could launch a serious attack."[48] Khe Sanh was to be left "a completely clean piece of real estate."[49] Even burned-out hulks of aircraft were to be cut apart and hauled away so that they not be used as war trophies by the Communists. Nothing must be left that would be of use to the enemy or that would suggest that the Americans had been chased out.

Almost eight hundred bunkers, 3 miles of concertina barbed wire, and several acres of steel matting for the air strip had to be buried, removed, or destroyed. The 3d Battalion, 9th Marines, would do the actual work of dismembering the base, while the 1st Marines provided the defensive force for the operation. Other Marine units guarded the dozens of convoys carrying the equipment and debris of the base along Route 9 to Ca Lu.

Abrams instructed his officers to keep the base closing secret as long as possible, then to provide the media only with carefully prepared statements. No "backgrounders" or additional information was to be provided, and reporters were prohibited from publishing any word of the base closing until the withdrawal was completed.

Despite those precautions, the story soon leaked and appeared in the *Baltimore Sun*. Angry American generals blamed the press for endangering the lives of their men, but the frantic activity at the base would have been difficult to conceal from North Vietnamese observers in any case. As the Americans emptied sandbags, filled in trench lines, and collected their gear, the Communists kept the base under intermittent rocket, mortar, and artillery fire. The North Vietnamese also made repeated attempts to capture Hill 689, 2.5 miles west of Khe Sanh, in order to have an observation post to direct their heavy weapons onto the combat base. A Company of the 1st Marines held the hill against repeated probes, culminating in a night attack on July 1 supported by Communist mortars and artillery from Co Roc Mountain. The North Vietnamese troops, unable to take the hill, were caught in daylight on the south and southwest slopes and suffered heavy casualties from U.S. artillery and air strikes.

For the Marines at Khe Sanh, the final two nights were the worst. Communist shells continued to rain down on the base, but the

Marines were unable to find cover in bunkers or trenches since all had been dismantled or filled in.[50] Finally, on the night of July 5 the last of the Marines, F Company, 2d Battalion, 1st Marines, moved out under cover of darkness to Ca Lu and a welcome five days of hot food and cold beer.[51]

Khe Sanh was declared officially closed at 8:00 P.M. on July 5. In place of the four or five battalions that had normally been stationed at the base, two hilltop artillery positions, Fire Base Shepherd and Fire Base Cates, each with a single battalion, covered the Khe Sanh area. Since Shepherd and Cates were supplied by air, the many troops needed to guard the lines of communications along Route 9 from Ca Lu to Khe Sanh were also freed for other duties.[52]

The decision to close Khe Sanh was viewed with incredulity and bewilderment in the United States. "I believe we have a serious problem—perhaps of substance, certainly of public relations," National Security Adviser Walt W. Rostow wrote when the news of the base closing became public. Rostow wondered whether "the situation had objectively changed" or whether "Abrams' plan [was] simply the way one field commander chooses to deal with the battlefield situation rather than another?" He pointed out that the intelligence estimates still placed about 40,000 enemy troops in the DMZ area. "If it was good to pin down two divisions with 6000 men, then why not now?"[53]

Rostow's questions were precisely those which the Pentagon and MACV wished to avoid answering, for they highlighted the strategic confusion and incoherence of the American approach to the war in the DMZ area. The question of the feasibility and desirability of the McNamara Line had never been systematically discussed by Washington and the various command echelons involved. Instead the project had proceeded in fits and starts, often by fiat from Washington or MACV, with the Marines taking scattered potshots at the plan and dickering with Saigon over manpower and material. The President and his advisers seemed only dimly aware of the terms of the debate or of what the barrier approach had actually entailed. It was at best debatable whether the border strong points like Khe Sanh and Con Thien had ever "pinned down" any sizable enemy forces. On the contrary, the North Vietnamese were free to mass their forces and initiate large-scale attacks, as they did at Hue during the Tet Offensive and at Dong Ha in May. Those unexpected attacks had to be met by American forces committed piecemeal from their scattered positions along the McNamara Line. As General Davis observed, the strong points on the DMZ, intended to target the enemy, had instead made targets of the Marines.[54]

The Pentagon's initial response to "the difficult public relations task" posed by the closing of Khe Sanh was to suggest that the enemy had experienced such a beating that the old posture was no longer necessary, and that the new posture was "reinforcing success" and the Americans had now "taken the initiative in western Quang Tri."[55] General Abrams was much more circumspect. Having witnessed the grim contest along the DMZ over the past year, he wanted no rosy predictions, no exaggerated statements that might "come back to bite us." Abrams believed that any public statement should "stick to the reason we are making the change—to get into a better position to meet the increased enemy threat. Mobile forces tied to no specific terrain must be used to the utmost to attack, intercept, reinforce, or take whatever action is most appropriate to meet the enemy threat."[56]

The inconvenient fact that Westmoreland had adamantly refused to close Khe Sanh despite Abrams's and Rosson's strong recommendations also had to be dealt with. The solution devised by the Pentagon was to tell the press that Westmoreland "had approved in principle the plan now being put into execution" but "did not make a decision as to details and date of implementation since he would not be in command at that time."[57]

While Washington and MACV pondered the public relations problems of the new mobile strategy, Davis proceeded to put it into effect. A new operating base, Vandegrift, was established on the site of the Cav's old base at LZ Stud. The new base made possible a short turnaround for helicopters operating in the western DMZ area by eliminating the long flight east to Dong Ha or Quang Tri. Centralized planning and new, more efficient techniques for staging and loading supplies made it possible for Vandegrift to support the operations of nine infantry and nine artillery battalions operating in the mountains to the north and west.

The infantry and artillery, no longer tied to fixed bases, now targeted the Communist network of supply trails, caches, and way stations in the dense mountain jungle. The Marines' artillery was positioned on a landing zone atop a razorback ridge or a high pinnacle, which engineers had blasted out of the thick, triple-canopy jungle. First on the ground would be the engineers, with chainsaws and axes, to clear an area large enough for lightweight bulldozers and backhoes to be lowered by helicopters. Within two hours these machines would have the landing zone ready to receive the first artillery pieces.

Under the protection of the fire bases, positioned about 8 kilometers apart so as to provide mutually supporting artillery coverage, the infantry fanned out to search for enemy trails and supplies. One rifle company, or part of it, normally remained behind to protect the fire base, while the other companies searched an area of 4–8 square kilometers. In the high mountains companies moved forward along the heavily wooded ridge lines and seized the first high knob. Then they hacked out a landing zone to evacuate casualties and bring in supplies. Another company would pass through the first, seize the next hilltop, search out the fingers, and hack out a second landing zone.

Using this new method of operations, the Marines cut and blasted their way into even the most inaccessible regions of the jungle-covered mountains. Areas that had not been entered by American forces for months were invaded and searched by Davis's helo-borne battalions, who would then withdraw only to return again a few weeks later.

To accompany these new, more mobile operations, Davis stepped up the employment of all long-range reconnaissance patrols. Four- or five-man teams were inserted deep into the jungle or mountains near the Laotian border, far beyond the range of supporting artillery. The four-man teams would be landed from small helicopters flying at low altitudes and accompanied by a chase ship and two gunships. The copters faked landings at several locations before dropping the team, then continued on to make more simulated landings to confuse enemy observers.[58]

Once on the ground the recon team attempted to remain hidden and reported on patterns of enemy movements and the locations of roads and trails. If the team was detected, its only hope of survival was quick extraction by helicopter, often supported by gunships and fighter-bombers.

Closer in, larger teams of eight to ten men, called "Stingray," patrolled inside the fire bases' artillery fan, seeking to find enemy units and direct fire on them. At times some forty to forty-five reconnaissance teams were in the field searching the wooded crags, ravines, and mountain trails of western Quang Tri.[59] The teams were credited with impressive successes. Defense Department analysts calculated that the Marines' long-range patrols accounted for thirty-six enemy dead for every U.S. casualty.[60] Yet the recon patrols were far from a super weapon. Only a few well-trained and experienced troops had the confidence and ability to conceal themselves effectively in the jungle and to handle the complex task of coordinating and directing air and artillery fire.[61] Even when large numbers of enemy could be located, artillery and air were sometimes too slow in responding. One Marine officer recalled that patrols outside Khe Sanh "could see thousands of them [the NVA] but our indirect fire system was not good enough" to respond quickly enough to hit a column of North Vietnamese moving rapidly down a jungle trail in single file.[62]

Davis's new operation methods were truly tested in August and September, when the 320th PAVN Division renewed its attacks into South Vietnam. Crossing the Ben Hai River, the division's three regiments, the 64th, the 52d, and the 48th, attempted to move south over the network of infiltration trails between the town of Cam Lo and the artillery base at the Rockpile a few miles west. This time they found the Marines astride the trail, and as the North Vietnamese moved south other Marines were helo-lifted in behind them.

In the intermittent, sharp encounters the North Vietnamese found themselves forced to abandon large quantities of their food provisions, equipment, and supplies. The Marines could now move freely in pursuit of the enemy, supported by their mobile fire bases. Air strikes by B-52s were closely coordinated with the movement of the Marines so that the big bombers became, at times, almost tactical support for the ground troops.

Where enemy bunkers were encountered, Davis borrowed Army CH-54 "Flying Crane" helicopters to lift in 155mm howitzers and blast away enemy defenses. At one point the giant 16-inch guns of the newly arrived battleship *New Jersey* supported an attack by a battalion of Marines on a bunker complex near the Ben Hai River. The Marines advanced World War I fashion behind a creeping barrage of 16-inch shells 1,000 meters to their front.[63]

The new high-mobility tactics strained the Marines' resources to the limit. The helicopters assigned to Davis's division were far fewer than for a comparable Army division and were not well organized to support the kind of fast-moving, high-tempo operations the Marines were now carrying out. The 1st Marine Air Wing, with headquarters far to the south near Da Nang, proved unable, at first, to respond to Davis's demands. "When [you have] troops on little pinnacles where you can't walk to them, you can't supply them, you can't extract them, you can't get your casualties out, you're totally dependent on air to make your operation work," the general later observed. "When we didn't have it, it was a shambles."[64]

Poor weather conditions posed an even greater problem. Frequent fog and rain and rapidly changing weather conditions meant that helicopters had to be available to respond within a few minutes to sudden breaks in the weather. The Marines dealt with these problems by establishing a provisional air group (MAG-39) at Vandegrift and by instituting procedures for critical resupply missions by helicopters on short notice.

In clear weather the air strip at Vandegrift came to resemble a giant aerial taxi rank, with helicopters dropping down to lift pre-positioned supplies on numbered pads. Choppers hovered above the pad while ground crews hooked large pallets loaded with rations or ammunition to the choppers' external sling. This activity continued from dawn to dark unless foul weather intervened.

In addition to the new problems posed by air-mobile operations, the battles with the 320th held all the old dangers of combat in the thick mountain jungles against a determined enemy. Combat in western Quang Tri was still exhausting, frequently harrowing, and bloody, but by early October it seemed clear that the Marines had the upper hand. The new leapfrog operations and systematic searches enabled the Americans to find and uproot the massive pre-positioned supplies that were the vital blood and arteries of North Vietnamese operations. In early September, on two ridge lines southwest of the Rockpile, the 2d Battalion, 9th Marines, discovered caches of supplies totaling 55,000 pounds of rice, 11,000 pounds of salt, 4,000 pounds of TNT, 3,400 82mm mortar rounds, and 400,000 rifle rounds. A few days later 3/9 found an even larger cache on a ridge line to the north, where the North Vietnamese had stored 13,000 hand grenades and hundreds of 122mm rockets.[65]

In mid-September two battalions of Marines were lifted into the southern half of the Demilitarized Zone, where they found a newly built road, underwater bridges spanning the Ben Hai River, and newly dug artillery positions for 152mm guns. Dug into the mountains to a depth of 7 feet and surrounded by underground bunkers, Communist gun positions were impervious to all but direct hits.

By late October North Vietnamese prisoners reported that the 320th's scattered regiments, plagued by shortages of food and ammunition, were withdrawing back across the Ben Hai River.

The Marines' return engagement with the 320th Division was the product of the Communist's Third General Offensive, launched in mid-August. Documents captured by the Americans and South Vietnamese suggested that Hanoi intended the Third Offensive to be both more gradual and more prolonged than the Tet and May attacks. The ultimate objectives remained Saigon and Da Nang, but the enemy's strategy was more flexible and opportunistic, aimed at drawing major forces away from the large cities.[66]

The offensive began on the evening of August 17 with attacks in the Da Nang and Tay Ninh areas and numerous rocket and mortar bombardments of American and South Vietnamese towns and bases. The Communist thrust at Da Nang was preempted on August 16, when three battalions of Marines silently converged on the village of Chau Dhong about 18 miles from Da Nang, where U.S. intelligence sources had reported the presence of the Viet Cong R20 Battalion and a battalion of sappers. The crash of artillery shells impacting in the village at 2:00 A.M. was the first warning the Viet Cong received that their presence had been detected. More than two hundred fled east into waiting ambushes laid by F and G Companies of the 7th Marines. More than fifty Viet Cong were killed, with almost no loss to the Marines. Moving further into Chau Dhong, the Marines encountered stiff resistance from Communists entrenched in the hamlets of La Phat and La Nam. It took G Company, 2d Battalion, 5th Marines, assisted by air strikes, five hours to force a Communist platoon from La Phat at the cost of seven Marines killed and nineteen wounded.

The North Vietnamese and Viet Cong had been well prepared. In Chau Phong the Marines found sufficient rice and ammunition to supply five hundred men. The troops opposing the Marines at La Thap had new weapons, helmets, and body armor.[67] Yet the Communist threat to Da Nang had died in the blasted, smoldering houses of Chau Dhong.

Elsewhere, the Third Offensive also sputtered to a halt. Many of the planned attacks had never materialized. U.S. forces had not been lured from the major cities, and many Communist units found themselves short of supplies and unable to mass for the attack in the face of heavy U.S. firepower. Only in Tay Ninh province, northwest of Saigon, did sustained fighting erupt. Communist forces, hoping to push past Tay Ninh toward Saigon, clashed with elements of the U.S. 25th Division in a series of bloody fights in the bamboo woods, hills, and rubber plantations near Tay Ninh.

The battles began with an attack on Fire Base Buell, which sat astride the main approach routes to Tay Ninh from the north about 4 miles from the town. The Americans had been alerted by intelligence to the danger of attack and were well prepared. The fire base's six 105mm and five 155mm guns and a battery of 4.2-inch mortars were protected by revetments and by a high chain-link fence for defense against rocket-propelled grenades. The entire base was protected by triple concertina wire with numerous trip flares concealed in its strands. The fire base's infantry company had been reinforced the previous day by a mechanized infantry company and a platoon of tanks, whose armored vehicles added to the already considerable firepower of the soldiers entrenched in Fire Base Buell's bunker line.[68]

The Communist attack began at 1:00 A.M. with a barrage of 82mm mortar fire. As the firing slackened illumination rounds from the 4.2-inch mortars revealed enemy forces advancing on the northern and southern ends of the base. The North Vietnamese mortar rounds hit an oil storage area near the 155mm battery, starting a large fire, and two of the tanks were damaged by rocket powered grenades (RPGs) fired by a group of North Vietnamese soldiers who had managed to crawl forward through the wire on the northwest sector of the perimeter—but the base was never in danger. Deadly high explosive rounds called "Killer Junior" burst in the air above the attackers. As the North Vietnamese closed to under 100 yards, the gunners switched to rounds of "Beehive" canisters fired at point-blank range. On the southern edge of the base, two Cobra helicopter gunships made repeated machine gun attacks on the North Vietnamese, then were replaced by Air Force fighter-bombers and "Spooky" gunships, which remained on station throughout the battle. By 5:30 A.M. enemy fire had all but ceased. Most of the attackers had not even come within 10 meters of the wire. The Americans lost one dead and twenty-six wounded, while the Communists left 104 bodies and eight wounded on the battlefield.[69]

Yet not all the clashes near Tay Ninh were as one-sided as the attack on Fire Base Buell. One week after that fight a large convoy from Long Binh to Tay Ninh was ambushed near the village of Ap Nhi on the road to Tay Ninh. It was nearly noon, and the convoy of almost a hundred vehicles had just passed the village when the ambush was sprung. More than one hundred Viet Cong and NVA were concealed among the young rubber trees to the left of the road. The ambushers allowed about half the convoy to pass through the killing zone, then opened heavy fire with automatic rifles, machine guns, and mortars.

A tanker toward the head of the column was hit and burst into flames, effectively blocking the road. The truckers leaped from their vehicles and took cover on the opposite side of the road, laying down a heavy volume of fire with their M-16s and machine guns as they desperately sought to prevent the enemy from crossing the road and flanking the convoy.[70]

Specialist 4 William Seay was driving a 5-ton tractor pulling a trailer load of artillery charges when the convoy came under fire. Snipers concealed in the trees added to the hazards of fire from the more numerous attackers concealed in the rubber fields. Jumping from his vehicle, Seay took cover behind the large rear wheels of his tractor, where he was joined by another driver, Specialist 4 David Sellman. Sellman and Seay were soon in the midst of a fire fight with a group of North Vietnamese who had left the cover of the rubber trees and were attempting to assault the vehicles. Sellman killed one NVA who had approached to within 15 meters of his position before his M-16 jammed. Seay killed or wounded two more, halting the enemy attack. Seay also accounted for a sniper in a tree to his right. Minutes later a grenade landed under Seay's trailer, which was loaded with 175mm shells. Shifting his rifle to his left hand, Seay scooped up the grenade and tossed it back at the Vietnamese concealed in the rubber.[71]

To the rear of the convoy, a squad of engineers of the 65th Engineer Battalion was returning from a mine-sweeping operation when it encountered the Communist ambushers. The engineers were accompanied by about a dozen infantrymen of the 1st Battalion, 5th Mechanized Infantry, riding in two armored personnel carriers. One of the .50 caliber machine guns on the APCs had been burned out in a previous fight and was inoperable, while the other continually jammed.

The NVA opened heavy fire with rifles and machine guns, supplemented by grenades from a captured M79 grenade launcher. The engineers and infantry fought back with rifles, grenades, and M-60 machine guns. As ammunition began to run low, Sergeant Gregory Haley, an engineer squad leader, worked his way to the rear of one of the APCs, climbed in, and brought out additional ammunition and two more machine guns. Jumping down from the APC, he emitted a string of curses as he noticed that one of the machine guns lacked a trigger. Haley fed a bandolier of ammo into the second machine gun, slammed the plate shut, and opened fire, only to have the gun jam. As he attempted to unjam the gun, the charging handle broke in his hand.[72]

After two hours of heavy fighting, an armored cavalry troop arrived on the scene, forcing the ambushers to break off their attack. At 9:00 P.M. the remnants of the shattered convoy limped into Tay Ninh. More than two dozen ruined vehicles had been left on the road, along with the bodies of several dozen of the attackers. Specialist Seay, killed by a sniper's bullet, was nominated by his commanding officer for a Medal of Honor. Sergeant Haley, after rescuing two of the wounded, drove them to safety in an APC.

As action around Tay Ninh gradually died down and further

planned attacks in I Corps and in the Delta failed to materialize, the Communists launched a final desperate attack on the Special Forces camp at Duc Lap near the Cambodian border in Quang Duc Province, perhaps hoping to repeat their earlier successes at Lang Vei and Kham Duc. Four thousand North Vietnamese soldiers from at least three regiments attacked the Duc Lap subsector headquarters astride the main routes to the large highland city of Ban Me Thuot and the nearby Special Forces camp, A-239. For more than a week the grim battle raged in the jungle-covered hills around the small, flat Duc Lap plateau. The outnumbered Vietnamese, Special Forces, and Montagnard tribesmen and their American advisers at A-239 fought off repeated NVA attacks and were reinforced by other Special Forces Mobile Strike Force companies fed in from Nha Trang and Ban Me Thuot.

The subsector headquarters was defended only by a company of Popular Forces and by a handful of American advisers, but the South Vietnamese, mostly former Catholic refugees who had fled North Vietnam in 1954, turned the defense of the small district headquarters into an epic worthy of the Alamo. The district chief, Lieutenant Nguyen Nhu Phu, refused to leave his post even after being wounded, and his officers and NCOs moved about among the outnumbered defenders continually encouraging them and positioning them to meet new enemy assaults. Wives of the Popular Force soldiers reloaded magazines and braved enemy fire to bring ammunition to the defenders.[73]

After two days of heavy fighting, two battalions of the South Vietnamese 23d Division were lifted by helicopter to attack the North Vietnamese positions ringing the Duc Lap subsector and A-239. An American Army officer watched as one of the South Vietnamese battalions assaulted a hill near the Duc Lap subsector five times during one day. "In the evening the hill was still in enemy hands. The commander pulled back to medevac his wounded and prepare to attack once more. . . . The battalion had been on combat operations continuously for the past thirty-one days. Casualties had claimed one-third of the unit. The troops were obviously tired. Still the plan and conversation were only of the impending attack."[74]

The North Vietnamese also fought well. A Special Forces sergeant watching the North Vietnamese withdraw under heavy fire observed that "one position would cover and pin us down while another was evading us. They fought hard and they left their positions only when they thought it was safe to do so. It was almost like a well-planned and rehearsed operation because each man seemed to know exactly what the other was going to do."[75]

Despite their excellent discipline and stubborn determination, the North Vietnamese were unable to breach the defenses of Duc Lap and A-239 completely. Under increasing pressure from South Vietnamese Army attacks and heavy air assaults by American gunships, fighter-bombers, and even B-52s, the North Vietnamese withdrew toward Cambodia, carrying with them the wreckage of the Third Offensive.

"The events that took place constituted a dismal failure" for the Communists, a MACV report on the fighting declared. The enemy lost 20,000 KIA in five weeks of fighting and attained not a single objective for his long touted "final and decisive phase."[76] The message omitted mention of the obvious: that the Communist failures were not final or decisive either. Yet after September, Abrams could breathe a little easier. On the battlefield, for the Americans, things would never be quite so bad again.

Eager to exploit the Communist August defeats, Abrams requested permission for American units in contact with enemy forces to pursue them across the Cambodian border to a distance of up to 20 kilometers. President Johnson remained unwilling, as he had been with Westmoreland, to extend the war across international boundaries. After studying Abrams's request for almost six weeks, the White House instructed the MACV commander to maintain "constant, relentless, persistent pressure" on the enemy but to "avoid any sudden or dramatic increase in out-of-country operation."[77]

Abrams repeated his request in October. From MACV's point of view, extending the war into Cambodia made perfectly good sense. The Communists, after their August failures, were vulnerable in a way they had never been before. From the perspective of Washington the proposal to widen the ground war even in "hot pursuit" was politically and psychologically suicidal. Any apparent move to escalate the war would undermine the President's remaining public support, reignite antiwar protests, further splinter the Democratic

Party, and probably deliver the November elections to the Republicans.

The President's March speech, designed primarily as a device to buy time and regain public support, had set in motion a train of events that was now irreversible. Many Americans, dissatisfied with the lack of progress in Paris, were calling for a total bombing halt. Secretary Clifford had also found himself obliged to fend off repeated questions and rumors about the imminent beginning of U.S. troop withdrawals from Vietnam.

The Americans had gained a decided edge on the battlefield as a result of the Communists' costly attacks of February, May, and August, but in the United States time was running out and options were narrowing. If the Americans were to achieve a favorable solution to their Vietnam predicament, they would have to find it in Vietnam, not in Paris or Washington, and they would have to find it soon.

CHAPTER 11

The End of Racial Harmony

In the United States, news of the new Communist attacks of August and September shared the headlines with a more novel story: a major riot at the largest military prison in Vietnam. On the night of August 29 a fight broke out between a small number of prisoners in one of the three medium security compounds of the U.S. army installation stockade near Long Binh, universally referred to as the LBJ, or the "Long Binh Jail." Guards who attempted to separate the fighters were overpowered by the prisoners, who stripped them of their keys and unlocked the gates at the entire medium security area. A wave of prisoners then streamed through the exercise area into the main yard of the stockade, overpowering and beating guards as they went.

The rioting prisoners, now swollen to several hundred, unlocked the maximum security cells and set fire to a number of buildings in the main compound, including the mess hall and the administration building, which contained prisoner records. The stockade commander, attempting to talk with the rioters, was severely beaten and had to be hospitalized.[1]

The rioters, almost all blacks, were stopped at the main gate by guards armed with machine guns and .45 pistols, but the compound remained in their hands. Reports circulated that white prisoners were being confined and beaten by blacks.

About forty-five minutes after the uprising began, custodial personnel, heavily reinforced by troops from the 557th and 284th Military Police companies, wearing steel helmets and protective vests, moved with fixed bayonets into the compound.[2] Advancing in a phalanx and lobbing tear gas canisters as they went, the MPs managed to restore control to most of the compound at the cost of several casualties. In all, eight of the stockade staff, including Colonel Johnson, the commander, and twenty-six prisoners were injured seriously enough to require hospitalization, and two dozen other prisoners and one guard received minor injuries. One prisoner died as a result of beatings by fellow prisoners.[3]

By 1:00 A.M., a semblance of order had been restored to the stockade, fires were out or under control, and ambulances were evacuating the wounded. However, more than two hundred hard-core "uncooperatives," all African-Americans, still held out, locked into the former work area called "Big Red" on the north side of the stockade. Military police sealed off the area but made no attempt to forcibly enter Big Red. Cans of C rations were tossed over the fence each day for the recalcitrant prisoners, and gradually handfuls of militants began to give themselves up. After almost a month of this, only about fifteen prisoners remained in Big Red. Most were serving long sentences for murder or other serious crimes. Finally a squad of guards with fixed bayonets and tear gas was sent in to round up the last holdouts. All surrendered without a fight except for one prisoner, "who picked up a board and swung it around his head threatening to clobber anybody who came near him." After a short scuffle, he too was subdued and led out of the compound.[4]

Meanwhile a new stockade commander, Colonel Ivan Nelson, had arrived. A hard-bitten veteran of World War II, in which he had received a battlefield commission, Nelson immediately took steps to ease the overcrowded conditions and restore discipline to the stockade. Men awaiting trial or guilty of minor offenses were returned to their units. For prisoners remaining, additional psychologists and lawyers were made available, but a stricter regimen was also instituted. A seemingly endless parade of flatbed trucks began arriving at the stockade gates, carrying CONEX boxes, large steel shipping crates about 6 feet high, 9 feet wide, and 6 feet long. Soon rows of boxes appeared, not only in maximum security but in the medium yard. The smallest offense was sufficient to land a prisoner in a CONEX box for a week or more. When not in the CONEX box, prisoners were put through an exhausting routine of drill and exercise, all in the sweltering heat of the Vietnamese autumn.

Virtually everyone in Vietnam, from newspaper reporters to stockade guards, joined in labeling the LBJ uprising primarily a race riot. The all-black composition of the rebel prisoners and their conduct toward their white fellow inmates left little room for doubt. First Sergeant William J. Davidson, an experienced African-American career soldier, reported that the prisoners talked of only two things, "to get out of the Army" and "how much they hate the chucks (whites)." As for the white prisoners, "they want to be segregated. They can't stand the beatings that were going on. They will stand together now just like the colored prisoners."[5] *Newsweek* concluded that in the Long Binh stockade

. . . black soldiers, rightly or wrongly, felt they faced the same kind of prejudice that they had in the ghettos of the U.S. and quickly rediscovered their built-in resentment of authority. All of which seemed to suggest that the vaunted egalitarianism of the Army cannot, by itself, eliminate the ingrained tensions that unfortunately exist between white and black Americans.[6]

For a long time the armed forces in Vietnam had appeared almost immune to the racial animosities tormenting American society. While race riots made nightly headlines in the United States during the summer of 1967, the troops in Vietnam showed few outward signs of racial trouble. Recounting the impressive battlefield achievements of African-Americans, *Time* declared in May 1967: "The performance of the negro GI under fire reaffirms the success—and diversity—of the American experiment. Black-white relations in a slit trench or a combat-bound Huey are years ahead of Denver and Darien, decades ahead of Birmingham and Biloxi."[7] Black soldiers still occasionally faced racism and prejudice and often shared the doubts of their fellow countrymen about the war, yet "all but a few volunteered the information that they were there to serve their country no matter how badly it may have treated them."[8]

As late as April 1968, General Abrams reported "racial problems among our men in South Vietnam are for all practical purposes insignificant." In the fall of 1968, when Judge L. Howard Bennett, one of the Pentagon's top civil rights officials, returned from Vietnam and warned that racial tensions had reached the point of explosion, his observations were dismissed as "alarmist" by armed services leaders.[9]

Among the thousands of African-American officers and NCOs in Vietnam, Lieutenant Eddie L. Kitchen seemed to epitomize the skilled, confident, upwardly mobile black soldier celebrated in *Time*. Kitchen had entered the Army in 1955 as an enlisted man and had risen through the ranks, becoming an officer in 1967. A former drill sergeant and Army boxing champion, Kitchen was "proud of being a negro. He knew discrimination existed but it didn't make him bitter."[10]

When he arrived in Vietnam in January 1968, Kitchen was surprised and annoyed to find that Confederate flags were being flown from some of the vehicles in his unit. "We are fighting and dying in a war that is not very popular in the first place and we still have some stupid people who are still fighting the Civil War," Kitchen wrote to his mother. "Black soldiers should not have to serve under the Confederate flag or with it. We are serving under the American flag and the American flag only."[11] Kitchen urged his relatives to bring the situation to the attention of the NAACP and the President. He also complained that almost all the men in his infantry platoon were African-American. In March he again complained about the Confederate flags in a letter to his mother and promised to send a photo of the offensive objects in his next letter. Kitchen was killed three days later. His mother presented his last letter to Senator Robert Kennedy on the day of his burial.

If even a disciplined career soldier like Eddie Kitchen had found reasons for anger and concern about the position of African-American GIs in Vietnam, many younger African-Americans serving their first tour in the military found it degrading and intolerable. Young African-Americans entering the Army after 1967 were far more sensitive to racial slights and had far less patience than their older relatives who had served in World War II and Korea. "In a day gone by, the reaction of the black to discrimination was to work hard and persevere," a Congressional subcommittee report on racial tension noted. "Today that enlistee has more racial pride, probably more bitterness, more sensitivity to real or fancied oppression, and often enters [the military] with a chip on his shoulder."[12] Many of the eighteen- and nineteen-year-old black GIs of 1968 had experienced at first hand the bitterness and frustration of the urban ghettos as well as a heightened pride and self-awareness encouraged by the movement for African-American rights and black consciousness of the 1960s. Little in their civilian life had encouraged these young men to put their trust in authority, least of all the white authority represented by military officers and NCOs. "The young black soldier is angry," a black journalist wrote. "He is angry because he feels that the armed forces discriminate against him, because when he goes off base he becomes a second-class citizen, because he must fight in Vietnam and sometimes against his brothers in the streets at home."[13]

The most common source of dissatisfaction was the feeling that African-Americans were discriminated against in promotions and job opportunities. A universal complaint was that blacks were overrepresented in combat units. It was also widely believed that in these line units African-Americans were always assigned the most dangerous jobs. "When you're on patrol and moving into an area it's always the negro who's walking point," declared one black Marine. "That means he is the first to get it if a mine explodes. That's the kind of harassment we get from the whites. . . . Look at the guys who go out on sweeps, who protect the hills. Brothers, as many brothers as they can find."[14]

Another source of friction was the alleged discrimination on the part of military police, most of whom were white. African-Americans believed that MPs singled them out for harassment and overzealous enforcement of rules that did not apply to whites. Large groups of African-American soldiers were routinely stopped and checked for ID cards or unauthorized weapons, while groups of whites were seldom bothered.[15]

A frequent area for trouble was the Enlisted Men's Club. Often located in ramshackle buildings or hooches, usually hot, crowded, and noisy, with beer and liquor readily available, clubs were often the scene of minor fights and arguments whenever the bored, tired, and irritable GIs gathered to drink, talk, and listen to music. By 1968 the almost endemic quarrels and bickering at the club had taken on racial overtones. "Now and then to help slice the monotony into endurable segments, floor shows came to LZ Gator," Tim O'Brien recalled. "The black soldiers would arrive an hour before show time, cameras poised for a shot of flesh, taking the front row seats. The white guys didn't like that much. A few whites tried arriving even earlier, but for the next floor show, the black soldiers were ready and waiting two full hours before curtain up."[16]

One common cause of arguments was music, with blacks frequently demanding that the clubs provide more soul music. One club at Cam Ranh Bay that featured almost exclusively country and western music was the scene of a near riot and "threats to burn the club down."[17]

The traditional source of leadership and discipline for new young soldiers was the noncommissioned officer. It was the NCO who was the GI's day-to-day boss; who assigned him to work details, sick call, and R&R; who settled pay disputes and found him quarters; and who decided on job assignments and minor promotions. In the noncommissioned officer ranks African-Americans had had outstanding success, and a substantial proportion of career NCOs in the Army and Marine Corps were black. Yet black or white, the noncommissioned officers of the "Vietnam only" military were poorly situated to deal with the challenge of growing racial tension. A Department of Defense study on race relations pointed out that most black senior NCOs were referred to as "Uniform Tangos," or "Oreos- Uncle Toms," by younger black GIs. "Otherwise, the reasoning goes, they could not have gotten ahead in an environment inherently hostile to blacks. Most are tagged as figureheads, promoted to appease or cool black troops. . . . Every time one is bypassed, overruled, or put down by other NCOs or officers, it reinforces the young troops' belief. To the black NCOs, many of whom had to work harder than their white counterparts to get rank, these youngsters 'want something for nothing.' "[18]

By 1968 the senior sergeants who in past wars had provided the experienced leadership and continuity for new soldiers and junior officers were fast disappearing from front line units. GIs in Vietnam frequently commented on the fact that few E-7s, E-8s, and E-9s could be found in infantry units in the field. A newly arrived infantryman recalled being told by a member of his unit "that the so-called cadres of the replacement company were all senior NCOs and had an 'in' somewhere so they never went to the field and none of them were ever in combat. . . . He also said that some of these

NCOs were on extended tours, some up to four years, all drawing combat pay. . . . Their hooches were all dry and clean as well as stocked with things like radios, refrigerators, and comfortable beds."[19]

This phenomenon of lifers in the rear, draftees in the field, was far more prevalent during the latter years of the war than during 1965–67. By the beginning of 1969 some career NCOs were on their third tour in Vietnam. Many had been wounded in earlier tours. It was an aging NCO corps that was not replicating itself either through "Shake and Bakes" or by normal promotion. "These individuals, E-7s and E-8s, are people who are over here right now, most probably on their third tour. Certainly none of them are here on their second," one division commander observed. "They have been wounded and they have had other things occur to them. . . . If you are over forty years old, there is no place for you in a platoon. . . . It is impossible to get those guys to hump about in the jungle."[20]

Whether in the rear or in the bush, the senior NCOs or "lifers," as they were universally called, inspired little respect or affection in the younger GIs they were expected to lead. The Defense Department's reports declared that the lifers

> . . . are regarded by many young troops, both black and white, as their biggest problem. . . . They live apart from the men they supervise as a reward for making rank and as a means of artificially creating sufficient professional distance to maintain discipline. . . . They even attend different clubs in the evening. . . . Long hair, soul, psychedelic, and black power are alien, suspect, little understood, and resented. . . . Yet they are expected to translate for the higher command the meaning of such concepts . . . and then interact with them [sic] on a working level in a manner productive of efficiency, harmony, and high morale.[21]

Junior officers, black or white, were probably the most knowledgeable about the actual state of race relations in their units, but they were distracted by many other urgent tasks and were, in any case, discouraged from bringing problems to the attention of their superiors. The traditional approach to military leadership called for problems to be resolved at the lowest possible level, and problems that traveled up the chain of command to reach the ears of senior officers were likely to be viewed as reflecting poorly on the abilities of the junior officers involved.

Senior officers were thus largely isolated from the reality of racial tension by the silence of their juniors and the inability of their NCOs to deal with the problem or even to understand it. In 1968 higher-level commanders tended to think of race relations in terms of memos to be initialed, statements to be promulgated, and reports to be filed. A Department of Defense report declared that most units seemed to devote more attention to the yearly Savings Bond Drive than to race relations and equal opportunity programs.[22]

With the murder of Dr. Martin Luther King in April 1968, signs of racial polarization and tension became clear and unmistakable. A black infantryman named Charles Taliaferro recalled that King's death first gave black soldiers in his unit "a feeling of unity and got them thinking about black issues."[23] Jim Heiden, a white GI, agreed. "Reactions to Tet and things like that, they were minimal, you know, . . . that was people confronting the war. But when Martin Luther King was assassinated reactions became—reactions were very, very visible. . . . People fought. People had fist fights. Black guys maybe hung a little tighter if that was possible. You know, people pretty much stuck to their own groups, but they sat around and they talked about it."[24] Paul Hathaway, a black reporter for the *Washington Star* spent a month interviewing large numbers of African-American GIs in Vietnam during April 1968. He found 80–85 percent of those interviewed "expressed negative feelings about the purposes and the objectives of the war or about the military's treatment of negroes. Usually it was both."[25]

In many cases African-American GIs directed their anger at the Confederate flags that had so annoyed Lieutenant Kitchen. The flags became a frequent source of complaints and arguments. Many black GIs wrote their relatives and Congressmen complaining about the widespread display of Confederate flags, which they saw as symbols of Southern racism. The *Daily Defender* of Chicago, a major African-American newspaper, carried reports that "Confederate flags [are] flying in most barracks and U.S. vehicles."[26] Barry Wright, a SeaBee stationed at Cam Ranh Bay, saw the flags as proof that "racial hatred has grown to the point where we never know whether we will get a bullet in the head from a Viet Cong or in the back from whitey."[27] Even Afro-Americans who took a less dire view than Wright found the flags hateful. "They didn't mean nothing by the rebel flag," recalled Richard Ford, a member of a long-range reconnaissance platoon of the 25th Infantry Division, "it was just saying 'We for the south,' it didn't mean they hated blacks. But after you in the field you took the flags very personally."[28]

Responding to the barrage of complaints by African-Americans and the press, U.S. Army Vietnam headquarters reminded subordinate commanders that "only official flags are authorized to be displayed in accordance with regulations."[29] Even earlier, the 1st Marine Division, following the news of the King assassination, had banned the display of Confederate flags, a ban that soon extended to all Marine units.

Yet that was not the end of the matter. It had long been customary for servicemen to write to their Congressmen or legislators for a flag from their home state. Such flags were flown from vehicles, buildings, and the tops of bunkers. In a kind of oneupmanship, GIs sometimes vied with one another to obtain the largest state flag or to display it in the most conspicuous place. Even soldiers who felt no strong identity with their states often felt obliged to join in the competition.[30]

In the ordinary course of events the state flags would have evoked no more interest than the graffiti customarily scrawled on helmet covers. In the tension-charged atmosphere of early 1968, however, many African-Americans were quick to note that the flags of some Southern states closely resembled the detested Confederate battle flag. To head off possible trouble, many commanders forbade the display of state flags as well as the Confederate flag.

Now it was the turn of white soldiers to write indignant letters home complaining that they could not even fly the home state flag, which, in many cases, had been sent to them by a member of the state legislature or a representative in Congress. A new rain of letters from irate Representatives, Senators, and state legislators now descended on the Pentagon demanding to know why their states' finest sons, serving their country in Vietnam, were forbidden to fly the state flag, etc., etc.[31] The Pentagon, backpedalling rapidly, issued a statement in mid-May assuring lawmakers that GIs would be permitted to display the state flag and that the ban had been only temporary, confined to Confederate flags, and aimed at easing racial tensions during the days following Dr. King's death.[32]

The affair of the flags, despite the publicity it attracted, was a mere tempest in a teapot beside the more fundamental racial tensions present in Vietnam in mid-1968. Among these, it was problems in the military justice system that led to the earliest sign of trouble. Experience in civilian life had given most young African-Americans little reason for confidence in systems of courts and police. Their experience with MPs and with the military justice system was even less happy. "People who are part of the system (staff judge advocates, commanders, reviewing authorities) are . . . automatically mistrusted" by African-Americans," a Department of Defense investigative report concluded. "As a result staff judge advocates complain that blacks particularly will not open up or level with them or take their advice; appeals are haphazardly filed or never filed at all. The [judicial] system itself is . . . not at all understood."[33]

By the summer of 1968 African-Americans formed almost half of the prison population at the Long Binh stockade and over 40 percent of those held in the III MAF brig, the two largest military confinement centers in Vietnam.

At that point the III MAF brig, a collection of tents and "southeast Asia huts" ("hooches") in the midst of the sprawling Da Nang base complex, already housed more than its maximum capacity of 250 prisoners. The majority of prisoners were Marines, but there were a number of prisoners from other services as well. Only a minority of the prisoners had committed offenses that would have been considered criminal in civilian life, and many had been sentenced to the brig for relatively minor infractions.

Once in the brig prisoners soon discovered that others guilty of the same offense had received lighter sentences. The brig's executive officer described a typical scenario: "So a guy went over the hill for six days and they gave him six months. No one comes to visit him. The kid wonders what is happening, so he talks to a buddy. The buddy went over the hill for nine days and he only got two months. Nobody ever explains to him the different command's policy [*sic*]."³⁴ Lieutenant Colonel Gambardello, the brig commander, recalled that a sailor "was sentenced to thirty days for possession of marijuana. I have people in the brig sentenced to one year and a dishonorable discharge for the same offense. That does not create any [feeling of] well-being among the prisoners."³⁵

Added to the general discontent of the prisoners was growing racial animosity. Several prisoners had been members of African-American Chicago street gangs in civilian life and, according to one prisoner who claimed to be a gang leader, had recreated their organization inside the brig.

> We would all stay in one line in the chow formation, eat at the same table, and associate only with each other. . . . In order to prove yourself to get in this group you had to do something like when we were to be standing at attention when a guard would enter our hooches, we would sit down; and when told to stand up we would say, "Fuck you" or something similar. Normally this would get us thrown in the cell block and then we would be one of the gang.³⁶

There was especially strong animosity between these prisoners and three of the warders, two African-American NCOs whom the prisoners labeled Uncle Toms and a white lance corporal whom they derisively called "John Wayne."³⁷

In the afternoon on Friday, August 16, one of the brig guards was overheard by the prisoners referring to "a dark motherfucker." Although the guard later claimed he was talking about a lack of lighting in the rear of the cell block, word of the "racial slur" quickly made the rounds of the compound. That evening, as the prisoners were returning from a movie, an argument followed by a shoving match broke out between "John Wayne" and a prisoner. As other brig guards moved to break up the fight, prisoners poured out of their huts to confront the guards, shouting threats and curses. When the outnumbered guards tried unsuccessfully to regain control, prisoners began throwing rocks, stones, and buckets of water at the turnkeys and encouraging others to join them. At the same time a prisoner in the maximum security cell block succeeded in breaking out and began to release other prisoners in the block. Warning shots from the tower guards failed to halt the riot, and the remaining guards left the compound.[38]

For the next twenty-four hours the compound was in a virtual state of siege. The prisoners, in complete control of the compound, burned the cell blocks, looted the offices and mess hall, and held bizarre "courts-martial" of fellow prisoners suspected of being informers. Some of those found "guilty" were savagely beaten; others more fortunate were sentenced to "clean up the hut and move out."[39]

After several unsuccessful attempts to negotiate with the prisoners, Colonel Gambardello concluded that the brig would have to be forcibly reoccupied, but he was concerned to avoid injuries to brig personnel and to innocent prisoners. Finally, in the afternoon of Sunday, August 18, Gambardello warned the prisoners that if they did not surrender in fifteen minutes the compound would be retaken by force.

First Lieutenant Jimmie W. Glenn selected twelve men from the 3d MP Battalion, most of them sergeants with combat experience, and armed them with baseball bats and shotguns. "I told the men with shotguns that if I pointed at a man, I wanted that man to be dropped right on the spot. . . . If they had time to fire a warning shot then shoot at the legs."[40]

At 2:30 Lieutenant Glenn's men were formed up just outside the compound. A rock thrown by one of the prisoners was deflected by a baseball bat, and Glenn's detail replied with tear gas, which quickly blanketed the compound. Within two minutes the first prisoners came streaming through the gate, some holding wet towels to their faces in an attempt to mitigate the effects of the tear gas.[41] By 7:00 P.M. the last of the recalcitrant prisoners had been rounded up. Most were returned to the huts in the compound, but thirty-one men, suspected of being the ring leaders, were moved to brigs in the Philippines and Okinawa for trial by general courts-martial on charges of mutiny, riot, and assault on other prisoners.[42]

Less than two weeks after the riot at the III MAF brig came the far more serious and prolonged disturbances at the Long Binh stockade. The LBJ had been established in 1966 as a "field" or temporary stockade designed to hold about four hundred prisoners. By the summer of 1968 there were more than seven hundred prisoners crowded into the compound on the hot, red mud flats of the Long Binh base complex.

Most of the prisoners were housed in hardback tents resting on wooden floors. The forty-odd tents, intended to accommodate seven or eight men each, now housed fourteen prisoners each, allowing about 37 square feet of living space per man.[43] More recalcitrant prisoners or those guilty of infractions were housed in maximum security cells—poorly lighted, 61 by 81 wood and sheet metal boxes with 8-inch wire mesh openings serving as the only windows. These were supplemented by large steel shipping crates called CONEX boxes, about 6 feet high, 9 feet wide, and 6 feet long. The roofs of the CONEX boxes had been removed and replaced by screens, but the heat within their narrow metal confines was all but unbearable during daylight hours.[44]

Experienced military police officers estimated that about 280 officers and men would be necessary to control the prisoner population adequately and provide the administrative requirements of the stockade. In August 1968, however, there were only ninety men assigned to duty at the LBJ. The shortage of personnel and the rapidly increasing prisoner population strained the stockade staff to the breaking point. "I have never experienced such a constant source of tension and rush about everything just to get the ordinary day's work done," the Catholic chaplain, Major Jerauld E. Vessels recounted. "It was a terribly uncomfortable place to work or visit. The administrative office, the kitchen, the control shack, the education office—there was tension everywhere."[45]

The crowded conditions of the stockade were made all the more intolerable by the almost total absence of any real work projects, training, or recreation to allow the prisoners to vent their energies and anxieties. As a means of escape from their anger and discomfort many prisoners turned to drugs. Prisoners who left the compound on work details during the day had little difficulty in obtaining marijuana, which they easily smuggled back into the stockade. The prisoners told a reporter that marijuana could also be purchased inside the stockade from Vietnamese who "would throw bundles of 'grass' over the fence." The prisoners complained that the guards often seized the drugs, then smoked it themselves and beat the prisoners to keep them quiet.[46] Army investigators later strongly denied that stockade guards used pot or abused prisoners but confirmed that "evidence is plentiful that marijuana was available to prisoners."[47]

Many of the enlisted men assigned as guards or prison chasers to the LBJ had little or no experience or training in custodial work. Mostly young men serving their first tour in Vietnam, they often coped with the daunting task of controlling large numbers of sullen, provocative, and belligerent prisoners either by adopting an attitude of Draconian severity or by turning their backs on all but the most flagrant infractions.[48]

Although the stockade housed a number of men accused or convicted of murder, rape, and other serious crimes, an even greater number had been incarcerated for relatively minor offenses or were simply confined while awaiting trial. Chaplain Vessels believed that the crowded conditions in the stockade were due in part to the number of men sentenced to confinement "for offenses that could easily be handled on the level of unit punishment." Many men confined for such offenses had been led to believe that a short period of good behavior in the stockade would win their early release. "Unit commanders time and again promised their men that if they behaved in the stockade and made parole they would take them out, and then reneged on their promises. There were an unbelievable number of men who had not only become parolees but had passed a clemency board months before the riot and who were still in the stockade."[49]

African-American soldiers confined in the stockade felt particularly angry and exploited. By August 1968 close to 48 percent of the prisoner population at the LBJ were African-Americans, although African-Americans constituted only about 11 percent of servicemen in Vietnam.[50] African-Americans believed that the Army's disciplinary and judicial systems were racist and unfair. They argued that African-Americans were overrepresented in the stockade not because they committed more offenses but because they were often subjected to punishment for offenses that were ignored or tolerated when committed by white soldiers and that generally blacks were disciplined for behavior that was permitted to whites. Once convicted of an offense, whether by court-martial or by company-level "Article 15s" (nonjudicial punishment), blacks believed they received harsher punishment than whites found guilty of the same offenses.[51]

By August racial tensions in the stockade were at an all-time high. Fights between whites and blacks became an almost daily occurrence. There were persistent rumors that a small group of militant "black power" advocates had been organizing among the African-American prisoners. The relative ease of movement between the different compounds of the stockade, with prisoners moving back and forth several times a day to obtain meals or to use the latrine and exercise yard, provided ample opportunity for militants to communicate with and organize fellow prisoners.

On August 12 a prisoner was murdered by being struck with a metal rod used as a bunk adaptor (to raise or lower beds). The newly arrived stockade commander, Lieutenant Colonel Vernon E. Johnson, ordered extra precautions taken to prevent further violence. Even the wooden stays were removed from the ends of canvas cots so that they could not be used as clubs. The canvas cots, never very comfortable to begin with, were thus reduced to sagging 4-foot hammocks, further adding to the anger and discomfort of the prisoners.[52]

It was not the search for weapons, however, but the subsequent crackdown on marijuana that, in the view of most observers, proved the final step toward precipitating an uprising. At the beginning of August, Colonel Johnson ordered strip searches for prisoners returning from work details outside the compound. This measure almost immediately reduced the flow of marijuana to prisoners. Denied their sole means of withdrawal from their inhospitable environment, many prisoners became even more angry and morose. Many also saw this measure as still another step by those in authority to abuse and harass them.[53]

On the night of August 29 a fight broke out between prisoners in one of the three medium security compounds of the stockade leading to what one magazine described as "the worst prison riot in the modern history of the U.S. army."[54]

In the weeks following the riot at the LBJ, racial animosity continued to grow. Most problems occurred "in the rear," at support units and large base complexes. The closer life in the rear approximated life in the United States, the more likely it was to mirror stateside racial tensions as well. One area where tensions were especially high was the major supply base complex at Qui Nhon on the South China Sea in Binh Dinh province. As usual, the clubs were the locus of most of the incidents, which began as early as July 1968. On July 19 a brawl broke out at the 58th Field Depot Enlisted Man's Club over complaints about the service provided to Afro-American servicemen. Two weeks later a similar brawl erupted at the club of the 85th Evacuation Hospital. Damage was so severe that the club was temporarily closed. On September 12 a black private named Collins was involved in an argument with a white sergeant of the guard and was charged with aggravated assault with his M-16 rifle. Released while awaiting trial, Collins became involved in another argument three days later with a black club sergeant whom he accused of being an Uncle Tom. According to military police reports, Collins then attempted to settle the dispute with a .45 caliber pistol, a hand grenade, and a switchblade knife. The club sergeant assaulted by Collins quit his job because of further threats against him by unidentified black soldiers. "Although on a voluntary extension of his overseas tour he has asked for immediate curtailment and rotation to continental United States." The other sergeant assaulted by Collins "also quit his job and requested transfer out of Qui Nhon."[55]

There were persistent stories and rumors that militant African-American GIs from the adjacent 88th Field Depot and the 85th Evacuation Hospital had organized a Black Panther chapter, which met in the nearby hamlet of Han Nghai, long a refuge for AWOLs and deserters.[56]

In October a series of small but ugly incidents broke out at the various installations in the sprawling complex of bases, airfields, and headquarters located east of Da Nang. On October 4 a black Marine in the 3d Amphibious Tractor Battalion arrived late at the mess hall for the evening meal. A white mess sergeant berated the Marine for being late, called him "nigger," and refused to serve him. The black Marine grabbed his rifle and fired two rounds through the mess hall. The sound of rifle fire brought other Marines to the scene, and the angry black Marine was quickly disarmed, but a shouting match ensued between black and white Marines in which threats and name-calling were exchanged. The battalion commander brought the situation under control and agreed to meet with all interested parties the next day.[57]

A more serious situation began to develop five days later at Camp Thien Shau, a naval shore installation across the river from the city of Da Nang. Thien Shau, with its relatively luxurious Navy Enlisted Club, was a popular gathering place and, like all popular clubs, the site of frequent arguments and brawls. On October 2 a group of thirty-five to forty African-American servicemen gathered at a "soul brothers" meeting at Thien Shau. They were soon confronted by a group of whites; fighting developed, and the groups had to be separated by armed Shore Patrol.

Three days later the Thien Shau club was again the scene of trouble. Soon after the club opened, a white sailor attempted to assault two black sailors with a 2-foot length of chain. The assailant was taken away by the Shore Patrol. Throughout the evening sailors who appeared about to become violent were led away by the Shore Patrol and, if they had not committed any crime, allowed to sleep it off in their quarters. However, one black sailor so released armed himself with a .45 pistol and began shooting at a Shore Patrol jeep. His shots missed the two occupants of the jeep, but a random bullet struck and killed a black sentry in a watchtower near the mess hall.[58]

A few miles from Thien Shau was China Beach, the site of an R&R center and a large PX. On October 11 a fight broke out between about a dozen black Marines and soldiers and four whites. Security guards at the R&R center tried unsuccessfully to stop the fight but were assaulted and disarmed by the blacks. Leaving the R&R center, the group of blacks, now grown to about forty Marines and soldiers, began walking east toward the compound of the 384th Quartermaster Company, which had a large number of African-American personnel. Truckloads of heavily armed military police intercepted the group and took five men into custody.[59]

News of the incidents at China Beach and Thien Shau spread quickly among the dozens of units and headquarters scattered around the Da Nang area. Many expected that full-scale race riots might erupt. Senior commanders ordered investigations into reports that militant black power groups such as the Black Panthers might be recruiting and organizing among troops in Vietnam. By the spring of 1969, less than one year after Gen Abrams had declared racial problems among GIs "insignificant," the Pentagon was openly acknowledging that the racial tensions convulsing much of the United States had also reached Vietnam.[60] Between January and September 1969, more than twenty serious racial incidents among U.S. forces in Vietnam were reported.[61]

One part of the Vietnam force did remain largely immune from racial animosities, however. Even as tensions grew worse and incidents increased in rear areas and in stateside bases, combat units in Vietnam maintained the solidarity that had so impressed newsmen in 1966 and 1967. Joel Davis, a black field artilleryman, observed that in 1969 "out in the field blacks and whites got along a whole lot better than in the units that was way back." It was one of the many ironies of the Vietnam War that the greater the degree of danger and discomfort for the combatants, the greater the racial harmony and solidarity. Davis concluded: "that's [one] thing about the Army that doesn't happen here . . . you see all races can work together. People would go out and risk their lives for each other. People would share clothes or share money. . . . Like one for all; no racial distinctions. And that was one of the good things that came out of the experience, you know—that it can work. Lots of times it doesn't work here. But it can work. I witnessed it working."[62]

In retrospect, it is easy to see that 1968 marked a clear dividing line between the relative racial harmony among Vietnam GIs of the 1965–67 period and the increasingly corrosive racial animosities of the early 1970s. By 1968, increasing racial antagonisms in the United States, growing black consciousness and a growing sense of injustice among African-American soldiers in Vietnam, and frustration with a war that appeared increasingly costly and pointless had all begun to converge to move the armed forces toward racial crisis.

CHAPTER 12

In the Rear with the Gear, the Sergeant Major, and the Beer

As in all wars, the burden of hardship and sacrifice in Vietnam fell most heavily on soldiers in combat units. Yet in 1968 it was GIs in combat support and service support units, men "in the rear," who first began to manifest the serious signs of demoralization and frustration produced by the war—a war whose purpose and progress had become hopelessly confused in the eyes of most Americans. The racial troubles of the summer and fall had begun in the rear, and by the end of the year an even more serious problem, growing drug abuse, had also made its appearance.

By 1968 service, support, and headquarters troops made up at least 70–80 percent of all U.S. military personnel in Vietnam. They were impatiently dismissed by combat soldiers as "Rear Area Mother Fuckers" (REMFs), and few passed up an opportunity to voice their disgust with those contemptible creatures. "I remember going back to division headquarters," the commander of a mechanized infantry company recalled, "and being invited to the general's mess. Here was a mess served with silver and china and a five- to six-course meal. . . . And I'm saying to myself, 'My God, am I in the same country as, you know, these guys?' "[1] Specialist Richard Ford, a member of a long-range reconnaissance platoon, "didn't believe Nha Trang was still part of Vietnam. . . . They were riding around on paved streets. . . . Nice, pretty bunks, mosquito nets even on top of the bunks, and they had the nerve to have camouflaged covers. Air

conditioning. Cement floors. We just came out of the jungles. . . .
We just went off. [We] said, 'Y'all the real enemy. We stayin' here.' "[2]

As in previous wars, headquarters and service troops were
suspected of unfairly appropriating for themselves equipment and
benefits rightfully belonging to front-line soldiers. "We didn't like
the people at the landing zone," infantryman Louis Pofi recalled;
"we thought they were getting over. We felt cheated, unappreciated,
the lowest fucking scum of the whole Vietnam war. . . . The last
fucking people to get to go on R&R. The whole fucking headquarters company went on R&R before the R&R even got down to the
fucking line."[3]

Support and service troops were well aware of the comparative
luxury in which they lived and their low estate in the eyes of the real
combat troops. "The feeling of guilt was brought to a peak of
embarrassment when one happened to meet . . . a friend in from
the field for a couple of days," a Marine lieutenant with an MP
company in Da Nang said. The REMF "stood there like a recruiting
poster—short hair, no stubble beard, pressed uniform, shiny brass,
and polished boots. Mr. Field Marine stood there displaying all the
opposites of those details. Explanations were futile."[4]

Despite pride in their superior status and in the awe and
embarrassment they inspired in lesser breeds of GIs, few soldiers in
combat units passed up any opportunity to transfer to a safer job. "If
foot soldiers have a single obsession," Tim O'Brien observed, "it's
the gnawing, tantalizing hope of being assigned a job in the rear."[5]

But where *was* the rear? Was it the fire bases with their modicum
of comfort and safety offered by sandbagged bunkers and their
relatively frequent hot meals. Was it the larger semipermanent
operating bases like An Khe and An Hoa? Was it the even larger
corps and division headquarters like Phu Bai and Bien Hoa? Was it
the sprawling logistics and support complexes like Long Binh and
Cam Ranh Bay, each the size of a small city? Or was it the cities
themselves, like Da Nang and Saigon, so far from "the war" that at
some commands GIs wore khakis rather than utilities or camouflage
uniforms.

Actually, the Tet Offensive had shown that no place in Vietnam
was truly safe. Men had been killed or horribly maimed in almost

every part of Vietnam. "You could be in the most protected space in Vietnam and still know that your safety was provisional; that early death, blindness, loss of legs, arms, or balls, major and lasting disfigurement—the whole rotten deal—could come in on the freaky fluky as easily in the so-called expected ways," the reporter Michael Herr wrote. "The roads were mined, the trails booby-trapped, satchel charges and grenades blew up jeeps and movie theaters, the VC got work inside all the camps as shoe-shine boys and laundresses and honey-dippers; they'd starch your fatigues and burn your shit and then go home and mortar your area. Saigon and Cholon and Da Nang held such hostile vibes that you felt you were being dry-sniped every time someone looked at you."[6]

To the combat rifleman anything from a remote fire base or landing zone to a division headquarters to an office complex in Saigon might be considered "the rear." Yet the largest proportion of supply, service, and administrative troops were stationed in or near one of the dozen-odd large American base complexes from Quang Tri and Dong Ha in the north near the DMZ to Phu Bai near Hue, to Da Nang and Chu Lai in southern I Corps, to Qui Nhon, Nha Trang, and Cam Ranh Bay along the central coast, to the Saigon–Bien Hoa complex, the largest of all. All were located near large airfield or port facilities and housed upwards of 10,000 U.S. troops—close to 60,000 at Cam Ranh Bay and Saigon. From the air the bases looked like middle-size cities of gray-green storage sheds, repair shops, barracks, motor pools, offices, mess halls, and bunkers. Often groups of buildings were divided into separate "compounds," each surrounded by barbed wire and sandbagged fences and wooden watch towers, which gave them the look of frontier forts or state penitentiaries. Close by many of the bases, often completely surrounded by them, were the older Vietnamese towns and cities, their whitewashed buildings with tile roofs and small open-front shops lining streets that were always crowded with motorscooters, bicycles, trucks, and American military vehicles.[7]

On the fringes of the bases were newer, less attractive Vietnamese cities, vast shanty towns of wood, cardboard, and sheet metal, housing refugees and squatters who eked out a living working for, stealing from, or scavenging from the Americans. Though these refugees appeared to live in dire poverty, they were in fact relatively well off compared with others relocated to more remote areas of Vietnam like Cam Lo, away from the large American bases.

Within the base complexes the standard of living often equaled or exceeded the fantasies and rumors of the grunts in the field. Most GIs lived in Southeast Asia huts, or "hooches" as they were universally called, single-story rectangular buildings raised slightly off the ground by piles as a defense against the monsoon. The roof was sheet metal and the sides plywood topped by screens to allow some ventilation. A few steps away from the hooch, or sometimes directly beneath it, was a sandbagged bunker for protection against rocket and mortar attacks.

In the larger complexes at Da Nang, Tan Son Nhut, and Cam Ranh Bay, large two-story wooden barracks replaced the Southeast Asia huts. These were dryer and usually featured indoor plumbing. Yet they had the significant disadvantage of being more dangerous to be in during an enemy rocket or mortar attack. To reach a bunker the thirty to forty men on the second story had to clamber single-file down one of only two sets of wooden stairs. If the attack came without warning, men on the upper story in the double-deck metal bunks were more exposed to flying shrapnel than those closer to the ground. Accidents in rolling out of the upper bunks or descending the wooden stairs during attacks or alerts were common.[8]

In general, the larger the base or headquarters, the greater were the amenities. As a minimum, however, troops at the major installations enjoyed beds with sheets, hot food, electricity, hot showers, a club, athletic facilities, movies, and plenty of beer. Barracks and hooches often had Vietnamese maids and laundresses. Many clubs were air-conditioned, and the larger ones featured dining rooms where hamburgers, french fries, fried chicken, or steak were always available.

By 1968 the task of providing recreation and entertainment for the 550,000 American troops in Vietnam had grown to mammoth proportions. As the number of troops in Vietnam rapidly increased from 23,000 in 1965 to more than half a million by late 1967, the Pentagon had hastily established a system of clubs, post exchanges, theaters, and athletic facilities. By 1968, there were forty-six "main store" PXs—similar in size to large one-story department stores—operating in Vietnam, and 168 smaller "troop and base stores."

There were also eight cafeterias, forty-eight snack bars, and twenty-two mobile retail stores. There were 765 officers and men assigned to the PX system, assisted by more than 150 civilians and nine hundred "third country nationals." The PXs also employed more than eight thousand Vietnamese.[9]

In addition to popcorn machines, pizza ovens, and vending machines, all but the smallest clubs provided slot machines. A good proportion of the Army's eight thousand slot machines were located in Vietnam, where they generated a profit of $23 million a year, a sum theoretically devoted to paying the operating expenses of the clubs.[10]

Many large clubs provided frequent "live" entertainment, ranging from Filipino bands with strippers and female impersonators (the latter often more popular than the former) to Australian rock groups to American movie stars and other celebrities. At one point during 1968 some sixty-six live shows were on tour in Vietnam.[11] Generally the five or six largest base complexes received most of the live shows. Only unusually adventurous or desperate entertainment troupes were willing to make the trip to outlying headquarters or fire bases.[12]

In addition to providing the troops with needed recreation, the Pentagon aimed to "keep our service men out of unwholesome Vietnamese establishments" and to prevent the adverse impact of a flood of dollars into the Vietnamese economy.[13] The availability of the extensive system of PXs and clubs undoubtedly did reduce the amount of money that GIs paid directly to the Vietnamese for goods and services. Yet the clubs and stores, with their multimillion-dollar purchases and payrolls, their constant flow of luxury goods and American-made gadgets, opened grand vistas of racketeering and theft to those Americans and Asians with even a minimal imagination and the slightest inclination toward larceny. "The leakage of PX goods onto the black market and elsewhere began at the docks in Vietnam with widespread pilferage of incoming cargos." During a single month in 1968 military police reported pilferage of goods from ships unloading at Cam Ranh Bay by both stevedores and members of the crew. There were also "large losses of PX items" at depots at Cam Ranh Bay and Nha Trang, and GIs at the beer and soda yard at Cam Ranh Bay were alleged to be selling entire pallets of beverages to members of the Vietnamese navy.[14]

In all parts of Vietnam GIs were involved with Vietnamese, often prostitutes or cab drivers, in purchasing PX items for resale on the black market. PX items and other American-made goods were displayed openly in Vietnamese markets and roadside stands from Cam Ranh Bay to Da Nang. Many Vietnamese entrepreneurs supplemented their traffic in black market goods with the sale of marijuana cigarettes. A relatively small-scale operator apprehended by Vietnamese police at Hue, perhaps because she had angered some official or failed to pay the proper bribes, was found to have 559 cartons of American cigarettes, twenty-nine boxes of cigars, 121 bottles of liquor, and more than seven hundred marijuana cigarettes in her possession.[15]

The reputed kings of the black market, however, were neither Vietnamese nor Americans, but members of Korean military units and Filipino advisers sent to Vietnam to aid the South Vietnamese in their struggle with the Communists. These "third country nationals" were often notified in advance of the arrival of big-ticket PX items such as televisions, stereos, refrigerators, and fans.[16] An investigation by military police in Da Nang led to the conclusion that "Republic of Korea personnel were heavily engaged in significant and widespread diversion of goods, intended for military use, to Vietnamese and third country national businessmen."[17] Traveling in trucks and jeeps from one PX to another, the Koreans, often using "spurious letters of authorization," efficiently scooped up large quantities of goods, most still in their packing crates, and drove on to the next store. At the III Marine Amphibious Force headquarters, a Korean helicopter landed near a PX a few hundred yards from General Cushman's office and quickly loaded aboard televisions, refrigerators, and radios that had arrived less than two hours earlier.[18] As a sideline to their specialty in electrical products, the Koreans also purchased and resold large quantities of beer and soda, as well as "significant quantities of food items issued for use of military messes."[19]

Yet though "third country nationals" were probably the most systematic and industrious black marketeers, the boldest and most flamboyant profiteers of the military recreation and welfare system were Americans. The understaffed, rapidly growing system of Vietnam clubs and messes, with their inadequate, sometimes nonexistent accounting controls, were easy prey to those who knew how to manipulate the system. In 1971 a Senate investigation would reveal that a ring of senior noncommissioned officers headed by Sergeant Major William O. Wooldridge, who had been appointed Sergeant Major of the Army in 1966, had managed to assume practical control over the management of many of the largest clubs and messes in the Saigon, Long Binh, and Chu Lai areas. The sergeants earned thousands in kickbacks for purchases of refrigerators, furniture, liquor, and food from favored suppliers, some of whom were alleged to have connections with criminal syndicates.[20]

Civilians could also get into the act. One American civilian converted his large Saigon house on Truong Minh Gian into a gambling casino complete with blackjack tables, American dealers and croupiers, and armed guards to keep out unwelcome visitors. An American officer reported that at certain times there were some $10,000 worth of chips on the crap table. The proprietors, in the spirit of internationalism, accepted both U.S. and Vietnamese money.[21] His twenty to thirty employees, many of whom also worked at the PX, were paid in American greenbacks and PX goods. His casino, which was reportedly "frequented by senior MACV officers, some not bothering to remove their uniforms," was so successful that food and drinks were provided *gratis* to the customers.[22] Power for the club came from a small gasoline-powered generator "of U.S. Army origin."

Although few Americans in Saigon were as resourceful as the casino owner, all who were stationed near a city or a large town could turn a profit by converting American money to piasters at the black market exchange rate, which far exceeded the official rate. To curb such activities and to discourage the flow of dollars into the Vietnamese economy, GIs in Vietnam received their pay in a special scrip called "military payment certificates" (MPC). This scrip was in theory good only for purchases at such U.S. facilities as post offices, laundries, PXs, and clubs. Obtaining dollars or piasters required special arrangements.

These measures slowed but failed to halt currency manipulation among GIs and Vietnamese. Prohibitions against using MPC for purchases from Vietnamese were routinely disregarded. Bar girls, prostitutes, drug dealers, and merchants soon came into possession of large amounts of the scrip. A lively trade then sprang up in the exchange of U.S. dollars for MPC. American GIs wrote home for cash and money orders, which could then be exchanged with the Vietnamese for MPC at a premium of about 35 percent.[23]

In an attempt to clamp down on such illegal exchanges, MACV, in a surprise order of October 1968, directed that all MPC then in circulation, called the "641 series" be turned in for new scrip called the "661 series." The time period for conversion was very short and, of course, only U.S. servicemen could legally make the exchange. Although many Vietnamese probably managed to convert their MPC in a final frenzy of illegal exchanges (at some bases local Vietnamese tossed stacks of bills over and through the barbed wire perimeters), more than $6 million of now-worthless scrip was left in the hands of Vietnamese and third country nationals at the conclusion of the exercise.[24]

Despite the relative amenities and inexpensive diversions, life in the rear was far from the country club existence imagined by the grunts in the jungles and mountains. Troops in the rear shared the same feelings of loneliness and depression, of separation from friends and family, the same problems of adjustment to an alien and unfriendly culture and environment.[25] "There was a song at that time," Nurse Laura Redman related, "called 'It's Saturday Night In The World,' and that's how we lived our year; because none of us really considered Vietnam to be in the world."[26]

Most clerks, technicians, medics, mechanics, and truck drivers in the rear worked a twelve-hour day, seven days a week (although more than a few suspected that an entire day's work could, in reality, be accomplished in four or five hours).[27] In addition to their primary work in the motor pool, supply depot, communication center, or office, the REMFs were frequently called upon to fill sandbags, collect and burn latrine refuse, help in the mess hall, stand guard, and make local patrols. Some officers and NCOs in rear areas managed to combine the worst of two worlds by requiring the REMFs to undergo stateside-style personal and unit inspections. More than a few angry letters to Congressmen from Vietnam demanded to know why service and support troops, admonished to work seventy-hour weeks and to limit their drinking "because they were in a combat zone," should nevertheless be expected to have immaculately shined boots and starched uniforms.

Despite all the work, make-work, and indignities inflicted by the lifers, most troops in the rear found themselves fighting a constant battle against boredom, for which the clubs and PXs provided only a weak antidote. Those willing to ignore the heat could find some relief in sports, weightlifting, and running. Letter-writing was a frequent and universal activity. Many GIs supplemented the traditional pen and paper with long tape-recorded messages mailed to the United States on the new plastic tape cassettes. Virtually every soldier owned at least one camera, and no scene was too mundane, grotesque, incomprehensible, or revolting to be recorded on film and sent to the folks back home.[28]

Some men had more imaginative ways of coping with boredom. Lieutenant Charles R. Anderson "once saw a battalion surgeon race through a monsoon downpour, throwing off another part of his uniform every few strides. Nude by the time he reached the motor pool, he grabbed an inflated inner tube and headed for the nearest drainage ditch. Sprawling over the inflated donut, he whooped in delight as the building spilloff carried him down the ditch past the mess hall. Dumbstruck staff officers, NCOs, and young cooks stared in disbelief."[29]

With several hundred thousand bored, lonely, and frustrated men under the age of twenty-five serving in Vietnam, sex was understandably a major preoccupation. "It seemed as if the Americans thought of nothing but sex," a Vietnamese woman who lived in Saigon recalled. "We Vietnamese women talked about this often and felt sorry for them. We wondered what kind of lives their wives must have lived in the States."[30] Porno magazines enjoyed a brisk sale, and some of the most heated arguments about Vietnam war issues among GIs took place in the correspondence pages of *Penthouse* and *Playboy*.

In principle, MACV expected Vietnam servicemen to save their libidinous urges for R&R. In practice, sex was relatively easy to obtain in the shanty towns surrounding many of the large bases. These areas were almost always "off limits," making those men found there liable to fines, demotion, or worse, and the venereal disease rate was high. But many GIs still found the shanty towns hard to resist. Many units established unofficial "clubs" that doubled as brothels. "We ended up setting up our own little club," one company commander recalled, "brought our own entertainment in. Very raunchy entertainment. Then what started off as 'we'll just have these girls come in here and dance'—well, after a while it becomes a little more rambunctious."[31]

These semiofficial brothels had the advantage of allowing medical personnel to examine both the women and their clients for possible disease. One soldier recalled that the 1st Cavalry Division "recreation area" called "Sin City" was so well managed that "nobody used rubbers because all the girls in Sin City were clean. . . . Medical personnel in the camp would always go and check 'em once a week, and if they got diseased, they'd get shots and wouldn't be able to work until they were clear."[32]

Sometimes in the field opportunities would present themselves. "We would set up our perimeter and . . . a girl would show up with Coca Cola and also some broads would show. . . . Normally those kind of deals, was a C Ration deal. . . . We would give the girl a C Ration meal. Ham and lima beans, 'cause nobody . . . would want to eat ham and lima beans. You would never give up spaghetti and meat balls."[33]

In Saigon and a few other large cities, which were usually not "off limits" to all GIs, sex was a growth industry similar to and closely connected with drugs and black marketeering. A "hostess" in a Saigon bar usually earned about $180 a month even if she confined her activities to hustling overpriced drinks. The drinks the GIs were expected to buy for the girls were in fact simply colored water, a fiction so transparent that the bar girl's beverage was universally referred to as "Saigon tea." In addition to tea, priced at $1.50 to $2.00 a glass, the girls often pressed their regular customers to bring them cigarettes, soap, or candy for resale on the black market.[34] Bar girls who were willing to sleep with some or all of their admirers could earn monthly incomes equal to three or four times the salary of South Vietnamese cabinet ministers.[35]

Many of the bar girls were widows of Vietnamese soldiers; others were young women from the country attracted by the high salaries or tricked into their trade. Most were supporting several relatives and often a child or two. Some girls arranged temporary "marriages" with GIs or American civilians. The American provided a small house and a monthly salary as well as access to PX goods. Sometimes two or more Americans shared a "wife," and girls might be "passed on by one GI to a buddy when a man's tour of duty was up."[36]

The personal closeness, camaraderie, and automatic cooperation found in combat units was far less common among men "in the rear." Arguments and fights were common, tensions between GIs and lifers were higher, and almost all racial incidents took place in the rear. "You have a [barracks] room full of very horny, very frustrated, bored men," observed one soldier who served at Cam Ranh Bay. "Give them a lot of beer and let them get fucked up and bring in those Filipino and Korean girls in those sequins and these bands that play imitation American rock, and get the heat going . . . and what are you going to do with all that energy? It's going to turn in on itself. So you always had fights. Guys being stabbed, killed, taking a jeep and driving it, turning it over."[37]

Some men found the boredom and military make-work intolerable and did their best to transfer to a combat unit. Others requested a transfer out of a desire to participate in the adventure of war, however dangerous, an attitude that GIs referred to as "getting grungy."

Commanders in "the rear" were well aware that action and danger, or at least the appearance thereof, could actually have a positive effect on morale and help to combat boredom among their men. Some officers discovered that their service troops *liked* being assigned to reaction squads or perimeter defense. The commander of a supply and transport company found that assigning men to convoy operations improved their morale.[38] The commander of an aviation maintenance detachment found that many of his men volunteered to fly combat assaults to give the crew chief or door gunner a day off. "I had no lack of volunteers from the maintenance folks, they jumped right out there. . . . We never had to order someone . . . we had them standing in line."[39]

A universal antidote for all morale problems in Vietnam, both in combat units and in the rear, was "R&R." Of the hundreds of special military projects and programs the Americans introduced in Vietnam, R&R was one of the few unalloyed successes. It was also one of the most improbable. That thousands of American GIs in their early twenties could be airlifted from the jungles and rice paddies of Vietnam to a large Asian city, left to their own devices for five or six days, and then returned to their duties in Vietnam without serious incident seemed so unlikely that only the actual record of success over more than six years could have proven otherwise.

During 1968 almost 32,000 men a month took the free commercial 707 flights provided by the Pentagon to Bangkok, Manila, Singapore, Taipei, Tokyo, Hong Kong, Kuala Lumpur, Penang, Sidney, and Hawaii for a five- or six-night vacation.[40] Married men generally opted for Hawaii, which provided an opportunity for a brief reunion with wives and children, while single men chose the more exotic sites and those with the best-developed night life. Many R&R cities soon sprouted dozens of cheap but comfortable "R&R hotels," complete with air-conditioning, telephones, televisions, refrigerators, cocktail lounges, and, most important of all, women.

Most GIs embarked on their R&R with the firm resolve to spend the entire 120 hours in pursuit of alcohol and sex. Hayden Thompson, a left-wing Australian journalist, described the King's Cross section of Sydney, "an area geared especially to the dollars of U.S. servicemen." King's Cross boasted

> . . . about twenty high-priced hotels, joints like the Texas Tavern . . . Whiskey A Go-Go, etc. Innumerable ice cream joints; head shops, striptease joints, men's clothes shops. . . . It is also the local dope center so there are very down and out hippies hustling frantically. And then there are the women. . . . Down in the Cross you've got to be young. . . . Most girls there are pretty close to twenty years old, a lot are definitely in their teens. Trouble is there just isn't enough to go around. I have seen girls desperately fighting over doorways. . . . A guy is assailed by a swarm of girls every step he takes.[41]

In Singapore, Lieutenant Charles R. Anderson found soon after checking in to his hotel that "a banquet room was being used as a . . . what else could it be called but a girl market. . . . The place where the lonely and horny GIs far from home could meet their five-day girl friend. Young Americans in civilian clothes were nudging and squeezing their way out with laughing girls, eager to get back to their rooms and try out their choices. The bustle of activity in the room reminded me of a fish market."[42] Despite this single-minded pursuit of booze and women, many GIs managed to see a good deal of the city they were in and came away with a not unsympathetic view of their host country—a view that balanced in a small way their strongly negative feelings toward Vietnam and the Vietnamese.

For infantryman Joel Davis, R&R became a kind of social experiment. Davis, an African-American, chose Australia, though "everybody had heard of Australia as being really prejudicial." Davis's buddies were surprised and skeptical. "My captain said, 'Come on, Davis, where you really want to go?'. . . . Like all of a sudden . . . it was like a lot of the white guys were really pulling for me, and the black GIs were really pulling for me that like I was a sort of race movement within myself. Everybody didn't want me to have a bad time. So all of the sudden the whole emphasis had gotten off the war as a result of me going. . . . For the next two weeks, I was the whole talk."[43] In the end, Davis was well received in Australia and had a memorable visit. "One day some of the Australian soldiers, they were sitting in one of these pubs—and we couldn't get out of that pub, they set us up so much for beer."[44]

In all, "R&R was a big factor" in helping combat troops keep their equilibrium, the commander of an air assault company recalled. "As he came back from R&R [the soldier] had sort of returning blues, but it sort of gave him another shot in the arm and helped him make it through the tour."[45]

As in all wars, soldiers turned to alcohol as a temporary escape from loneliness, boredom, and fear. "I was drinking two quarts of Old GrandDad, 100 proof, every day," a soldier who served four tours in Vietnam recalled. "You drank it and you'd just sweat it out. You needed it to keep going I guess. I got tired, real tired. You saw so much happening."[46] In Vietnam the clubs and PXs made access to booze cheap and convenient, almost effortless in the rear areas. "You could go to the PX and buy . . . a whole fifth for a dollar," recalled one GI, "and some of the high-grade alcohol, even J&B scotch, only three dollars."[47] Some commanders prohibited the sale of hard liquor to men below the rank of E-5. Yet these men could easily obtain what they desired through purchases from other GIs not so restricted, and in any case had access to virtually unrestricted quantities of beer.

Senior officers and career NCOs expected that soldiers far from home and in a war zone would do a good deal of drinking. Drunkenness was not exactly encouraged, but drinking was widely viewed as an acceptable outlet for the stress, fatigue, and tension of military life. So long as a man indulged himself while off duty and kept his behavior within certain broad bounds, heavy drinking was tolerated or ignored. Indeed, the tough, experienced soldier was almost expected to be a hard-drinking man as well.

The generals recognized that there was a price to be paid in accidents, fights, and even occasional homicides, yet this price was understood and accepted, while the traditional apparatus of military control ranging from the tough old sarge who knew how to handle drunks to the Military Police to unit punishment to the military justice system was expected to keep a lid on things.

By 1968, however, many younger GIs had begun to indulge another habit which the military was ill-prepared either to understand or to control: the widespread use of drugs. Beginning with the vogue for psychedelic drugs on college campuses in the mid-1960s, recreational drug use, widely popularized and celebrated in movies and the media, had become increasingly acceptable to American teenagers and college students.[48] Men entering the armed forces in the late 1960s had radically different attitudes toward drug use from those of their fathers and older brothers of World War II and Korea, or even the Vietnam GIs of 1965–66.

By 1968 a significant number of soldiers had already experimented with or used drugs as teenagers before entering the service.[49] "Many members of the 18–26 age group feel the use of marijuana is a shared experience of their generation," a 1968 Army report concluded. "Consequently they possess a willingness or desire to participate."[50] The chairman of the Second Field Force Drug Suppression Council, Major General Jack Wagstaff, observed that "young soldiers, and to a lesser extent young officers . . . seem to equate marijuana with social drinking; they attach no moral stigma to its use."[51]

Marijuana was as readily available in Vietnam as whisky or cigarettes. The plant could be easily grown throughout large areas of the country and was widely sold in the form of cigarettes by laundrymen, bar girls, street urchins, and taxi drivers. A marijuana cigarette could be purchased for one dollar in the Da Nang area and as little as twenty cents in Saigon, where it was also available in bulk for only about thirty dollars a kilo.[52] Vietnamese law did not specifically prohibit the possession and use of marijuana, and, whatever its legal status, American leaders soon discovered that cultivation and sale of the drug had become a major industry involving entire villages in the countryside and many high-ranking officials in the military and civil bureaucracy. Five of the largest farms in the Mekong Delta alone produced a 3200-kilogram crop with an estimated retail cash value of over more than $2.2 million. The head of the Vietnamese customs service, the director of the Saigon police, President Thieu's intelligence adviser, and the commander of the II Corps were all suspected by U.S. intelligence and police agencies of involvement with the drug trade.[53]

How many soldiers actually used drugs in Vietnam is impossible to estimate with any degree of precision. Use of marijuana was a crime subject to fairly harsh punishment, including possible imprisonment under the Uniform Code of Military Justice. Although many young GIs argued vehemently in private that "marijuana was cheaper and less harmful than liquor," few were willing to risk jail by openly championing such convictions.[54]

In the absence of direct evidence, the Pentagon was obliged to rely on two types of indirect measures: statistics on cases of possession and use of drugs compiled by the provost marshal and other law enforcement agencies, and anonymous questionnaires administered by military physicians and psychologists. The law enforcement figures showed an increase of over 260 percent in the number of soldiers involved with possession or use of marijuana during 1968 as compared with the previous year.[55] These disquieting statistics the Pentagon explained as "primarily attributable to an increased awareness of the problem and to more vigorous application of enforcement measures."[56] Lieutenant General Bruce Palmer, a plain-spoken, cerebral soldier, was not so sure. As he prepared to turn over command of U.S. Army, Vietnam, in May 1968 and become Westmoreland's vice chief of staff, Palmer warned Abrams that "the number of incidents of possession and use of marijuana by

U.S. Army personnel in Vietnam has steadily risen since 1965 and there is nothing to indicate that there will be a reversal of this trend." He also pointed out that drugs were becoming a major South Vietnamese industry.[57]

Unofficial polls of enlisted men appeared to bear out Palmer's warnings. The earliest surveys of drug abuse in Vietnam were undertaken by medical officers between August 1967 and September 1968. The first survey polled about five hundred enlisted men, E-6 and below, who had finished their tours in Vietnam and were completing their preparation for departure at the 90th Replacement Battalion at Long Binh. About 30 percent of these soldiers indicated that they had used marijuana at least once in Vietnam, and over 7 percent had used it twenty times or more. Less than 5 percent reported using any other drug.[58] Two other studies, by Dr. Wilfred Postal, 4th Infantry Division psychiatrist, who polled patients at the 71st Evacuation Hospital near Pleiku, and Dr. E. Caspar of the American Division, produced similar results. About 30–35 percent of the GIs queried admitted to using marijuana while in Vietnam. Casual users and experimenters outnumbered heavy users almost three to one. Amost half of the users indicated that they had begun the practice before arriving in Vietnam. Among both heavy and casual users, marijuana smoking was a social activity, almost always engaged in with others. Few if any soldiers used drugs in combat, although some believed that using it after a battle helped to calm their nerves.[59]

As rumors of drug abuse among troops in Vietnam began to reach the United States at the end of 1967, journalists speculated that over three-quarters of American GIs were probably "doing drugs." The *Washington Post* writer Nicholas von Hoffmann reported that at Fort Hood, Texas, 75 percent of the men, a number of junior officers, and even the military police used drugs and that most had acquired the taste for them in Vietnam.[60] Writers and academics speculated that the 1960s "counterculture" had finally spread to the fighting forces in Vietnam. They warned that the Army brass and the lifers, with their fondness for booze, were separated by an unbridgeable cultural and psychological chasm from the new generation, which preferred "consciousness raising drugs."

They were half right. The lifers were puzzled and contemptuous of the younger soldiers' tolerance for drugs. But most GI drug users were more than happy to supplement their smoking with alcohol. For most men and women in Vietnam, marijuana use was neither a cultural statement nor a protest but a means of escape, like beer, scotch, and porno magazines.

A soldier with the 1st Battalion, 5th Mechanized Infantry, described a brief respite from operations. "Everybody was sitting with his feet dangling off the side. . . . You know, playing music on tape recorders, getting high, you know, smoking marijuana, drinking. All we could think about was when we got back home. . . . You don't think about the bad things in America, all you think about is the good things."[61]

By the end of 1968 more and more GIs were turning to drugs to help them escape the heat, tedium, fear, and loneliness of Vietnam and to hold on to thoughts and memories of life "back in the world." The younger the GI and the lower his rank, the more likely he was to be a drug user. In a study of marijuana use in the 173d Airborne Brigade, a clear majority of all E-1s and E-2s were characterized as either regular or chronic marijuana users, as against only 8 percent of E-6s. Among E-7s, who would normally incude only "lifers," there were no chronic or regular users. The chronic user was most likely to be a high school dropout, least likely to be a college graduate. However, college dropouts were almost as heavily represented among heavy users as those who had failed to finish high school. High school graduates fell somewhere in between.[62]

By March 1969 the MACV Provost Marshal was reporting "twice as many apprehensions had been made for possession of marijuana in that single month than in the entire year of 1968."[63] A survey of more than two thousand soldiers at a Vietnam transit center revealed that over half of the enlisted men completing their tour of duty admitted to having tried marijuana; 31 pecent of that group reported having used the drug two hundred times or more during their one-year tour. Of new troops arriving in Vietnam, close to 35 percent were already marijuana users. A more disquieting finding was that 17 percent of the departing troops also reported using opium or marijuana cigarettes laced with opium.[64]

Then, in the spring of 1970, the Vietnam drug scene took an abrupt turn for the worse. At some time in the spring of 1970, 92–96 percent-pure heroin became available in South Vietnam for the first time. The reasons for the flood of heroine are obscure. The so-called Golden Triangle area of mainland southeast Asia, comprising portions of Thailand, Burma, Laos, and southern China, had always been a center of large-scale opium cultivation. However, before 1970 there were no facilities in southeast Asia for processing this opium into high-grade acetylmorphine, or heroin. At the end of 1969 laboratories in the Golden Triangle, reportedly supervised by master chemists from Hong Kong, achieved the capability to produce high-grade heroin.[65] The U.S.–South Vietnamese incursion into Cambodia in 1970, by opening the border between the two southeast Asian countries, may also have served to provide an easy route for the importation of Thai and Laotian heroin.

For whatever reason, within a few weeks of the Cambodian incursion, cheap, high-quality heroin was everywhere in Vietnam. Packaged in small plastic vials, the powdery white substance was available for less than three dollars for 250 grams. Laundrymen, bar girls, taxi drivers, maids—all the Vietnamese who had served as the source of supply for marijuana—now began to deal in the more potent "smack." Heroin was easier to transport and less easy to detect than the strong-smelling marijuana and gave a far better "high."

Unlike heroin addicts in the United States, who usually employed a syringe to inject heroin directly into their bloodstream, Vietnam users often ingested the drug by "snorting" it through the nostrils or smoking heroin-laced cigarettes. Vietnam heroin was so pure that only a small amount was necessary to cause addiction in the user.[66] Once he became hooked, an addict in Vietnam could maintain his habit for as little as fifty to sixty dollars a month, a tiny fraction of what it would have cost him back in the States.[67] Reported deaths from drug overdose among servicemen in Vietnam increased from about two a month in the spring of 1970 to around two a day by the early fall.[68] Word of the military's growing drug problem soon reached the United States. In August 1970, the nationally syndicated columnist Jack Anderson declared that drug abuse had become a serious problem among GIs in Vietnam, where it "gnaws at U.S. combat efficiency." According to Anderson, one group of GIs, stoned on marijuana, had attempted to shoot down an American helicopter.[69] Three different Congressional committees announced inquiries into drug abuse in the military. In Vietnam, MACV redoubled its efforts to crack down on drug use; instituted surprise searches, shakedowns, and urine testing; pressured the South Vietnamese to get tough on traffickers and smugglers; churned out films and pamphlets to warn young soldiers about the perils of addiction; and experimented with amnesty, counseling, and rehabilitation programs, all with indifferent success. By 1971 many commanders in Vietnam had begun to view drug abuse as a more formidable enemy than the North Vietnamese or the Viet Cong.

CHAPTER 13

The War for the Countryside

Although the Communists had suffered some sharp defeats in their May and August offensives, the South Vietnamese government still appeared farther than ever from winning the contest for the villages. More than 40,000 civilians had been killed or wounded in the Tet fighting, and 1 million new refugees had been created. The damage to homes and property was staggering. Almost 170,000 houses alone had been damaged or destroyed.[1] Government projects in rural areas were abandoned or in tatters, and many government functionaries, police, and technicians had fled the countryside. Yet to a few men the aftermath of the Tet attacks spelled not disaster but opportunity.

Robert Komer, Deputy COMUSMACV (Command U.S. Military Assistance Command Vietnam) for Civil Operations and Revolutionary Development, or CORDS, was known as "the blowtorch." A Harvard graduate and a longtime CIA analyst, he had made his career in the federal bureaucracy. Yet he was an inveterate enemy of red tape, sacred cows, and vested interests. A short, slightly balding man in his mid-forties, he had a loud voice, a ready temper, and did not suffer fools gladly. Alongside the cautious, canny bureaucrats and staff officers of "Pentagon East," with their reverence for proper procedure and organizational boundaries, his behavior resembled that of Attila the Hun.

Brought to the White House in March 1966 as a special Presidential assistant to direct and coordinate Washington-level support for pacification, Komer soon concluded that the U.S. programs in support of the "other war," as the struggle for the countryside was frequently called, were underfunded, uncoordinated, ill-conceived, and often mutually competing. Henry Cabot Lodge, who had resumed the post of U.S. Ambassador in Saigon in August 1965, emphasized the importance of pacification in his public and private pronouncements but had done little to bring order out of the confusion of agencies, programs, and strategies that was Saigon's pacification effort.

A graduate of the Harvard Business School, Komer placed great faith in the importance of sound management and clear lines of authority and control. His solution to the problem of ensuring effective direction and control for the many programs and agencies engaged in pacification was novel yet logical: assign responsibility for all aspects of pacification, civil as well as military, to Westmoreland's Military Assistance Command, Vietnam (MACV). All civilian programs of the Agency for International Development, State Department, and the U.S. Information Agency, as well as the CIA's intelligence and area security programs, would come under the authority of MACV. To manage this new array of organizations and programs, Westmoreland would have a deputy commander for pacification who would be a civilian. Komer argued that the military was by far the most powerful and wealthy "player" in the American war effort in Vietnam and controlled most of the assets that would be needed to establish regional security in the countryside as well as having the most clout with the Vietnamese government and army.[2]

Several months before Komer began his push for a single manager for pacification, an independent study by the Army staff had reached similar conclusions. In the summer of 1965 Army Chief of Staff Harold K. Johnson had directed some of his most capable officers to develop a long-term plan for bringing the Vietnam conflict to a successful conclusion. The PROVN study, as it came to be called, concluded that "the critical actions are those that occur at the village, district, and provincial levels. This is where the war must be fought; this is where that war and the object which lies beyond it must be won."[3] The PROVN study also recommended creation of an organization to integrate the U.S. effort in pacification and U.S. involvement in Vietnamese government activities designed to achieve rural security.

In addition to the Army, Defense Secretary McNamara had also become a convert to the concept of a single manager for pacification. Yet President Johnson, although he had often expressed impatience with the slow pace of "the other war," was reluctant to override the loud objections of the State Department, the CIA, and Ambassador Lodge against giving control of their Vietnam programs to the military.

Perhaps as a stopgap, perhaps as a last chance experiment, the President agreed to the creation of a new Office of Civil Operations under Deputy Ambassador William Porter to plan and coordinate the work of all the nonmilitary agencies engaged in pacification. OCO made notable progress on the organizational level, particularly in creating regional directors to control all civilian activity in the four corps areas of Vietnam. The new regional directors included three men who would later form the backbone of many of the 1968 and 1969 pacification efforts: Henry Koren, an experienced diplomat, became I Corps coordinator; and John Paul Vann, a forceful and controversial former Army adviser and outspoken critic of the American approach to the war, became regional coordinator in III Corps. The IV Corps, or Delta, region was assigned to Vince Heymann, an able CIA administrator.

Yet, the OCO arrangement had little chance of achieving real success in the few months' trial that the President and his increasingly impatient advisers were willing to allow it. Ambassador Lodge departed on a one-month vacation soon after the startup of the new organization, leaving Porter to manage the business of the Embassy. Most of Porter's OCO functions were, in turn, assigned to a career USAID official whom a *Pentagon Papers* study described as "a methodical and slow worker with strong respect for the very interagency system he was supposed to supersede."[4] It says much about the mindset of the bureaucrats manning OCO that relocating their offices to a new chancery building apparently consumed far more of their energy and attention than any of the programs they were expected to implement.[5]

In May 1967 the blow fell. The newly appointed Ambassador, Ellsworth Bunker, with the strong support, if not direction, of the White House, announced his decision to place all U.S. activities in support of local security and development under unified management. Robert Komer was named as Westmoreland's deputy, with the personal rank of Ambassador, to head the new civil and military organization now known as CORDS.

All the vast and confusing array of U.S. programs in support of activities, ranging from regional security and paramilitary forces to propaganda to agricultural development, now came under the sway of CORDS, with its unique structure of unified province- and district-level advisory teams composed of both military personnel and civilian specialists. Just as Komer was the first U.S. Ambassador to serve in a direct military chain of command, so throughout CORDS's hybrid organization civilians sometimes "commanded" teams composed of colonels, majors, and captains, while just as often Army officers "commanded" Foreign Service officers, economists, and information specialists.

As they surveyed the wreckage of Tet, Komer and his newly appointed civilian generals thought they saw a unique opportunity to strike a blow for Saigon in the protracted war for the countryside. The Viet Cong had suffered heavy casualties in the Tet battles and more in the fighting in April and May. Of course, the Communists had suffered heavy casualties before and had returned to fight another day. This time, however, there was to be little respite.

The prolonged fighting in the Second and Third Phase offensives in May, June, and August took a heavy toll of experienced fighters. Main force Viet Cong from Long An, for example, had had to remain near their objectives in the Saigon area for almost five months, subject to constant shelling and air attacks.[6] The long absence of the main force units left the Communist-controlled villages and hamlets vulnerable to attacks by U.S. and South Vietnamese forces and left political warfare and guerrilla operations in the hands of the least experienced and worst equipped cadres.[7] Viet Cong forces in the Delta province of Kien Hoa had been ordered to supply three full battalions—more than 1,000 men—for offensive operations far from their home villages, leaving too few experienced cadres to train new recruits and form new battalions.[8] Everywhere in South Vietnam, many of the most able and experienced Viet Cong cadres, administrators, and combat leaders were dead or prisoners by the end of 1968. Now was the time for a maximum effort to establish Saigon's control in the hundreds of villages and hamlets of rural Vietnam.

As early as March 1968 John Paul Vann, one of the brightest and most experienced of Komer's civilian generals, was proposing a more vigorous new approach to pacification. In the past, Vann observed, the United States had experimented with a large number of pacification programs, all of which had failed "because the first, basic requirement, security, was not met. You cannot expose the population to the inroads of the enemy every night and expect them to willingly cooperate with the government or overtly reject the Viet Cong." The essential requirement, Vann argued, was security. "Whether security is ten percent of the total problem or ninety percent, it is inescapably the *first* ten percent or the *first* ninety percent." Moreover, the U.S. and Saigon governments had to be prepared to provide long-term security, not simply a temporary occupation by Army or security forces.[9] Vann proposed that pacification be undertaken on a villagewide scale rather than by separate hamlet and that a Regional Force company be assigned to the village on a long-term basis with a Popular Force platoon stationed permanently in each hamlet.[10]

The emphasis on achieving government control ("security") through a massive, long-term military presence was to be the hallmark of the new pacification programs begun in the summer of 1968. And, for the first time, Americans believed they had sufficient forces to do the job. While the Viet Cong had been decimated in the winter and spring battles, U.S. force strength was at an all-time high. In addition, President Thieu, finally yielding to U.S. pressure, had significantly widened the manpower pool available to the Saigon government by signing a new General Mobilization Law, which made all Vietnamese men ages 18–38 liable for service in the army, and older men liable to serve in a new People's Self-Defense Corps. Draft deferments were drastically curtailed, and terms of service were extended indefinitely. By the end of 1969 the South Vietnamese army and security forces had added almost 200,000 men to their ranks, many of them armed with the new M-16 rifle and other modern U.S. equipment.[11] The new militia-style People's Self-Defense Corps enrolled 80,000 more for the war.

The People's Self-Defense Corps was the pet project of William Colby, a tough, low-key CIA career officer whose experience in Vietnam extended back to the Diem era and who had succeeded

Komer as head of CORDS in late 1968. Colby believed that arming virtually every able-bodied man and woman remaining in the villages, not already in the army or security forces, would show Saigon's confidence in its rural citizens and would involve them more closely in the anti-Communist struggle. In the past, arms supplied to Saigon forces had often ended up in the hands of the National Liberation Front. Colby argued, with unconscious irony, that there was now a small risk of that, since the Communists already had all the weapons they needed.[12]

After the war Colby would note that of the 170,000 weapons distributed to the People's Self-Defense Corps, less than 3 percent were lost. But though the PSDF managed to hang on to their rifles, in many areas they accomplished little else. A careful study of Hau Ngia province found that on the few occasions when the Viet Cong bothered to attack the PSDF, the Saigon forces were always badly defeated. More frequently front cadres entered a hamlet at night, disarmed the local PSDF, gave the members a lecture, and left, sometimes taking new recruits with them. "Front losses to PSDF activities numbered only a handful."[13]

By 1970 almost one-third of the adult male population of South Vietnam was at least nominally enlisted in some element of the armed forces or constabulary, with about one in nine serving in the army.[14] With these new forces and with more U.S. money than ever before available for pacification, Komer persuaded Thieu to take the offensive in an all-out effort to establish government control over large areas of the countryside. In a briefing for Thieu in June 1968, Komer laid out the basic objectives for such a new campaign. They included the establishment of local security, elimination of the Viet Cong local-level political and military cadres, and inducements to Communist forces to surrender or join the government side.

As he listened to Komer, Thieu was aware that the Viet Cong had been busy in the countryside establishing "liberation committees" to assert control over disputed areas and to be in a stronger position should the Paris negotiations lead to a ceasefire.[15] The possibility of an early ceasefire with the Communists still in nominal control of much of the countryside was a nightmare Thieu was determined to avoid.

By the fall of 1968 the Vietnamese and their American advisers had begun an Accelerated Pacification Campaign. The campaign was to last from November 1, 1968, to the end of January 1969. The objectives were to establish some degree of government "presence" and control in one thousand contested hamlets throughout South Vietnam.

General Abrams also promised to devote a maximum number of troops to operations in direct support of pacification. By September 1968, Abrams's staff was emphasizing a new approach to the ground war called the "One War" strategy, which sought to give the improvement of the South Vietnamese armed forces and the attainment of territorial security equal priority with offensive operations against the enemy's large units.[16] Hazy in concept and slow in starting, the One War approach nevertheless promised far better coordination between Abrams's big battalions and the myriad security and paramilitary forces engaged in pacification.

The U.S.–South Vietnamese efforts to establish greater government presence in the countryside were accompanied by programs specifically designed to weaken the Viet Cong and to attack its organization and leadership. One of these programs, the Chieu Hoi (literally Opened Arms), had been instituted as early as 1963. It was designed to induce Communist fighters and administrators to defect to the government by promises of amnesty and fair treatment.

The Chieu Hoi idea was based on a program implemented with great success by Philippine President Ramon Magsaysay during his campaign against the Huk insurgents in the 1950s. The program did not easily take root in Vietnam, however. Vietnamese officials and police were highly suspicious of Viet Cong defectors and little interested in converting them into productive citizens. An experienced American adviser observed that "status-conscious Vietnamese" may have believed that "the relative low rank and unimportance of most defectors places them beneath official notice." For the same reason the idea of attempting to induce higher-level defections "remains unpopular with those Vietnamese in official positions who perhaps fear the competition of more aggressive, determined former Viet Cong leaders. . . . This concept of accepting a defector and turning him into a useful citizen just doesn't fit within the Vietnamese philosophy of how to fight a war."[17]

Like so many other American-initiated programs in Vietnam,

Chieu Hoi also provided opportunities for a little larceny. Beginning in 1967, South Vietnamese citizens who induced or persuaded a Viet Cong to defect were eligible for a monetary reward, and local officials soon developed a convenient arrangement whereby every "Hoi Chanh" who turned up in their area was persuaded to state that he had been "induced" to defect by the district chief, police chief, hamlet chief, or other local worthy. That zealous official would then split the reward with the newly arrived defector. More enterprising officials, not content to await the chance appearance of a genuine Viet Cong defector, often arranged to have their relatives or subordinates turn themselves in as Chieu Hoi, then claimed the reward for inducing these "defections." The third-party inducement program was finally terminated in 1969.

Whatever the shortcomings of the Chieu Hoi program, there were always significant numbers of defections, more than 75,000 between 1963 and 1967.[18] It may be, as some critics charged, that the program simply provided a mechanism for those who would have defected in any case.[19] They included those who had grown weary of the hardships of Viet Cong life in the mountains, jungles, or swamps and those who were concerned for the economic welfare of their families. This was especially true of Viet Cong fighters in units serving far from their home villages.

Prolonged combat and heavy losses also were frequent inducements to rally.[20] B-52 strikes were especially feared. CIA interrogator Orrin de Forrest recalled many defectors who "had survived the attacks, though often with ruptured eardrums, but had witnessed the horrifying results, the concussion that killed many of their friends or buried them alive in their bunkers."[21]

Few Hoi Chanh rallied for ideological reasons or because they found life under the Saigon regime more appealing. Indeed, Rand interrogators found that "the defector often retains a high regard for VC aims, and he may be proud of his service record."[22]

Defectors were a valuable source of intelligence for U.S. and South Vietnamese forces, but American advisers and intelligence professionals frequently complained that these valuable sources were not thoroughly or effectively interrogated and that information that was developed was often not properly exploited. "Typically when a Hoi Chanh defected he was debriefed on the spot by South

Vietnamese army field interrogators. . . . Often the debriefings weren't gentle. . . . Once they were debriefed, the Hoi Chanh would be sent to the province Chieu Hoi center where they might be interrogated further but where more commonly they would just sit around until their identities were confirmed and their official ID cards were issued."[23]

While Chieu Hoi was a staple of the pacification effort by 1968, a second basic program, Phuong Hoang, or "Phoenix," was only a few months old. Phoenix was an effort to assist the South Vietnamese in developing a coordinated intelligence program to identify and map the Communist covert political and administrative organization called the Viet Cong infrastructure, or VCI. Once individuals were identified, they could be targeted as potential Chieu Hoi, recruited as spies, or captured.[24]

The national police were nominally in charge of the Phoenix program, but massive support came from the CIA, which also armed and trained special paramilitary forces called Provincial Reconnaissance Units, or PRU. The PRU were, in theory, placed at the disposal of the province chiefs for difficult and dangerous missions.[25] In practice, the PRUs, tough, experienced, and ruthless teams of Viet Cong defectors and others with special grudges or hatred for the Communists, remained under the firm control of the CIA. The PRU's main target was the Viet Cong infrastructure, the network of tax collectors, secretaries, intelligence agents, and propagandists who formed the backbone of the Communist organization at the village and district levels. In principle these individuals were to be captured and exploited for intelligence. In practice, they were more often than not killed; both because the Viet Cong's own security system and fighting qualities made capture difficult and because the PRU squads were seldom very solicitous about the fate of their prisoners.[26]

Critics of the war castigated the PRU as brutal assassins, while American officials nervously insisted that the PRU and the entire Phoenix effort were "a Vietnamese program." Privately, military and CIA leaders spoke warmly of the PRU's "effectiveness." Yet even if all of the PRU's claims regarding Viet Cong captured or killed are accepted at face value, they accounted for only about 7 percent of all Viet Cong killed or captured by U.S. and South Vietnamese forces.[27]

Indeed, critics of the Phoenix program in Saigon were quick to point out that most Viet Cong losses occurred as a result of "normal" military and security operations, not because of "neutralizations" under Phoenix.

CORDS developed an elaborate questionnaire called the Hamlet Evaluation Survey (HES), filled out monthly by hundreds of CORDS advisers down to the district level in order to measure the progress of pacification. A computer read the data and placed every hamlet in South Vietnam on a six-level scale ranging from A (adequate security forces, Communist infrastructure eliminated, public projects under way) through C (subject to infrequent Communist harassment, infrastructure identified, some self-help programs) to VC (under Communist control, no government or American presence except in military operations).[28] The immediate goal of the accelerated pacification program was to move as many of the thousand target hamlets as possible into the A, B, or C category.

By early 1969 it was apparent that the security situation in the countryside was improving. Defections under the Chieu Hoi program reached an all-time high, and thousands of Viet Cong agents and functionaries were reported killed or captured. The HES rating showed continued improvement, and by the end of 1969 over 70 percent of the population were rated as living in areas under government control, as opposed to 42 percent at the beginning of 1968.[29]

Even those who had come to regard all Saigon reports and statistics with deep skepticism could not deny the physical evidence of improved security. Roads and rivers that had been closed to government forces for years were reopened to civilian traffic. Bridges were repaired, and even the railroad began regular service again. By 1970 the dangerous "Street Without Joy" area of coastal Quang Tri province had been cleared of major enemy units for the first time since 1963.[30]

Route 9, the east–west road just south of the DMZ, which ran from the coast to Khe Sanh, had been dangerous for even the most heavily protected convoys in early 1968. During the Khe Sanh siege it had taken most of the 1st Cavalry and two regiments of Marines to force open the route. Ten months later Major General Raymond Davis would drive along the route at night alone in his jeep. "We totally controlled Quang Tri Province," the general recalled.[31] While this was an exaggeration, even as measured by the HES system, there was no doubt that the North Vietnamese and Viet Cong had suffered severe setbacks. In a meeting at Hanoi with a high-ranking party official in May 1969, Major General Le Trung Tin, who commanded Communist forces near the DMZ, was urged to "strive to improve the overall situation because no progress had been noted for some time due to various difficulties."[32]

Elsewhere in Vietnam the story was much the same. In the Delta, John Paul Vann discovered that many hamlets previously classified as under Viet Cong control had less than a dozen active cadres.[33] A party report on one of these Delta provinces observed that by 1971 "Ben Tre (Kien Hoa) which used to have seventy-two liberated villages comprising two-thirds of all the land area, was now an occupied province. . . . The enemy . . . took the initiative in cutting up the rural areas. They concentrated on pacifying one area completely before moving to the next, and hence were able to make us lose our control of the land and the people."[34]

The North Vietnamese troops sent south to replace Viet Cong losses could not really take up the slack. Strangers to the people and the region, they could not operate effectively away from the border areas without the logistical support, coordination, leadership, and local knowledge of the southerners. "The North Vietnamese are like you," a Vietnamese interpreter told a Marine in 1969. "They wander around in the jungle and can't do anything without our local people to act as guides."[35]

As Communist theorists never tired of pointing out, the basis of military success rested on close coordination and mutual support of the main force regular battalions, the local forces at provincial and district level, and the guerrilla militias, scouts, porters, and self-defense forces.[36] By 1969 the increased U.S.–Saigon presence in the countryside and heavy Viet Cong losses threatened to kick away one of the three legs of this military tripod.

When the northerners tried to operate on their own, they often came to grief. The 320th Independent Regiment, composed largely of northerners sent to the southern part of Long An to try to obstruct the government's pacification efforts, suffered such heavy losses that according to a Viet Cong source "the inhabitants of Long

An came to them in tears begging them to leave for the Cambodian borders or some other sanctuary."[37] Many of the main force Viet Cong and North Vietnamese Army units were already there recovering from their heavy losses in 1968 and waiting for the Americans to begin their withdrawals.

Early in 1970 President Thieu promulgated a sweeping land reform law, which at one stroke ended rents, put a ceiling of 15 hectares on the ownership of rice land, and transferred the title to persons actually farming the fields. The percentage of tenant farmers in Vietnam fell from almost 60 in 1970 to 7 percent by 1973. By South Vietnamese standards this was a radical program of almost breathtaking boldness and success. Yet it came many years too late; the stakes in the war had moved well past questions of land tenure. It was now a matter of settling old scores, supporting comrades, avenging relatives, driving out the foreigners, vindicating the cause, or the many other reasons that have always prompted angry and embittered combatants in a long civil war to call for each other's blood.

The Communists could and did proclaim that Thieu had only done in 1970 what they had done in 1954. In any case, after half a dozen years of American-assisted modernization of agriculture and the steady movement of people to the city, land was no longer as vital as other considerations—access to credit, for example, to be able to afford the new fertilizers and irrigation pumps on which the South's more productive new agricultural system now depended.[38]

Between 1969 and 1971 the Americans and their South Vietnamese allies came as close as they would ever come to winning the war for the countryside. Yet it was not close enough. The Viet Cong, beset by losses and shortages of supplies, hounded by government security forces, often reduced to eating manioc and bindweed grown in bomb craters created by B-52 strikes, still hung on and did not disintegrate.[39] They retained a number of their base areas in the more inaccessible parts of the Delta, along the Cambodian and Laotian borders, and in southern I Corps. Even in the provinces that appeared to be most firmly under Saigon's control, Communists were far from extinct. "We rid the country of larger enemy forces and armed every South Vietnamese who could stand still, Colonel

Jack Weissinger, a senior adviser with extensive experience in Vietnam, stated. Yet the government forces were still fearful. "They were more afraid of the dedication, persistence, and uncompromising attitude of [the Viet Cong] than they were of their numbers. In some villages we got the Front cadres down to two or three but that was just enough to hang in there."[40]

During 1969, 264 people were assassinated by the Communists in a single province, one in which pacification was reputed to be proceeding very well.[41] In I Corps, at the supposed height of U.S.-Saigon control in 1971, a senior adviser reported that "the enemy can use the vast majority of the land with total and complete impunity. Intelligence reports indicate that there are massive hospital complexes, enemy headquarters, staging areas, and heavily traveled supply routes. . . . American advisors have themselves seen vast areas of land being cultivated by enemy forces. One advisor even reported seeing mechanized agricultural equipment being used."[42] De Forrest, the CIA interrogator, estimated on the basis of information supplied by defectors that in 1970 the number of Vietnamese still actively working for the Viet Cong by providing food, delivering rice or ammunition, tending the wounded, or acting as couriers numbered at least 100,000 in III Corps alone.

Even when U.S. and South Vietnamese military ascendancy was at its height, the countryside was far from being either safe or peaceful. July 1970 was arguably the quietest month of the war. Just how fragile an equilibrium had been achieved can be seen by examining events in the Vietnamese countryside during that month. In July 250 North Vietnamese Army troops entered Hai Lang district in Quang Tri province and raided the town of Gio Linh, killing seventeen civilians and destroying dozens of houses. Fifty more civilians died when their boat was hit by a mine on the Dong Ha River, one of four such incidents during the month.[43] In Binh Dinh province U.S. advisers reported the beginning of the Communists' "most extensive terror campaign since the autumn of 1963." In the Central Highlands near Pleiku, American advisers reported eighty-three enemy-initiated incidents, including an attack on a Regional Forces unit by three North Vietnamese Army companies.[44]

The province of Kanh Hoa experienced relatively little combat, but two districts, Dien Khanh and heavily populated Ninh Hoa, were reported by U.S. observers to be receiving "regular nightly visits" by the Viet Cong in search of food and recruits. In the western half of Dien Khanh "reconnaissance reveals fearsome enemy crop production."[45] Kontum in the Central Highlands was another relatively quiet province, but U.S. advisers reported large enemy forces massed just across the Laotian and Cambodian borders and complained that ARVN and territorial forces "had failed to exploit fully the absence of the enemy from the province."[46]

The HES reports themselves revealed that in 1971 nearly 45 percent of rural villagers in I Corps lived within 1,000 meters of a recent terrorist incident. In Hau Ngia Province in III Corps near Saigon during the same period, an official or a Hoi Chanh was killed or wounded every few days throughout the year.[47] "You have to remember that even in the period of 1971 when the enemy was pretty well down, there was not a single official, nobody, who spent the night outside the barbed wire," a province senior adviser recalled, "because it was so quiet most people considered Hau Ngia secure. But it was totally insecure at night and that's all the enemy needed."[48]

More important, while the Communist forces had grown weaker, the Saigon government's forces had grown stronger only in terms of men under arms. The top leadership of the government and army remained as dependent as ever upon the United States, not only for military support but for ideas, strategy, doctrine, and tactics. No one in Saigon or Washington had a clear plan or even a good idea about how the southern forces were to achieve success under the changed conditions brought about by the progressive withdrawal of U.S. combat forces.

The same problems of sloth, incompetence, corruption, and nepotism that had plagued the military and administrative organs of the South Vietnamese government remained generally unchanged. A province or district chief might be removed here, a more competent and honest commander or administrator might be promoted there, usually as a result of CORDS's relentless prodding, but the general picture remained unchanged. In 1971, at the height of the seeming success of pacification, a senior U.S. adviser, after assessing the security situation in I Corps, concluded that "advisors are in complete agreement in [*sic*] that the largest problems facing Vietnamese units, in particular the RF and PF, is the absence of good leadership and the absence of motivation of the individual soldier. . . . Only the most naïve would argue with the contention that the majority of the Territorial Forces are interested primarily in their own personal fortunes and welfare in preference to winning the war."[49]

Although support for the NLF had become far more difficult and dangerous for the rural Vietnamese, he still felt no strong incentive to cast his lot with the Saigon government. "True, we were building schools and clinics and the like, but the government still was viewed with basic cynicism," Colonel Stuart Herrington, an Army intelligence officer in Vietnam, wrote. "Reason: corruption at all levels generally had the effect of angering people."[50]

At all times the danger of falling victim to terrorism remained high. Government security forces had come and gone before in many parts of rural Vietnam, and few Vietnamese, whatever their political or ideological inclination, were any more willing to take the risk of openly opposing the Front. The same U.S. studies that indicated an improvement in the security situation also showed a steady growth of fatalism and apathy among the population.[51] Lieutenant Colonel Carl Bernard, one of John Paul Vann's province senior advisers, observed in 1969 that "there are at least four Vietnamese officers I know who are withdrawing their commitment to the GVN. . . . They do not want to 'offend the VC' any more than is absolutely necessary." Lieutenant Colonel Bernard saw this not just as a sign of South Vietnamese laziness or inefficiency, but as representative of "malaise that is coming over the middle ranks of the GVN as they prepare for our withdrawal."[52]

Le Ly Hayslip recalls that "lots of Vietnamese concluded about this time that the American effort was doomed despite its success in the field. . . . We Vietnamese had a saying . . . 'by sticking together the tiny ants can carry the elephant.' By 1968 the American elephant could rage and stomp on the Vietnamese anthill but time and weight of numbers guaranteed that it would be the ants, not the elephant who danced on the bones of the victims."[53]

In the end, despite a promising land reform program, despite continued U.S. development efforts, despite attempts to restore "traditional" village government, the success of pacification rested only on superior military forces. As American forces began to thin out in 1971 and 1972, the government's hold on the countryside began to slip, and the patient, supremely confident Front cadres began rapidly rebuilding their military forces and their shadow governments in the villages and hamlets.

CHAPTER 14

"It Is the Right Thing to Do"

As October waned and the hot sunny days gave way to clouds and damp chilling rain, the people of the Democratic Republic of Vietnam prepared for another winter, the fourth winter of their war with the Americans and of living under constant threat of air attack. Despite the April bombing halt most government agencies still operated out of air raid shelters in the suburbs of Hanoi, and factories dispersed to outlying areas had remained in place. Food and clothing shortages were still common despite repairs to roads and bridges made possible by the cessation of bombing. Air raid alerts sounded upon the appearance of American reconnaissance flights, and the authorities attempted to discourage evacuees from returning from the countryside to the larger cities and towns.[1]

In the south, rain and tropical storms whipped across the narrow coastal plains of central Vietnam, causing widespread flooding and mud slides. Some districts received more than 20 inches of rain in September, 29 in October. Bridges were carried away, roads were inundated, and houses were buried in mud or borne away by water. The much-heralded Communist Third Offensive had sputtered to a halt with heavy losses. By October many large North Vietnamese and Viet Cong units had withdrawn to remote bases in swamps or jungles or across the border to refit, reorganize, and replace their losses as best they could. Three North Vietnamese Army regiments that had operated from the Demilitarized Zone had withdrawn 6 miles into North Vietnam. Fifteen other North Vietnamese regiments and two Viet Cong regiments, by now manned mostly by northerners, had also withdrawn into Cambodia.[2]

Abrams and his commanders, aware that the Communists had suffered heavy losses and that their logistical system was in disarray, felt more confident than at any time since Tet. Militarily, Abrams reported, the United States faced "a moment of supreme opportunity."[3] In the White House, however, the mood was far less upbeat. U.S. casualties continued at a near-record high, even in the absence of major battles. Most community leaders, educators, journalists, and politicians not closely associated with the President were weary and disillusioned with the war and impatient about the lack of progress in Paris.

At the Democratic National Convention in Chicago, more than a thousand of the 2,600 delegates voted for a platform plank calling for a complete bombing halt and an early withdrawal of U.S. troops from Vietnam. As the voting ended, "a priest knelt on the convention floor and prayed for peace. McCarthy delegates put on black arm bands and chanted 'Stop the war,' and peace delegates sang chorus after doleful chorus of 'We Shall Overcome.' "[4] Outside the convention hall thousands of antiwar demonstrators clashed with police under the glare of television lights on Michigan Avenue. While delegates listened to speeches supporting Vice President Humphrey's nomination, police pursued and beat demonstrators with nightsticks, and the smell of tear gas filled the downtown streets.

On September 30, in a nationally televised speech, Humphrey openly broke with the Johnson White House by declaring that as President he would completely halt the bombing of the north "as an acceptable risk for peace because I believe it would lead to success in the negotiations."[5] The Republican candidate, Richard Nixon, announced that he had a plan to end the war, which he could disclose only after the election.

At Paris, in secret negotiations with the North Vietnamese representative, Ha Van Lau, U.S. negotiator Cyrus Vance had offered a halt to the bombing if three conditions were met. The North Vietnamese had to promise to respect the sanctity of the Demilitarized Zone and refrain from rocket attacks on large cities; promise to begin "prompt and productive" negotiations; and agree to allow

South Vietnamese to participate in those negotiations.[6] The North Vietnamese promptly rejected this proposal, repeating their old slogan that they would never accept conditions for an end to U.S. bombing.

President Johnson was probably not particularly surprised by the North Vietnamese response. He had grown increasingly impatient and angry at what he saw as Communist procrastination in Paris. At a press conference on July 31, the President indicated that the United States might re-escalate the war if there was no progress at the peace talks. Johnson was inclined to listen sympathetically to Walt Rostow, who argued that the bombing seriously impeded the Communist military effort in South Vietnam. At Rostow's request General Abrams attempted to estimate the impact a complete bombing halt would have on the Communist war effort and on U.S. casualties. He projected a "several-fold increase in U.S. and allied casualties."[7] With the defeat of the Third Offensive, however, Abrams and his subordinates became far less apprehensive.

From Paris Averell Harriman urged the President to treat the battlefield lull and the withdrawal of Communist troops across the border as an occasion for stopping the bombing while making it clear that the next move was up to Hanoi. On October 12 the Soviets informed Washington that they had assurances that if the United States ended the bombing, Hanoi would agree to Saigon's participation in the Paris talks and to substantive negotiations. Informed of the Soviet message, Ambassador Bunker and General Abrams reported that they would support a bombing halt if it included safeguards for the cities and respect for the Demilitarized Zone. Bunker also reported that President Thieu had agreed to go along with the bombing halt provided Washington was prepared to "press the offensive" in the South and resume bombing if the Communists violated the understanding.[8]

The Russian message, with its offer of North Vietnamese concessions, left the President mired in doubt and indecision. He was suspicious of the Communist proposal, mindful of the fruitless earlier bombing halts of 1966 and 1967, convinced he would be charged with seeking popularity and partisan advantage or endangering American forces in Vietnam. There was some basis for his concern. Less than a month before, General Wheeler had returned from a meeting of the Senate Armed Services Committee to report that Senators Richard Russell, John Stennis, and Gordon Allott believed that the March bombing halt had been a mistake and were discouraged at the lack of progress in the war. Senator Stennis said that "we should have brought [more] military force to bear."[9]

Johnson continued to hesitate and seek reassurance from his advisers. Secretary of State Rusk and CIA Director Richard Helms saw Hanoi's acceptance of South Vietnamese participation in the talks as a major concession. Rusk pointed out that this was tacit recognition "that there can be no settlement in Vietnam without the assent of the GVN. . . . GVN participation could have a major effect on the political and psychological situation inside South Vietnam: the Chieu Hoi rates should go up." Helms observed that "all his experts" had believed that Hanoi would "never accept the GVN at the table" and that therefore Hanoi's concession on this point was "very significant."[10]

Defense Secretary Clifford pointed out that the North Vietnamese had long insisted that they would never sit down with Saigon representatives and that the U.S. bombing must stop unconditionally. Their recent offer indicated that "something has occurred to weaken the resolve of the North Vietnamese" and to induce them to make a "substantial concession."[11]

The Air Force Chief of Staff, General John P. McConnell, advised the President, "if you are to stop bombing now is the time." The weather below the 19th Parallel and in the Laotian panhandle was expected to be poor for the next several weeks. Heavy monsoon rains would, in any case, do more to slow Communist supply trucks than bombing and strafing.[12] The Chief of Naval Operations and the Commandant of the Marine Corps agreed with General McConnell. JCS Chairman Wheeler pointed out that the bombing could be easily restarted if the Communists violated the DMZ or attacked the cities.[13]

Still the President hesitated. "I know I will be charged with doing this to influence the election," he told Senator Richard Russell of the Armed Services Committee, in a meeting on October 14. "The doves will criticize us for not doing it earlier. The hawks will say it shouldn't have been done at all."[14] Russell observed that the war had been "miserable—worse than Korea" and that the bombing halt was "worth a try."[15]

On October 15 Harriman and Vance finally received the green light to inform the North Vietnamese that the bombing would cease provided the North Vietnamese agreed to observe the "facts of life: no shelling of cities or violation of the DMZ" and promised to set a definite and early date for the beginning of negotiations, which would have to include the South Vietnamese.

At this point the Saigon government, faced with the prospect of real negotiations, began to drag its feet. Thieu, Ky, and their entourage might be venal and corrupt, but they were far from stupid. They probably sensed that the United States was getting tired of the war and that men like Clifford and Harriman might be willing to disengage America even at considerable risk to South Vietnam. For his part, Clifford was convinced that the Saigon oligarchy "did not want the war to end—not while it was protected by half a million troops and a golden flow of money."[16] In addition, the Thieu government had established secret contacts with Nixon's campaign headquarters. The White House suspected that Nixon's managers, worried that the beginning of serious peace talks would provide a boost to the Humphrey campaign, were encouraging the South Vietnamese to delay their participation in the Paris conference until after the elections.

For the next ten days the Saigon government continued to raise doubts and objections while most of President Johnson's advisers urged him to take the decision to halt the bombing. General William Momyer, recently returned from his tour as the top air commander in Vietnam, reported that the weather was now so bad that bombing between the 17th and 19th parallels could be done only by radar. Most of the air effort would now "normally concentrate on trucks coming through Laos. If we can still do this, the risk undertaken by the President is minimal at this period for the next few months."[17] Secretary of Defense Clifford commented that if ten steps originally separated the United States and North Vietnam, "they had taken eight and we have taken two." "I would say it is even nine to one," Secretary of State Rusk added.[18] Still, the President hesitated, insisting on a personal meeting with General Abrams to discuss the bombing halt.

One reason the President's military advisers could feel confident about halting the bombing of North Vietnam was the knowledge that in recent weeks the most important part of the air war had shifted from North Vietnam to the Ho Chi Minh Trail. The Trail began at two main mountain passes between Vietnam and Laos, Mu Gia and Ban Karat, and led south through the rugged Annamite Cordillera, which the Vietnamese called the Truong Son, to the Central Highlands of South Vietnam.

By 1968 the "trail" had become a complicated network of motor roads, bypasses, fords, and bridges totaling some 16,000 kilometers. On any given day at least two thousand and sometimes as many as three thousand trucks would be on the trail, serviced by twelve major storage depots, repair shops, barracks, bunkers, and infirmaries, all hidden in caves or limestone karsts deep underground. Somewhere between 30,000 and 100,000 engineers, mechanics, technicians, laborers, and antiaircraft artillerymen made their permanent home on the trail, helping to maintain the road, keep the trucks moving, and defend them against the constant threat of American air attack.[19]

The trail was far more than a major Communist supply route, however. It was itself a major part of the North Vietnamese logistical system, with hundreds of well-concealed, widely dispersed storage areas for food, ammunition, fuel, and medical supplies. Communist planners calculated the supply requirements of their units in the South and then stocked the trail with supplies far in excess of the anticipated requirements. Even heavy and repeated air attacks would be unlikely to destroy all the pre-positioned supply sites and the high degree of "redundancy" built into the Communist supply system ensured that the surviving supplies would be sufficient to meet operational needs.

The Americans and South Vietnamese attempted to keep track of traffic on the trail through highly secret long-range reconnaissance teams, which infiltrated from Vietnam, and through local tribesmen organized by CIA and Special Forces. Aircraft dropped tiny sensors that could burrow into the ground with only their plantlike antennae exposed or hang concealed in the leaves of trees. Air Force reconnaissance planes used infrared photography to locate major choke points, bridges, and storage areas.

To attack the endless stream of trucks along the Ho Chi Minh Trail, the Air Force employed everything from high-flying B-52s to helicopter gunships and small propellor-driven observation planes. Yet many trucks still got through, aided by excellent use of camouflage in daytime and the limited ability of most U.S. planes to find targets at night. The North Vietnamese also made good use of darkness to repair quickly the roads, bridges, and fords damaged by bombing.[20]

American electronic warfare experts and North Vietnamese engineers played a deadly cat-and-mouse game with the array of mines and reconnaissance devices the Americans constantly seeded along the trail. North Vietnamese combat engineer companies were responsible for ensuring the continued movement of traffic along the trail. Each engineer company was responsible for a segment of the trail, and its observation posts and reconnaissance teams continually monitored the route for American mines and surveillance devices. Men assigned to these tasks soon learned to tell by an aircraft's flight pattern, or even by the sound of its engines, whether the plane was on an attack mission or dropping electronic devices along the trail.

As soon as a mine or sensing device was spotted, a team was dispatched to deal with it.[21] Often the team had no other equipment than shovels, ropes, levers, and explosives. Tripwire bombs, cluster bombs which attached themselves to trees or foliage by tiny green wires, had to be disarmed by a man carrying a "mobile shield made from half of a 200-liter gas drum and padded with straw." With this as protection, a bomb demolition man used a long pole to knock lightly against the wires, triggering the bomb. Sometimes satchel charges were hurled into an area thought to be mined in the hope that their explosion would trigger a chain reaction. Magnetic mines could be triggered by pulling steel bars with magnets attached across the suspected area.[22] In all, the North Vietnamese Army estimated it had neutralized more than 80 percent of American electronic devices dropped along the trail.[23] The cost in lives of this mine-clearing effort was not recorded.

Whatever the success of their counterelectronic warfare, there could be no gainsaying the fact that large numbers of Communist vehicles continued to survive the gauntlet of American bombs, bullets, and booby traps. By early 1968 U.S. intelligence was reporting evidence of a "truck kill plateau." That is, the number of trucks sighted or detected on the trail had increased over 160 percent from 1966 to the end of 1967, but the number of "truck kills" by aircraft remained roughly the same.[24] This was due in part to the pattern of U.S. bombing. The Air Force's "stereotyped" operations —concentrating attacks on the same roads, junctions, bridges, or passes month after month. This predictable pattern of bombing the same targets enabled the enemy to repair them more quickly by pre-positioning repair crews, construction equipment, and supplies near the areas he knew in advance would be bombed.[25] The Air Force's ability to bomb at night and in bad weather was also severely limited, and intelligence on truck traffic, despite all the electronic gadgetry, was never as good as the aviators desired.

By mid-1968 the Defense Department, MACV, and the Air Force brass in Washington were all pressing for better results against the trail. The Seventh Air Force, which ran the air campaign against the trail, responded with a plan for a stepped-up campaign called COMMANDO HUNT. Yet Abrams and MACV were reluctant to go along with all the Air Force requests for more planes and more sensors. Some of the sensors were needed by the Marines to help police the DMZ, and Abrams refused to commit planes that might be needed for tactical missions inside South Vietnam. The real reason for Abrams's lukewarm reaction, Air Force generals suspected, was that COMMANDO HUNT was an Air Force rather than a MACV program. The Air Force was reluctant to share responsibility for COMMANDO HUNT for "fear it might develop into a joint operation and thereby threaten the Tactical Air Control System."[26]

While the generals continued their arcane squabbles over command and control, technical developments seemed to promise a more effective attack on the trail. The Air Force's research and development program, called Shed Light, was yielding a number of devices for night attack, such as the Starlight Scope, capable of picking up and magnifying even the smallest light from the ground, and new low-light television cameras, which worked on similar principles. Improved sensors, tied by relay aircraft to a surveillance center in Nakhon Phanom, Thailand, transmitted information to the Seventh Air Force command and control center, which selected and dispatched aircraft to suitable targets. In addition, a new and more deadly threat to the slow-moving trucks had appeared, the AC-130 gunship.

Nicknamed Spectre, the AC-130 was a large four-engine cargo plane modified to carry flares, rockets, and 20mm automatic cannon, and equipped with the newest heat and light sensors. These included infrared detectors, which picked up the heat of truck engines and exhausts, low-light television; and ignition detectors, code-named BLACK CROW, which registered the electrical emissions of the truck's internal combustion engine. Flying at night at low speeds and relatively low altitudes, escorted by fighters, the AC-130 proved a formidable threat to the trucks plying the Ho Chi Minh Trail. By early 1969 the four AC-130s operating against the Ho Chi Minh Trail were accounting for more than 40 percent of trucks destroyed.

The North Vietnamese responded to the new threat by bringing in more trucks and more antiaircraft guns. As one Air Force squadron commander observed, "Where there are trucks, there are very many 37mm [antiaircraft gun] positions."[27] From late 1968 to early 1970 the number of antiaircraft guns defending the trail quadrupled.[28] The North Vietnamese also had some success in countering the airborne sensors carried by the AC-130s. Alerted to the capabilities of BLACK CROW by an American aeronautics magazine, the Vietnamese truckers and engineers began to wrap their ignition systems in aluminum foil to suppress electromagnetic emissions. Mats of banana leaves and bamboo were employed to shield hot spots on vehicles from detection by infrared-sensitive instruments.[29]

For the hapless Vietnamese truck driver, there was only one defense against bombs, rockets, and shrapnel: keep moving. Jolting along a darkened road filled with bomb craters, directed by a guide's dimly lighted lamp, the truckers seldom made more than 20 kilometers a day. Vehicles that broke down and blocked traffic were quickly unloaded and pushed off the road into a ravine or stream bed while the driver joined the workmen, mechanics, and soldiers traveling the road on foot.[30]

The trail took its toll of the attackers as well. "The illuminator operator who used the drop flares, would hang out the back of the aircraft, actually hang his chest out, . . . and was able to see the muzzle flashes and then watch the AAA come up," Lieutenant Colonel Steven Opitz, a fire-control officer aboard an AC-130, recalled. "Thirty-seven and fifty-seven millimeter took about six seconds to come up to our altitude. So he would call, 'AAA 6 o'clock, coming up' and you'd listen to him, he'd get your attention . . . and then he would holler at the last minute, 'break right,' or 'break left.' And the pilot would turn the bird, break it out of orbit and the shot would come relatively close. They would go off and you would hear them and smell the cordite."[31]

One AC-130 reconnoitering a road intersection was hit by two 37mm rounds, which knocked out the plane's two hydraulic systems, fatally wounded the illuminator operator, and pitched the aircraft into a steep climb. The pilot, Lieutenant Colonel William Schwehm, braced the control column in full forward position and brought all the crew members to the flight deck, where their combined weight helped to trim the plane. In a few more seconds Colonel Schwehm had the aircraft back under control and turned for home. A quick inspection revealed that the rudder, autopilot, and elevator trim were all inoperable. Using the aileron trim and engine power, Colonel Schwehm and his copilot, Major Gerald Piehl, nursed the plane back to Udorn, Thailand, then ordered most of the flight crew to bail out.

With only four crewmen still aboard, Colonel Schwehm brought the badly damaged AC-130 in for a landing. As the aircraft bounced along the field, Colonel Schwehm vainly attempted to reverse engines. Two thousand feet down the runway the plane suddenly veered to the right, shearing off a wing, and burst into flames. Colonel Schwehm, his copilot, and a crew member managed to escape the burning plane, but Staff Sergeant Jack Troglin, the illuminator operator, and Staff Sergeant Cecil Taylor, the flight engineer, were killed[32]—two of the more than two hundred airmen who were to die in operations against the Ho Chi Minh Trail.

On October 29, General Creighton Abrams secretly left Tan Son Nhut airport for the long flight to Washington and an early morning meeting at the White House. Two days before, the Hanoi delegation had conceded the last point demanded by the Americans. They secretly agreed to begin talks within four days of a bombing halt instead of several weeks, as they had previously proposed, and dropped their proposal that the enlarged meetings be called "the four power conference."[33]

Abrams found the President about to make his final decision on a bombing halt for all of North Vietnam. After a long review of the negotiations, the President asked Abrams, "if the enemy honors our agreement will this be an advantage militarily?" "Yes," Abrams answered. "Will it compensate for the lack of bombing?" "Yes," he replied again. How, demanded the President, could Abrams say in August that a bombing halt would lead to greater U.S. casualties yet now advise that a bombing halt was advantageous? Abrams referred to the successful interdiction bombing on the Laotian panhandle and to the heavy enemy losses in the August–September offensives, losses that had not been replaced.

"If you were President would you do it?" Johnson asked. "I have no reservations about doing it," the general replied. "I know it is stepping into a cesspool of comment. I do think it is the right thing to do. It is the proper thing to do."[34]

From Saigon came word that President Thieu was still not ready to go along. He now claimed that the Vietnamese National Assembly would have to authorize sending a delegation to the Paris talks. After two days of fruitless efforts to persuade Saigon to come around, President Johnson finally announced the end of American bombing at 8:00 P.M. on October 31. Saigon's response was to declare that South Vietnam would send no representatives to the new round of talks scheduled to begin on November 6.

On November 5 Nixon won a narrow victory over Humphrey, and Saigon agreed a few days later to join the talks. No sooner had they arrived in Paris, however, than the South Vietnamese representatives raised procedural objections. These soon took the form of a prolonged and "famously stupid" argument over the shape and arrangement of the conference table.[35]

The South Vietnamese professed to believe that a square table, desired by the North Vietnamese, or a round table, suggested by the United States, implied recognition of the National Liberation Front (the Viet Cong) as a separate and equal party to the negotiations. Clifford and Harriman angrily dismissed the controversy as a deliberate stall by Saigon. After two months of haggling, the conferees finally agreed on a compromise "shape"—two rectangular tables placed at opposite ends of a round table.

While the Vietnamese and Americans argued in Paris over the shape of the conference table, other Americans and Vietnamese continued their more deadly arguments in the rice paddies and jungles of the south.

In Quang Nam province, south of Da Nang, the Marines returned to the area near Go Noi Island, which had been the scene of the bloody encounters in Operation ALLEN BROOK in May. Unlike many other areas of South Vietnam, the mountains and river valleys of Quang Nam continued to be heavily occupied by Communist troops. In mid-September, the 7th Marines had suffered 120 casualties in wiping out the command post of the 2d Battalion, 36th North Vietnamese Regiment, during Operation MAMELUKE THRUST in this area.

In late November the Marines resumed operations in the area with seven battalions in Operation MEADE RIVER. The seven Marine battalions, two of them aboard the amphibious assault ships of the Seventh Fleet, were under the overall command of Colonel Robert G. Lauffer. The plan was to form a giant ring or cordon around the area just north of Go Noi Island, a densely populated region of villages and rice paddies, which the Marines had nick-named Dodge City in reference to the many fire fights, ambushes, and booby traps encountered there.

The Marines and Army had often employed the cordon approach to seal off and search a suspicious area, but this method had previously been confined to hamlets or villages. Now the area to be cordoned comprised some 36 square miles and contained an unknown number of North Vietnamese troops and local guerrillas.

In the evening of November 19, men of the 2d Battalion, 26th Marines, watched the nightly movie sprawled on the spacious hangar deck of the amphibious assault ship USS *Tripoli* riding the gentle swells in the South China Sea just south of Da Nang. The *Tripoli* was shaped like a small aircraft carrier, but her lower decks contained a complete hospital with operating rooms, X-ray machines, a pharmacy, and beds for about two hundred patients. In these hospital spaces doctors, technicians, corpsmen, and pharmacists were completing their final preparations to receive casualties from Operation MEADE RIVER, scheduled to begin early the following morning.

For the Marines on the hangar deck there was little to do but wait as they munched candy and potato chips from the ship's store and watched Dustin Hoffman and Katharine Ross in *The Graduate*. Although they yelled and hooted at the appropriate places, most watched the movie with a certain hunger and sadness, well aware that this would be their last glimpse of life "in the world" for many days, perhaps forever.

A few hours later, in the predawn darkness, flight deck guides led squads of Marines to waiting helicopters positioned on the *Tripoli's* flight deck; squat black shapes, already bouncing and vibrating to the roar of their engines, exhausts emitting flashes of blue and orange flame. Ashore and aboard other ships, Marines were climbing into other helicopters for the assault on Dodge City. Almost fifty CH-46s and CH-53s carried the Marines to their landing zones, escorted by more than a dozen "Huey" gunships. All together there were seventy-three helicopters from three Marine air groups, making MEADE RIVER one of the largest Marine helo assault operations of the war.[36] Only one landing zone proved to be hot, and a CH-46 of Marine Medium Helicopter Squadron 265 was lost to ground fire.[37]

Once on the ground, companies and platoons spread out and began slowly to tighten the noose of the cordon. The Dodge City area was a flat, heavily cultivated region of rice paddies broken by occasional tree lines. Forming the cordon were two battalions each from the 5th, 7th, and 26th Marines.

First to find the enemy was Colonel Neal A. Nelson's 2d Battalion, 7th Marines, who found themselves, in the late afternoon of November 20, in the midst of a deadly Communist bunker complex near a large bend in a stream, which the Marines called "the Horseshoe." The North Vietnamese fought from mutually supporting diamond-shaped bunkers constructed of concrete reinforced by logs, railroad ties, and rails from the nearby right-of-way of the national railroad. One Marine company was immediately pinned down and managed to extricate itself only after suffering six killed.[38]

The Marines withdrew to the opposite bank of the stream and called for artillery support, which continued intermittently throughout the night. Colonel Nelson was reinforced the following morning by two additional companies but was still unsuccessful in forcing the North Vietnamese from their bunkers.

In a third attack on the Horseshoe on November 22, D Company managed to cross the stream and fight its way to within 100 yards of the bunkers, but E Company was caught in the middle of the stream after American fire support had lifted and the Communists managed to return to their firing positions. In a few minutes E Company suffered more than thirty casualties and withdrew to the north bank of the stream.

In the meantime, D Company had fought its way to within 300 meters of the Communist positions but then was stopped by continuing heavy fire. By this point the company had suffered nineteen casualties, including the radio operators for the forward air controller and the artillery observer. Unable to call in fire support, D Company finally withdrew to the stream bank and set up a landing zone to evacuate casualties. As the medevac helicopters approached the landing zone, heavy fire from the nearby bunkers caused them to break off. It was only with the coming of darkness that D Company was able to evacuate its wounded.[39]

The following morning the 3d Battalion, 26th Marines, advancing from the southwest corner of the cordon, made a coordinated attack on the Horseshoe and captured some of the Communist positions, but others still remained. The Communists, as usual, fought from "beautifully constructed bunkers" with mutually supporting fields of fire. Built low to the ground with their firing ports at ground level, the bunkers were hard to spot. "Troops moving through the area could pass those holes and not be aware they were there." The bunkers' occupants would hold their fire until the Marines were well inside the bunker complex then "open up and get a lot of first hits." The Marines soon learned to treat any piece of earth "so much as a foot high" with suspicion.[40]

After further unsuccessful efforts on November 24 to take the remaining Communist positions, the Marines pulled back and blasted the area with artillery. When the rain of shells ceased, the Marines again attacked the bunkers, only to find the enemy gone.

Documents captured in the battle for the Horseshoe made clear that enemy strength in the Dodge City area totaled three full North Vietnamese regiments reinforced by two local force Viet Cong battalions.

Over the next four days the Marine battalions steadily tightened the cordon around the Dodge City area. The constantly shrinking ring created fire support problems as the battalions drew closer together. At one point a plane supporting the 1st Battalion, 1st Marines, fighting near the Co Ca River, dropped a napalm bomb that landed directly on the positions of H Company, 2d Battalion, 5th Marines, heavily engaged on the opposite side of the river. Fortunately the bomb bounced away from the Marine positions before exploding.[41]

By the end of November the Marines were closing the ring around the last enemy positions between the Co Ca and the trace of the national railroad. On December 2 elements of the 3d Battalion, 5th Marines, were halted by heavy fire near a small bend in the Co Ca. This time the Marines made no attempt to overrun the Communist bunkers but called for artillery, carefully adjusted by the forward observers. After three days of heavy bombardment, the Marines swept through the Communist positions with little resistance. They found seventy-five bodies in the complex of thirty bunkers in the river bend and captured five prisoners.[42]

H Company, 2d Battalion, 5th Marines, was less fortunate. Three days after 3/5 had cleared out the bunkers at the bend of the Co Ca, Hotel ran into heavy fire while crossing a rice paddy. In a tree line near the river the Marines could see a large bunker, which appeared to be the center of the Communist defenses.[43] H Company was now so close to other Marines operating just across the river that air strikes on the bunker posed the danger of causing friendly casualties. The company commander, Captain Ronald Dreez, tried to arrange for a supporting attack by a nearby troop of Vietnamese army armored personnel carriers, but the Vietnamese commander refused to attack the bunkers.

Dreez then turned to his "combat engineer," a young PFC named Michael Emmons, temporarily attached to H Company from an engineer company, and ordered him to prepare a satchel charge to blow up the bunker. Emmons could find only 12 pounds of C-4, the standard Marine Corps demolition explosive, barely enough to do the job. To make sure, Emmons added all the grenades he could find plus two 3.5-inch rocket rounds, which had failed to explode. With this doubtful mixture, Emmons, Dreez, and the company gunnery sergeant picked their way around the flank and onto the top of the bunker, covered by heavy fire from the rest of the company. Emmons lit the five-second fuse, and Dreez and the gunny leaped back into the rice paddy. Delaying a few seconds to make sure the fuse was burning, Emmons was tossed into the air by the force of the explosion but landed with only minor injuries. The blast killed thirty-nine North Vietnamese inside the bunker and effectively ended the battle on the river bank.[44] The following day H Company reached the river and linked up with 1st Battalion, 1st Marines, on the other side.

III MAF and Saigon pronounced MEADE RIVER "highly successful." Marine commanders claimed to have killed more than a thousand North Vietnamese. They captured 123 prisoners and six Chieu Hois and destroyed more than 20 tons of rice.[45] Yet by the end of December the Communists had reoccupied most of the Dodge City area, and the Americans were busily planning another operation against the twenty-four Communist battalions estimated to be still in Quang Nam Province.[46]

In Washington, President Johnson, preparing to leave office, took a positive view of developments in Vietnam. The Communists "could still knock out a window light," he observed, but "they have been out of it since September."[47] The enemy's main forces had been "pulled back into North Vietnam, Laos, and the Cambodian border area," he told President-elect Nixon, and the "pacification progress is moving about three times our best sustained period in the past."[48]

Yet the Administration was as uncertain as ever about how to translate these gains into a peace settlement. "I spent most of yesterday making calls and meeting people in Washington," Abrams's deputy, General Andrew Goodpaster, reported in late December. "Already it is apparent that there is wide and deep disagreement as to the situation [in Vietnam] and as to the course we should take in Paris."[49] So 1968 ended as it had begun, with heavy fighting, uncertain policies, and renewed proclamations of success.

EPILOGUE

Our campaign is over and there has nothing come of it on one side or the other but the loss of a great many worthy people, the misery of a great many poor soldiers, crippled forever, the ruin of some provinces, the savage pillage and conflagration of some flourishing towns. Exploits these, which make humanity shudder.

FREDERICK II, 1753

On December 19, 1968, Ambassador Ellsworth Bunker sat down to draft his weekly personal assessment for President Johnson, then in the waning days of his Administration. "I believe 1968 will go into history as the year in which the strength and love of freedom of South Vietnam was most sorely tested and not found wanting," Bunker wrote. "I am convinced if we continue, patient and confident in our strength, we will get, next year, the kind of peace we have sought through so many grim trials."[1]

Two days later General Vo Nguyen Giap, Minister of Defense, Commander in Chief of the People's Army of Vietnam, and legendary victor of Dien Bien Phu, delivered a speech at an Army Day rally in Hanoi. "Our strength, military and political, has grown unceasingly while that of the United States' puppets have suffered heavy losses," Giap told his listeners gathered in the damp chill of the Hanoi winter afternoon. "The enemy battle order has been upset and they are sinking ever deeper into passive defense and into a strategic position of being attacked and encircled on all battle-fields."[2]

Despite these proclamations of success, 1968 ended as it had begun, with bloody yet inconclusive struggles on the battlefield and continued diplomatic deadlock. Yet by not deciding anything, the battles of 1968 decided much. In the long run the costly struggles of 1968, which began with Tet and continued through August and September, were a political success for the Communists. They convinced almost all influential Americans that the war could not be won at an acceptable price or in an acceptable time. Yet because they failed to break the political and military deadlock in Vietnam itself, the Communists doomed themselves to four more years of war.

Indeed, the balance of forces in South Vietnam by early 1969 had shifted in such a manner as to put the Communists at a disadvantage from which it took them more than two years to recover. This was not because the Communist losses in the 1968 battles had been high, although they had been. More important were the timing and unrelenting scope and intensity of the attacks demanded by Hanoi strategists.[3] Each of the Communist offensives, January and February, May–June, and August–September, had attempted to follow the same script, and each had been less successful and more costly than the last. Indeed the Communists, by August 1968, seemed almost to be imitating the American habit of following the same predictable patterns of operations.

It was not until early 1969 that Hanoi began to change its operational method to emphasize carefully planned attacks on towns and bases by highly trained small units and sappers, and not until late 1969 did Communist strategists decide to reduce the level of combat.[4] By then the damage had been done. The heavy manpower losses could be made good by sending more men from the north, but without the experience, organization, and local knowledge provided by the Viet Cong they would inevitably be less effective.

The Americans in Saigon, dimly perceiving that something like this was taking place, responded with a determined attempt to win control of the countryside for Saigon and smash the remaining large enemy units. In this they had considerable success, although that would not be evident until late 1969 or early 1970.

Yet the Americans and South Vietnamese were never able to turn their advantage to a decisive victory. The Communists survived and husbanded and rebuilt their forces. As the American troop withdrawals proceeded, the Viet Cong and North Vietnamese once again moved to challenge Saigon's control.

It is tempting to speculate that had the United States only been more patient and slowed or halted the withdrawal of its forces during 1969 and 1970, the favorable stalemate might have continued longer or Saigon might have found a road to victory. Yet the Saigon government seemed no more able in 1970 or 1971 to put its house in order, end corruption, and win the loyalty of the people than it had been in 1967 or 1968. And the cost of maintaining the favorable stalemate continued to be very high. Almost as many Americans died in Vietnam in 1969 as in 1967, and even casualties for 1970, the last year that sizable numbers of U.S. combat troops remained in Vietnam, still almost equaled those of 1966. South Vietnamese casualties kept right on increasing in every successive year after 1968.[5]

The battles of 1968 were decisive, then, because they were so indecisive. Despite the drama of the Tet attacks, the ruin of the Johnson Administration, the agonizing attempts at peace negotiations, and the sanguinary trials on the battlefield, the Vietnam War remained what it had been and would remain until 1973: a stalemate.

American generals attempted to explain the apparent pointlessness of most Vietnam military operations by arguing that this was an "unconventional war" without front lines or normal military objectives. Yet the inconclusive, repetitive, and costly style of U.S. operations was also due, in large part, to American military policies and practices, which served, in effect, to institutionalize inexperience. The short command tours for officers, the one-year tour for enlisted men, the lack of any systematic attempt to pass on lessons or develop doctrine, and the dearth of interest in any information that could not be quantified all helped perpetuate the tentative, clumsy, and indecisive style of American operations even after three years of experience of war in Vietnam.

After 1968 both sides recognized that they could never completely destroy or drive out the opponent from the mountains, jungles, rice paddies, and villages of South Vietnam. As in World War I, the war in Vietnam was a stalemate. As in World War I, it had been a stalemate since the early months of the meeting between U.S. and Communist forces in 1965. Like the leaders of the powers in World War I, the leaders in Hanoi and Washington sensed that the war was stalemated, indeed sometimes spoke of it openly. Yet neither side was willing to accept the implications of that situation.

As in World War I, each side grossly underestimated the determination and staying power of the other. Both sides believed that if they persevered, the opponent would finally capitulate. Both sides always conceived themselves to be on the offensive, always on the brink of winning against an opponent who was near the breaking point. Thus Westmoreland calling for "maximum pressure on the enemy" following the Tet attacks; Abrams describing the "moment of supreme opportunity" in the autumn of 1968; Lyndon Johnson repeating the call for "maximum pressure" in the last weeks of his presidency; and the Hanoi strategists calling for further reprises of the costly Tet attacks in May, August, and February are psychologically closely akin to the generals of World War I, Haig in 1916, Nivelle in 1917, and Ludendorf in 1918.

In the end, the American failure was a failure of understanding and imagination. The American leaders did not see that what for them was a limited war for limited ends was, for the Vietnamese, an unlimited war of survival in which all the most basic values—loyalty to ancestors, love of country, resistance to foreigners—were involved. As Le Ly Hayslip, who grew up in a village near Da Nang and joined the Viet Cong at twelve, observed, "everything we knew commanded us to fight. Our ancestors called us to war. Our myths and legends called us to war. Our parents' teachings called us to war. Uncle Ho's cadre called us to war."[6]

The North Vietnamese leadership also suffered from a failure of imagination and understanding. Because they knew that the materially superior French and Americans undervalued will, determination, dedication, and patience in warfare, they built their military system on these foundations. Yet by 1968 they had reached the point of far overvaluing these qualities. The result was the bloodletting of 1968. So, caught between an American government that could never make up its mind and a Communist government that refused ever to change its mind, thousands of brave and dedicated men and women gave up their lives to no good purpose.

Just as there were no "good solutions" for the Great Powers in 1917, so there were no "good solutions" for the United States in Vietnam in 1968. The costs of Johnson's and Nixon's decisions to "stay the course" are well known. We are living with them still. What the consequences of an early unilateral withdrawal or a steep escalation of the war may have been can only be the subject of speculation. There is good reason to suspect that they may have been equally unfortunate. In 1968 the public was frustrated and disillusioned about the war, but only a minority were then prepared to accept a Communist takeover of South Vietnam as the price of peace. A May 1969 Harris poll found that only 9 percent of Americans were willing to accept a peace settlement that might allow an eventual Communist victory. Like Johnson and Nixon, the majority of Americans in 1968 and 1969 wanted to "get out" but "didn't want to lose."

As for escalation, it is hard to say what, if any, measures might have induced the Communists to capitulate. Political scientist John Mueller has argued that "the military costs accepted by the Communists in Vietnam were virtually unprecedented historically." Their battle deaths as a percentage of the prewar population are approximately equal to those of Germany, Austria-Hungary, France, and England in World War I, "probably twice as high as those suffered by the fanatical, often suicidal Japanese in World War II," and about twelve times as high as the Chinese and North Koreans in Korea.[7] As a former Saigon station chief, John Limond Hart, observes, "even if we Americans had by our criteria 'won' the Vietnamese war, it is unlikely the Vietnamese would have credited us with the victory . . . they would have treated their reverses more as a temporary setback than a defeat . . . then would have geared down once again to prolonged guerrilla struggle."[8]

Americans dislike problems without solutions. Almost from the beginning of U.S. involvement in Vietnam they have attempted to find "lessons" in the war. The controversy about the appropriate lessons to be learned continues with the same vigor and lack of coherence as the debates about the war itself.

Lessons are controversial and fleeting but memories are long. The memories of 1968 have remained and served to influence attitudes and expectations well into the 1990s. The ghosts of Vietnam haunted all sides of the recent deliberations about the Gulf War. In the wake of that war, President Bush hastened to announce that "we've kicked the Vietnam syndrome."

Doubtless many Americans would like to agree. It is easier to think of the Vietnam War as a strange aberration, a departure from the "normal" kind of war, like World War II and the recent war in the Gulf, where the course of military operations were purposeful and understandable and the results relatively clear cut. Yet the Vietnam War may be less an aberration than an example of a more common and older type of warfare, reaching back before the Thirty Years' War and including World War I. A type of warfare in which a decision is long delayed, the purposes of the fighting become unclear, the casualties mount, and the conflict acquires a momentum of its own. In a world which has recently been made safe for conventional, regional, and ethnic wars, Vietnam rather than World War II may be the pattern of the future.

APPENDIX 1

KIA Rate for Maneuver Battalions Jan 67-Sep 6 as Compiled by OSD Systems Analysis (Annual Rate per 1,000 Average Strength)[a] (These figures demonstrate that, contrary to frequent Pentagon statements, the casualty rate for combat troops in Vietnam was comparable to those in World War II and Korea.)

	1967				1968			
	Jan–Mar	Apr–Jun	Jul–Sep	Oct Dec	Jan Mar	Apr–Jun	Jul–Sep	Jan 67–Sep 68
Maneuver Bns[b]								
Army	103.9	95.2	55.8	92.2	147.3	123.8	79.7	99.9
Marines	85.8	175.0	133.2	78.6	148.9	188.3	102.1	130.2
Overall	97.9	106.1	79.9	88.2	147.8	141.9	85.3	108.9
Non-maneuver Bns								
Army	3.9	2.8	2.9	4.7	10.5	9.3	5.3	5.5
Marines	9.0	12.4	14.0	17.9	29.0	15.6	17.3	15.9
Overall	4.7	4.8	5.0	5.6	13.6	10.4	7.3	7.3
All forces								
Army	25.8	20.9	12.9	22.3	39.3	34.5	21.3	25.2
Marines	33.6	63.3	51.6	33.1	73.1	76.0	47.7	54.5
Overall	25.1	30.2	21.1	24.4	46.1	42.7	26.4	31.3

[a]Operating strength only. *(Continued on p. 318)*
[b]Includes attached cavalry units (Army) and battalion landing teams (Marines).
SOURCES: OSD Directorate for Statistical Services, DOD Forms 1300 , MACV Strength Report, Army Build-up Progress Report.

*World War II**
   All theaters [2]   37.4
   European theater only [b]   51.9
Korean War [c]   45.1

[a]Based on strength and casualties in the European theater of operations (Jun 44–May 45), the Mediterranean theater (Nov 42–May 45), and the Pacific (Apr 42–Aug 45).
[b]European theater including Air Corps (Jun 44–May 45).
[c]Jul 50–Jul 53.

* Note that the KIA rate for *Army* is HIGHER than the World War II rate during Jan–Mar 1968 and only slightly lower during Apr–Jun 1968. For the *Marines* the rate is HIGHER during the entire period Jan–Sep 68. During Jan–Jun the Marine casualty rate exceeds even the rate for European theater in World War II.

APPENDIX 2

U.S. Casualities for February–May 1968 as Compiled by the White House Situation Room.*

Week	Killed	Wounded Not Hopitalized	Hospitalized
27 Jan–			
3 Feb	203	499	543
4–10 Feb	421	666	720
11–17 Feb			
18–24 Feb	584	775	839
25 Feb–			
2 March	536	989	1,070
3–9 March	520	1,262	1,398
10–16 March	356	913	991
17–23 March	371	948	1,026
24–30 March	335	1,800	2,000
31 March–			
6 April	290	1,500	1,600
7–13 April	369	1,251	1,356
14–20 April	287	694	752
21–27 April	324		
28 April–			
4 May	374		
5–11 May	616	1,139	1,235
12–18 May	552	1,149	1,244
19–25 May	443	1,360	1,475
26 May–			
1 June	459		

* Note that the highest casualties in any single week occur during May 1968, not during TET.

319

NOTES

Introduction

1. KIA Rate by Force Component: Jan 67–Sept 68, Southeast Asia Analysis Reports, November 1968, SEA-RS-193L, p. 22, Table 2. Copy in U.S. Army Center of Military History (hereafter CMH). This table is reproduced as Appendix 1.

1. "I Want to Speak to You Tonight of Peace in Vietnam"

1. 1st Battalion, 26th Marines Command Chronology, February 1968. Marine Corps Historical Center (hereafter MCHC).
2. This was not a "heavy" bombardment by World War I or World War II standards, and even the French at Dien Bien Phu had received an average of 2,000 mortar and artillery rounds per day. However, it was almost unprecedented in the American war in Vietnam.
3. Quoted in Ray Stubbe, "Khe Sanh Chaplain," Unpublished ms., p. 700. Copy in MCHC.
4. Interview with Lieutenant J. W. Dillon, USMC, 3 January 1969, Tape 3716; interview with Lance Corporal Michael H. McCauley, 8 June 1968, Tape 2810. Both in Marine Corps Oral History Collection. This account of the March 30 action is based primarily on these interviews and on the material by Stubbe. It differs in important respects from both the 1st Battalion 26th Marines after-action report and the published accounts in Moyers S. Shore, *The Battle for Khe Sanh* (Washington: Historical Branch G-3 HDQTRS USMC, 1969), pp. 128–30, and Robert Pisor, *The End of the Line: The Siege of Khe Sanh* (New York: Norton, 1982) pp. 244–45.
5. Letter, PFC Jeff Culpepper to Madalyn Culpepper, April 2, 1968. Reproduced in Stubbe, "Khe Sanh Chaplain," p. 704.
6. Lieutenant J. W. Dillon interview.
7. 1st Battalion, 26th Marines Command Chronology, March 1968, Part III, p. 5.
8. Kathleen Turner, *Lyndon Johnson's Dual War: Vietnam and the Press* (Chicago: University of Chicago Press, 1985), p. 246.
9. Notes of President's Meeting with the Democratic Congressional

Leadership, February 6, 1968, LBJ Library, CBS Subpoenaed Case No. 38, Lyndon Johnson Library, Austin, Texas (LBJ Library).

10. *Time,* April 5, 1968, p. 20.

11. "The Logic of the Battlefield," *Wall Street Journal,* February 23, 1968.

12. Herbert Y. Schandler, *Lyndon Johnson and Vietnam* (Princeton, N.J.: Princeton University Press, 1977), p. 224.

13. *Frank McGee Sunday Report,* March 10, 1968, cited in Don Oberdorfer, *Tet!* (New York: Doubleday, 1971), p. 273.

14. William C. Westmoreland, *A Soldier Reports* (Garden City, N.Y.: Doubleday, 1976), p. 332.

15. Schandler, *Lyndon Johnson and Vietnam,* p. 107.

16. The fullest discussion of the developments leading up to the troop request may be found in Schandler, *Lyndon Johnson and Vietnam,* pp. 93-100, 105-16.

17. Oberdorfer, *Tet!* pp. 84-85.

18. On this point, see John E. Mueller, *War, Presidents and Public Opinion* (New York: John Wiley, 1973), pp. 83-106.

19. Schandler, *Lyndon Johnson and Vietnam,* p. 220.

20. Telegram, MacNamara to President, April 21, 1965, *The Senator Gravel Edition of the Pentagon Papers* (Boston: Beacon, 1972), vol. III, pp. 705-6.

21. Quoted in Guenter Lewy, *America in Vietnam* (London: Oxford University Press, 1978), p. 49.

22. Schandler, *Lyndon Johnson and Vietnam,* p. 49.

23. Evidence about the conception and planning of the Tet attacks is confused and fragmentary. My conclusions are based on a careful reading of available documents and secondary sources. Some alternative approaches to explaining the Tet attacks may be found in William J. Turley, *The Second Indochina War: A Short Political and Military History* (New York: NAL, 1987), pp. 101-2; William J. Duiker, *The Communist Road to Power in Vietnam* (Boulder, Colo.: Westview Press, 1981), pp. 263-65; Gabriel Kolko, *Anatomy of a War* (New York: Pantheon, 1965), pp. 294-96; Eric M. Bergerud, *The Dynamics of Defeat* (Boulder, Colo.: Westview Press, 1991); and Philip Davidson, *Vietnam at War* (Novato, Calif.: Presidio Press, 1988), pp. 391-404.

24. Schandler, *Lyndon Johnson and Vietnam,* p. 122.

25. *Ibid.,* p. 23.

26. Charles Mohr, "Departure of Westmoreland May Spur Shift in Strategy," *New York Times,* March 24, 1968.

27. Letter, Brigadier General John R. Chaisson to Mrs. Chaisson, March 23, 1968. Chaisson Papers, Hoover Institution.

28. Letter, Chaisson to Mrs. Chaisson, March 28, 1968, Chaisson Papers.

29. Tom Johnson's Notes on Meeting, President, General Wheeler, General Abrams, 26 March 1968. Meeting Notes File, Johnson Papers, LBJ Library.
30. Tom Johnson's Notes on Meetings: Notes on President's Meetings with Senior Foreign Policy Advisers, March 4, 1968. Meeting Notes File, Johnson Papers, LBJ Library.
31. Except where noted, this discussion of the air war against North Vietnam is based on the studies and documents in *Gravel Edition of Pentagon Papers,* vol. IV, pp. 1–232.
32. *Ibid.,* p. 26.
33. A single raid on Berlin in early 1945 resulted in 25,000 casualties. An American incendiary attack on Tokyo in March 1945 caused more than 80,000 deaths.
34. *Gravel Edition of Pentagon Papers,* vol. IV, p. 18.
35. Mark Clodfelter, *The Limits of Air Power: The American Bombing of North Vietnam* (New York: Free Press, 1989), pp. 47, 51, 53–54, 76–79.
36. Jack Broughton, *Going Downtown: The War Against Hanoi and Washington* (New York: Orion Books, 1988), p. xv.
37. Clodfelter, *Limits of Air Power,* p. 43.
38. Drew Middleton *et al., Air War Vietnam* (New York: Arno Press, 1978), pp. 216–22 and *passim.*
39. *Gravel Edition of Pentagon Papers,* vol. IV, p. 39.
40. *Ibid.,* p. 40.
41. *Ibid.,* p. 111; Clodfelter, *Limits of Air Power,* pp. 93–99.
42. *Gravel Edition of Pentagon Papers,* vol. IV, pp. 125–26.
43. John Duffet, ed., *Against the Crime of Silence* (New York, 1970), p. 18.
44. Wilson to LBJ, June 3, 1966, *Gravel Edition of Pentagon Papers,* vol. IV, p. 102.
45. U.S. Senate Committee on Armed Forces, Preparedness Investigating Subcommittee, *Air War Against North Vietnam,* Hearings, 90th Cong. 1st Sess., 31 August 1967, p. 719.
46. President's Meeting with Senior Foreign Policy Advisers, March 20, 1968. Meeting Notes Files, Johnson Papers, LBJ Library.
47. Memo, George Christian to President, subj.: Luncheon Meeting with Senior Advisers, March 22, 1968. Meeting Notes Files, Johnson Papers, LBJ Library.
48. Schandler, *Lyndon Johnson and Vietnam,* p. 255.
49. Tom Johnson's Notes of Meetings, March 27th Briefings. Meeting Notes File, Johnson Papers, LBJ Library.
50. Summary of Notes, Advisory Group Meeting, March 26, 1968. Meeting Notes File, Johnson Papers, LBJ Library.

51. Schandler, *Lyndon Johnson and Vietnam,* p. 262.
52. "Top of the Week," *Newsweek,* April 15, 1968, p. 3.
53. Turner, *Lyndon Johnson's Dual War, p. 248.*
54. News Analysis, April 23, 1968. National Security Files, Vietnam Country File, LBJ Library.
55. David Watt, "How in One Year Americans Changed Tack on Vietnam," *London Financial Times,* August 28, 1968.
56. CIA–DOD Briefings by General Dupuy and George Carver, March 27, 1968. Tom Johnson's Notes of Meetings, LBJ Library.
57. Message, Westmoreland to Lieutenant General Robert Cushman, CG III MAF, *et al.,* MAC4534, 4 April 1968. Creighton Abrams Papers, Message Files, CMH.
58. CDEC Doc. No. 60275562–68, 31 May, 1968, U.S. Mission Vietnam, Press Release No. 102–68, 25 May 68. Both in Douglas Pike Collection, University of California at Berkeley.
59. Memo for the President by the Duty Officer, White House Situation Room, subj: Casualties, June 9, 1968. DSDUF Files, LBJ Library.
60. Jeffrey J. Clarke, *Advice and Support: The Final Years* (Washington: CMH, 1988), Table 14, p. 275.

2. "You Don't Know How Lucky We Are to Have Soldiers Like This"

1. For an analysis of the performance of American troops in the initial engagements in North Africa and Korea, see Martin Blumenson, "Kasserine Pass," and Roy K. Flint, "Task Forces Smith and the 24th Division: Delay and Withdraw," in Charles E. Heller and William A. Stofft, eds., *America's First Battles* (Lawrence: University of Kansas Press, 1986), pp. 226–65, 266–99.
2. Lawrence M. Baskir and William A. Strauss, *Chance and Circumstance: The Draft, the War, and the Vietnam Generation* (New York: Vintage, 1978), p. 6.
3. Captain James C. Edwards, December 1968, Tape 3733, Marine Corps Oral History Collection.
4. Interview with First Sergeant Walter A. Sabralowski, Operation Hawthorn, 20 June 1966, CMH interview file.
5. Interview with Captain George A. Joulwen, 1/26 Inf., 1st Infantry Division, 3 April 1967. For similar views by a Korean War veteran, see Colonel A. P. Abood interview, 1st Battalion (ABN), 327th Inf., 101st Airborn Division, June 3, 1966. Both in CMH interview file.
6. James M. Gavin, *Crisis Now* (New York: Random House, 1968), p. 48.

7. John D. Stuckey and Joseph H. Pistorius, "Mobilization for the Vietnam War: A Political and Military Catastrophe," in Lloyd J. Mathews and Dale E. Brown, eds., *Assessing the Vietnam War* (Washington: Pergamon-Brassey, 1987), p. 123.

8. *Ibid.,* p. 126.

9. Lyndon Johnson, *The Vantage Point* (New York: Popular Library, 1971), p. 146.

10. For various interpretations of Johnson's decision, see Chester L. Cooper, *The Last Crusade* (New York: Dodd Mead, 1970), p. 280; David Halberstam, *The Best and the Brightest* (New York: Random House, 1969), pp. 593–94; Doris Kearns, *Lyndon Johnson and Vietnam* (New York: Harper & Row, 1976), pp. 295–96.

11. Baskir and Straus, *Chance and Circumstance,* pp. 49–51.

12. James M. Gerhardt, *The Draft and Public Policy: Issues in Military Manpower Procurement 1945–1970* (Columbus: Ohio State University Press, 1971), pp. 147–60, 225–27.

13. *Washington Post,* February 20, 1967.

14. "Statement of Thomas D. Morris, Assistant Director of Defense, (Manpower), Before the House Committee on Armed Services, 30 June 1966." Copy in CMH. James W. Davis, Jr., and Kenneth M. Dolbeare, *Little Groups of Neighbors: The Selective Service System* (Chicago: Markham, 1968), pp. 131–33.

15. Gerhardt, *Draft and Public Policy,* pp. 286–92; Robert K. Griffith, Jr., "To Raise and Support Armies" and "The Evolution of U.S. Military Manpower Systems," in Len Austin, ed., *The Anthropo Factor in Warfare: Conscripts, Volunteers, and Reserves* (Washington: National Defense University Press, 1987), pp. 30–31.

16. Davis and Dolbeare, *Little Groups of Neighbors,* p. 117.

17. *In Pursuit of Equity: Who Serves When Not All Serve? Report of the National Advisory Committee on Selection Service* (Washington: GPO, 1967), Appendix I, Section I, pp. 73–74.

18. *Hearings Before the Subcommittee on Armed Forces of the Committee on Appropriations,* 89th Cong., 2d Sess., Part 3, p. 19.

19. Roger W. Little, "Procurement of Manpower: An Institutional Analysis," in Roger W. Little, ed., *Selective Service and American Society* (New York: Russell Sage, 1964), pp. 15–16; Davis and Dolbeare, *Little Groups of Neighbors,* p. 97.

20. Gary L. Wamsley, "Decision Making in Local Boards: A Case Study," in Little, *Selective Service,* p. 88.

21. Davis and Dolbeare, *Little Groups of Neighbors,* pp. 18–19.

22. G. David Curry, *Sunshine Patriots: Punishment and the Vietnam Offender* (Notre Dame, Ind.: Notre Dame University Press, 1985), pp. 80–86 and *passim.*

23. Andrew V. Glass, "Defense Report: Draftees Shoulder Burden of Fighting and Dying in Vietnam," *National Journal*, August 15, 1970, p. 1747.

24. Robert R. Palmer, *The Procurement and Training of Ground Combat Troops* (Washington: Office of the Chief of Military History, 1948), p. 158.

25. Ronald Spector, "The Vietnam War and the Army's Self-Image," in John Schlight, ed., *Second Indochina War Symposium* (Washington: Center of Military History, 1986), p. 177.

26. *Ibid.*

27. Robert L. Ruhl, "NCOC," *Infantry*, May–June 1969, pp. 32–39.

28. "Congress and the Corps." *Marine Corps Gazette*, April 1968, p. 1. The Marine Corps eventually reached 313,000 men in 1969, the largest Marine Corps since World War II.

29. Allan R. Millett, *Semper Fidelis: The History of the United States Marine Corps* (New York: Macmillan, 1980), p. 578.

30. *Ibid.*, p. 579.

31. John A. Hottell III, Captain, Infantry, "The Motivation of the Infantry Soldier in Vietnam." Copy in CMH.

32. Glass, "Draftees Shoulder Burden," p. 1747.

33. *Report of the Director of the Selective Service System: Selective Service in Wartime* (Washington: GPO, 1943), p. 55, Table 28.

34. "Median Age of Involuntary Inductees, FY 1954–65," in statement of Thomas D. Morris, July 30, 1966.

35. Summary of Findings, Quantitative Phase, Army Recruiting Study, May 1969. Copy in CMH.

36. Sue E. Berryman, *Who Serves? The Persistent Myth of the Underclass Army* (Boulder, Colo.: Westview Press, 1988), p. 35.

37. *Ibid.*, p. 54, Table 27. "Survey Estimate of Educational Level of Male Enlisted Personnel, OPOPM Report 17-269-E, 30 November 1968. Office of Personnel Operation, DCSPER. Copy in Shelby Stanton Collection. "Estimated Educational Level of Military Personnel on Active Duty, Selected Dates, 1952–1967," in DOD, *Selected Manpower Statistics*, April 15, 1969, p. 36.

38. "Estimated Educational Level," p. 37.

39. Cited in Baskir and Straus, *Chance and Circumstance*, p. 8.

40. On the question of the representativeness of the American military, see Richard H. Kohn, "The Social History of the American Soldier: A Review and Prospectus for Research," *American Historical Review*, 86 (1981), pp. 553–67. Neil D. Fligstein, "Who Served in the Military, 1940–1973," *Armed Forces and Society*, Spring 1980, pp. 279–311; Berryman, *Who Serves;* and Curry, *Sunshine Patriots.*

41. Fact Sheet: Negro Participation in the Armed Forces and in Vietnam,

Tab. C to Memo, Director of Military Personnel Policy to Chief of Staff, subj: Evaluation of Marshall Report Pertaining to Negro Distribution and Casualties. Casualty figures are from Tab. C, "Extract from the Report of the National Advisory Commission on Selective Service." Copies in CMH.

42. *Ibid.,* Tab. F.

43. *Ibid.,* Tab. D. Bernard Nalty, *Strength for the Fight: A History of Black Americans in the Military* (New York: Free Press, 1986), p. 298.

44. Charles Moskos, Jr., "The American Dilemma in Uniform: Race in the Armed Forces," *Annals of the American Academy of Political and Social Sciences,* vol. 40 (1973), pp. 94–106.

45. Army Casualties in Vietnam by Race Through May 31, 1969, BUPER 53-R, June 24, 1969. Copy in CMH. Black marines accounted for about 13 percent of Marines in Vietnam and suffered around 12.5 percent casualties. Reference Notebooks Item: Assignment of Negro Marines. Manpower Div., Headquarters Marine Corps, 1970. Copy in MCHC.

46. Fact Sheet, *Negro Participation,* Tab. C.

47. Stan Goff interview, Winter Soldier Collection, Columbia University Oral History Collection.

48. Gilbert Badillo and G. David Curry, "The Social Incidence of Vietnam Casualties: Social Class or Race?" *Armed Forces and Society,* Vol. 2 (Spring 1976), p. 402.

49. Maurice Zeitlin *et al.,* "Death in Vietnam: Class Poverty and the Risks of War," *Politics and Society,* vol. 3 (Spring 1973), pp. 313–28; Baskir and Strauss, *Chance and Circumstance,* pp. 7–10. Baskir and Strauss conducted their own survey of draft-age men in South Bend, Indiana; Ann Arbor, Michigan; and Washington, D.C. They also claim to have used data furnished by the Defense Department on the likelihood of Vietnam service by educational level. However, the survey data presented on page 9 of their book differs in important respects from the DOD data presented on page 10. The authors made no attempt to analyze or explain the differences and indeed appear unaware of them.

50. See especially Fligstein, "Who Served in the Military," pp. 304–5, 307.

51. Charles R. Anderson, *The Grunts* (San Rafael, Calif.: Presidio Press, 1977), p. 23.

52. Peter Cameron interview, p. 10, Winter Soldier Collection.

53. Joel Davis interview, p. 5, Winter Soldier Collection.

54. Memo for Commanding Officer by Lieutenant Colonel William V. Koch, AG, HQ USASC, Cam Ranh Bay, September 3, 1968, subj: Impressions Gained upon Arrival in Country; Attachment to Ltr, CO HQ USASC, to 1st Log Command, September 5, 1968, Records of 1st Logistical Command. Record Group, National Archives.

55. Al Santoli, ed., *Everything We Had: An Oral History of the Vietnam War* (New York: Ballantine Books, 1981), p. 104.

56. Diary of Sergeant Michael Forrisi, Viet Nam War Miscellaneous Collection, U.S. Army Military History Institute, Carlisle, Pa.

57. U.S. Military Strategy in South Vietnam, no date (June 1968), Clark Clifford files, LBJ Library.

58. Message, Abrams to Wheeler, 2810587 April 1969. Abrams Papers, Message Files; Anthony Herbert, *Soldier* (New York: Holt, 1972), pp. 140–41.

59. Harry G. Summers, Jr., *Vietnam War Almanac* (New York: Facts-on-File, 1985), p. 165.

60. ASD (Systems Analysis), "Southeast Asia Analysis Reports: Army and Marine KIA," November 1968, p. 24

61. Jack Shulimson, *The U.S. Marines in Vietnam: An Expanding War, 1966* (Washington: History and Museums Division, Headquarters USMC, 1982), pp. 281–82.

62. Herbert, *Soldier,* p. 141.

63. Lieutenant General Julian J. Ewell and Major General Ira A. Hunt, Jr., *Sharpening the Combat Edge: Vietnam Studies* (Washington: Department of the Army [hereafter DOA], 1974), pp. 19–22.

64. *Ibid.,* pp. 23–24.

65. James Jay Carafano, "Officership, 1966–1971," *Military Review,* vol. 69 (January 1989), pp. 50–51.

66. Message, Abrams to General Earle Wheeler, 2810587, April 1969. Abrams Papers, Message Files, CMH.

67. The most complete account is in Lieutenant General Carrol H. Dunn, *Base Development in South Vietnam 1965–1970* (Washington: DOA, 1972). See also Richard Tregaskis, *Southeast Asia: Building the Bases* (Washington: GPO, 1975).

68. Message, Abrams to Wheeler 2810587, April 1969.

69. Diary of Sergeant Michael Forrisi, p. 2.

70. Hottell, "Motivation of Infantry Soldier in Vietnam."

71. Captain Jerome Dowling, MC, "Psychological Aspects of the Year in Vietnam," *USARV Medical Bulletin,* vol. 2 (1967), p. 45.

72. Roger W. Little, "Buddy Relations and Combat Performance," in Morris Janowitz, ed., *The New Military* (New York: Free Press, 1966), p. 220.

3. "You're Going Home in a Body Bag"

1. Ernie Boitano interview, Winter Soldier Collection, Columbia University.

2. Bernard Edelman, *Dear America: Letters Home from Vietnam* (New York: Norton, 1985), p. 50.

3. Captain Blake K. Thomas interview; L/Cpl Paul A. Wood, Jr., interview and Lance Corporal Luis Calderon interview, I Co., 3/27 Marines, Tape 2875, Marine Corps Oral History Collection.

4. James Martin Davis, "Vietnam: What It Was Really Like," *Military Review,* vol. 69 (January 1989), p. 35.

5. Colonel A. W., A Co., 2/12th Infantry, 25th Division, 1968–69, Company Command in Vietnam Interview Collection, U.S. Army Military History Institute, Carlisle, Pa.

6. Elmo Zumwalt and Elmo Zumwalt, Jr., *My Father, My Son* (New York: Macmillan, 1986), p. 82.

7. "Army of Rats Plagues Khe Sahn Marines," *Pacific Stars and Stripes,* March 28, 1968, p. 6.

8. Ernie Boitano interview.

9. Fact Sheet by Lieutenant Colonel Delieve, MACMD, Subj.: Medical support in RVN, 22 May 68; Fact Sheet by Lieutenant Colonel Joseph Bartley, MC, Preventive Med Div., USARV, Subj.: Disease in a hostile environment, May 18, 1968. Both in U.S. Army Vietnam Files (USARV Files), National Archives.

10. Commandant Lavisse, *Comparative Studies of the Field Equipment of the Foot Soldier,* trans. Captain Edward P. Lawton (Washington: GPO, 1906), pp. 139–40.

11. S. L. A. Marshall, *Soldier's Load and the Mobility of a Nation* (Washington: Combat Forces Press, 1949), p. 71 and *passim*.

12. Shelby Stanton, *U.S. Army Uniforms of the Vietnam War* (Harrisburg, Pa.: Stackpole Press, 1989), p. 11.

13. Enclosure 4 (Lesson Learned by Co. B 2/35th Inf., March 1–22, 1969) to Combat After-Action Report, *Green Thunder,* 18 April 1968. Copy in CMH, Oral History Collection.

14. Letter, Igor Bobrowsky to author, March 17, 1992.

15. This discussion of uniforms and equipment is based primarily on Shelby Stanton's comprehensive *U.S. Army Uniforms of the Vietnam War,* and on personal observation by the author.

16. Stanton, *U.S. Army Uniforms of Vietnam War,* pp. 72–74.

17. *Ibid.,* p. 52.

18. *Ibid.,* p. 40.

19. Message, COMUSMACV to various commands, R250947, 25 September 1971, Abrams Papers, CMH.

20. Quoted in James Fallows, *National Defense* (New York: Vintage, 1982), p. 93.

21. *Ibid.,* p. 92.

22. *Ibid.*

23. Thomas L. McNaugher, *The M-16 Controversies: Military Organizations and Weapons Acquisition* (New York: Praeger, 1984), p. 141, 158.

24. *Ibid.,* p. 140.

25. Memo, Lieutenant Colonel M. C. Ross, AC of S, G-3, subj.: M-16 rifles, 5 March 1968, 1st Air Cavalry Div. Records, National Archives.

26. Fallows, *National Defense,* p. 91.

27. McNaugher, in his insightful and comprehensive study, suggests that there may in fact have been "a complex and subtle interaction" between the problem of the powder and the problem of proper maintenance. See *M-16 Controversies,* p. 159.

28. M. E. Arnstein and F. J. West, Jr., "A Tabular Method for Comparing Friendly and Enemy Casualties: A Case Study of Marine Mortalities Resulting from Patrols and Six Offensive Operations in Quang Nam Province" (RM-6378-ARPA, December 1990), pp. iii–iv. Copy in J. R. Chaisson Papers, Box 19.

29. Southeast Asia Analysis Reports, May 1969, Tactical Initiative in Vietnam, p. 7, copy in CMH; Thomas C. Thayer, *War Without Fronts: The American Experience in Vietnam* (Boulder, Colo.: Westview Press, 1985), pp. 45–46.

30. Taped interview and documentation sheet, Brigadier General J. R. Chaisson, USMC, subj.: Analysis of Vietnam by Corps Areas as Seen at the MACV Level, May 1968. Copy in Marine Corps Oral History Collection.

31. Southeast Asia Analysis Report, SEA-RS-193K, November 1968, p. 22, Table 2. Copy in CMH.

32. Colonel William T. Dabney oral history interview transcript, pp. 18-20, Marine Corps Oral History Collection.

33. John Sack, *M* (New York: New American Library, 1966), p. 189.

34. Andrew J. Glass, "Draftees Shoulder Burden of Fighting and Dying in Vietnam," *National Journal,* August 15, 1970, p. 1749.

35. Lieutenant Colonel Thomas G. Rhame interview, "Company Command in Vietnam," Interview Collection.

36. Memo by Lieutenant Colonel G. A. Aaby, Office of the Surgeon General, 19 May 1968, subj.: Combat Deaths per Thousand Troops. Copy in CMH.

37. Major General Spurgeon Neel, *Medical Support of the U.S. Army in Vietnam 1965-1970* (Washington: DOA, 1973), p. 65.

38. *Ibid.*

39. Peter Dorland and James Nanney, *Dust-off: Army Aeromedical Evacuation in Vietnam* (Washington: CMH, 1982), pp. 67–68.

40. 14th Military History Detachment, 1st Cavalry Division (Air Mobile),

"Medical Evacuation Within the 1st Cavalry Division," 5-70, 10 March 1970, p. 6, 1st Cavalry Div. Records, National Archives.

41. *Ibid.*

42. Dorland and Nanney, *Dust-off,* pp. 116–17.

43. *Ibid.,* pp. 63–66. Brady became the first dust-off pilot to receive the Medal of Honor.

44. Lieutenant Colonel Delieve, Fact Sheet: Medical Support in RVN. Copy in CMH.

45. Fact Sheet, Office of the Surgeon General, subj.: Combat Deaths per Thousand Troops, 19 May 1968, USARV Records; Lawrence A. Palinkas, "Combat Casualties Among U.S. Marine Personnel, Vietnam 1964–1972," Report No. 85-11, Naval Health Research Center, San Diego, 1985, p. 11.

46. Elizabeth A. Paul and Jacqueline S. O'Neill, "American Nurses in Vietnam: Stresses and After-effects," *American Journal of Nursing,* vol. 86 (May 1986), p. 526; Dan Freedman and Jacqueline Rhoads, eds., *Nurses in Vietnam: The Forgotten Veterans* (Austin: Texas Monthly Press, 1987), p. 1.

47. Paul and O'Neill, "American Nurses," p. 526.

48. Freedman and Rhoads, *Nurses in Vietnam,* p. 13.

49. Kathryn Marshall, *In a Combat Zone* (Boston: Little, Brown, 1985), p. 31.

50. Douglas R. Bey, M.D., "Group Dynamics and the 'FNG' in Vietnam: A Potential Focus of Stress," *International Journal of Group Psychotherapy,* vol. 23 (1972), p. 24.

51. Sack, *M,* p. 108.

52. See, for example, Stanley Goff and Robert Sanders, *Brothers* (Novato, Calif: Presidio Press, 1982), pp. 132–33.

53. Charles Taliaferro interview, p. 35, Winter Soldier Collection.

54. Bey, "Group Dynamics and 'FNG' in Vietnam," p. 26.

55. *Ibid.*

56. The author served with some former members of this unit in Vietnam.

57. Lieutenant Colonel Thomas G. Rhame interview, p. 20, Company Command in Vietnam Collection.

58. Corporal Gerald Brown interview, Tape 3620; Corporal Gilbert A. Lemmon interview, Tape 3738; and Lance Corporal Terry C. Toombs interview, Tape 3663, all in USMC Oral History Collection.

59. Lieutenant Colonel Allan Wetzel interview, p. 19, Company Command in Vietnam Collection.

60. Major F——— interview, p. 42, Company Command in Vietnam Collection. See also Jim Heiden interview, pp. 31–32, Winter Soldier Collection; Lieutenant Colonel G. A. L., interview, p. 61, Company

Command in Vietnam Collection; Al Santoli, ed., *Everything We Had: An Oral History of the Vietnam War* (New York: Ballantine, 1981), pp. 20, 22.

61. Arnold Abrams, "South Vietnam: Everybody, USA," *Far Eastern Economic Review*, February 12, 1970.

62. Interview with Major 5451, former Commanding Officer, E Company, 1/8 Infantry, 4th Infantry Division, March 1982, p. 2, Company Command in Vietnam Oral History Collection, U.S. Army Command General Staff School.

63. Interview with Major 5341, former Commanding Officer, E Company, 3/503rd, February 1982, p. 42, Company Command in Vietnam Collection.

64. Samuel A. Stouffer *et al.*, *The American Soldier: Combat and Its Aftermath* (New York: John Wiley, 1965), pp. 172–73.

65. Tim O'Brien, *Going After Cacciato* (New York: Delacorte, 1978), p. 61. For similar views, see Winston Groom, *Better Times than These* (New York: Summit, 1978), pp. 220–21, and Philip Caputo, *A Rumor of War* (New York: Ballantine, 1977), p. xix.

66. Peter G. Bourne, "Military Psychiatry and the Vietnam Experience," *American Journal of Psychiatry*, vol. 127 (October 4, 1970), p. 125.

67. *Ibid.*, p. 126. The most comprehensive guide to the psychological aspect of the Vietnam experience is Norman M. Camp, Robert H. Stortch, and William C. Marshall, eds., *Stress, Strain and Vietnam: Bibliography of Two Decades of Psychiatric and Social Science Literature* (annotated) (Westport, Conn.: Greenwood Press, 1988).

68. Neel, *Medical Support of U.S. Army in Vietnam*, p. 45.

69. *Ibid.* For a useful overview, see Norman M. Camp and Caren M. Carney, "U.S. Army Psychiatry in Vietnam: Preliminary Findings of a Survey," *Bulletin of the Menninger Clinic*, vol. 51, pp. 6–18, and Norman M. Camp, "U.S. Army Psychiatry in Vietnam from Confidence to Dismay," paper presented at the Annual Meeting of the American Historical Association, 1987.

70. Bourne, "Military Psychiatry and Vietnam Experience," p. 125. On World War II, see Samuel A. Stouffer *et al.*, *The American Soldier: Combat and Its Aftermath*, pp. 168–70 and *passim*.

71. For one of the rare discussions of "short-timer's syndrome" in the social science literature, see Charles C. Moskos, Jr., "Surviving the War in Vietnam," in Charles R. Figley and Seymour Leventman, eds., *Strangers at Home: Vietnam Veterans Since the War* (New York: Praeger, 1980), p. 76.

72. Igor Bobrowsky letter.

73. Major WGR interview, p. 39, Platoon Command in Vietnam Oral History Collection, Combat Studies Institute, U.S. Army Command and General Staff College, Fort Leavenworth, Kansas.

74. Robert J. Graham, "Vietnam: An Infantryman's View of Our Failure," *Military Affairs,* vol. 48 (July 1984), pp. 137–38.

75. Moskos, "Surviving War in Vietnam," p. 76.

76. Major WGR interview, p. 41.

77. Major General Richard G. Lawrence interview, p. 15, Battalion Command in Vietnam Collection, U.S. Army Military History Institute, Carlisle, Pa.

78. Major R.W. interview, p. 6, Platoon Command in Vietnam Collection.

79. Lieutenant Colonel Joseph Gross interview, p. 10, Company Command in Vietnam Collection.

80. Colonel William P. Boyd interview, p. 17, Company Command in Vietnam Collection.

81. Based on an analysis of the interviews cited above and seven additional interviews in the Carlisle and Leavenworth collections.

82. William P. Boyd interview, p. 17.

83. Lieutenant Colonel Thomas C. Rhame interview, p. 12.

84. Igor Bobrowsky letter.

85. Ronald H. Spector, *Advice and Support: The Early Years of the U.S. Army in Vietnam* (New York: Free Press, 1985), pp. 293–94 and *passim.*

86. Memo for the Vice Chief of Staff by Acting DCSPER, subj.: Study of the 12 Month Vietnam Tour, 29 June 1970, DCSPER-DRO, 570-0071. Copy in CMH.

87. *Ibid.,* Appendix C.

88. *Ibid.*

89. MACV Fact Sheet, no date, subj.: Increasing Tour Length, Item F, Westmoreland Briefing Book, Westmoreland Papers.

90. Talking Paper, CS AVCS-FAG, subj.: Extension in Vietnam, Feb 69. Copy in Shelby Stanton Files.

91. Tim O'Brien, *If I Die in a Combat Zone (Box Me Up and Ship Me Home)* (New York: Dell, 1989), pp. 69–70.

92. Based on an analysis of some 117 summary court-martial records of the 1st Cavalry Division (Air Mobile) and the 101st Airborne Division, Federal Records Center, Saint Louis, Missouri.

4. "Born in the North, to Die in the South"

1. Richard Blanchfield interview, Winter Soldier Oral History Collection, Columbia University, p. 18.

2. Wallace Terry, *Bloods: An Oral History of the Vietnam War by Black Veterans* (New York: Random House, 1984), p. 64.

3. David Chanoff and Doan Van Toai, *Portrait of the Enemy* (New York: Random House, 1986), p. 58.

4. Ellen Hammer, *Vietnam: Yesterday and Today* (New York: Holt, Rinehart, 1966), pp. 220-21.
5. Le Ly Hayslip, *When Heaven and Earth Changed Places* (New York: Doubleday, 1989), pp. xiii-xiv.
6. Douglas Pike, *PAVN: People's Army of Vietnam* (Novato, Calif.: Presidio Press, 1986), p. 13.
7. *U.S.-Vietnam Relations* ("The Pentagon Papers"), Vol. 2, IV A-5, p. 25.
8. Ronald Spector, *Advice and Support: The Early Years of the U.S. Army in Vietnam* (New York: Free Press, 1985), p. 338.
9. The most graphic and thorough account of Ap Bac is in Neil Sheehan, *A Bright Shining Lie* (New York: Random House, 1988), pp. 204-75.
10. *Ibid.*, p. 274.
11. Spector, *Advice and Support,* pp. 305-9, 335-38, and *passim.*
12. The best account of how the Diem regime alienated the rural population is Jeffrey Race, *War Comes to Long An: Revolutionary Conflict in a Vietnamese Province* (Berkeley: University of California Press, 1972). See also Roy F. Prosterman, "Land Reform in Vietnam," *Current History,* vol. 57, December 1969.
13. J. J. Zasloff, *Origins of the Insurgency in South Vietnam, 1954-1960,* Rand Memorandum, RM5163/2-ISA/ARPA (Santa Monica, Calif.: Rand, 1968), pp. 8-14 and *passim.*
14. *Ibid.*
15. Pike, *PAVN,* p. 215.
16. Combined Intelligence Center, Vietnam Study 69-02, "The Viet Cong Guerrilla," June 20, 1969. Copy in MACV Records, J-2 Files.
17. Douglas Pike, *Viet Cong: The Organization and Techniques of the National Liberation Front of South Vietnam* (Cambridge, Mass.: MIT Press, 1966), pp. 235-38.
18. William Darryl Henderson, *Why the Vietcong Fought* (Westport, Conn.: Greenwood Press, 1979), p. 55.
19. CIC, "Viet Cong Guerrilla," p. 4.
20. Combined Intelligence Center (CIC), Vietnam Study 69-02, "The Viet Cong Guerrilla," June 20, 1969. Copy in MACV Records, J-2 Files.
21. Hayslip, *When Heaven and Earth Changed Places,* pp. 70-71.
22. CIC, "Enemy Soldier, 1968."
23. Combined Intelligence Center, Vietnam Study ST-76-013, "Update: The NVA Soldier in South Vietnam," October 18, 1966. Copy in MACV Records, J-2 Files.
24. Combined Intelligence Center, Vietnam Study ST-70-05, "North Vietnam Personnel Infiltration into the Republic of Vietnam," December 16, 1970. Copy in U.S. Army Military History Institute, Carlisle, Pa.

25. DIA Fact Sheet, North Vietnamese Presence in South Vietnam, May 17, 1968, LBJ Library, CBS subpoena case no. NLS/CBS4, doc. 16.
26. *Ibid.*
27. CIC, "North Vietnamese Personnel Infiltration."
28. "A Monograph of 2d Lieutenant Nguyen Van Thong, 320th Regt. 1st NVA Division, I Field Force, G-2 Section, September 1968." Copy in CMH.
29. Lieutenant Colonel Thomas G. Rhame interview.
30. Major General Richard Lawrence interview, pp. 31–35; Captain James B. Hollis interview, Company Command in Vietnam Collection.
31. Southeast Asia analysis reports, May 1969, Tactical Initiative in Vietnam, p. 9.
32. *Ibid.*
33. The literature on American code-breaking in World War II is large and growing. Three general accounts are Wilford J. Holmes, *Double-Edged Secrets* (Annapolis: Naval Institute Press, 1979); Ronald Lewin, *The American Magic* (New York: Farrar, Straus & Giroux, 1982); and Ronald Spector, *Listening to the Enemy: Key Documents on Communications Intelligence in the War With Japan* (Wilmington, Del.: Scholarly Resources, 1988).
34. Combined Intelligence Center, Vietnam Study ST 67-061 "VC/NVA Electronic Warfare Capability," July 1, 1967. Copy in MACV Records.
35. Commanding General's Debriefing Report by 13th Signal Battalion, March 9, 1970, 1st Air Cavalry Division Records.
36. Colonel William P. Boyd interview, pp. 25–26.
37. John D. Bergen, *The United States Army in Vietnam: Military Communications—A Test for Technology* (Washington: CMH, 1986), p. 403.
38. CIC, "VC/NVA Electronic Warfare Capability."
39. Combined Intelligence Center, Vietnam, Technical Study ST-67-007, "Viet Cong Structures and Field Fortifications." Copy in CMH; Tom Mangold and John Penycate, *The Tunnels of Cu Chi* (New York: Random House, 1985).
40. USMACV, Vietnam Lessons Learned, no. 71: "Countermeasures Against Standoff Attacks," MACJ3-053, March 13, 1969. Copy in MACV Records.
41. Lieutenant General Bui Phung, "Rear Services Support," *Tap Chi Cong Son,* December 12, 1984, p. 35.
42. AVDAGI, "The Shadow Supply System in the 1st ACD AO," October 19, 1970, Records of 1st Air Cavalry, National Archives.
43. *Ibid.*
44. Senior General Hoang Van Thai, "Some Lessons and Experiences in

Building the Vietnamese People's Armed Forces," *Tap Chi Cong Son* December 12, 1984, p. 23.

45. Chanoff and Toai, *Portrait of the Enemy*, pp. 63, 83.
46. War Participant interview, Hoang Tat Hong, no date, 1970, p. 27, Indochina Archive.
47. War Participant Interview, Mai Van So, no date, 1969, p. 12, Indochina Archive.
48. *Ibid.*
49. Chanoff and Toai, *Portrait of the Enemy*, pp. 44, 46, 53, 113.
50. *Ibid.*
51. *Ibid.*, p. 64.
52. *Ibid.*, p. 64-65.
53. CIC, "North Vietnamese Personnel Infiltration," p. 12.
54. Chanoff and Toai, *Portrait of the Enemy*, p. 44.
55. CIC, "North Vietnamese Personnel Infiltration," pp. 12-14; CIC, "Update: NVA Soldier in South Vietnam," p. 34.
56. Combined Document Exploitation Center MACV, Report 6028068470, August 6, 1970, p. 4, Indochina Archives.
57. War Participant Interview, Hoang Tat Hong, pp. 30-31.
58. Combined Document Exploitation Center, MACV Report 6028068470, p. 6.
59. CIC, "Update: NVA Soldier in South Vietnam," pp. 34-35.
60. *Ibid.*
61. Combined Document Exploitation Center Report 6028068470, p. 4.
62. "A Monograph of 2d Lieutenant Nguyen Van Thong."
63. Lieutenant Colonel Merrill L. Bartlett, "Nhuyen 'Who Shall Be Victorious': An NVA Officer 1969," *Marine Corps Gazette*, November 1990, p. 100.
64. CIC, "Update: NVA Soldier in South Vietnam," p. 34.
65. Combined Intelligence Documentation Center, Report 602802611, April 30, 1971, p. 3, Indochina Archives.
66. Konrad Kellen, "Conversations with Enemy Soldiers in Late 1968/Early 1969: A Study of Motivation and Morale," Rand Report RM-6131-1 ISA/ARPA, September 1970, p. 1.
67. *Ibid.*, p. 66.
68. *Ibid.*, p. 64.
69. Henderson, *Why the Viet Cong Fought*, p. 69; Kellen, "Conversations," p. 28.
70. CIC, "Update: North Vietnamese Soldier in South Vietnam," p. 10.
71. *Ibid.*
72. "A Monograph of 2d Lieutenant Nguyen Van Thong."
73. Henderson, *Why the Viet Cong Fought*, p. 45.
74. *Ibid.*

75. Alexander George, *The Chinese Communist Army in Action: The Korean War and Its Aftermath* (New York: Columbia University Press, 1967), pp. 167–68, 171, 189–94.

76. William R. Corson, *The Betrayal* (New York: Norton, 1968) p. 148; CIC, "Update: North Vietnamese Soldier in South Vietnam," p. 27.

77. Kellen, "Conversations," pp. 8–9. Combat intensity increased during 1968, but Kellen still found it "well within the limits of what soldiers seem able to endure."

78. *Ibid.*, pp. 10–11.

79. Pike, *PAVN*, p. 220.

80. Chanoff and Toai, *Portrait of the Enemy*, pp. 48, 60, 63, and 155; CIC, "Update: NVA Soldier in South Vietnam," p. 41.

81. "A Return to Human Nature," English translation of letters by forty-five members of the Quyet Thang Regiment, June 1968. Copy in Indochina Archives, University of California, Berkeley.

82. Kellen, "Conversations," p. 39.

5. "Corruption Is Everywhere"

1. Jeffrey J. Clarke, *The U.S. Army in Vietnam: Advice and Support— The Final Years 1965–1973* (Washington: GPO, 1988), p. 275.

2. Quoted in Herbert Y. Schandler, *Lyndon Johnson and Vietnam* (Princeton, N.J.: Princeton University Press, 1977), p. 295.

3. Lyndon Johnson, *The Vantage Point* (New York: Popular Library, 1971), p. 415.

4. Schandler, *Lyndon Johnson and Vietnam*, p. 296.

5. For a discussion of the origins of the Second Indochina War, see William J. Duiker, *The Communist Road to Power in Vietnam* (Boulder, Colo.: Westview Press, 1981), pp. 186–201; Ronald H. Spector, *Advice and Support: The Early Years of the U.S. Army in Vietnam* (New York: Free Press, 1985), pp. 310–15, 327–30; and William S. Turley, *The Second Indochina War* (New York: NAL, 1987), pp. 22–27, 30–31.

6. Clarke, *U.S. Army in Vietnam: Final Years*, pp. 20, 293; Peter Braestrup, "Saigon's Fighting Role Grows," *Washington Post*, February 2, 1969.

7. Allan E. Goodman, *Politics in War: The Basis of Political Community in Vietnam* (Cambridge: Harvard University Press, 1973), pp. 31, 38, and *passim*.

8. Bui Diem, *In The Jaws of History* (Boston: Hougton-Mifflin, 1987), p. 158.

9. *Ibid.*; Clarke, *U.S. Army in Vietnam: Final Years*, pp. 23–24.

10. Diem, *In Jaws of History*, p. 157.

11. Clarke, *U.S. Army in Vietnam: Final Years,* pp. 130–44, has the most detailed account. See also Lewis W. Walt, *Strange War, Strange Strategy* (New York: Funk & Wagnalls, 1970), pp. 118–23; Nguyen Cao Ky, *Twenty Years and Twenty Days* (New York: Stein & Day, 1976), pp. 94–102; and Goodman, *Politics in War,* pp. 39–41.

12. Clarke, *U.S. Army in Vietnam: Final Years,* pp. 259–66.

13. *Ibid.*

14. Goodman, *Politics in War,* pp. 57–60.

15. *Ibid.,* p. 61.

16. *Ibid.,* p. 37; Frances FitzGerald, *Fire in the Lake* (Boston: Little, Brown, 1972), p. 330.

17. Alfred McCoy, *The Politics of Heroin in Southeast Asia* (New York: Harper & Row, 1972), p. 176.

18. Clarke, *U.S. Army in Vietnam: Final Years,* pp. 262–63.

19. Goodman, *Politics in War,* p. 56.

20. FitzGerald, *Fire in the Lake,* p. 336; Robert Shaplen, "Letter from Saigon," *The New Yorker,* October 7, 1967, pp. 151–57.

21. Don Oberdorfer, *Tet!* (New York: Doubleday, 1971), pp. 164–70.

22. "The War: Saigon Under Fire," *Time,* June 21, 1968.

23. McCoy, *Politics of Heroin,* p. 179.

24. Stephen T. Hosmer et al., *The Fall of South Vietnam: Statements by Vietnamese Military and Civilian Leaders* (New York: Crane Russek, 1980), p. 64.

25. *Ibid.,* p. 69.

26. FitzGerald, *Fire in the Lake,* p. 408.

27. Clarke, *U.S. Army in Vietnam: Final Years,* pp. 47, 59, 321, 365–66, and *passim.*

28. George W. Ashworthe, "Some Glaring Weaknesses in Saigon Military," *Christian Science Monitor,* January 5, 1970.

29. George W. Ashworthe, "Thieu's Next Move," *Christian Science Monitor,* January 8, 1970.

30. Allan E. Goodman, "A Social and Political Profile of the Republic of Vietnam's Officer Corps," p. 13. Copy in CMH. A revised version of this study was published as *An Institutional Profile of the South Vietnamese Officer Corps* (Santa Monica, Calif.: Rand, 1970). All page references are to the draft study.

31. In 1968, Rand Corporation researchers could find only fifteen RVNAF officers, out of 24,000 studied, who had ever fought against the French. Of thirty-four retired officers serving in the National Assembly, all but five had fought *with* the French. Goodman, "Social and Political Profile," pp. 50, 60.

32. Cf. comments of Major General Richard E. Lee in Clarke, *U.S. Army in Vietnam: Final Years,* pp. 162–63.
33. Goodman, "Social and Political Profile," p. 64.
34. *Ibid.,* p. 102.
35. Bernard Weinraub, "Major Deplores Saigon's Forces," *New York Times,* August 13, 1968.
36. USAID Office of Education Briefing Materials, 1969, 1970. Copy in CMH.
37. Goodman, "Social and Political Profile," p. 43.
38. Donald Lancaster, *The Emancipation of French Indochina* (London: Oxford University Press, 1961), pp. 248–49.
39. Melvin Gurtov, *Viet Cong Cadres and the Cadre System* (Santa Monica, Calif.: Rand, 1967), pp. 14–15 and *passim.*
40. Tran Dinh Tho, *Pacification,* Indochina Monographs (Washington: CMH, 1980), p. 193.
41. Goodman, "Social and Political Profile," p. 55.
42. Major General Nguyen Duy Hinh and Brigadier General Tran Dinh Tho, *The South Vietnamese Society,* Indochina Monographs (Washington: CMH 1980), p. 112.
43. *Ibid.*
44. Clarke, *U.S. Army in Vietnam: Final Years,* p. 230.
45. McCoy, *Politics of Heroin,* pp. 169–73 and *passim.*
46. Clarke, *U.S. Army in Vietnam: Final Years,* p. 230.
47. McCoy, *Politics of Heroin,* p. 171.
48. Arnold R. Isaacs, *Without Honor* (Baltimore: Johns Hopkins, 1983), pp. 112–13.
49. Goodman, "Social and Political Profile," 99–100; Clarke, *U.S. Army in Vietnam: Final Years,* pp. 308–9.
50. Hosmer, *Fall of South Vietnam,* pp. 74–75.
51. Goodman, "Social and Political Profile," pp. 41–42.
52. Hinh and Tho, *South Vietnamese Society,* p. 113.
53. Clarke, *U.S. Army in Vietnam: Final Years,* p. 275.
54. William R. Corson, *The Betrayal* (New York: Norton, 1968).
55. Memo, Vann to Deputy, CORDS, subj: Improvement of Security Within South Vietnam, November 13, 1967, John Paul Vann Papers, U.S. Army Military History Institute.
56. Corson, *Betrayal,* p. 98.
57. Ly K. Tran, "The Advisor and His Counterpart: A Study of the Vietnamese Officer's Perception of His American Advisor," Junior Paper, Princeton University, Department of History, May 1991, p. 17.
58. Goodman, "Social and Political Profile," p. 7.

59. Memo, John Paul Vann to AC of S, CORDS, 13 Aug 70, subj.: Inquiry from Ambassador Bunker, Vann Papers, Military History Institute.

60. Clarke, *U.S. Army in Vietnam: Final Years,* pp. 42–43, 314.

61. *Ibid.,* pp. 152–53.

62. *Ibid.,* pp. 31–32, 308–11; General L. Nguyen Khang interview, Marine Corps Oral History Collection.

63. Comments by Colonel Leroy Vance Corbett on Working Draft, "U.S. Marines in Vietnam 1969," chapter 17, Comment Files, Marine Corps Historical Center.

64. *Ibid.*

65. Clarke, *U.S. Army in Vietnam: Final Years,* p. 252 and *passim.*

66. Nguyen Ngoc Ngan, *The Will of Heaven,* p. 36.

67. George W. Ashworthe, "Being No. 1 Division Can Be An Experience," *Christian Science Monitor,* December 9, 1969.

68. Comments by Colonel Corbett.

69. William Ezzard interview, pp. 177–79, Winter Soldier Oral History Collection.

70. Ashworthe, "Being No. 1 Division."

71. *Ibid.*

72. Clarke, *U.S. Army in Vietnam: Final Years,* p. 251.

73. Ngan, *Will of Heaven,* p. 36.

74. Clarke, *U.S. Army in Vietnam: Final Years,* pp. 292–93, 295, 303–5.

75. On Williams's career in Vietnam, see Spector, *Advice and Support,* pp. 275–352.

76. *Ibid.,* pp. 340–42.

77. Cao Van Vien *et al., The U.S. Advisor,* Indochina Monograph Series (Washington: CMH, 1980), pp. 31–32.

78. Gerald C. Hickey, "The American Military Advisor and His Foreign Counterpart: The Case of Vietnam," Rand Monograph RM 4482 ARPA, March 1965, p. 20.

79. Spector, *Advice and Support,* p. 288, 340–42.

80. Interview with Major John E. Ciccarelli, Senior Adviser, Cau Ke District, Vinh Binh Province, 24 Sep 68, VNIT 242, p. 13, CMH Oral History Collection.

81. Hickey, "American Military Advisor," pp. 16–17.

82. Interview with Major Ciccarelli, p. 8.

83. William Ezzard interview, p. 43.

84. Interview with Major Ciccarelli, p. 5.

85. Clarke, *U.S. Army in Vietnam: Final Years,* pp. 189–90.

86. MACV Directive 525-20, January 26, 1967, subj.: Combat Operations: Guidance for U.S. Advisors, copy in CMH.

87. Clarke, *U.S. Army in Vietnam: Final Years,* p. 330.

88. *Ibid.,* pp. 88–90, 112, 231, 263.
89. Neil Sheehan, *A Bright Shining Lie* (New York: Random House, 1988), p. 556.

6. The Relief of Khe Sanh and After, April 1968

1. Letters, Brigadier General J. R. Chaisson to Mrs. Chaisson, January 28, 1968, and February 1, 1968, Chaisson Papers.
2. Message, Abrams to Westmoreland 2683267 February 1968, Abrams Papers, Back Channel Files.
3. Lieutenant General Carl W. Hoffmann interview, p. 168, Marine Corps Oral History Collection.
4. Lieutenant General John J. Tolson, *Airmobility 1961–1971* (Washington: DOA, 1973), p. 167.
5. Combined Intelligence Center (CIC), Vietnam Special Study 68-08, "Arc Light Effectiveness," March 16, 1968, p. 1. Copy in MACV Records, National Archives.
6. MACV, "Khe Sanh Analysis," July 8, 1968, p. 13, MACV Records.
7. Robert Pisor, *The End of the Line: The Siege of Khe Sanh* (New York: Norton, 1982), p. 247; Truong Nhu Tang *et al., A Vietcong Memoir* (New York: Vintage, 1986), p. 168.
8. CIC, "Arc Light Effectiveness," p. 10.
9. Dang, *Viet Cong Memoire,* p. 168.
10. Peter Braestrup, *Big Story* (New Haven: Yale University Press, 1977), pp. 256–58.
11. See for example, Charles Mohr, "Khe Sanh and Dien Bien Phu: A Comparison," *New York Times,* March 8, 1968. Dien Bien Phu was in fact far more desperate. See Braestrup, *Big Story,* pp. 263–64.
12. Don Oberdorfer, *Tet!* (New York: Doubleday, 1971), p. 110.
13. Michael Herr, *Dispatches* (New York: Avon, 1978), p. 120.
14. Oberdorfer, *Tet!* p. 250.
15. MACV, Command History 1968, vol. I, pp. 158–59. Copy in CMH.
16. Tolson, *Airmobility,* p. 169.
17. Herr, *Dispatches,* p. 165.
18. Tolson, *Airmobility,* p. 170; III MAF Periodic Intelligence Report, No. 17-68, May 5, 1968, III MAF Records, MCHC.
19. Lance Corporal Francis Gonway interview, Tape 2755, Marine Corps Oral History Collection.
20. MACV, "Khe Sanh Analysis," p. 15.
21. Ray Stubbe, "Chaplain at Khe Sanh," unpublished ms. in MCHC, p. 714.
22. *Ibid.,* pp. 227–28; 1/9 Command Chronology, April 1968, MCHC.

23. Stubbe, "Chaplain At Khe Sanh," p. 728.
24. Captain Charles B. Hartzell interview, Tape 2803, and Captain Francis B. Lovely interview, Tape 2803, Marine Corps Oral History Collection.
25. Tolson, *Airmobility,* pp. 175-77.
26. Pisor, *End of the Line,* pp. 26-33, Lieutenant Colonel J. C. Studt, "Battalion in the Attack," *Marine Corps Gazette,* July 1970, pp. 39-40.
27. Moyers S. Shore, *The Battle for Khe Sanh* (Washington: Historical Branch, G-3 USMC, 1969), pp. 1-2.
28. Second Lieutenant Charles W. King interview, Tape 2776, Marine Corps Oral History Collection.
29. Corporal Eldridge Patterson, Jr., interview, Tape 2776, Marine Corps Oral History Collection.
30. Studt, "Battalion in the Attack," p. 44.
31. Letter, Dennis Mannion to Joe Doherty, April 19, 1968. Cited in Stubbe, "Chaplain at Khe Sanh," p. 754.
32. Stubbe, "Chaplain at Khe Sanh," p. 826.
33. *Ibid.,* p. 756.
34. Chaisson to Mrs. Chaisson, April 17, 1968, Chaisson Papers.
35. Cited in Stubbe, "Chaplain at Khe Sanh," p. 756.
36. Concept of Operation SCOTLAND II, 180527Z, April 1968, III MAF COC Files, MCHC.
37. Unless otherwise noted, this account of 1/9's fight near Hill 689 is based on "Informal investigation of a night operation conducted by 1st Battalion 9th Marines in the vicinity of Khe Sanh, RVN, on the night of 16-17 April 1968 and supporting documents." All in Third Marine Division, mixed topics file, MCHC.
38. First Lieutenant David D. Carter interview, Tape 3950, Marine Corps Oral History Collection.
39. Corporal Dewey E. Troup interview, Tape 2803, Marine Corps Oral History Collection.
40. Corporal Glenn R. Horne interview, Tape 2776, Marine Corps Oral History Collection.
41. Brigadier General John H. Cushman, "How We Did It in Thua Thien," *Army,* May 1970, pp. 50-51. The author was present during General Cushman's debriefing following the operations at Phuoc Yen and Le Xa Dong described here.
42. Headquarter, 1st Air Cavalry Division Combat After-Action Report, Operation DELAWARE, July 11, 1968, p. 2. 1st Cavalry Division Records, National Archives.
43. Tolson, *Airmobility,* p. 178.
44. *Ibid.,* pp. 178, 192.
45. Combat After-Action Report, Operation DELAWARE, p. 8.

46. Tolson, *Airmobility,* p. 187.
47. Combat After-Action Report, Operation DELAWARE, p. 8.
48. *Ibid.,* p. 10; Shelby Stanton, *Anatomy of a Division* (Novato, Calif.: Presidio Press, 1987), pp. 147–48.
49. Combat After-Action Report, Operation DELAWARE, pp. 6–7.
50. *Ibid.,* p. 13.
51. Message, Thompkins to CG, PCV, 160725Z May 1968, III MAF, SPECAT File, III MAF Records.
52. Brigadier General Carl W. Hoffman interview, February 16, 1969, Tape 3918, Marine Corps Oral History Collection.
53. *Ibid.*

7. The May Offensive: Dai Do

1. Chester Cooper, *The Lost Crusade: America in Vietnam* (New York: Dodd, Mead, 1970), p. 395.
2. *Time,* May 10, 1968, p. 21.
3. *Ibid.*
4. *Ibid.,* p. 24.
5. David Halberstam, *The Best and the Brightest* (New York: Random House, 1972), p. 191.
6. *Ibid.,* p. 73.
7. Summary Notes of 586th NSC Meeting, May 22, 1968, Case NLJ 83-45, Doc. 2, LBJ Library.
8. *Ibid.*
9. CINCPACFLT, "Navy Interdiction Campaign, North Vietnam, 16 October 1969," p. 161 and *passim.* Vietnam Command File, Naval Historical Center, Washington, D.C.
10. Notes of President's Meeting with Policy Advisers, May 25, 1968, Meeting Notes File, LBJ Library.
11. Summary Notes of 586th NSE Meeting.
12. Cited in William J. Duiker, *The Communist Road to Power in Vietnam* (Boulder, Colo.: Westview, 1981), p. 274.
13. Memo, W. W. Rostow to President, June 11, 1968, subj.: relative strength in combat effective equivalents, NSC Country Files, LBJ Library.
14. See Chapter 2, pages 41–44.
15. Message, COMUSMACV to LTG Goodpaster, subj.: Assessment of Military Position and Forecast of Operations, 131148Z May 68, MACV Message Files, MACV Records.
16. "Analysis of Vietnam by Corps Areas as Seen by MACV," briefing by Brigadier General J. R. Chaisson, May 1968, p. 2. Copy in MCHC.

17. Colonel Marion C. Dalby interview, Tape 2781, and HN2 Robert J. Dourlain interview, Tape 2781, Marine Corps Oral History Collection.

18. Unless otherwise indicated, the following account is based on Major William H. Dabney, "The Battle of Dong Ha, 1968," unpublished paper, copy in U.S. Marine Corps Command and Staff College Library, Quantico, Va., and Brigadier General William Weise, "Memories of Dai Do," *Marine Corps Gazette,* September 1987. I am grateful to General Weise for allowing me to use and quote from the unpublished manuscript.

19. PFC Cecil F. Whitfield interview, Tape 2804, Marine Corps Oral History Collection.

20. Sergeant Bruce Woodruff interview, Tape 2804.

21. First Lieutenant A. F. Prescott interview, Tape 2804.

22. Weise, "Memories of Dai Do," p. 11.

23. Woodruff interview.

24. Michael D. Harkins, "Magnificent Pressure Exerted," *Vietnam,* Summer 1989.

25. Corporal William Patton interview, Tape 2804.

26. Whitfield interview.

27. *Ibid.*

28. Sergeant Robert Ward interview, Tape 2804. See also Weise, "Dai Do," note 7.

29. Weise, "Dai Do," p. 28; Dabney, "Battle of Dong Ha," p. 62.

8. Lessons of the May Offensive

1. This description of American countermeasures is derived from Lieutenant General Ormond R. Simpson interview, Marine Corps Oral History Collection, pp. 430–34.

2. Message, Bunker to Secretary of State, 100820Z May 1968, LBJ National Security Files (DSDUF) LBJ Library.

3. Edward Doyle, Stephen Weiss, *et al. A Clash of Cultures* (Boston: Boston Publishing, 1984), p. 78; Don Oberdorfer, *Tet!* (New York: Doubleday, 1971), p. 134.

4. Gene Roberts, "Saigon Is Vehicle Jungle," *New York Times,* June 23, 1968.

5. Neil Sheehan, *A Bright Shining Lie* (New York: Random House, 1988), p. 626.

6. Robert Shaplen, *The Road from War* (New York: Harper & Row, 1970), p. 211.

7. *Ibid.,* p. 212.

8. Peter Braestrup, "U.S. Seeks to Cut Harm to Viet Cities," *Washington*

Post, May 23, 1968; John H. Thompson, "No 100% Security," *Chicago Tribune,* May 28, 1968.

9. "Viet Cong Step Up Attacks in Saigon Neighborhoods," *New York Times,* May 8, 1968.

10. Vietnam Lessons Learned No. 71, "Countermeasures Against Standoff Attacks," March 13, 1969, pp. 42–43.

11. "Enemy Steps Up Terror in Saigon," *New York Times,* May 8, 1968.

12. Gene Roberts, "People of Saigon," *New York Times,* May 16, 1968.

13. Message, Abrams to Admiral U. S. G. Sharp, MAC7605, 091112Z June 1968, Copy in Abrams Papers, Backchannel Files.

14. Donald Kirk, "Air Strikes at Reds Inside Saigon Trigger Bitter Row," *Washington Star,* May 30, 1968.

15. William M. Hammond, "Press Coverage and the Political-Military Consequences of the Tet Offensive," paper presented at the 1990 Annual Meeting of the American Historical Association, p. 7.

16. Vietnam Lessons Learned, No. 71.

17. Letter, General Ormond R. Simpson to Brigadier General Edwin Simmons, August 18, 1986, Comment File, U.S. Marines in Vietnam, 1969, MCHC.

18. Vietnam Lessons Learned No. 71.

19. "The War in Vietnam: Deadly Tide," *Newsweek,* June 10, 1968, p. 61.

20. "Rocket Mistake No Error, Saigon Paper Intimates," *Washington Star,* June 7, 1968.

21. "War in Vietnam: Deadly Tide."

22. Hammond, "Press Coverage," p. 7.

23. "War in Vietnam: Deadly Tide."

24. Hammond, "Press Coverage," p. 10.

25. *Ibid.,* p. 12.

26. Message, Abrams to Sharp, AC7605 091112Z June 1968, MACV Message Files.

27. Kenneth Sams and A. W. Thompson, "Kham Duc," Project CHECO Report, July 8, 1968, p. 1. Copy in Air Force Historical Research Center, Maxwell AFB, Alabama.

28. Alan L. Gropman, *Air Power and the Airlift Evacuation of Kham Duc,* USAF Southeast Asia Monograph Series, vol. V, Monograph 7, Air War College, Maxwell AFB, Alabama, 1979.

29. On the CIDG, see Charles M. Simpson III, *Inside the Green Berets* (New York: Berkeley, 1984), pp. 103–12 and *passim;* Shelby L. Stanton, *Green Berets at War: U.S. Army Special Forces in Southeast Asia* (New York: Dell, 1985), pp. 56–66, 85–87.

30. Fact Sheet (with attachments), subj.: Attack at Kham Duc, RVN in May 1968, February 10, 1970, MACV Records National Archives. Gropman, *Airlift Evacuation,* p. 6.

31. After-Action Report, Ngoc Tavak, Annex A to 5th Special Forces Group (Airborne) After-Action Report, Kham Duc, May 31, 1968. Copy in Stanton Collection.

32. Statement by Captain Silva, Attachment to Annex A to 5th Special Forces Grp. (Airborne) After-Action Report.

33. *Ibid.;* statement of Captain Eugene Makowski, Attachment to Annex A.

34. Statement of Makowski.

35. Letter, Tim Brown to Shelby Stanton, June 25, 1985, Stanton Collection.

36. Gropman, *Airlift Evacuation,* p. 41.

37. *Ibid.,* pp. 41–42; Fact Sheet, Attack on Kham Duc.

38. Message, CO, 5th Special Forces Group, Nha Trang, to Director I & CA, ODCSOPS, DA 2208257 May 68, Attachment to Fact Sheet, Attack on Kham Duc.

39. Stanton, *Green Berets at War,* pp. 233–36.

40. Letter, Chaisson to Mrs. Chaisson, May 14, 1968, Chaisson Papers.

41. Message, CO 5th Special Forces Group Nha Trang, to Director ICA, 2208257 May 68.

42. Sams and Thompson, "Kham Duc," p. 9.

43. Letter, Todd Regon to Shelby Stanton, March 2, 1981. Copy in Stanton Collection; C Co., 5th SF Group (Airborne) After-Action Report, Battle of Kham Duc, May 31, 1968, p. 5.

44. Gropman, *Airlift Evacuation,* p. 34.

45. *Ibid.*

46. Company C, Fifth Special Forces, After-Action Report, p. 8.

47. Company C After-Action Report, Personal Statement of Staff Sergeant Richard F. Campbell.

48. Major James M. Meade interview, May 13, 1968, Tape 3146, Marine Corps Oral History Collection.

49. *Ibid.;* Gropman, *Airlift Evacuation,* p. 50.

50. Message, Abrams to Lieutenant General Cushman CG III MAF, 061125 June 68, Abrams Papers, Back Channel Files.

51. Chaisson to Mrs. Chaisson, May 14, 1968, Chaisson Papers.

52. Message, Abrams to Lieutenant General Cushman, 0611257 June 68, Abrams Papers.

53. PFC Ray E. Fisher *et al.* interviews, May 30, 1968, Tape 2876, Marine Corps Oral History Collection.

54. Sergeant Douglas M. Paulson interview, May 30, 1968, Tape 2876.

55. Corporal Charles D. Huckaby interview, Tape 2875, Marine Corps Oral History Collection.

56. 3d Battalion, 27th Marines, Combat After-Action Report, Operation ALLEN BROOK, June 11, 1968, p. 6. Copy in MCHC.

57. Huckaby interview.
58. 3d Battalion, 27th Marines, After-Action Report, p. 7.
59. Captain B. K. Thomas interview, Tape 2873, Marine Corps Oral History Collection.
60. 3d Battalion, 27th Marines, After-Action Report, p. 10.
61. Huckaby interview.
62. Letter, Lieutenant General Metzger to Brigadier General Edwin Simmons.
63. See the description of the fight for Hill 881 South in Sheehan, *A Bright Shining Lie,* pp. 647–49.

9. "The People in the Middle"

1. John T. McAlister and Paul Mus, *The Vietnamese and Their Revolution* (New York: Harper & Row, 1970), pp. 45–51.
2. *Ibid.*; Jeffrey Race, *War Comes to Long An,* (Berkeley: University of California Press, 1972) pp. 3–5.
3. Race, *War Comes to Long An,* pp. 41–120; J. J. Zasloff, *Origins of the Insurgency in South Vietnam: The Role of the Southern Cadre,* RM51627-ISA-ARPA (Santa Monica, Calif.: Rand, 1968), pp. 9–10; William J. Duiker, *The Communist Road to Power in Vietnam* (Boulder, Colo.: Westview Press, 1981), pp. 181–86; Ronald H. Spector, *Advice and Support: The Early Years of the U.S. Army in Vietnam* (New York: Free Press, 1985), pp. 320–27.
4. This "myth of the village" is discussed more fully in Samuel Popkin, *The Rational Peasant: The Political Economy of Rural Society in Vietnam* (Berkeley: University of California Press, 1979), pp. 137–65.
5. Memo, Williams to Ambassador Elbridge Durbrow, February 25, 1960, subj.: Balance Between Security and Development, Samuel T. Williams Papers, LBJ Library.
6. MACCORDS, *The Vietnamese Village: Handbook for Advisors,* 1971 ed., p. 4, MACV, CORDs records, CMH.
7. William E. Colby, *Lost Victory* (Chicago: Contemporary Books, 1989), pp. 71, 215.
8. Milton Taylor, "South Vietnam: Lavish Aid, Limited Progress," *Pacific Affairs,* vol. 3 (Fall 1961), p. 243.
9. Race, *War Comes to Long An,* p. 176.
10. Le Ly Hayslip, *When Heaven and Earth Changed Places* (New York: Doubleday, 1989), pp. xv–xvi.
11. Race, *War Comes to Long An,* p. 98.
12. Memo, Williams to Colonels Rasor and Barnett, subj.: Loss of Weapons, May 23, 1960; Memo of Conversation, Williams with Ngo Dinh Diem, May 27, 1960, both in Williams Papers.

13. Quoted in Roger Hilsman, *To Move a Nation* (New York: Dell, 1967), p. 414.

14. Andrew F. Krepinevich, Jr., *The Army and Vietnam* (Baltimore: Johns Hopkins University Press, 1986), pp. 43-50.

15. *Gravel Edition of Pentagon Papers,* vol. IV, pp. 506-8.

16. Krepinevich, *Army and Vietnam,* pp. 131-94.

17. Richard Hunt, "The Challenge of Counter-Insurgency," in John Schlight, ed., *Second Indochina War Symposium* (Washington, D.C.: CMH, 1985), p. 123.

18. *Gravel Edition of Pentagon Papers,* vol. IV, pp. 506-8.

19. Michael E. Peterson, *The Combined Action Platoons: The U.S. Marines' Other War in Vietnam* (New York: Praeger, 1988), pp. 45-49; Bruce Allnutt, "Marine Combined Action Capabilities: The Vietnam Experience," *HUMRO Inc,* December 1969, pp. 11-22. The author served briefly with the Second, Third, and Fourth Combined Action Companies, November-December 1968 and February-March, 1969.

20. Peterson, *Combined Action Platoons,* p. 73.

21. Allnutt, "Combined Action Capabilities," p. 27.

22. *Ibid.,* p. 41.

23. *Ibid.,* pp. 36-39.

24. Major Edward F. Palm, "Tiger Papa Three: A Memoir of the Combined Action Program—Part II," *Marine Corps Gazette,* vol. 72 (February 1988), p. 67.

25. Peterson, *Combined Action Platoons,* p. 86.

26. Corporal Roosevelt Johnson interview, Tape 3679, Marine Corps Oral History Collection.

27. Palm, "Tiger Papa Three," p. 75. The author observed a similar change of attitude among the PFs in Huong Tra district across the river from Hue. Their villages had suffered extensively at the hands of the Communists during Tet.

28. Letter, Igor Bobrowsky to author, March 17, 1992.

29. Francis J. West, "Something of Significance," unpublished paper, undated (1968?), p. 4. Copy in MCHC.

30. *Ibid.*

31. *Ibid.,* p. 5.

32. Peterson, *Combined Action Platoons,* p. 44.

33. William R. Corson, *The Betrayal* (New York: Norton, 1968), p. 197.

34. Lieutenant Colonel Earl R. Hunter, "Individual Research Paper on the Most Effective Utilization of Combined Action Units, 1972," pp. 13-14. Copy in Archives, USMC Command and Staff College, Quantico, Va.

35. Peterson, *Combined Action Platoon,* pp. 87–88.
36. Corson, *Betrayal,* pp. 241–42.
37. Hunter, "Utilization of Combined Action Units," p. 13–14.
38. *Ibid.*
39. Peterson, *Combined Action Platoons,* pp. 22, 32, 50.
40. Michael A. Hennessy, "Divided They Fell: America's Response to Revolutionary War in I Corps, Republic of Vietnam," M.A. Thesis, University of New Brunswick, 1987.
41. *Ibid.,* pp. 311, 329–30.
42. Palm, "Tiger Papa Three," p. 76.
43. Quoted in Peterson, *Combined Action Platoons,* p. 61.
44. Allnutt, "Marine Combined Action Capabilities," p. 54.
45. William C. Westmoreland, *A Soldier Reports* (Garden City, N.Y.: Doubleday, 1976), p. 166.
46. Peterson, *Combined Action Platoons,* p. 83.
47. Allnutt, "Marine Combined Action Capabilities," Appendix C.
48. Palm, "Tiger Papa Three," p. 76.
49. Peterson, *Combined Action Platoons,* p. 90.
50. Palm, "Tiger Papa Three," p. 76.
51. Telford Taylor, "Vietnam and Nuremberg Principles," in Richard A. Falk, ed., *The Vietnam War and International Law,* vol. IV (Princeton, N.J.: Princeton University Press, 1976), p. 369. The most thorough discussion of the Rules of Engagement, their relationship to international law, and their enforcement is in Gruenter Lewy, *America in Vietnam* (London: Oxford University Press, 1978), pp. 233, 235, 238–39 and *passim.*
52. Lewy, *America in Vietnam.* Douglas Kinnard's survey of 173 U.S. Army generals who served in Vietnam found that only 29 percent believed the ROE were "well understood"; 49 percent said they were "fairly well understood," and 17 percent believed they were "frequently misunderstood." Douglas Kinnard, *The War Managers* (Hanover, N.H.: University Press of New England, 1972).
53. Major WJR interview, pp. 14–15, Company Command in Vietnam Collection, U.S. Army Combat Studies Institute, Card GSC, Leavenworth, Kous.
54. Arthur Salzer interview, p. 361.
55. Le Ly Hayslip, *When Heaven and Earth Changed Places* (New York: Doubleday, 1989).
56. Memo, Senior Adviser, subj.: Policy for Combat in Populated and/or Built Up Areas, April 4, 1972, II Corps Senior Advisers File, CORDs files, CMH.
57. Colonel Charles K. Nulsen, Jr., "The Use of Firepower in Counterin-

surgency Operations," Army War College Student Essay, December 2, 1968. Copy in CORDs file, CMH.

58. Message, Johnson to General Creighton Abrams, October 2, 1967, Abrams Papers.

59. Thomas C. Thayer, *A Systems Analysis View of the Vietnam War, 1965-1972*, vol. IV, p. 208. Copy in Army Library.

60. Robert H. Scales, *Firepower in Limited War* (Washington: NDU Press, 1990), pp. 141-42.

61. Memo, Major General G. S. Eckhardt to DepCORDs, no subject, April 4, 1968, IV Corps Senior Adviser File, CORDS Files, CMH.

62. Lewy, *America in Vietnam*, p. 141.

63. *New York Times,* February 9, 1968, p. 12.

64. Quoted in Joseph C. Goulden, *Korea: The Untold Story* (New York: Times Books, 1982), p. 171.

65. Human Resources Research Institute, Military Management Research Directorate, Maxwell AFB, "Human Factors Affecting the Air War Effort," Report No. MM-1, December 1951, pp. 4-5. Copy in Air University Library, Maxwell AFB.

66. Ellen Frey-Wouters and Robert S. Laufer, *Legacy of a War: The American Soldier in Vietnam* (Armonk, N.Y.: M. E. Sharpe, 1989), p. 121.

67. *Ibid.*

68. Corporal Gilbert Lema interview, December 1968, Tape 3733, Marine Corps Oral History Collection.

69. Bernard Edelman, *Dear America: Letters Home from Vietnam* (New York: Norton, 1985), p. 54.

70. Kathryn Marshall, *In a Combat Zone* (Boston: Little, Brown, 1985), p. 49.

71. Charles C. Moskos, Jr., *The American Enlisted Man,* pp. 148-49.

72. Robert G. Kaiser, "Many GIs Dislike Viet Allies," *Washington Post,* October 18, 1969.

73. Brigadier General Richard J. Allen interview, October 9, 1968, VNIT 151, CMH.

74. Frey-Wouters and Laufer, *Legacy of a War,* p. 185.

75. Lewy, *America in Vietnam,* p. 324; William Anderson, "Analysis of Misconduct in Combat in Vietnam," June 1986, in Solis Backup File, MCHC.

76. *Ibid.* Anderson, "Analysis of Misconduct."

77. Vietnam Veterans Against the War, *The Winter Soldier Investigation* (Boston: Pantheon, 1972); Citizens Commission of Inquiry, *The Dellums Committee Hearings on War Crimes in Vietnam* (New York, 1972). For a critique of these inquiries, see Lewy, *America in Vietnam,* pp. 313-24.

78. Major WJR interview, Company Command in Vietnam Collection. Combat Studies Institute, p. 14; Major General William Lawrence interview, pp. 37–39, and Lieutenant Colonel Allen R. Wetzel interview, p. 49–50, both in Company Command in Vietnam Collection, Military History Institute; Wallace Terry, *Bloods: An Oral History of the Vietnam War by Black Veterans* (New York: Random House, 1984), p. 233.

79. Lewy, *America in Vietnam,* p. 329.

80. Fact Sheet by Brigadier General Edward Boutz, Director of Military Personnel Policies, DCSPER-SARD, subj.: Torture of PW by U.S. Officers, no date (July 1971). Copy in CMH.

81. Anderson, "Analysis of Misconduct."

82. William R. Peers, *The My Lai Inquiry* (New York: Norton, 1979), p. 180.

83. *Ibid.,* p. 175; Seymour Hersh, *My Lai 4* (New York: Random House, 1970), pp. 49–50.

84. Peers, *My Lai Inquiry,* pp. 283–85.

85. Hersh, *My Lai 4,* pp. 104–113.

86. A good brief description of the prosecution of the My Lai cases is in Lewy, *America in Vietnam,* pp. 356–65.

87. Peers, *My Lai Inquiry,* pp. 287–89.

88. *Ibid.,* pp. 232–33.

89. Quoted in Lewy, *America in Vietnam,* p. 327.

90. Private communication to the author, March 6, 1979.

91. Al Santoli, ed., *Everything We Had: An Oral History of the Vietnam War* (New York: Ballantine Books, 1981), pp. 114–15.

92. OASD (Public Affairs) Atrocity Fact Sheet, CORDS Files, CMH.

93. Race, *War Comes to Long An,* p. 83.

94. "The Massacre of Dak Son," *Time,* December 15, 1967, pp. 32–33.

95. Don Oberdorfer, *Tet!* (New York: Doubleday, 1971), p. 229.

96. *Ibid.,* p. 215.

97. *Ibid.,* p. 201.

98. The Senate Subcommittee on Refugees estimated civilian casualties at about 43,000 dead a year. I have used Lewy's more conservative figure of 25,000. Lewy, *America in Vietnam,* p. 445.

99. *Ibid.,* p. 447. As Lewy notes, considerable doubt exists as to the accuracy of these figures, since they are often based on the testimony of the injured person or his relatives or a quick examination by a nurse or orderly. The author recalls a particularly sad injury, a baby hit by shrapnel. As they waited for a medevac helicopter, the relatives and village officials engaged in a heated discussion about whether the shrapnel had come from a Viet Cong booby trap or a U.S. artillery shell.

100. Lewy, *America in Vietnam*, p. 108.

101. Edward Doyle, Stephen Weiss, *et al.*, *A Clash of Cultures* (Boston: Boston Publishing, 1984), p. 77.

102. DCSOPS, "Program for the Pacification and Long Term Development of South Vietnam," March 1, 1966, pp. 4-35. Copy in CMH.

103. Doyle and Weiss, *Clash of Cultures*, p. 145.

104. Hayslip, *When Heaven and Earth Changed Places*, p. 174.

105. Bernard Rodgers, *Cedar Falls-Junction City: A Turning Point*, Department of Army, Vietnam Studies (Washington, D.C.: GPO, 1974), p. 74. Cedar Falls was one of the few large-scale forced evacuations to receive much attention in the U.S. media, primarily due to the eloquent account published in *The New Yorker* and later in book form by Jonathan Schell, *Village of Ben Suc* (New York: Random House, 1967).

106. Schell, *Village of Ben Suc*, p. 70.

107. "Study of Mass Population Displacement," Part II, p. 101.

108. *Ibid.*, p. 9.

109. *Ibid.*, p. 13.

110. *Ibid.*, pp. 10, 13, 71, 101, 105-6.

111. *Ibid.*, pp. 24, 115-16, 148-50.

112. Quoted in Lewy, *America in Vietnam*, p. 111.

113. III Marine Amphibious Force Command Chronology, October 1967, Part II, p. 53.

114. *Ibid.*

115. *Gravel Edition of Pentagon Papers*, vol. IV, p. 508.

116. Study of Mass Population Displacement, Part I, p. 77.

117. *Ibid.*

118. A. Terry Rambo *et al.*, *The Refugee Situation in Phu Yen Province* (Human Sciences Research Corporation, 1967), p. 67.

119. Colby, *Lost Victory*, p. 238.

10. The August Offensive

1. Biographical information on Abrams from "Changing the Guard," *Time*, April 19, 1968, pp. 21-25; Kevin P. Buckley, "General Abrams Deserves a Better War," *New York Times Magazine*, October 5, 1969, pp. 120-27; and George C. Wilson, "Creighton Abrams: From Agawam to Chief of Staff," *Washington Post*, September 5, 1974, pp. 4-5.

2. Wilson, "Creighton Abrams."

3. Message, Abrams to General Brown, Lieutenant General Mildren, *et al.*, MAC 12145, 081000Z September 1968, Abrams Papers, Back Channel Files.

4. David Halberstam, *The Best and the Brightest* (New York: Random House, 1972), p. 549.

5. Buckley, "Abrams Deserves Better War," pp. 120–22.

6. Message, Abrams to General Momyer, Lieutenant General Palmer, *et al.*, MAC7236, 020158Z June 1968, Abrams Papers.

7. Elmo Zumwalt, Jr., and Elmo Zumwalt, III, *My Father, My Son* (New York: Macmillan, 1986), p. 46.

8. Buckley, "Abrams Deserves Better War," pp. 35, 120.

9. Organization and Function, Headquarters, USMACV, Vietnam, May 31, 1968. Copy in Historical Files, CMH.

10. Admiral Arthur Salzer Oral History interview p. 365, Naval Historical Center.

11. Typed list of questions, South Vietnam trip, Miscellaneous Notes, Clark Clifford Papers, LBJ Library.

12. Abridged MACV JSOP, Preliminary Version for Staff Comment, p. FO-2, Marshall Papers, Indochina Archive.

13. Clay Blair, *Korea: The Forgotten War*, (New York: Times Books, 1987), pp. 570, 575, and *passim.*

14. Jeffrey J. Clarke, *Advice and Support: The Final Years,* 1965-1973 (Washington: GPO, 1988), p. 89.

15. 18th Military History Detachment, 25th Inf. Div., Small Unit After-Action Interview, A Co. 3rd Battalion, 187th Airborne, September 5-6, 1968, VNIT-249, pp. 4-5, CMH, Oral History Collection.

16. Francis J. West, "Problem Recognition and Organizational Adaptation in a Counter-Insurgency Environment," unpublished paper, pp. 5–6. Copy in J. R. Chaisson Papers.

17. Memoirs of Colonel Donald Seibert, unpublished ms., pp. 1164–66. U.S. Army Military History Institute, Carlisle, Pa.

18. Lieutenant Colonel William R. Rindberg interview, p. 40, Company Command in Vietnam Collection, U.S. Army Military History Institute Oral History Collection.

19. Interim Report by the Department of Army Management Review Team, March 29, 1968, vol. II, Annex C-I. Copy in USARV Records, Record Group 319, National Archives.

20. Lieutenant Colonel Thomas Weitzel interview, Company Command in Vietnam Collection, p. 27.

21. For a discussion of the influential role of statistical reports in measuring the "progress" of the war, see Douglas Kinnard, *The War Managers* (New York: Da Capo, 1991), pp. 68–70.

22. Lieutenant Colonel NSV interview, Company Command in Vietnam Collection, p. 44.

23. John Limond Hart, "The Statistics Trap in Vietnam," *Washington Post*, December 22, 1982.

24. Quoted in Lieutenant Colonel Richard A. McMahan, "Let's Bury the

Body Count," U.S. Army War College essay, December 13, 1968, p. 2. Copy in U.S. Army Military History Institute.

25. Kinnard, *War Managers,* p. 72.
26. McMahan, "Let's Bury the Body Count."
27. Salzer interview, pp. 433-34.
28. After-Action Report, Operation SPEEDY EXPRESS, December 1, 1968-June 1, 1969, June 30, 1969. Copy in CMH.
29. Guenter Lewy, *America in Vietnam* (London: Oxford University Press, 1978), p. 142.
30. Salzer interview, p. 434.
31. Kevin Buckley, "Pacification's Deadly Price," *Newsweek,* June 19, 1972, pp. 42-43.
32. Major Garry L. Telfer *et al., U.S. Marines in Vietnam: Fighting the North Vietnamese 1967* (Washington: History and Museums Division, HQMC, 1984), pp. 86-87.
33. *Ibid.,* pp. 90-91, 94.
34. Human Sciences Research, Inc., "Study of Mass Population Displacement in the Republic of Vietnam, Part II: Case Studies of Refugee Resettlement," Advanced Research Projects Agency, Department of Defense, July 1969, p. 36.
35. *Ibid.,* pp. 13, 26.
36. *Ibid.,* pp. 29-30.
37. Telfer, *U.S. Marines in Vietnam,* pp. 131-32.
38. *Ibid.,* p. 93.
39. Major General Raymond G. Davis interview, January 1, 1969, p. 271, Marine Corps Oral History Collection.
40. General Raymond G. Davis interview 1978, p. 34, Marine Corps Oral History Collection.
41. *Ibid.,* p. 20.
42. See Chapter 7 above.
43. 3d Marine Division Command Chronology, June 1968, pp. 24-27; Brigadier General Carl W. Hoffman interview, p. E-2, Marine Corps Oral History Collection.
44. Carl. W. Hoffman interview, Tape 3825, p. E-5, 3d Marine Division Command Chronology.
45. 3d Marine Division Chronology.
46. *Ibid.*
47. *Ibid;* Davis interview, January 1, 1969, p. 272.
48. Hoffman interview, p. 151.
49. *Ibid.*
50. Lance Corporal Guadaloupe E. Rentario and HM3 Robert L. Gruba interviews, Tape 8034, Marine Corps Oral History Collection.
51. *Ibid.*

52. Davis interview, January 1, 1969, p. 282.

53. Memo, W. W. Rostow to President, June 18, 1968, CBS Subpoena Case No. NLS CBS 21, LBJ Library.

54. Davis interview, January 1, 1969.

55. Message, Abrams to Chairman, JCS, MAC 8515 281202Z June 1968, Abrams Papers, Back Channel Messages.

56. *Ibid.*

57. Message, Westmoreland to Abrams, HWA2165, 272357 June 1968, Abrams Papers, Back Channel Files.

58. Carl W. Hoffman interview, Tape 2781, Marine Corps Oral History Collection.

59. Davis interview, January 1, 1969, p. 285.

60. Thomas C. Thayer, "System Analysis View of the Vietnam War, Vol. IV: Allied Ground and Naval Operations," p. 37. Copy in Historian's Files, CMH.

61. Robert H. Scales, *Firepower in Limited War* (Washington: National Defense University Press, 1990), p. 117.

62. *Ibid.*

63. Major General Raymond G. Davis and First Lieutenant H. W. Bravier, "Defeat of the 320th," *Marine Corps Gazette,* March 1969, p. 28.

64. Davis interview, 1978, p. 24.

65. Davis and Bravier, "Defeat of the 320th," pp. 28–29.

66. Military Assistance Command Vietnam, *Command History 1968,* pp. 131–33; Message, Abrams to Wheeler and McCain, MAC 14451, 281816 Oct 68, LBJ Library, CBS Subpoena Case NCJ7CBS 8, Document 9, November 30, 1983; Beverly Dreps, "Viet Cong Battle Plans Captured," *Christian Science Monitor,* August 20, 1968.

67. 5th Marines Command Chronology, August 1968, Part IV, p. 5.

68. Major General Ellis W. Williams, "Defense of a Firebase," *Infantry Magazine,* November 1969, pp. 146–47.

69. *Ibid.,* pp. 148–50.

70. Synopsis of interview with Specialist Steven Bozoich, 62d Transportation Co (Med Trk); Synopsis of interview with Sergeant William E. Adrian, Jr., 86th Transportation Co.; Enclosures 46 and 48 to Recommendation for Award, William M. Seay, by CO, 62d Transportation Company, November 8, 1968, USARV Records, Record Group 319, National Archives. .

71. Enclosures 46 and 48, Seay award recommendation.

72. Interview with Gregory Haley, Sergeant, 1st Squad, 3d Platoon, A Co., 65th Eng. Bn.; Enclosure 45 to Recommendation for Award, William M. Seay.

73. Combat After-Action Report for the Battle of Duc Lap; Enclosure 1 to letter, Lieutenant Colonel E. M. Carter to Dr. Walter G. Hermes,

December 17, 1968; 21st MHD, 5th Special Forces Group (Airborne), After-Action Report, Battle of Duc Lap, A-239, all in CMH Oral History Collection.

74. Enclosure 1 to letter, Carter to Hermes, p. 32.

75. After-Action Report, Battle of Duc Lap, A-239, pp. 1-89.

76. Message, Abrams to Wheeler, 281816Z October 1968, CBS Subpoena Case no. NLJ7CBS8, Document 9, LBJ Library.

77. Message, Abrams to Wheeler, September 1, 1968, MAC 11819; Message, Abrams to McCain; Message, Wheeler to Abrams, October 16, 1968, JCS 11890.

11. The End of Racial Harmony

1. Report of Investigation Concerning USARV Installation Stockade by Lieutenant Colonel Baxter M. Bullock, President of Investigatory Board, September 13, 1968, p. 7, USARV Records, National Archives, Record Group 319.

2. *Ibid.,* p. 5.

3. *Ibid.,* p. 2.

4. "Race Riot at Long Binh," *Newsweek,* September 30, 1968.

5. Sworn statement by First Sergeant William Davidson, September 3, 1968, in Bullock, Report of Investigation.

6. "Race Riot at Long Binh," p. 35.

7. "Democracy in the Foxhole," *Time,* May 26, 1967, pp. 15-16.

8. *Ibid.,* p. 16.

9. Message, Abrams to Lieutenant General Palmer *et al.,* MAC 04599, 0608347 April 1968, Abrams Papers, Back Channel Files; Jack White "The Angry Black Soldiers," *The Progressive,* March 1970, p. 22.

10. *Jet,* April 4, 1968.

11. *Ibid.*

12. House Armed Services Committee, Special Subcommittee Report on Camp Lejeune Incident, December 15, 1969, HASC 91-2, pp. 5055-56.

13. White, "Angry Black Soldiers," p. 25.

14. Paul Hathaway, "The Negro at War: There Is Anger at Problems at Home," *Washington Star,* May 7, 1968.

15. Post-Southeast Asia Trip Overview of Interracial Relations and Equal Opportunity, p. 5, Enclosure 2, to Joint OSD-Military Departments Southeast Asia Equal Opportunity Base Visit Report, no date (1969). Copy in USARV Records, Record Group 319, National Archives.

16. Tim O'Brien, *If I Die in a Combat Zone (Box Me Up and Ship Me Home)* (New York: Dell, 1989), p. 68.

17. Report of Inquiry Concerning a Petition of Redress of Grievances by a

Group of Soldiers of the 71st Transportation Battalion, May 23, 1968. Copy in IG Files, USARV Records.

18. Post–Southeast Asia Trip Overview, p. 8.
19. Diary of Sergeant Michael Forrisi, Vietnam Miscellany Collection, U.S. Army Military History Institute, Carlisle, Pa.
20. Transcript, USARV Commander Conference, August 1971, USARV Records.
21. Post-Southeast Asia Trip Overview, p. 8.
22. *Ibid.,* p. 6.
23. Charles Taliaferro interview, Winter Soldier Oral History Collection, Columbia University, pp. 35–38.
24. Jim Heiden interview, Winter Soldier Collection, p. 41.
25. Paul Hathaway, "The Negro at War: He Asks Himself Some Disturbing Questions," *Washington Star,* May 6, 1968.
26. Thomas Picou, "Negro Seabee Raps Bias in Vietnam," *Chicago Daily Defender,* March 20, 1968.
27. *Ibid.*
28. Wallace Terry, *Bloods: An Oral History of the Vietnam War by Black Veterans* (New York: Random House, 1984), p. 40.
29. Memo, MPP to Assistant Secretary of the Army (MRA) subj.: Complaints Alleging Discrimination/Prejudicial Treatment in Vietnam, May 24, 1968. Copy in USARV Files.
30. In a further effort at oneupmanship, the author's hooch displayed a large blue banner that read: "For God, For Country and For Yale."
31. "G.I.s Are Allowed to Fly Their Home-State Flag," *Washington Post,* May 17, 1968, p. 22.
32. *Ibid.*
33. Enclosure 3 to Joint OSD-Military Departments Southeast Asia Equal Opportunity Base Visits Report, p. 9.
34. Testimony of Major Donald F. Milone, USMC, 3d MP Battalion, September 1968. Unless otherwise noted, all testimony cited in connection with the III MAF Brig is from documentary material collected by John C. Reynolds for Lieutenant Colonel Gary D. Solis, *Marines and Military Law* (Washington: History and Museums Division, Headquarters USMC, 1989). It is filed with Lieutenant Colonel Solis's other research material at MCHC.
35. Solis, *Marines and Military Law,* p. 114.
36. Testimony of Private Talmadge D. Berry, August 29, 1968, Reynolds Folder, Solis Files.
37. *Ibid.*
38. Testimony of Sergeant James E. Bean, USMC, 3d MP Battalion, no date, Reynolds Folder.
39. Testimony of PFC Graves S. Johns, August 19, 1968, Reynolds Folder.

40. Solis, *Marines and Military Law*, p. 116.
41. *Ibid.*, Testimony of Major Donald F. Milone, Reynolds Folder.
42. Solis, *Marines and Military Law*, p. 119.
43. Report of Investigation Concerning USARV Installation Stockade.
44. Robert Sherrill, "Justice Military Style," *Playboy*, January 19, 1970, p. 217; USARV IG Report, February 24, 1970, subj.: Playboy Magazine Article: "Justice Military Style," encl. to Memo, Deputy Asst Sec Army (Manpower) to Deputy Asst Sec Def (Military Personnel Policy), March 25, 1970, USARV Records.
45. Memo, Major Jerauld E. Vessels to Major General Francis Sampson, Chief of Chaplains, subj.: Report and Personal Analysis of Riot in USARV Confinement Facility, Long Binh Post, Vietnam, September 9, 1968. Copy in USARV Records.
46. Sherrill, "Justice Military Style," p. 217.
47. USARV IG Report, February 24, 1970.
48. Report of Investigation Concerning USARV Installation Stockade, pp. 9–10.
49. Vessels, Report and Personal Analysis, p. 14.
50. USARV IG Report, February 24, 1970. About 47 percent of the prisoners were white, and 5 percent "other."
51. Sworn Statement by First Sergeant William Davidson, September 2, 1968, p. 1; Attachment to Report of Investigation Concerning USARV Installation Stockade.
52. Vessels, Report and Personal Analysis, p. 3.
53. Report of Investigation Concerning USARV Installation Stockade, p. 13.
54. "Race Riot at Long Binh," p. 35.
55. Special Police Intelligence Report by Provost Marshal, I Field Force, October 1, 1968, I Field Force Records, CMH.
56. *Ibid.*
57. Message, Deputy CINC, USARPAC, to Deputy CG, USARV, 221913Z October 1968, USARV Records.
58. *Ibid.*
59. Summary of Significant Racial Incidents at Marine Corps Installations, Aug68–Aug71. Copy in General References Files, MCHC.
60. "Tensions of Black Power Reach Troops in Vietnam," *New York Times*, March 13, 1969, p. 1.
61. "Detailed Breakout of Disturbances," Annex E to MACV J-1 Monthly Report, no date (June 1970). Copy in USARV Files.
62. Joel Davis interview, Winter Soldier Oral History Collection, p. 47.

12. In the Rear with the Gear, the Sergeant Major, and the Beer

1. Lieutenant Colonel Wetzel interview, Company Command in Vietnam Collection, U.S. Army Military History Institute, p. 85.
2. Wallace Terry, *Bloods: An Oral History of the Vietnam War by Black Veterans* (New York: Random House, 1984), pp. 38, 40-41.
3. Al Santoli, ed., *Everything We Had: An Oral History of the Vietnam War* (New York: Ballantine, 1981), p. 112.
4. Charles R. Anderson, *Vietnam: The Other War* (New York: Warner Books, 1990), p. 21.
5. Tim O'Brien, *If I Die in a Combat Zone (Box Me Up and Ship Me Home)* (New York: Dell, 1989), p. 164. Stouffer and his colleagues discovered a similar pattern of attributes and behavior in World War II troops. Samuel A. Stouffer *et al., The American Soldier,* vol. II: *Combat and Its Aftermath* (New York: Wiley, 1965), pp. 290-319.
6. Michael Herr, *Dispatches* (New York: Avon, 1978), pp. 13-14.
7. Anderson, *Vietnam: The Other War,* pp. 2-4.
8. Captain James E. Citrano interview, December 14, 1968, Tape 3587; Sergeant Albino Perez interview, December 22, 1968, Tape 3602. Both in Marine Corps Oral History Collection.
9. Memo, Staff Exchange Officer to AC of S, G-1, USARV, subj.: Exchange Service, Vietnam, no date (1968), USARV Records, Record Group 319, National Archives.
10. Info brief by DCSPER-PSD, subj.: Slot Machines, June 24, 1971, copy in USARV Records.
11. Memo by Special Services Division, AG, subj.: Leave, Rest, and Recreational Facilities, May 19, 1968, USARV Records.
12. Lieutenant Colonel Lawrence Karjola interview, May 10, 1981, Company Command in Vietnam Collection, p. 14.
13. Letter, Acting Secretary of Army to Honorable Abraham A. Ribicoff, Acting Chairman, Permanent Investigation Subcommittee, Government Operations Committee, U.S. Senate, May 11, 1971, Chief of Staff Files, Westmoreland Papers, LBJ Library.
14. Headquarters, 18th Military Police Brigade, Police Intelligence Report, July 31, 1968, USARV Records; Peter Cameron interview, Winter Soldier Oral History Collection, p. 19.
15. 18th Military Police Brigade Report.
16. *Ibid.*
17. Headquarters, USMACV, "Provost Marshal History 1964-1973," MACV Records 334-75-211, National Archives, p. I-51.
18. The author was present during this business transaction.
19. "Provost Marshal History," p. I-51.
20. The most extensive documentation is in U.S. Senate Committee on

Government Operations Permanent Investigation Subcommittee, *Fraud and Corruption in Management of the Military Club System*, 91st Cong., 2d sess., and 92d Cong., 1st sess., parts 1–4 (Washington, D.C.: GPO, 1972).

21. Memo for Record by CWO4 K. B. Hon, Enforcement/Security Branch, MACV J-5, subj.: Illegal Gambling Establishment, August 22, 1967, attachment to William C. Westmoreland to Hon. Eugene Locke, Deputy American Ambassador, subj.: Illegal Gambling Establishment, Westmoreland Papers, Signature File.

22. Anonymous letter from U.S. Army officer to Representative Wayne Teague, July 13, 1967. Copy in Westmoreland Papers, Signature File.

23. HQ, 18th MP Brigade, Police Intelligence Report; Terry, *Bloods,* p. 39.

24. Provost Marshal History, p. I-44.

25. H. Spencer Bloch, M.D., "The Psychological Adjustment of Normal People During a Year Tour in Vietnam," p. 619.

26. Dan Freedman and Jacqueline Rhoads, *Nurses in Vietnam* (Austin: Texas Monthly Press, 1987), p. 154.

27. Colonel Ivor Manderson interview, p. 17, Company Command in Vietnam Collection; Charles R. Anderson, "Survival in the Rear," *Vietnam,* August 1989, p. 22.

28. The author recalls a helicopter hovering high above the rolling deck of a small destroyer to pick up a liaison team. While the men in a harness were slowly winched up to the swaying, vibrating helicopter, the crew chief divided his time between managing the winch and photographing the process through the open deck hatch. See also Terry, *Bloods,* p. 217.

29. Anderson, "Survival in the Rear," p. 24.

30. Le Ly Hayslip, *When Heaven and Earth Changed Places,* p. 168.

31. Lieutenant Colonel JLT interview; Lieutenant Colonel RAO interview. Both in Company Command in Vietnam Collection.

32. Terry, *Bloods,* p. 28; Anderson, *Vietnam: The Other War,* pp. 144–45.

33. Terry, *Bloods,* p. 29.

34. Robert Shaplen, "The Girls They Leave Behind in Saigon," *McCall's,* July 1968, pp. 81–82.

35. *Ibid.*

36. *Ibid.,* p. 132.

37. Peter Cameron interview, Winter Soldier Oral History Collection, pp. 33–34.

38. Lieutenant Ivor Manderson interview, Company Command in Vietnam Collection.

39. Lieutenant Colonel Pat E. Brown interview, Company Command in Vietnam Collection, p. 11.

40. MACV-13 Memo, subj.: Out-of-Country R&R Program—All Ser-

vices, May 22, 1968, MACV Records. Transportation to Manila was provided by Air Force C-54s.

41. Letter, Hayden Thompson to U.S. Servicemen's Fund, August 14, 1971, U.S. Servicemen's Fund Records, State Historical Society of Wisconsin.
42. Anderson, *Vietnam: The Other War,* pp. 180–81.
43. Joel Davis interview, Winter Soldier Oral History Collection, p. 71.
44. *Ibid.,* p. 77.
45. Lieutenant Colonel RAO interview, Company Command in Vietnam Collection, Military History Institute.
46. Terry, *Bloods,* p. 91.
47. Joel Davis interview, p. 32.
48. Allen J. Matusow, *The Unravelling of America* (New York: Harper & Row, 1984), pp. 287–92, 299–304, and *passim.*
49. Peter S. Cookson, "Marijuana and Drug Abuse in the Twenty-Fifth Infantry Division, Republic of Vietnam, 1970: An Exploratory Field Survey," copy in CMH. Cookson found that "more than two-thirds of all users began their drug pattern as civilians."
50. Supplemental Data Sheet D to USARV AG Report, subj.: Use of Marijuana in Vietnam, May 1, 1968. Copy in USARV Records.
51. Quoted in Memo, CG, II Field Force, to Lieutenant General W. J. McCaffery, September 17, 1970, subj.: Marijuana and Drug Suppression, USARV Records.
52. Provost Marshal History, p. I-34.
53. *Ibid.,* pp. I-38-39; Alfred McCoy, *The Politics of Heroin in Southeast Asia* (New York: Harper & Row, 1972), pp. 168–201; Memo, Lieutenant General Bruce Palmer to General Creighton Abrams, subj.: sub Marijuana Investigation, May 15, 1968, MACV Records.
54. Memo, Major General Robert W. Strong, USAF, to Mr. Robert E. Jordan, III, subj.: Working Paper, re Survey of Use of Marijuana and Dangerous Drugs by Members of the Armed Services, September 9, 1968. Copy in Westmoreland Papers.
55. Provost Marshal History, p. I-38.
56. Testimony of Honorable Alfred Fitt, Assistant Secretary of Defense, in *Drug Abuse In the Military: Report of the [Senate] Subcommittee to Investigate Juvenile Delinquency* (Washington, D.C.: GPO, 1971), p. 9.
57. Memo, Palmer to Abrams, subj.: Marijuana Investigation in the Delta.
58. R. A. Roffman and E. Sapol, "Marijuana in Vietnam: A Survey of Use Among Army Enlisted Men in the Two Southern Corps," *International Journal of the Addictions,* vol. 5 (1970), pp. 1–42.
59. W. B. Postal, "Marijuana Use in Vietnam: A Preliminary Report," *USARV Medical Bulletin,* September–October 1968, pp. 56–59; E. Caspar, J. Janacek and H. Martinelli, Jr., "Marijuana in Vietnam,"

USARV Medical Bulletin, September–October 1968, pp. 60–72.

60. Nicholas Von Hoffman, "Even the MPs Smoke Pot at 'Fort Head'," *Washington Post,* July 14, 1968.
61. Joel Davis interview, p. 25.
62. Captain Robert Sellers and Sergeant Lawrence E. Urban, "Marijuana in a Tactical Unit," unpublished paper, no date (Spring 1970), copy in CMH; M. Duncan Stanton, "Drugs, Vietnam, and the Vietnam Veteran: An Overview," *American Journal of Drug and Alcohol Abuse,* vol. 3 (1976), p. 563.
63. Provost Marshal History, p. I-49.
64. Colonel Harry C. Holloway, "Epidemiology of Heroin Dependency of Army Soldiers in Vietnam," *Military Medicine,* vol. 139 (1974), p. 103.
65. McCoy, *Politics of Heroin,* pp. 180–81.
66. Stanton, "Drugs, Vietnam, and Vietnam Veteran," pp. 561–62.
67. Holloway, "Epidemiology of Heroin Dependency," p. 109.
68. *Report of Proceedings, Hearings Held Before the [Senate] Subcommittee on Juvenile Delinquency of the Committee on the Judiciary,* October 30, 1970 (Washington, D.C.: GPO, 1972), p. 338.
69. Quoted in message, CGUSARV to COMUSMACV 140406Z August 1970, Abrams Papers.

13. The War for the Countryside

1. AC of S. CORDs to SJS MACV, Staff Contribution to Overview Report on MACV 1968–1970, p. 3. Copy in CMH.
2. *The Senator Gravel Edition of the Pentagon Papers,* vol. IV (Boston: Beacon, 1972), pp. 573–74; Richard Hunt, "The Challenge of Counter-Insurgency," in John Sehlight, ed., *Second Indochina War Symposium* (Washington: CMH, 1985), pp. 130–31.
3. *Gravel Edition of Pentagon Papers,* vol. III, pp. 576–77.
4. *Ibid.,* vol. II, p. 612.
5. *Ibid.,* p. 613.
6. Ngo Vinh Long, "The Tet Offensive and Its Aftermath: Perspectives from Southern Revolutionary Veterans," unpublished paper. Long's paper is based, in large part, on conversations with former Viet Cong leaders.
7. *Ibid.,* pp. 44–45.
8. *Ibid.,* p. 57.
9. John Paul Vann, "Thoughts on Pacification," no date, attachment to memo, Deputy CORDS, II Field Force to CORDS, April 1, 1968. Copy in Jeffrey Race Papers, Center for Research Libraries, Chicago.
10. *Ibid.*
11. Staff Contribution to Overview Report on MACV 1968–1970, p. 5.

12. William Colby, *Lost Victory* (Chicago: Contemporary Books, 1989), pp. 241–43.

13. Eric Bergerud, *The Dynamics of Defeat: The Vietnam War in Hau Ngia Province* (Boulder, Colo.: Westview Press, 1991), p. 268.

14. Michael A. Hennessy, "Divided They Fell: America's Response to Revolutionary War in I Corps, Republic of Vietnam," M.A. thesis, University of New Brunswick, 1987, p. 297.

15. Special National Intelligence Estimate 14-69, Pacification Effort in Vietnam, January 16, 1969, NSC Country File, LBJ Library, pp. 3–4.

16. Message, COMUSMACV to Senior Commanders 280929Z Sept 68, subj.: Operational Guidance, 4th Quarter, CY68, MACV Message Files, Abrams Papers.

17. Earl J. Young, "Pacification in Theory and Practice," August 1967, p. 10. Copy in CORDS Files, CMH.

18. Guenter Lewy, *America in Vietnam* (London: Oxford University Press, 1978), p. 91.

19. Jeffrey Race, *War Comes to Long An* (Berkeley: University of California Press, 1972), p. 194.

20. Leon Goure and C. A. H. Thomson, "Some Impressions of Viet Cong Vulnerabilities: An Interim Study," RM-4699-ISA-ARPA (Santa Monica, Calif.: Rand, 1965); Leon Goure, A. J. Russo, and D. Scott, *Some Findings of the Vietcong Motivation and Morale Study, June–December 1965,* RM-4911-ISA-ARPA (Santa Monica, Calif.: Rand, 1966), p. 33.

21. Orrin de Forrest, *Slow-Burn: The Rise and Bitter Fall of American Intelligence in Vietnam* (New York: Simon & Shuster, 1990), pp. 100–101.

22. Goure and Thompson, "Some Impressions," p. 40.

23. De Forrest, *Slow-Burn,* p. 70.

24. "Phuang Hoang Advisor Handbook," 1971, pp. 2–7, CORDS Files, CMH.

25. Colby, *Lost Victory,* pp. 216–17.

26. Dale Andrade, *Ashes to Ashes: The Phoenix Program and the Vietnam War* (Lexington, Mass.: D. C. Heath, 1990), pp. 172–75, 185–86.

27. *Ibid.,* p. 186. The importance and effectiveness of the Phoenix program and, indeed, many other programs associated with pacification remain subject to debate. The lack of hard evidence about the impact of various programs on the Viet Cong remains a major obstacle. Even what evidence exists is open to conflicting interpretation. For example, Eric Bergerud has suggested that the Communists may have used the term "Phoenix Program" to refer to the *entire* U.S. pacification effort. The conclusions presented in this chapter are my own, based on a

careful reading of the secondary literature, a portion of the records, and limited personal experience during 1968-69. Many academic specialists and former pacification advisers would take issue with some or all of them.

28. Race, *War Comes to Long An,* p. 215.

29. Hunt, "Challenge of Counter-Insurgency," p. 134.

30. Hennessy, "Divided They Fell," p. 318.

31. Raymond G. Davis interview, 1978, p. 63.

32. Personal Notebook of NVA Commanding General, Tri-Thien-Hue Military Region, CDEC Document 10-1327-69, 7 Oct 68. Copy in Indochina Archives.

33. Neil Sheehan, *A Bright Shining Lie* (New York: Random House, 1988), p. 732. For a discussion of the impact of the new security situation and pacification programs on politics and administration at the village level, see Samuel L. Popkin, "Pacification, Politics and the Village," *Asian Survey,* August 10, 1970, pp. 20-26.

34. Nho Vinh Long, "The Tet Offensive and Its Aftermath," pp. 20-21.

35. Igor Bobrosky interview, Marine Corps Oral History Collection, p. 87.

36. Senior General Hoang Van Thai, "Some Lessons and Experiences in Building the Vietnamese People's Armed Forces," *Tap Chi Cong San,* no. 2, December 1984.

37. Nho Vinh Long, "The Tet Offensive and Its Aftermath." The experience of the 320th Independent Regiment is discussed in Tran Van Tra, *Concluding the Thirty Years War* (Hanoi: Ho Chi Minh Publishing House, 1982), pp. 63-84.

38. A perceptive interpretation of the changing Vietnamese agriculture is in Gabriel Kolko, *Anatomy of a War* (New York: Pantheon, 1985), pp. 489-94 and *passim.*

39. The practice of growing greens in bomb craters is mentioned by one of Long's former Viet Cong informants. Nho Vinh Long, "The Tet Offensive and Its Aftermath," pp. 62-63.

40. Bergerud, *Dynamics of Defeat,* p. 306.

41. *Ibid.,* p. 261.

42. Memo, Colonel Joseph E. Pizzi to Headquarters I Corps, MR2, subj.: Study Directive, Assessment of Combat Power, October 2, 1971, MACV Records.

43. Quang Tri Province Report, Period Ending July 30, 1970 (August 4, 1970), MACCORDS, 31.01, p. 2, CORDS Files.

44. Pleiku Province Report for Period Ending July 31, 1970 (August 3, 1970), CORDS Files, p. 3.

45. Khanh Hoa Province Report for Period Ending July 31, 1970 (July 31, 1970), CORDS Files, p. 1.

46. Kontum Province Report for Period Ending July 31, 1970 (August 1, 1970), CORDS Files, p. 1.
47. Bergerud, *Dynamics of Defeat,* p. 311.
48. *Ibid.,* p. 306.
49. Memo, Colonel Joseph E. Pizzi, subj.: Study Directive, October 2, 1971.
50. Bergerud, *Dynamics of Defeat,* p. 315.
51. JUSPAO Attitudes in Danang and Hue, May–June 1970, Office of Policy, Plans, and Research Survey, June 1970, CORDS Files.
52. Bergerud, *Dynamics of Defeat,* p. 304.
53. Le Ly Hayslip, *When Heaven and Earth Changed Places* (New York: Doubleday, 1989), p. 222

14. "It Is the Right Thing to Do"

1. Based on intelligence reports summarized in MACV Command History 1968, pp. 48–49. Copy in CMH.
2. Memo, JCS to General Ginsburgh, October 16, 1968, Attachment to Rostow to President, October 16, 1968, Rostow Memos to President File, DSDUF, LBJ Library.
3. Abrams to Admiral John McCain, MAC 1340, October 13, 1968. Cited in William H. Hammond, "The American Withdrawal From Vietnam: Some Military and Political Considerations," unpublished paper, p. 81.
4. Allen J. Matusow, *The Unravelling of America* (New York: Harper & Row, 1984), p. 419.
5. *Ibid.,* p. 431.
6. Dean Rusk oral history interview, July 28, 1969, p. 17, LBJ Library; Clark Clifford, "Serving the President: The Vietnam Years—III," *The New Yorker,* May 20, 1991, p. 68.
7. Draft cable, Abrams to Rostow, August 23, 1968, NSC Country File, LBJ Library.
8. Clifford, "Serving the President," pp. 76–77.
9. Tom Johnson's Notes of Meeting, Tuesday Lunch, September 17, 1968, Meeting Notes File, LBJ Library.
10. Meeting with the President, Monday, October 4, 9:40 P.M., in the Cabinet Room; Mandatory Review Case no. NLJ 82-86, Document 68-N, LBJ Library.
11. Summary Notes of President's Meeting with Joint Chiefs on Vietnam, October 14, 1968, 11:50–4:40 P.M., Cabinet Room; Mandatory Review Case No. NLJ 85-05, Document 57, LBJ Library.
12. Tom Johnson's Notes of Meeting, October 14, 1968, 1:40 P.M., Foreign Policy Advisory Group Meeting, Notes File, LBJ Library.
13. *Ibid.*

14. Clifford, "Serving the President," p. 77.
15. *Ibid.*
16. *Ibid.*, p. 70.
17. Memo for Record, Meeting with the President, Walt Rostow, General Momyer, October 23, 1968, President's Appointment File, Diary Backup, Box 105, LBJ Library.
18. Clifford, "Serving the President," p. 79.
19. *The Ho Chi Minh Trail* (Hanoi: Foreign Languages Publishing House, 1985), p. 16; Robert Shaplen, *Bitter Victory* (New York: Harper & Row, 1984), p. 157.
20. Jack S. Ballard, *Development and Employment of Fixed Wing Gunships 1962-1972* (Washington D.C.: Office of Air Force History, 1982), pp. 110-11.
21. Senior Colonel Nguyen Viet Phuong, "Electronic Warfare and Counter Electronic Warfare on the Truong Son Route," *Tap Chi Quan Doi Nhan Dan*, nos. 2-3, January-February 1984.
22. *Ibid.*, pp. 77-78.
23. *Ibid.*, p. 77; Shaplen, *Bitter Victory*, p. 160.
24. Ballard, *Fixed Wing Gunships*, p. 111.
25. *Ibid.*, p. 283.
26. *Ibid.*, p. 284.
27. *Ibid.*, p. 118.
28. *Ibid.*, p. 118.
29. Eduard Mark, ed., *Case Studies in Interdiction* (Washington: Office of Air Force History, forthcoming), pp. 176-77.
30. *Ho Chi Minh Trail*, p. 16.
31. Interview of Lieutenant Colonel Stephen J. Opitz by Lieutenant Colonel Robert G. Zimmerman, July 18, 1972, p. 6. U.S. Air Force Oral History Collection, Maxwell AFB, Alabama.
32. Ballard, *Fixed Wing Gunships*, pp. 122-23.
33. Notes of President's Meeting with President-Elect Richard Nixon, November 11, 1968, Meeting Notes File, LBJ Library.
34. President's Meeting with Foreign Policy Advisers, October 29, 1968, Tom Johnson's Notes of Meeting, Meeting Notes File, LBJ Library.
35. Clifford, "Serving the President," p. 87.
36. Major Robert D. Palmer interview, Tape 3588, Marine Corps Oral History Collection.
37. *Ibid.*
38. Lieutenant Colonal A. A. Laporte interview, Tape 3733, Marine Corps Oral History Collection; Captain Leonard Blasiol, "Counter-Offensive Operations in Southern I Corps," draft ms., MCHC, p. 21.
39. Blasiol, "Counter-Offensive Operations," p. 23.

40. Captain Anthony A. Johnson interview, Tape 3733, Marine Corps Oral History Collection.
41. Blasiol, "Counter-Offensive Operations," p. 31.
42. 3d Battalion, 26th Marines, Command Chronology, December 1968, p. 5, MCHC.
43. Blasiol, "Counter-Offensive Operations," p. 31.
44. *Ibid.,* pp. 31–32.
45. *Ibid.,* p. 3.
46. Charles R. Smith, *U.S. Marines in Vietnam: High Mobility and Stand Down, 1969* (Washington, D.C.: History and Museums Division USMC, 1988), pp. 82, 84.
47. Henry F. Graff, *The Tuesday Cabinet* (Englewood Cliffs, N.J.: Prentice-Hall, 1970), p. 163.
48. Notes for 5:30 P.M. Briefing of Mr. Nixon, December 12, 1968. CBS Subpoena Case No. NLJ/CBS21, Document 98, LBJ Library.
49. Message, Goodpastor to Abrams, JCS14865, 191924Z December 1968, Abrams Papers, Backchannel Files.

Epilogue

1. Message, Bunker to President, December 19, 1968, Bunker Papers Microfilm, Department of State.
2. Vo Nguyen Giap, "The Final Phase of Battle," in Russell Stetler, ed., *The Military Art of "People's War": Selected Writings of General Vo Nguyen Giap* (New York: Monthly Review Press, 1970), pp. 309–18.
3. The devastating impact of the *post*-Tet battles is well documented in Ngo Vinh Long's interview with former Viet Cong leaders. Long, "The Tet Offensive and Its Aftermath: Perspectives from Southern Revolutionary Veterans," unpublished paper.
4. Information about these high-level decisions is still sketchy. The conclusion is based on William J. Duiker, *The Communist Road to Power in Vietnam* (Boulder, Colo.: Westview, 1981), pp. 278–79; William J. Turley, *The Second Indochina War: A Short Political and Military History* (New York: NAL, 1987), p. 131; and the author's conversations with General Tran Van Tra and David Elliot in New York in October 1990.
5. On this point see Jeffrey Clarke, "On Strategy and the Vietnam War," in Lloyd Matthews and Dale E. Brown, eds., *Assessing the Vietnam War* (London: Pergamon-Brassey, 1987), pp. 73–74. In his memoirs Kissinger implies that the Nixon Administration ultimately reached the same conclusion. "We finally rejected the military option because we did not

think we could sustain support for the length of time required to prevail; because its outcome was problematical and because had we succeeded Saigon might still not have been ready to take over." Henry Kissinger, *White House Years* (Boston: Little, Brown, 1979), p. 288.

6. Le Ly Hayslip, *When Heaven and Earth Changed Places* (New York: Doubleday, 1989), p. xiv.

7. John E. Mueller, "The Search for the 'Breaking Point' in Vietnam: The Statistics of A Deadly Quarrel," *International Studies Quarterly,* December 24, 1980, p. 498.

8. Hart, "The Statistics Trap in Vietnam."

A NOTE ON SOURCES

The most important published sources for this study are discussed in the footnotes. Those interested in the large and growing secondary literature on Vietnam should consult Richard Dean Burns and Milton Leitenberg, *The Wars in Vietnam, Cambodia, and Laos 1945–1982* (Santa Barbara, Calif., 1983), a comprehensive bibliography of books and articles in English published through the early 1980s. An unusual and extremely useful bibliographic guide is Norman M. Camp, Robert H. Stretch, and William C. Marshall, *Stress, Strain, and Vietnam: An Annotated Bibliography of Two Decades of Psychiatric and Social Sciences Literature Reflecting the Effect of the War on the American Soldier,* a mine of information on medical and psychological studies relating to combat and military service. I have attempted to discuss some of the unpublished records of the Vietnam War in two earlier publications, *Researching the Vietnam Experience* (Washington, D.C.: US Army Center of Military History, 1984) and "In the Nam and Back in the World: American and Vietnamese Sources on the Vietnam War," *Journal of American History,* vol. 75, June 1988. What follows is merely intended to provide some indication of the nature and condition of some of the more important records used in this book.

While the records of the National Security Council, the State Department, and the Central Intelligence Agency remain closed to researchers, decisions at the White House level may be followed through the records available at the Lyndon B. Johnson Library in Austin, Texas. For purposes of this study, the most important records there included the NSC Vietnam country file, the meeting notes file, the March 31 (1968) speech file, Tom Johnson's notes of meetings, and the Clark Clifford papers. I also consulted the messages and reports of Ambassador Ellsworth Bunker, so far declassified by the State Department, and the papers of Brigadier General John R. Chaisson at the Hoover Institution.

Materials on high-level decisions in Hanoi are far rarer, but a large number of captured Communist reports, messages, and diaries shed light on Communist organization, activities, and decisions at the operational level. A major source of documents concerning the NLF and North Vietnamese side of the war are the records of the MACV Combined Documents Exploitation Center (CDEC). The Center was established in 1966 as part of an American and South Vietnamese effort at combined intelligence collection and exploitation. Enemy documents captured by U.S. and allied units were sent to the CDEC for translation, analysis, and appropriate dissemination. The most important documents were translated in full; those of lesser importance were excerpted, and the least important were summarized. Microfilm copies of these documents are held by the National Archives and a few other repositories in the United States. I utilized mainly CDEC documents in other collections, such as the Indochina Archive at the Institute of East Asian Studies at the University of California, Berkeley, and the MACV and USARV intelligence files. Wherever possible, such documents are cited by CDEC file number. However, there are at present no usable indexes or finding aids for the CDEC files. Translations of histories and reminiscences of the war produced by Vietnamese authors since 1975 have been published by the Joint Publications Research Service and are available in government repository libraries.

Many of the records of specific Army units in Vietnam as well as higher-level headquarters, such as MACV and USARV, were transferred by the Army to the National Archives and may be found in Record Group 338 and Record Group 319. These include the records of U.S. Army Vietnam, records of XXIV Corps, 1st Infantry Division, 4th Infantry Division, 1st Cavalry Division (Air Mobile), and 9th Infantry Division. The division records are of widely varying quality but usually contain Operations Reports/Lessons Learned (ORLLs), intelligence reports, operation plans, and maps.

Many of the files of the U.S. Army Center of Military History pertaining to Vietnam were also transferred to the Archives and may be found in Record Group 319. The CMH records contain interviews, histories, and documents collected by Army historians in the field and in Washington. Among the documents are back channel messages, intelligence studies, records of investigations, and captured Communist documents. Since this book was begun before the transfer of many CMH records, some of the items described in the notes as located at the Center of Military History may now be in the National Archives.

Still at the Center of Military History are copies of the papers of General William Westmoreland and General Creighton Abrams, including sensitive "back channel" messages. The Center also has an extensive oral history collection created by Army military history detachments in Vietnam. Tapes and transcripts are sometimes accompanied by historical summaries, maps, and other documentation. A unique resource is the Center's collection of CORDS records arranged chronologically and by province, which provide extensive material on pacification and on South Vietnamese government, politics, and administration.

At the U.S. Marine Corps Historical Center, the most important documentary collections are the Command Chronologies submitted monthly by Marine units from battalion to division size. The Marine Corps oral history holdings relating to Vietnam are of two types: transcripts of interviews with retired Marine Corps general officers and interviews conducted by Marine Corps field historians with Marines in Vietnam at the scene of, or soon after the conclusion of, operations. Most of these latter interviews have not been transcribed and are cited by tape number in the notes. Also of interest are the "comment editions" of volumes in the *U.S. Marines in Vietnam* series. These contain the reminiscences, criticisms, and comments of former participants in the operations described. Unfortunately the volume for 1968 has not been completed, but "comment editions" for other years were helpful.

In the Operational Archives of the Naval Historical Center, I used the records of COMNAFORV and various task forces, particularly River Assault Flotilla One in the command histories file for information on the Navy's riverine operations in the Delta. Among the oral histories, the most valuable was the "Reminiscences of Vice Admiral Robert Salzer."

Many Air Force operational records were still classified at the time this history was written. However, I was able to examine declassified portions of the relevant CHECO studies prepared by Air Force historians. Project CHECO, an acronym that at various times referred to Contemporary Historical Evaluation of Counterinsurgency Operations, Contemporary Historical Evaluation of Combat Operations, and finally Contemporary Historical Evaluation of Current Operations, was an Air Force project to prepare historical monographs on Air Force operations and activities in Vietnam.

In addition to published collections of oral histories and those discussed above, three other collections were extensively utilized in the preparation of this book. They are the Company Command in Vietnam collections at the U.S. Army War College at Carlisle, Pennsylvania, and the Army Command and General Staff College at Leavenworth, Kansas. Consisting of lengthy interviews with War College and Staff College students who were young captains and lieutenants in Vietnam, they provide an unusually frank and candid perspective on the war from men who were at the critical leadership level. Another useful collection are the interviews conducted by Professor Clark Smith with Vietnam veterans in the late 1970s. Two of these interviews were published in Stanley Goff and Robert Sanders, *Brothers: Black Soldiers in the Nam* (Novato, Calif.: Presidio Press, 1982). Transcripts of the others are in the "Winter Soldier Collection" in the Columbia University Oral History Collection.

Shelby Stanton generously allowed me access to the extensive files accumulated in the preparation of his books on the Vietnam War. These include copies of official records and correspondence with participants in various Vietnam operations and battles.

The Reverend Ray W. Stubbe, former chaplain at Khe Sahn, kindly allowed me access to his immense collection of material accumulated over two decades concerning the siege of Khe Sahn. Some of this material has since been incorporated into *Valley of Decision: The Siege of Khe Sanh,* by John Prados and Ray W. Stubbe, published in 1991.

INDEX

Ladd, Jonathan, 169–70
Lam-Son 87, Operation, 209
Land reform, 74, 290
Landsdale, Edward, 205
Lang Binh, resettlement of, 209
Lang Vei Special Forces Camp, fall
    of, 122, 126
Lanier, William, 125–26
Lauffer, Robert G., 306
Lawrence, Richard G., 65
Leadership, military, 247, 248–49
Le Nguyen Khang, 108, 110
Le Trung Tin, 289
Le Van Thuong, village of, 135
Leverage, 217
Le Xa Dong, village of, 135
Life magazine, 28, 204
Lippmann, Walter, 7
Little, Roger, 45
Lodge, Henry Cabot, 96–97, 280,
    281
Logistical support, 43–44
Logistics infrastructure, 43
Long An, anti-pacification efforts
    in, 289–90
Long Binh Jail, 242–44, 251,
    253–57
Long-range reconnaissance patrols,
    232–33, 300
Loon, Fire Base, 227
Lovely, Francis B., 130

M-16 rifle, 52–54, 111, 153
McCarthy, Eugene, 7, 296
McCloy, John J., 20
McConnell, John P., 298
McGee, Frank, 5
McGonnigle, Richard, 194
McNamara, Robert, 8, 10, 11,
    16–17, 68, 95, 219, 222,
    225, 280

McNamara Line, 209, 222–25,
    230–31
McNaughton, John, 21
Magsaysay, Ramon, 285
Mai Van So, 83
Malaria, 48, 86–87
MAMELUKE THRUST,
    Operation, 306
Maneuver battalions, 41, 42, 55,
    317–18
Mannion, Dennis, 128
Manpower system, military, 27–35
Mansfield, Mike, 111
Marijuana, use of, 254–55, 256,
    265, 273–75, 276, 361n49
Marshall, S. L. A., 36, 49
Ma Sanh Nhon, 104
May Offensive, 144–83
    on Central Highlands, 166–76
    Dai Do, 145, 148–56, 225–26
    lessons of, 182–83
    Marines' Operation ALLEN
        BROOK, 47, 176–82
    on Saigon, 158–66
MEADE RIVER, Operation,
    306–10
Medevac helicopters, 56–58
Media, 214–15. See also specific
    publications
Medical care, American, 42, 56–59
Medina, Ernest, 205
Mekong Delta region, 111, 145–46
Military Assistance Command,
    Vietnam (MACV)
    headquarters, 215–16
    inability to learn from experience
        or pass on lessons, 217–18
    overcentralized command,
        218–19
    responsibility for pacification,
        280